Making God the Joy of Our Soul

Homilies Of
Fr. McLean Cummings

Dedicated to the Memory of
Audrey Stevenson
Also
To Edward and Hilere Cummings,
Rose, and all of Fr. Cummings' Family,
in gratitude for their love and sacrifice
as he answers the Call to serve God in Russia.
May that sacrifice bear much fruit.

Special thanks to Father Cummings for his kind
permission to print these homilies.
To the St. Thomas Aquinas Men's Group, the Knights of Columbus,
Rev. Mr. Matthew Buening, Patrick O'Donnell, Fr. McNamara,
Servants of Christ Ministries, and so many St. John the Evangelist's
parishoners who helped to make this book possible.
Also to Father Mitch Rozanski, in appreciation for
his support of so many ministries.

+

We ask your prayers for the repose of the soul of
Marguerite McCann whose initial encouragement and
generosity allowed the beginning of this endeavor.

Printed in the United States of America
by
Catholics United for Life
New Hope, KY

To order additional copies of this book,
call John or Miriam Lademan 410-757-5682.

Making God the Joy of Our Soul

Advent

Making God the Joy of Our Soul

In my God is the joy of my soul. This line sums up all the sentiments that should be in our hearts today. Great joy, because God is
coming very soon to enter into our souls. The Savior, by becoming
man, united Himself to each of us. Everyone who approaches Him,
purifies Himself as He is pure, in the words of John. This is what Advent is, a time of hope, a time of joy, a time of purification. This joy of
union with God depends not only upon the fact that a Savior was sent,
but upon the fact that we are capable of being saved, that we have a
soul that was made in the image of God, and naturally seeks union
with God. St. Augustine says, " Our hearts are restless 'til they rest in
Thee." Many today have ceased to ask the question from the psalm,
What art man that Thou art mindful of Him? Our greatness lies in the
fact that we alone, of all visible creatures, have an invisible soul. We
alone are enough like God, to be made for Him. Our dignity lies in
our potential for a relationship with the most Holy Trinity. We can
speak to, worship, love and obey God. We're able to receive His gifts,
even the gift of Himself, which is eternal life, union with the Eternal
One.

What a mistake it would be, therefore, and what a tragedy it has
been, to try to emancipate ourselves from God. This is death to all that
is noble in us. Ah, what a choice we have! We either answer the call to
be more than man is, to be elevated by grace, or we sink back down
even to the point of inhumanity. We are ordered to this glory, but how
to attain it? We need God to reach down from Heaven and take us up
to Himself. This is the joyful message, the wonderful enactment that
Christmas is about. A Savior is born to you who is Christ the Lord. He
is the Son of the Most High and yet His mother is one of us. And that
is the key to our liberation, that is the Incarnation. As one of the
Church Father's put it, "The Son of God is the first born of many
brothers, He became the Son of Man and made many men the sons of
God, uniting us to Himself by His love and power, so that they became
as one." Christ, therefore, opened the way to Heaven. His infinitely
abject humility by becoming man, mirrors the ascent that is our des-

1

tiny. He poured out upon the soul of all those who obey Him, His very own Spirit, His very own life. Through Him, we have obtained access to this grace, and we rejoice in our hope of sharing in the glory of God. Hope does not disappoint us. God's love is poured out into our hearts through the Holy Spirit. The Spirit of Truth is drawing unbelievers also toward the waters of Baptism and the Sacraments. God is not stingy with His gift of the Spirit but are we not often lacking in generosity in return? We have that terrible, perverse streak in us to resist the pull of things above, the transcendent. We seek to be happy, and yet the only source of happiness, the Heavenly Father, the infinite God, we tend to ignore and disobey.

So as Christmas approaches, my brothers and sisters, Christ once again calls out, *Open your hearts! I have come to cast fire upon the earth and how I wish it were burning already!* The fire of Divine Charity in the souls of all the elect! St. Paul reminds us, *your souls were made for higher things, for converse with angels,* not the trash the media serves up so often, not fit even for humans. Your ears were made for beautiful sounds, not for vulgar things. Your minds were made to contemplate the mysteries of God, to know things that are eternal, so why fret over things that will be forgotten in a month. Grace gives life to your spirit. Do you delicately protect it from every attack and seek to build it up? More than simply protecting the gift that is within us, we have to stir it up into a strong blaze. How do we do this if it is all a gift from God? St. Paul tells us, *Pray without ceasing.* Prayer is the answer, it is the proper action of a transcendent being, of a being made for God, having a trajectory towards Him. It's the voicing of our hope for union with Him. It's the constant striving for the things that are above. It's to gaze Heavenward like a fledgling bird that can't yet fly on it's own. It's to raise up our heart and mind and soul to God in earnest, longing to see His face. Never think of prayer as a mere obligation, it's not a few words we owe to God. It's not words at all. It's making God the joy of our soul.

Awaiting the Messiah

Having celebrated the consummation of salvation history on the Feast of Christ the King, we return now to its origins, to Advent, the waiting for the Promised Messiah. A dark and sinful human race waiting for the Light of the World to dawn. As we know the Lord comes not once but twice. First, He came in a surprising, hidden, humble way — *as a man like us in all things but sin* — even as a tiny little baby. Some day, however, He will come in glory on the clouds preceded by all the signs to which He Himself refers in the Gospel. These comings, different though they are, are similar in one respect: they can be easily missed. Hence the importance of watching, waiting, constantly training our souls not only to look back to Bethlehem two millennia ago, but ahead towards Heaven. *whence we also await a Saviour, the Lord Jesus Christ (Phil. 3.20)*.

The state of readiness for Our Lord's return is described in terms of the "heart". We just heard from Paul's letter to the Thessalonians: *May* [the Lord] *establish your hearts unblamable in holiness before our God and Father, at the coming of our Lord Jesus with all his saints. (I Th.3.13)* In the Gospel, Jesus points to two behaviors which, if we are not careful, will weigh down our hearts, so that the day of His coming catches us by surprise. The first is carousing and drunkenness. We are reminded of the Lord's parables of the wicked servants who are not ready upon the master's return. Hopefully we can all say, well that's not me, carousing and drunkenness! But then our Lord adds a second cause of downfall: *the anxieties of daily life*. That one is much harder to deny!

Yes, lack of peace of heart, lack of tranquility and serenity is an obstacle to the advent of Christ in our life, and could obscure being ready for His return. *The anxieties of daily life*. This is the kind of trap which may not be so very deep but is very wide: everyone can succumb to the fretting, cares and concerns of daily life. The constant crises that are forgotten in a week. The frantic activity that keeps us from relaxing. The sense that one is squeezing Mass and prayer in on top of our life, rather than building our life on that solid foundation. Is it a serious fault? After all, usually we're worried about something good and useful. Still, nowhere does a vice masquerade so easily as a virtue as in this case. If it wasn't a problem, Jesus wouldn't have brought it up and more than once: *Let not your hearts be troubled; believe in God, believe also in me. ... Let not your hearts be troubled, neither let them be afraid.(Jn. 14.1,27) Martha, Martha, you are anxious and troubled about many things; one thing is needful. (Lk. 10,41-42)* And then a long passage speaking directly of what we are to eat and wear, and our inability to add time to our life by worrying, He concludes: *Therefore do not be anxious about tomorrow, for tomorrow will be anxious for itself. Let the day's own trouble be sufficient for the day.(Mt. 6.34)*

Being anxious is a serious danger because it tends to cause a fourfold blindness in us. First, our worries keep us from seeing our neighbors' problems. The second blindness is that we get blinded to the major trends in the world, what the Second Vatican Council called the "signs of the times". The third blindness is more critical still. If our life is frenzied we will never be able to hear the voice of God in prayer. We will never be drawn to prayer. Contemplating beauty in general — nature, art — takes time. It requires periods of leisure well spent on what fills the soul. Paramount among our "leisure" activities is contemplating Beauty Himself, the source of all goodness. But this takes silence of the heart.

So, anxieties of life can blind us to neighbor, to the world, to God... what's left? It can blind us to our very selves. In fact the chief reason why we hustle and bustle and fret and frazzle so much is because we want to. We don't want to look at ourselves and see ourselves as we really are. This anyway is the opinion of the great Blaise Pascal, a French philosopher: "What people want is not the easy peaceful life that allows us to think of our unhappy condition, ... but the agitation that takes our mind off it and diverts us... take away all their cares, and then they would see themselves and think about what they are, where they come from, and where they are going. That is why men cannot be too much occupied and distracted ..." In this respect, you can see how similar worrying is to "carousing and drunkenness"!

What then are we to do? First of all: make God's will paramount in your life. Strive to desire only what God wants. So for instance, if God's providence makes a traffic jam appear out of nowhere so you're late for a meeting, say, Lord I accept. I accept completely. This is Your choice, this is God's will. So anxieties can disappear at once if love of God is greater than love of self. God's plans, not ours. God's will never asks us to do more than we can do in twenty-four hours. It wouldn't make sense. All God asks us to do for Him is simple. So we have to learn to simplify our lives by reducing our wants. That includes very noble and even unselfish wants. We can all simplify our lives a great deal, and simply wanting only what God wants is how to do it. The next step is to pray that God's will be done, and then cooperating with our prayers. We have to admit that we're unable to achieve the good that God wants, to fix problems on our own. So Peter advised, *Cast all your anxieties on Him, for He cares about you. (I Ptr. 5.7)* Promise Him you will take care of His things, and trust Him to take care of yours. *Have no anxiety about anything, but in everything by prayer and supplication with thanksgiving let your requests be made known to God. (Phil. 4.6)*

This is true even, and especially, when one's problems are great and intractable: the nephew on drugs, the husband who may have cancer, the unemployed family member, the culture of death, the divisions in the Church. In all these things turn to God in confidence. To refuse to worry or be anxious about such things is not the same as ignoring them. I was so struck by this when I met the Bishop of Sudan, Maxim Gassis, who is so widely known for his international campaign to make people aware of the terrible persecutions going on there. He told us about the terrible things, but he also had a ready smile, a simple, hopeful and peaceful heart. It was striking! Likewise, Mother Teresa's nuns are always cheerful even though they live in the midst of the greatest misery. Someone asked the head of the order, "How do you do it? How do you keep smiling?" She responded, "I put all my burdens on God, so that I can have joy."

My prayer, then, for you this Advent is a familiar one to us all: Protect us Lord from all anxiety as we wait in joyful hope for the coming of our Savior, Jesus Christ.

Christ the Way

The Advent season always has a two-fold purpose: first, to prepare us to live the mystery of Christ's coming in the flesh, but also, to prepare us for His return, in His glorified body at the end of time. Today, let us look to Christ as the Way, the one we hope for. The first reading taken from the prophet Isaiah calls upon the people to prepare for Christ's coming; they did not then know that there would be two comings — one in humility, and one in glory. That is why some of the prophecies refer to a suffering servant and some to a king triumphant. But there is a mysterious way in which these two aspects of the mystery of Christ remain intertwined. During His humble coming, He was treated as a king, from the adoration given Him by the three kings, to His triumphal procession into Jerusalem before His execution, simply for being *the king of the Jews.* Conversely, in His glory, Christ retains His cross and His wounds. Who is near the throne, in the vision of Heavenly glory given to St. John, but *a Lamb standing as though it had been slain? (Rev. 5)*

Likewise for us, that mysterious mixture of humility and glory is the essence of the Christian life. As we make our way to Heaven, in the footsteps of Christ, it is the royal road of the Cross that we must follow. It is visible most clearly in the radical way of the evangelical counsels: those who profess poverty, chastity and obedience. They are lacking nothing in their poverty; they enjoy love and spiritual parenthood without marriage; they find freedom and honor in humble obedience. It is hard to find the way to happiness, since it appears to go in the opposite direction. It was hard to recognize the King of Kings, because He appeared as a poor child turned away from the inns. By becoming Man, Christ opened the only way to God. In so doing, Christ became *our hope*. Before man had groped in vain. Moreover, the way that He opened is so attractive, so sweet, even if it is not wide and easy. He made the narrow path sweet by walking on it Himself; He made the cross, His yoke, easy, His burden light so that we could follow Him.

The Lord never really left his Church in this time between the first and second comings. He said *I will be with you always even until the end of the age*. Thus, He is trying to come into our souls every day, but we can be too preoccupied with the dreamworld of urgent matters. Like someone who puts off getting out of bed, we can put off a serious attempt to reorder the spiritual life, to read scripture, to make regular confessions, to learn to meditate upon the mysteries of Christ's life. *Why do you let us wander, O Lord, from your ways...There is none who calls upon your name, who rouses Himself to cling to you*. Yes, Christ knew that Christians would walk through this world like sleepy men. Tired out by all the distractions, weighed down by attachments, mired by venial sin, starving through lack of prayer Christians would seek easier paths; they would rest by the side of the road. *Oh, that you would rend the Heavens and come down*, the prophet cried. Would that Christ would break through the cloudy, foggy skies of our hearts with His bright countenance and wake us up! Every day is of immense value, every minute, and we must take advantage of it. Christ is a bottomless mystery that we must plumb every day, regardless of our walk in life, through study and personal meditation.

Come, my heart says, *seek His face (Ps.27.8)* The Christian life allows for constant advancement; we have virtues to form, vices to overcome, offenses to make reparation for, people to tell the Good News to. To be awake, to be vigilant, means to take advantage of every moment. The virtue of Hope tells us that the Way to God has been opened for us, not to walk down, but to run down. *Widen my heart that I might run in the way of your commands.*

Immaculate Conception

The infallible declaration that Mary was immaculately conceived was a long time in coming. Finally, Pius XI spoke infallibly in 1854; the Universal Church rejoiced, and his words were soon confirmed by the Blessed Virgin Mary herself at Lourdes: I am the Immaculate Conception.

Why is this doctrine so important? Why should we want to know about this privilege of the person of Mary at the very moment she was conceived? God's requirement that the human vessel that was to carry his Incarnate Son be totally free of any stain of sin, original or actual, speaks volumes about the holiness of God and the sinfulness of man. And it speaks of God's love: the lengths to which He will go to bridge that infinite gap between us. He wants each of us to become a worthy spouse, *finding favor with God, a bride without spot or wrinkle, holy and without blemish.* In Mary, God shows that this is possible for Him to do; all things are. By a unique privilege, Mary, from the first instant of her existence, was untouched by moral imperfection. She had no source of temptation from within, neither from a darkened mind or a weakened will. Although she was able to grow in holiness, she nonetheless received in full measure the benefit of her Son's redemptive sacrifice in advance.

So we call her Mother most Pure. To imagine what Mary was like, *is* like, we can only think of children. They are so innocent and pure. Christ extolled this quality of children: *to such as these belong the kingdom of Heaven.* Imagine Adam's confusion when that childlike purity, which he took for granted, was all of a sudden lost. How ashamed he was as he sunk into the bushes, the first victim of what we call Original Sin. For him, and for all his children to follow, save Mary, purity of intention would no longer be a given, but a goal. The capital sins seethe in us all, spoiling our choices, diverting our hearts. This is what Christ demanded we purify: not just *the outside of the dish, but the inside...* The spiritual life is a constant purification of intellect, will, memory...

The good news is that God knows we cannot purify ourselves, make ourselves worthy of Him on our own. It is the same power which made Mary so pure that we must appeal to: the passion and death of Christ, the love of God in action. Our God is a *consuming fire* of love. If we approach Him, if we plunge into this furnace, we will not regret it. Let us not wait for Purgatory! We can be cleansed by his Love now, through prayer, sacraments and a virtuous life. The experience will be painful, difficult, involving suffering both physical and moral, but bit by bit we will remove all obstacles to the grace which will make us beautiful, fitting sons and daughters of so lovely a mother as Mary.

This feast should lead us to turn to Mother Mary, not only as our example, but also as the one through whom all these graces come. Just as the Son of God came to us through her, so all of His blessings come to us through her. We have to excite our devotion to her and rejoice in the opportunity that the Church gives us to set aside a day like today in her honor. I just want to close with a poem written in her

honor. Written actually by a young girl who comes to church here at
St. John's. It shows how much if one turns ones mind to her, one can
be inspired by her to base ones whole life upon her. Her poem is
called *A Woman's Hand and Heart*:

> A woman's hand and heart have tended those of God,
> Have raised Him from a child that all might give Him laud,
> A woman's tears were shed and heart was heavy laden,
> when upon the cross He bled and in the tomb they laid Him.
>
> A woman gently smiled and raised her tearful eyes,
> When her Child Divine ascended to the skies.
> A woman born in Nazareth, who saw the Resurrection,
> Mary, Queen of Heaven, the Immaculate Conception.

True Humility

In the gospel we see how humble St. Elizabeth is, acknowledging
her unworthiness to be visited by the mother of the Lord, *Who am I
that the mother of my Lord should come to me?* And of course Mary's
humility is greater still, in the next paragraph she begins to sing out
that God has looked upon the lowliness of His maidservant and has
done great things for her.

This humility that we see in all of these readings is the virtue that
is most characteristic of Christianity. It was unknown to classical
thinkers and has been consistently rejected by non-Christians
throughout time. It seems to make no sense that God should accomplish more with worse instruments, but that's His plan. Listen to St.
Paul, *God chose what is foolish in the world to shame the wise, God
chose what is weak in the world to shame the strong, God chose what
is low and despised in the world, even the things that are naught to
bring to nothing the things that are so that no human being might
boast in the presence of God.* Here St. Paul gives us a small idea of
what humility is meant to lead to, of what perfect humility would be, the
confession that we are absolutely nothing in front of God. It's only when
we really accept this truth, that God can begin to do great things through
us as He did through the Blessed Virgin, as He did through St. Paul who
could go on to say, *I can do all things in God who strengthens me.*

Humility is not only the condition for us to be useful to God, to do
His work, it's essential for us to have any real relationship with Him.
It's the cornerstone of the Christian spiritual life, for only when God
is recognized for who He is, and we for who we are, only then are we

able to pray in truth, only then meditate, only then worship. If we have a fictional idea of God or a inflated idea of self, then we aren't worshipping in Spirit and truth. We're like the Pharisee in the Lord's parable, the prideful Pharisee with the publican behind Him. He prayed in vain and returned to his house without being justified. St. Bede puts it as bluntly as one possibly could, "Those who refuse to be humbled, cannot be saved. They cannot say with the prophets, *See God comes to my aid, the Lord is the helper of my soul.*

So humility then, properly understood, is more than a social grace, it's not simply good manners, refusing to blow one's own horn or refraining from boasting about one's talents or accomplishments. Many of us have those good manners, we don't want to appear arrogant or obnoxious. But how many of us have this true humility, this attitude of truth in front of God, for it's not easy to attain, in fact it's a life's work. It's a continual seeking to grow in humility and it is learning to stand before God in truth. This is the spiritual life. Humbling ourselves, emptying ourselves, purifying ourselves. For everything that is from us must go, our rights, our preferences, our desires, our plans, everything is to be sacrificed if we are to have complete union with God. This kind of humility, which is to be led by the grace of God to what is described as annihilation, is in fact, ironically, the road to fulfillment, the only road to fulfillment because it's the road to union with God.

Here for instance, St. Bernard says, "I would say that that man is blessed and holy to whom it's given to experience something of this perfect love of God so rare in this life, even if it be but once and for the space of a moment. To lose yourself as if you no longer existed, to cease completely to experience yourself, to reduce yourself to nothing, is not a human sentiment, but a divine experience." What it really is, is a foretaste of Heaven, where God will be "all in all." It's what mystics experience in this life, at least every now and then, and it was the constant experience of Mary, the mother of God. So marvelously humble was she, so emptied of self, that she simply reflected God, and as she said in the next line, her soul magnified the Lord. She's likened in Christian writing and poetry to the moon, because the moon reflects the splendor of the sun. C.S. Lewis, a well known Christian writer, says that we're all called to give up any hope of standing out as a moral or spiritual genius in our own right and instead to seek to "acquire a fragrance that is not our own, but borrowed, and become clean mirrors filled with the image of a face that is not ours." The face of Christ.

In practical terms, humility means we have to obey. We mustn't think that our fulfillment and our happiness lies in doing our will but the will of God. Who was more successful, more perfect, more free, more fulfilled, than Jesus Christ; and yet He's the one who we heard in the second reading came into the world, saying, *Behold I come to do Your will.* This He did willingly, even eagerly. He recommended that we learn from Him who was "meek and humble" of heart. Jesus emptied Himself, *taking the form of a servant, being born to the likeness of men and being found in human form He humbled Himself and became obedient unto death, even death on a cross.*

So Christmas gives us the chance to contemplate the ultimate example of humility: the Son of God, receiving a body that God prepared for Him, so that He could die for us. And just as Christ emptied Himself to become like us, so we must be willing to empty ourselves so as to be transformed into Him.

Lowliness

We're coming to the end of the very ancient "O" Antiphons, which describe the coming of the Lord from titles of the Old Testament. Today we speak of Christ as the King of all Nations and the Cornerstone of the Church. This helps us understand what a great condescension the Incarnation was. We should be meditating very much on this great mystery, this great condescension that the Lord of all nations, King of all nations, the Son of God should come to live among us. More than live among us, He should come and share our flesh and blood, which is to share this very mud, the elements of which we are made. We see how very lowly is the self emptying of the King of Heaven to come and share our human nature. We have to always remember it wasn't just out of some great, crazy act of love and solidarity that He was going to share our poverty and that's all. No, we have to remember the great exchange that St. Augustine talks about. He came down to share in our lowliness with the purpose of raising us up to share in His Divinity.

So as a result, we should be striving to free ourselves from our lowliness, from our tendency to wriggle about in slime, but to keep our mind always fixed on terrestrial things. We have to really strive to do that, especially when we are confronted with these mysteries. We have to not only rise above the trite worries of daily life, but even our greatest concerns, "Do I have cancer?" Whatever. The greatest concerns we can think of, compared to this great mystery, shouldn't even compare. We should say, "Lord, everything that has to do with my lowliness means nothing, now that You've assumed my lowliness." Now our minds are fixed on things above, now we can look forward to leaving behind all of these worldly things, leave them all in the hands of the Lord. We should think of the image we have at Christmas of Mother Mary holding the child Jesus: she's holding the Lord who's come down from Heaven. We can also think of her, because she's our mother, lifting us up, picking us up out of this mud that we are born in. Lifting us up toward Heaven and that is how we'll raise our minds up to things above.

Rejoice Always

Today the Liturgy enjoins us, in the words of St. Paul, to *Rejoice in the Lord always; I say it again, rejoice!* Oddly enough, of all the commands given us by the Lord and his Apostles, this one may be the hardest to keep: *rejoice always*. Aren't we as a nation still sorrowing? As a Church, we're suffering some very great trials, and many individuals have their own private agonies which do not go on holiday at Christmas time. Yet, when St. Paul says *Rejoice always* he means it, and he knows that his audience had troubles. But we have to understand that he wants us to rejoice because of, not in spite of, our troubles.

Yes, we mustn't miss that point. The key to Christian joy, the key to a perpetual, indomitable, contagious joy is recognizing that — amazingly — weakness, hardship, temptation and trial need not diminish our joy but can actually replenish it. How is that? The answer is in the next sentence of St. Paul's admonition: *Again I say rejoice. The Lord is near.* Because we have these woes, because we are sick, blind, little, wretched — because God knows this, He comes to save us. He is near at hand, *an ever present help in time of need*, and precisely for that reason it is good that we are in need, and not self-sufficient. God preserve us from ever being able to say: "I've got it all together, I'm happy and successful in life on my own; I have no need for a Savior." Then the undying cry of Christians, the last line of Scripture, *Come Lord Jesus* would fade from our hearts; and the joy of caring that *the Lord is near* would die with it.

John the Baptist's whole entire life, like that of all good Jews, was oriented towards the coming of the Messiah. This hope, this longing, is what sustained him in the desert and fired his heart to preach so that the whole region came out to see him. This hope is what made him brave enough to confront that murderous couple, Herod and Herodias, and it made the rigors of confinement seem light. All that mattered to him was the Christ. Without question: this is the secret of Christian joy: *The Lord is near*. Even in his own mother's womb, John the Baptist had leaped for joy when Mary drew near with the Lord inside her. When *the voice of your greeting came to my ears,* Elizabeth told Mary, *the babe in my womb leaped for joy.* Later in the desert, when his cousin came out to be baptized, John felt like *the friend of the bridegroom, who stands and hears Him, [and who] rejoices greatly at the bridegroom's voice; therefore [John said] this joy of mine is now full.* The Lord's word was sufficient to lift up his heart. To quote St. Peter: *rejoice, though now for a little while you may have to suffer various trials, so that the genuineness of your faith... may be tested in fire. (I Pet. 1.6-7)*

Now our greatest danger, and the reason why we do not continually rejoice, is that we also forget that the Lord is near, here, living and active, in our hearts and in our Church. Or worse, perhaps we begin to question whether He really is the Messiah. *Are you the one or are we to wait for another? If you really are the Messiah* why am I suffering? *Save yourself and us*! This is a terrible thing: to allow our troubles, or even just the hum-drum routine of life or its distractions to begin to make us forget that the Lord is near, that He knows our needs and desires, defects and challenges, and that He cares about our cares. We can begin to doubt his Love. And then surely we lose any chance of real and lasting joy.

St. Paul practiced what he preached. He was proud to show his life, as a living example of the paradox wrought by the transformation of nature by grace: *behold we live; as punished, and yet not killed; as sorrowful, yet always rejoicing; as poor, yet making many rich; as having nothing, and yet possessing everything. (2 Cor 6.9-10)* How did he do this? By embracing his sorrow, poverty, and emptiness for Christ's sake. When we thus pick up our cross, we will find Christ by our side lifting it with us. His presence at our side will more than compensate for the suffering. Listen to the words of a wise French priest: "Take advantage, take advantage of these dark hours when nature groans, where the heart is like ice, where you believe, wrongly, that Jesus is very far from you, and even perhaps that He has turned his eyes from you, because you seem to yourself so imperfect and miserable; take the occasion to make heroic acts of faith and of confidence by your will alone. These are the most precious, having immense merit because then it is pure faith without consolation or sensible help" *(Pere Elbee)*.

So nothing must shake our confidence that the Lord is close by to us with His loving concern and almighty Providence. Our wretchedness, even our sinfulness, will not repel Him as long as we do not deny it. Rather, as soon as we admit humbly: "Lord, look how useless, weak and unworthy I am" then the Lord will fly to our side to save us. This is not a one time action, but a change of attitude. We must develop the habit of embracing our miseries as a most precious magnet for attracting the Merciful Saviour. He cannot stay away from the humble; we must decisively reject as the most terrible temptations any thought that we are too ugly, too insignificant, too ordinary or too sinful for the Lord to bother about us. On the contrary: the uglier, dumber, or more insignificant our soul, the more ordinary our life and the more sinful our past – all the more will the Lord seek us out on these accounts and want to be with us and have us with Him. That is the logic of love and mercy and the reason why joy should be our most abundant commodity.

Joy In Our Hearts

The antiphon for today sets the tone for our hearts. Our mother the Church tells us how we must feel. The first word of this antiphon "Gaudete", lends itself to the name of the Sunday: Gaudete Sunday. The rose colored vestments are a clear sign that we are to have joy in our hearts, for the Lord's coming is at hand. We rejoice, not only because of his imminent coming at Christmas, made ever actual by the Church's liturgy, but for his coming into our souls by new graces which He holds out to us in this holy season. The joy that we speak of, Christian joy, is a "fruit of the Holy Spirit", enumerated by St. Paul. That is a perfection that the Holy Spirit forms in us as the first fruits of eternal glory, the joy that never ends *(CCC1832)*. It is a fruit that is found only on those who have been grafted onto the vine, Jesus Christ. "By the power of the Spirit, God's children can bear much fruit" *(736)*. While it is known only by God's children, it is meant for all. The announcement of the angels — *Behold I bring you good news of a great joy which will come to all the people (Lk. 2.10)* — was to all mankind, past, present and yet to come. Christian joy is not only universal, but inalienable: *Your hearts will rejoice, and no one will take your joy from you (Jn. 16.22)* This is because it comes from Christ who is the same yesterday, today and forever, and no one can separate us from the love of God that comes to us in Christ Jesus. The character of Christian joy was explained so well during the Jubilee year of 1975, by the Servant of God, Pope Paul VI:

"In essence, Christian joy is the spiritual sharing in the unfathomable joy, both divine and human, which is in the Heart of Jesus Christ glorified". O, if we could understand this sentence which brings together so many mysteries of our holy religion that we speak blithely of and delve into but little. We are members of the Mystical Body. By grace, we share now the divine nature. We must have within us the same joy that Christ feels in looking upon his Father with human eyes. This is "the secret of the unfathomable joy which dwells in Jesus and which is special to Him" but which we are called to share: namely, "the inexpressible love by which He knows that He is loved by His Father." From the first moment of his Incarnation, to the last moment when the depths of Christ's trust was tested by seeming abandonment on the Cross, to the resurrection "the seal placed by the Father on the value of His Son's sacrifice". "Henceforth, Jesus is living forever in the glory of the Father, and this is why the disciples were confirmed in an ineradicable joy when they saw the Lord on Easter evening". It was the Lord's mission to bring joy to the world. Before leaving He prayed: *But I am now coming to thee [Father] and these things I speak in the world, that they may have my joy fulfilled in themselves. (Jn. 17.13)*

Christ rejoiced especially in saving the weak. He loved to bring sight the blind and make lame men walk. "This is the paradox of the Christian condition which sheds particular light on that of the human condition: neither trials nor sufferings have been eliminated from this world, but they take on a new meaning in the certainty of sharing in the redemption wrought by the Lord and of sharing in His glory" *Though the fig tree does not blossom, nor fruit be on the vines, the produce of the olive fail and the fields yield no food, the flock be cut off from the fold and there be no herd in the stalls, yet I will rejoice in the Lord, I will rejoice in the God of my salvation. (Heb. 3.17-18)*

But "His happiness is above all to see the Word accepted, the possessed delivered, a sinful woman or a publican like Zaccaheus converted, a widow taking from her poverty and giving". It is spiritual healing that especially brings joy to the Heart of Christ. Similarly, *there is more joy in Heaven over one sinner who repents than over ninety-nine who have no need of repentance.* "The Lord wishes above all to make us understand that the conversion demanded of us is in no way a backward step, as sin is. It is rather a setting out, an advancement in true freedom and in joy. It is the response to an invitation coming from Him — an invitation that is loving, respectful, and pressing at the same time." "Following the line of the best spiritual tradition, we remind the faithful and their pastors that the confessing of grave sins is necessary and that frequent confession remains a privileged source of holiness, peace, and joy". *Fill me with joy and gladness; let the bones which thou hast broken rejoice...Restore to me the joy of thy salvation, and uphold me with a willing spirit. (Ps. 51)*

We rejoice because we are dependent upon God, and that He is near. The Lord is never nearer than at this Holy Eucharistic sacrifice. This Sunday celebration should be the most joyful moment of the week.

"Joy gives the heart a catholic openness to the world of people, at the same time that it wounds the heart with a longing for eternal bliss" and consequently a desire to please God in all things. Who is a clearer example of this love for all men and desire to please God than the sinless virgin? To whom was the Lord more "near" than she who had Him within her womb? Mary is "the incomparable dwelling place of the Spirit". So joyful because she was so far from that enemy of Joy which is sin. So the Church acclaims her as "Mother full of holy joy" and "cause of our joy". And she herself proclaims: *My soul magnifies the Lord and my spirit rejoices in God my Savior*. Let the anthem of Mary as her time drew near, be also the expression of our hearts at Christmas!

Mary as Mediatrix

Seeing in the gospel today Mary's beautiful song of praise and thanksgiving to the Lord, it reminded me that we're almost midway between the greatest Marian Feasts we have on our calendar, December eighth, the feast of the Immaculate Conception, and the feast of Mary the Mother of God, January first. So perhaps it's a good moment to remind ourselves of why we have such a great devotion to the Blessed Virgin Mary. I'm sure all of you pray to her all the time, but why? Is it perhaps just because it's part of Catholic tradition, because it's what you've grown up doing, what you've gotten used to doing, a habit? That certainly wouldn't be the best reason for praying to the Blessed Virgin Mary. You have to ask yourself, why is it part of Catholic tradition, why is it such an intimate part of our Catholic tradition? We might answer, well, because God decreed it, God wished it so, God revealed that we're to go to Him through Christ and to Christ through Mary. True enough. He wished to give all things to the world through her, just as He gave His only Son to the world through her. It was His plan, and the Church has constantly taught that it was His plan, that Mary was an essential part of His plan of salvation. But still if we stopped at that, because God decreed it and the Church teaches it, therefore we must do it, out of more or less blind obedience, without asking again, why did God decree it, then perhaps we don't still have as firm a footing, as we could, in our devotion to the Blessed Virgin.

Why then did God include her, make her such an essential part of the plan of salvation? The answer seems to be because we need her,

because *we* need her. And that's important because so often when we
defend this doctrine against those who don't believe it, we get caught
up because, why should God need mediators? That's what many of
our non-Catholic brothers and sisters say. Why does God need mediators? He doesn't, obviously, He's all powerful. But that's not the point.
The point is we need mediators, *We* need them. And that's brought
home beautifully in this little excerpt from a letter from a holy
Cistercian to one of his brothers, writing to him saying, "You tell me
in your letter what damage the world does to you. I believe it. You're
made of flesh, and the world drags you about by your passions and
ties you up to ruin your spirit and matter triumphs... It does you damage, I know it, but you have to fight and you will win." And then he
adds, "What else is the Most Holy Virgin Mary for?"

That's why we have her, because we need her so much. And therefore it's only the humble who realize, yes, God can do all things, He
has no need of helpers, it's we who have need of helpers and we would
not be able to respond to all of His graces, we would not be able to
persevere as we ought, we would not be able to love God as we ought
if we didn't have the help of the angels and the saints and especially
the Blessed Virgin Mary.

Marian Season

The Advent season and the Christmas season are, among other
things, very much Marian seasons. This should help us live it with the
same sentiments that Mary had. This would be to live the Christian
life perfectly, of course. St. Bernard says a beautiful thing, "The
Christian life is life in the heart of Mary." We not only see her as a
model, very distant from us, or as an intercessor, far away from us,
but as someone so close to us. Living in God means somehow living
in her and with her every moment of the day, thinking the way she
would think and having in our hearts what she would have. What she
had more than anything else was joy, as she says here, *My spirit finds
joy in God my Saviour and all ages to come will call me blessed*".
Mother Mary more than anything has joy in her heart and if we're going to have the true Christmas Spirit, which of course is a joyful one,
we're going to have to somehow get the secret of her joy.

The first and most important thing to realize is that joy isn't a
mere feeling, it isn't a mere mood. It's not right when people say, Are
you in the Christmas spirit yet? Are you in the mood yet for these parties and so forth? The Christmas Spirit has to be way much more than
that. That would be a very superficial kind of joy which would pass as

soon as the decorations were taken down and the tree was thrown away. All of those things that we do to make this season special, such as delicious food and so forth, help us rejoice, but they are only there as supports and especially as expressions of a deeper joy, a joy which is truly in our hearts and which comes from love. Joy is always one of the first and greatest effects of love. This of course is the kind of love that only God can give us and it's because Mary had this tremendous love of God that her heart was full of joy.

So this is the love that we have to ask for. We can't manufacture it, God has to pour it into our hearts through the Holy Spirit. There is something we can do besides ask for it and that's fight against everything that opposes love, every form of selfishness or egoism, envy, worries, human respect, laziness, all those things that are going to squelch our love. We can and must fight against those, and in this fight, again Mother Mary must be at our side. In our regard, her reason for being is to help us win this battle, to increase love in our hearts, the presence of Christ Jesus in our hearts and, as a result, joy in our hearts. So let us spend these last three days before Christmas really and truly asking ourselves whether or not we have a great love for the Lord Jesus and a joy that springs from that, or whether perhaps our joy is a little bit superficial and if so, let's ask the Lord to make it deep.

Preparing Our Hearts

We know the importance of Zacharia's first words he spoke after having been silenced by the angel Gabriel for not believing that his wife Elizabeth would bear a son. When the child was named his tongue was loosed and he began to speak. We usually think of this as nothing more than a punishment that the Angel Gabriel put upon him, at least it seems that way. But the Lord's punishments are also often medicinal. So perhaps we can think that perhaps Zacharia had that silence imposed upon him so that he could begin to fathom and respect the mystery that was before him. And this is no doubt true for all of us, that here as Christmas approaches, this mystery of mysteries, that we need silence imposed upon us, that we can learn, even these last few hours to respect, to rejoice in a holy way, in the mystery that is before us.

There was a pagan Roman who wrote that every time he went out of his house into the forum he came back less a man. It was just the contact with human beings that sort of emptied him and made him less able to recollect his thoughts and be a genuine human being. How much more true that would be for a Christian, who has so much more in his soul, so much more that's sacred, Christians going, for instance, to a mall on Christmas eve. How much more true it is that, if we're not careful, we'll come back less a man, less a Christian. We have these precious mysteries that have to be focused upon and, of course, it's very difficult for people who live in these times, for people who live in the world. But none the less, be aware, the world's sapping us of all kinds of things, and yet this precious mystery we have to be focused upon. We have to remember those words of St. John of the Cross, "The Father spoke one Word, which was His Son and this Word we speak always in eternal silence and in silence it must be heard by the soul."

So what we do, of course, is we go to the Blessed Virgin Mary. We draw close to her on this last day. Because she had many things to do to prepare for the birth of her Son but she did them with simplicity, only the ones that were essential, always with that focused reason 'I'm doing this for Christ the Lord' and so her heart remained very calm. She pondered this mystery in her heart and she was ready to receive the Lord when at last her eyes could see the face of God. So let us ask Mother Mary to form our hearts, be in our hearts, so that we can receive the Lord Jesus worthily this Christmas.

Christmas

Christmas

Christmas is certainly the best-loved of all holidays in the Western world – by the devout, the lukewarm, even by non-believers. By absolutely everyone. There's a fascination, a nostalgia, about this holiday which indicates that there is a very deep need in the human heart that finds some satisfaction in all the images and traditions, gatherings and decorations. We flock willingly to the celebration of Christmas, like shepherds and wisemen, to the stable in the cave outside Bethlehem, — to find an oasis in a world which so often seems to be barely holding together. Here for a time, peace reigns; angels and humans sing together, rich and poor kneel side by side, even the donkey and the cow watch with reverent attention. All are brought into one and there is peace on earth – a foreshadowing of the Kingdom to come.

How novel is this atmosphere; how unlike the rest of the year are the days filled with Christmas spirit. Life is a lonely journey. No matter how many friends we may have, no matter how much sympathy and compassion they may show, we are — on a certain level — inevitably alone on the pilgrimage of life, especially at its most difficult moments of pain and death. Our loneliness and the ultimate threat of eternal loneliness, cries out for a Savior.

This accounts for the universal appeal of Christmas: the deepest longings of our hearts for peace and unity are satisfied by, as they can only be satisfied by — Emmanuel. God with us. As of the first Christmas, we are alone no longer. God says to man in general and every man in particular: I am by your side, I love you – I've sought you out, and come to find you wandering in the dark valleys of egotism and selfishness and I will reunite you to me and so also to the rest of creation. For this reason Christ came among us: by uniting his divinity to human nature He opened up the possibility for every partaker in that nature to share also in the nature of God. *But to all who received Him, who believed in his name, He gave power to become children of God (Jn 1:12)* He established the Church as "a sign and instrument of communion with God and unity among all men". Eventually, when the Savior's work is done, all those who did not cling to their ego, their loneliness, will be united to God and neighbor in a manner which defies imagining, which we call Heaven. God has come to dwell with us so that we might dwell with Him forever.

As we contemplate these truths of faith, we must resolve not to let them pass in one ear and out the other. We must not leave the stable, forgetting what we have seen: proof that God really does love us. It's because God so loved the world that He gave us His only son. And not just the world, but each person in it. This is, in a way, the most essential and difficult to accept tenet of our faith: God loves even me. We may feel loveable, because we love ourselves, but it is a rare person – we call them saints – who really knows, and practically perceives to even a minimal degree, God's infinite love for him. We know that Christ died for all, but do we really believe that He died for me? Just for me? If we did, we'd be constantly brimming with joy. That is why we must not pass by the manger too quickly. We must stop and see how low God has stooped, how poor and simple He became. This is so that He can approach us – the lonely ones, the wretched, the outcast – without scaring us off. Sinners sin because they cannot accept that God really wants to be with them and have an intimate friendship with them. If they did, they would want to stay beautiful for this great friend. *Every one who thus hopes in Him purifies Himself as He is pure. (I Jn. 3.3)*

How do we grow in friendship with Christ, in purity, with the help of the Church? There are three essential steps. First, we must stop to meditate at least once a day – not superficial prayers, but a dialogue of love, quality time, begging that this knowledge of God's love for me will sink in, and that I will respond to it. Second, we must go to Mass and Communion (if our souls are ready) at least once a week. Third, we must go to the sacrament of reconciliation at least once a month. That's easy to remember: daily prayer, weekly Mass, monthly confession – as a minimum. That is the way to have your friendship with God in Christ Jesus take off. The only way we know. Even God can't maintain a one-sided relationship: it's contradictory. We must do that minimum part. Then our peace of heart and harmony with others at home and work will grow. With all mankind and creation too. Then, gradually, the joy of Christmas will begin to illumine every day, and we will say: thanks to you, Lord, I'll never be lonely again.

Feast of St. Stephen

What a dreadful shock this Gospel, this liturgical celebration, is so close on the heels of Christmas, where so much was said and thought, and contemplated during the last few days about peace and unity, goodness, and beauty, the Lord Jesus being accepted by the Shepherds and everybody. But then, a complete shock today, red vestments and opposition, even brother against brother. Very sad, but a very good reminder that even in the midst of the Christmas season, even in the midst of those celebrations, the difficulty of the Lord's mission was very much present. It's symbolized we're told by the holly berries, for instance being red, that idea of the Passion of the Lord. Even the red in Santa's suit, St. Nicholas would also share in the Lord's Passion. It's there in our Christmas celebrations too.

See for instance, when St. Paul is describing the coming of the Lord, *Though he was in form of God , he did not deem a equality with God something to be grasped at. Rather, he emptied himself and took the form of a slave, being born in the likeness of men,* this is what we saw at Christmas, being born in the most humble surroundings. *He was known to be of human estate, it was thus that he humbled himself obediently accepting even death, and death on a cross.* This is why the Lord Jesus came. From the very beginning, He met with opposition. He was the Light coming to illumine those who walk in darkness. But for some mysterious reason, people cling to the darkness and they don't want to be enlightened by the Lord. Nonetheless, even though that threat, that hint of battle is present even from the very beginning, the victory is very clear. It is also true that the darkness will not overcome the Light. So, we should all take heart, even when we fight this battle, which we must, within in our own selves, because the message that our Lord brought finds opposition, even in our own hearts.

The glorious thing about the grace of our Lord is that tremendous power. So it makes fighting the battle for goodness within ourselves and in our world much easier, knowing how powerful is the Lord's message. In the little reading given for this day, for instance, it tells in a beautiful way how it was the triumph of goodness in the heart of Stephen that converted Saul. Saul standing there guarding the coats is of course St. Paul, later to be converted. But the seeds of that conversion, according to this Father of the Church, were sown by the goodness he saw there on the face of Stephen. So he writes, "Strengthened by the power of his love, Stephen overcame the raging cruelty of Saul and won his persecutor on earth as his companion in Heaven. In his holy and tireless love, he longed to gain by prayer those he could not convert by admonition. Now, at last, Paul rejoices with Stephen. With Stephen he delights in the glory of Christ. With Stephen he exalts, with Stephen he reigns. Stephen went first, slain by the stones thrown by Paul, but Paul followed after, helped by the prayer of Stephen. This surely is the true life, my brothers, a life in which Paul feels no shame because of Stephen's death and Stephen delights in Paul's companionship, for love fills them both with joy."

Holy Families

We're still celebrating Christmas of course, when Christ came into the world to renew it, *Behold*, He said, *I make all things new*. Thanks to Him, civilization is being transformed, through the Church, into something altogether new, the Kingdom of God. And how did Christ begin? He spent thirty years at home, in His own home. The home, the family, is the first thing that Christ sanctified. Notice also, what was His first sign that made His disciples believe in Him? He changed the water into wine at Cana. By that sign, He showed that He was elevating married love, from natural love to supernatural love, and henceforth, marriages were to be holy and the beginning of holy families. As our present Holy Father says, "The Holy Family is the beginning of countless other holy families."

Just as Christ began His mission with the family, so also we must begin with the family. The family is the cell of society, likewise, the Christian Family is the cell of the Church, of the Kingdom of God. That's why St. Paul calls it the Domestic Church. Our families are to be the agents of change in our culture. The time for renewal of our families is long overdue. Now we have no choice, either return our families to sanity and to sanctity or the Church and our society falls totally apart. Obviously we have to look to the Holy Family as our model. We must remember that the Holy Family is also the model of Religious Life, those who live out the vows of poverty, chastity and obedience. But recall that all Christians, though they do not take those formal vows, they have to live those evangelical counsels according to their state in life. Poverty, chastity and obedience are the antidotes to the three enemies of our soul, the world, the flesh and the devil. They're what St. John mysteriously called the lust of the flesh, the lust of the eyes and the pride of life. And so how you live poverty, chastity and obedience in your families, makes a good examination of conscience of how holy your family is.

Poverty, you have to remember, is a virtue not a problem. It means simplicity, austerity, self denial. Financial strain that is voluntarily chosen and embraced out of love, either because of tithing or because of welcoming more children is a blessed thing. Likewise reduced income resulting from having only one income is a most beautiful way of choosing poverty out of love. It brings a family together like glue. Remember the Holy Family was poor. That's clear when they brought two turtledoves as their offering, that was the offering of the poor. It's a blessing to wear hand-me-downs, to share rooms, to have to make up simple games instead of having computer ones. A simple life, remember, leads to a prayerful life, leads to more dependence upon God and His providence. And a family that prays together, stays together.

An early Christian document written only fifty years after the death of the last Apostle, written to the emperor of the time, describing Christians, reads, "And their wives, O king, are pure as virgins, their daughters modest and their men refrain themselves from all unlawful intercourse and uncleanness." How much we wish we could still describe Christian families that way. Every Christian mother should be looked up to as a genuine reflection of the Blessed Virgin Mary, totally beautiful, by husband and by children on account of her purity of heart. Chaste hearts are hearts which are selfless. The body is to express self-giving, never self-seeking. For conjugal love to be wholesome and even holy, it is essential that spouses always remain in Christ's grace and never separate their married love from its orientation of procreating children. Only chaste parents can raise chaste children, especially in a culture that is demonically set on destroying these ideals. At a very young age personalities are getting warped, vocations are getting lost and the seeds are being sown for the broken families of tomorrow. The greatest evil of all, the inability to see God, even permanently, is also occurring. Chastity, we must remember, cannot flourish in isolation, without all of the other virtues that we just heard St. Paul list; patience, self-sacrifice, humility, piety, self-discipline, most of all, bound together by love. The family has to be a gymnasium of all the virtues.

Then finally obedience: Paul speaks in another place, of mutual submission of husband and wife, out of reverence for Christ. This may be the most important element in this triad of Poverty, Chastity and Obedience. The most important and also, the most overlooked. Our culture prides itself on independence and personal choice as the highest of all goals. But no, the husband and wife should freely submit themselves to each other in their respective areas of authority. Each has a place where their authority should be unquestioned. As one of the Holy Fathers said, "If the man is the head of the house, the woman is the heart." Children, of course, should obey your parents in everything for this pleases the Lord, as we just heard from St. Paul. There is no law of psychological development that says that all teenagers must become rebellious and disrespectful. That's an aberration, even if it's the norm, not to be expected or accepted but resisted with the help of the sacraments, careful training at a young age, and great respect for each child. For which reason Paul adds, *Fathers, do not provoke your children, lest they become discouraged.*

Poverty, Chastity and Obedience. Let us use this time of purification, to purify our families, convert our hearts to be more like those in the house at Nazareth. Let us ask the Lord for forgiveness for all the errors of our past, so that we'll not only find happiness in our life, but we'll lead society a step closer to being one big family in Christ Jesus.

Mary, Mother of God

Pope Paul VI restored an almost fifteen hundred year old tradition of the Church of Rome when he decreed the celebration of the Maternity of Mary on this day. Originally, perhaps, the motive of choosing this day was to Christianize the pagan feast day dedicated to the god, Janus, at the beginning of the New Year. In our day, too, we have to remind ourselves that there is a much better reason for fireworks and parties than simply marking off another milestone on man's march through time – for we know that history has a transcendental trajectory, that it has become *salvation* history, ever since God intervened in it to bring us to Himself.

These two motives for celebrating this day do not vie for our attention by accident; they are essentially opposed. In a sense, history without Christ and history with Him go in opposite directions. All those who celebrate the mere passage of time should stop and wonder, why? Time is the measure of motion, and motion of material things as the Greeks knew, and as modern physics has formulated, is, ultimately, corruption, decay. Time came into existence with the created world, the material world, and it will cease to be when the laws of entropy have run their inexorable course. Our souls, because they are not corruptible, are in a very real sense timeless, but we observe time in our flesh as aging. Now what Christians come to celebrate today is salvation, that is, the overcoming of the laws of decay and death. Because the Immortal God came in the flesh, our aging bodies will one day share in the timelessness of our souls, resurrected to an eternal youth. One of the great lessons that this feast teaches us, that Mary our Mother, in particular, teaches us, concerns time and our approach to it. It reminds us that God is not constrained by time; it fits into His plan, not his plan into it. Mary did not have to fret that she would not have her baby before having to go to Bethlehem or that they would not get off to Egypt before Herod grew suspicious. Joseph and Mary knew that if they did what God wanted, at once, all would get done.

Mary did not dread the future, she did not rue the past, she did not rush through the present: She dwelt in the present moment, peacefully. The future was in the hands of God, the past – though it may be hard to see now – will give Him glory one day; the present is for contributing to the unfolding of His marvelous plan. Mary's obedience to the will of God did not make her passive, a pawn in God's plan – far from it: at Cana, so active was her collaboration, that she even appears to change the immutable will of God. When she requests the first public miracle, Jesus notes that His *time has not yet come* – yet at His Mother's word, He begins His public ministry. Mary teaches us the lesson of peace of heart. There are many causes of losing peace of heart, but a common one is anxiety over time. Mary felt no such pressure from time, the only thing that weighed upon her, and that gently, was the will of God. What do you, God, want me to do **now**? If I am doing it, I am at peace, I leave the big picture to you.

If God's Providence governs all things, directing their movement without violating their natures, they will not decay before his purposes are achieved. He has not given us a mission to complete that we cannot finish before our bodies fall apart. So let us not fear unexpected illnesses, however serious. Nor does He expect us to do more before the sun goes down than He wishes us to do. God will not let the forces that lead to destruction operate without pulling that which must be renewed forward simultaneously, not only despite the evil, but by means of it: . *So we do not lose heart. Though our outer nature is wasting away, our inner nature is being renewed every day. (2 Cor 16)* or again, *We know that in everything God works for good with those who love Him. (Rom. 8.28).* If we simply do the will of God, we will not only have peace in our hearts, but we will contribute to peace in the world. Such peace is evidence of the progress of the Kingdom. So we pray: Mary Queen of Peace bring true and lasting peace to our hearts and to the world, by bringing us the Prince of Peace, Christ your son.

Epiphany

Put out into the deep! Every word that came from the lips of Our Lord Jesus was a message from God to Man, not just to this man, Peter, but to each and every one of us. *Put out into the deep! Duc in altum!* in the Latin. His words have inexhaustible meaning, containing hidden truths, and a living message to each generation and every single believing heart. Our Lord was speaking in a special way to Peter the fisherman, who was to be St. Peter the first bishop of Rome, and He was speaking in a special way to every one of his successors. On the Feast of the Epiphany, the last day of the Holy Year, Pope John Paul II relayed that phrase to us, to you and to me: Duc in altum! *Put out into the deep!* Or in other words "Go forward in hope!" *(NMI 58)* The beginning of the New Millennium is not a time to complain of our tiredness, our failures, our frustrations – it's a time to look to Christ, to be filled with a supernatural confidence, to strive and with His help, succeed.

"*Duc in altum!* These words ring out for us today, and they invite us to remember the past with gratitude, to live the present with enthusiasm and to look forward to the future with confidence: *Jesus Christ is the same yesterday and today and forever"*. Thus writes the Holy Father. A human outlook will simply not suffice. If, on the threshold of the third millennium, we were to look at the looming shortage of priests, the rapid spread of new cults and non-Christian religions, the ongoing construction of a culture of death by men and women who call themselves "Christian"... we might easily despair: We might say *we have labored all night in vain and we've caught nothing*. But, in the phrasing of the Holy Father, with "discerning eyes" we can see "the Son of God, who became incarnate two thousand years ago, out of love for humanity, ... at work even today" *(NMI, 58)*. Then we can accept his call to keep on trying and with "a generous heart to become the instruments of his work" *(NMI 58)*.

The Pope invites us to examine our "spiritual and pastoral responsibilities", and significantly in that order. We will be unable to make disciples of the world until we ourselves are following Him consistently, ardently, enthusiastically. For this reason, the seven pastoral priorities suggested by the Holy Father begin with "Holiness". Christians will be effective in building the Kingdom of God to the degree that that Kingdom is within them. The Church will be as strong and holy as the domestic churches, the families that make it up, are strong and holy. To ask catechumens: "Do you wish to receive Baptism?" means at the same time to ask them: "Do you wish to become holy?". Are you a Christian? Then you must be a Saint-in-progress.

"Altum" means not only deep, but also "high". So, "Duc in altum" might also be translated "set out for the heights". In a spiritual reading of Christ words, then, his message might well be for Peter and for us to set our sights high, to be ambitious for the best in life. Remember the introduction to St. Paul's incomparable hymn to charity: *But earnestly desire the higher gifts. And I will show you a still more excellent way...* That is the way for us also to trod, but we have this impatience that Peter had, *I am a sinful man!* Or Isaiah also, *I am a man of unclean lips, living among people of unclean lips.* I can't be a saint! I read the Bible once in college – it just didn't grab me. Mass bores me, and I've got "issues" with the "official" church. I keep confessing the same sins. I get distracted when I pray. I'm always tempted. So I've packed in the nets, after laboring all night in vain.

No. There's Jesus who says: Don't pack it in! Put out into the deep! Go farther than you have ever gone before. With no rational hope of succeeding, but only trusting in Me, you will make progress. You will. Indeed, you will have success that boggles your mind. Peace, joy, understanding beyond anything you imagined, even here below. Just look at St. Paul and what our Lord did for him. The great danger is in giving up too soon, and lowering our sights – settling for mediocrity. If we strive until we feel our powerlessness, then God's grace can work; *when I am weak, then I am strong.* In dealing with God there's a sort of mystery, a paradox, that sense of laboring all night in vain and also that experience of pulling in scads of fish seem to happen simultaneously. So we can easily be deceived by perceived futility in our prayers and we mustn't. We may be making great progress even when it seems that we're not.

Likewise, in our efforts to bring Christ to the world. We must set our sights high. Remember, God has entrusted to us, the Catholics of this parish, the evangelization of the area within our borders – at least. Now, every time a man dies in one of our nursing homes without much religion, though he's lived in our midst for the last twenty years or so... we have to ask ourselves, "Did we do enough?" Did that fish get away because of our timidity, our pusillanimity? Why do we have thirty new converts every Easter vigil and not three hundred? Do we only catch the fish that jump into our boat on their own accord? Or do we continue to labor when it seems we've labored enough? Mediocrity can masquerade itself as humility. It isn't. We are made for great things: to be saints and to transform the face of the earth. The Christian spirit is anything but what we might call wimpy. Remember St. Paul, *For you did not receive the spirit of slavery to fall back into fear, but you have received the spirit of sonship...* this makes Paul bold: *I consider the sufferings of this present time are not worth comparing with the glory that is to be revealed to us.* So, "Put out into the deep, try again, you will succeed. The only reason a Christian fails is that he doesn't persevere.

"Duc in altum", the latest command of the Holy Father to us, comes twenty-two years after his first command to the world: Be not afraid! A man who knew the Pope, a dissident from a communist country, expressed something about him which is so rare and so revealing: He is a man without fear. He wants us to understand that every Christian should be a person without fear. We must not fear failure, or effort, or sacrifice, or great odds, or past sins, or temptations... in all these things we are more than conquerors in Him who loves us.

Here at Mass, we draw close to this One who loves us. "Every Sunday, the Risen Christ asks us to meet Him as it were once more in the Upper Room where, on the evening of 'the first day of the week' He appeared to His disciples in order to 'breathe' on them his life-giving Spirit and launch them on the great adventure of proclaiming the Gospel". Let us put out deeply into the mystery of Christ in the Eucharist so as to get strength to be "fishers of men" for He is asking each of us also. "Whom shall I send?" And like Isaiah, let us each one answer, according to our particular vocation, no matter how tired or discouraged we may be: Here I am Lord send me!

Love of God and Neighbor

God is Love

The revelation of the name of God to Moses in the desert, from the burning bush, was thought by the Jews to be his ultimate self-revelation: *I am who am.* Yet, Jesus Christ came to reveal more about

God, and this revelation which is the ultimate revelation about the divinity was expressed by the beloved disciple with no fanfare at all, in his first letter: God not only is, *God is love*. It is this Love, with a capital L, — that is bigger than we are, stronger than death, and pre-existing the universe — that is our concern today. We as Christians should have no time to stop and admire the natural loves, the petty loves, the self-interested loves, that the world enjoys. As Christ said, *If you love those who love you, what good is that? Do not the pagans do as much?* This is not the love to which Christ refers when He says *Remain in my love.* He is talking about that Love which is a mystery, which is an acting as God acts. *Love one another as I*, God incarnate, *have loved you.* By love, we can be perfect as our Heavenly Father is perfect. And this is not an option but a command; indeed, the command. *This is my command, love one another....*

We can only love our neighbor, even our enemy, with this love, a love that would lay down our life for him, if we have loved God first. Many people forget that. Love that comes naturally is of no consequence — the pagans do as much; it's supernatural love that counts. For this reason, it's impossible to love our neighbor — even a spouse, child or friend — unless we love God first. When we love our neighbor out of love of God, then we can love him without limit; we break out of the limitations of a natural love. It seems simple then. We love God and then we will love our neighbor. But there is a problem. On our own we cannot love God. St. Philip Neri cried out, "How is it possible for him who believes in God to love anything but God?" It would seem that we would be drawn naturally to love God and yet, it is our common experience as believers that it is very hard to love Him as we ought. We could not love Him at all, John tells us, if He had not loved us first. Paul describes this to the Romans: *"The love of God has been poured into our hearts through the Holy Spirit who has been given to us".*

This love that we received, we must make it grow. Rather, we must ask God to make it grow, for it is always His gift. St. Alphonsus Ligouri tells us how: "To obtain and preserve Divine Love, three things are necessary: meditation, communion, and prayer. First, meditation is necessary. He who thinks but little on God, loves Him but little. In meditation, a fire shall flame out. Meditation, and particularly meditation on the passion of Christ, is the blessed furnace, in which the love of God is kindled and fanned. Holy Communion is another holy furnace in which we are inflamed with Divine Love." "The Holy Eucharist," says St. John Chrysostom, "is a fire which inflames us so that, like a lion breathing fire, we may retire from the table, being made terrible to the devil." (and beloved to God) Thirdly the prayer of petition is necessary. It is by means of prayer that God dispenses all of His favors, but particularly, the great gift of Divine Love. To make us ask for this love, meditation is a great help. Without meditation we shall ask little or nothing from God. We must then always, every day and several times a day ask God to give us the grace to love Him with our whole heart.

This is the practical method we must take away. Every day we must ask the Lord: Widen my heart! Enable me to love You as I ought! Let me never offend you, O Lord! We can be sure that these prayers will never go unanswered and a by-product of this love of God will be what the Lord promises in the Gospel, joy in our hearts. *All this I tell you that my joy may be yours and your joy may be complete.*

Growth in Love of God

Can this first and greatest commandment be kept? If this really is the essence of Gospel morality, we had better know the answer to these questions! Is it an ideal, a horizon to aim for or a bare minimum? Is the perfection implied, possible for a chosen few saints or expected of all Christians? Some have wanted to see our Lord prescribing the total love of God, as a counsel, that is, as an invitation for some, but requiring some lesser degree of love of God for others. However, in another version, Christ is responding to the question: *What must I do to have eternal life?* Jesus is, therefore, expressing a commandment for all people, necessary to gain Heaven.

In fact, it is not really possible to love God in any other way than with our whole heart. Even human relationships indicate that it's impossible to love in half-measures. Love is gift of self. An irrevocable gift too. You either give a gift or you don't. This is true with respect to God as well. For Christ, each person falls into one of two classes and *he who is not with Me is against Me (Lk 11.23)*. Upon careful reflection, we can see that it is possible to love God totally but with more or less intensity. We might see an analogy in human relationships too: a husband loves his wife totally, but not always in an actual, evident, intense manner. We call it "taking for granted". Likewise, everyone who has sanctifying grace, who loves nothing contrary to God, or equally to God, loves Him with his whole heart. He may not love Him in the best manner, but he fulfills the law. There are, in other words, different orders of perfection: just as a baby is perfect when born, but when it grows it gains in perfection still.

So Christ is telling his disciples who love totally, but weakly, to love totally and ever more intensely. This is a call to continual conversion Since we can always increase our love for God in this way, the precept is in a sense never going to be fully satisfied. In this sense, the great commandment is a horizon. Thus, there is no place at which to rest in one's spiritual life. St. Thomas says explicitly: "the love of God and of our neighbor is not commanded according to a measure." This is because love of God is the end for which we were made; it is not a means to get there. "We can never love God as much as He ought to be loved, nor believe and hope in Him as much as we should" (Aquinas)

Now, if our love of God can continually grow more intense in this life, and Christ commands us to do so, what are we doing about it? How will our love grow? All growth must come from God. *The love of God* must be *poured into our hearts through the Holy Spirit who has been given to us.* Of course we must be disposed, we must be eager, but God must give us his grace. This habitual disposition to grow in love of God is prayer. Prayer is turning in love towards God. It is there that we receive from Him. It is there that we experience His love, and we will love to the degree that we have been loved by Him. *We love, because He first loved us.(I Jn 4.19)* Yes, it is imperative that we take time to recognize God's great love for us. We must do more than think about it — it must penetrate into our hearts and transform them so that they can go and do likewise. The fact is that this most obvious datum of our creed — that God loves us — is probably the one that we have the hardest time really believing. The proof is that we are not saints.

This change is the work of prayer. Do not say that you pray if you only read out of a book. The prayers you say must reach down into your heart. You have to be speaking to the personal God. It must be communion with Him. Vocal prayer must lead to meditation. Considering the mighty works of God: Creation, Redemption — the Cross; the Church and Eucharist. In time, your relationship of love, your time of prayer will be an awareness of presence, a communication that surpasses concepts, a union of hearts which is called contemplation. Contemplative souls live in a state of prayer. Here, we have people who are coming very close to fulfilling the precept, even in the second sense of an intense, actualized total loving and not a minimal, habitual total loving. My dear brothers and sisters, we have much to do. It takes a lot of time to learn to pray. And time is short. Let us learn to love, for *In the evening of life we will be judged on love.* (St. John of the Cross)

Loving God Above All Things

The Beatitudes are, first and foremost, promises. As the Catechism tells us, "the Beatitudes fulfill the promises of the Old Testament by ordering them no longer merely to the possession of a territory, but to the Kingdom of Heaven." Christ asks us to trust, to trust that God, and God alone, can fulfill all the longings of the human heart. Only by loving Him above all things will we ever be happy. Since we can only have perfect union with God in the hereafter, we can't find perfect happiness here below. What's more, Christ seems to be saying that if we try to seek happiness in this life, we're putting up an obstacle to our ultimate goal, because in order to love God above all things, we must turn, now, from all that is not Him, all that might substitute for Him. Thus He says, *Woe to you rich, for you have received your consolation...* and so on. In other language St. John of the Cross, a faithful interpreter of the Gospels, writes, "The further you withdraw from earthly things, the closer you approach Heavenly things."

Now to accept this teaching, which is the high point of the moral teachings of Jesus Christ, requires great trust in God. It's so much easier to grasp after happiness we can see, that's not merely promised for the hereafter. In Jeremiah we see these two paths. The path of the wicked, which he said leads to destruction, is the path of those who trust in finite goods, who seek their strength in the flesh, who turn from the Lord. People love created things for themselves, not as gifts of God which speak of Him and lead us to Him. In this way the gifts of God get misused, which is what we call sin. The just man, on the other hand, loves the Giver, not the gifts. That's why he has no worries in the year of drought, that's why when he loses his finite goods, he's not distraught, because he's set his heart on their source. Those who follow the Beatitudes find not only happiness in the hereafter, but even right here on earth. Didn't Christ promise as much? That those who give up everything for His sake and the sake of the Gospel would receive everything back now, that they gave up, and eternal life as well.

So if we want to be happy, now and forever, this is the time to examine where we place our treasure, where our hearts are. Are they set on Heaven or things that will pass away? A good place to start may be to examine what we tend to think about when we are alone and what we tend to pray about. While it's good to pray for temporal gifts, is that all we turn to God for? Or do we ask Him to fill us with His Spirit and His virtues? When we do ask for finite goods, is it with the purpose of serving Him better and helping Him spread His Kingdom? St. Paul's words must never leave us, If we hope in Christ for this world only, then we are the most pitiable persons of all. If, however, we have hoped in Him for eternal life, than blessed shall we be even now.

Divine Love

Today is the feast of the apostle Matthias. Our joy in recalling this apostle's life is muted however, by the circumstances of his coming to be an apostle. He replaces Judas who, we are told, *deserted the cause.* Our Lord had chosen Judas even though He knew that Judas would not remain in his love. In the Gospel Jesus tells us that we, too, have been chosen and exhorts us, too, to remain in his love. We will take a great stride towards succeeding where Judas failed if we understand correctly what this love is that Jesus speaks of. In particular, it is not something of ours but a gift from God; it is not natural love but divine charity. Our Lord is referring to the theological virtue of charity infused at baptism, not our own human love. His grace transformed our natural love into something much greater.

Why is this point so important? Because if we try to love God and neighbor with our own human love we will fail. We cannot fulfill the commandments with our own will power. Besides, the commandments are just the minimum He expects of us, for He has called us to heroic charity, to laying down our lives for others. Those who try to love as Jesus did, by their own human love, get frustrated quickly. Then they claim that the commandments are impossible, just ideals to shoot for, and really God doesn't expect us to keep them. The Church is unfair, they say, to hold fast in proclaiming them without exceptions, and then they, too, *desert the cause...* No, the Church is not unfair, and Christ expects the commandments to be kept. But He expects us to do all this with the supernatural power He gives us. He equips us for the life He has called us to: *you did not choose me, but I chose you and appointed you to go and bear fruit, fruit that will endure.* Our deeds endure forever, that is, they merit an eternal reward, because they are the fruit of Divine Love working in us. Let us welcome that Divine Love now poured out into our hearts in this Holy Sacrament.

Where Your Treasure Is

The Lord's parable about the pearl of great price and the treasure buried in the field are amongst the many images He uses to teach about the Kingdom of Heaven. The key thing about these two is that, in both cases, it took all that the man had to buy the field, to buy the pearl. What's indicated is the necessity of a total response in order to enter into the Kingdom of God. Christ made this point in so many ways, not putting your hand to the plow and turning back, and in many, many ways. We see the point in regard to money in that famous story of Ananias and Sapphia, in the Acts of the Apostles, how they gave a great deal to the Church, but they didn't give everything. Compare that to the widow's mite, who gave very little but she gave all that she had and won the praise of the Lord. So what we see in these examples of giving money is true of everything we need to give to the Lord, our energy, our time, our obedience, everything.

It's so easy for a Christian to give ninety-nine percent, to do a lot of good things, going to visit someone in the hospital, let's say, but to do it begrudgingly, or do it while thinking that they are doing a good work, with some kind of lack of self emptying. This is what we have to avoid. We have to give ourselves totally to Christ, for the reason, He gave Himself totally for us. St. Teresa of Avila tells us He would have died to save one single soul, He poured Himself out for us, so our response can't be anything but total.

Let me just read you a little section of this book by one of the greatest thinkers of the twentieth century, Deitrich Von Hildebrand, where he makes this point. "True self surrender consists in giving ourselves to Christ absolutely, in a spirit of loving admiration, in our full renunciation of our sovereignty, in our becoming empty with regard to other things…So long as we draw the line somewhere in us, we have not given ourselves to Christ in a way that is a true self surrender. We must really push our skiffs off from the shore and burn the boats behind us. The important thing is to do away with all conditions and reservations, overt or hidden. In this matter, very much is of little avail, it has to be all. It is only by the totality of our surrender, by our leap into the dark, that we achieve the loss of our soul." Of course he means the loss of our soul in the sense that those who lose their soul will find it. Let's ask the Lord for that gift of self knowledge today, to see where we hold back in giving our all.

Total Conversion

Where your treasure is there shall your heart be also. The heart is another way of saying the depths of a person, his soul. The eyes also refer to the interior of man; we can see what a person is really like from his eyes, the "window to the soul". They tell us what a person desires and if his will is crooked. Light and dark are obvious metaphors for good and evil desires. If he longs for "dark" things his soul will be dark.

It is significant that Our Lord's discussion of the interior of man comes soon after He preached the Beatitudes. The essence of his New Law was that it must consist of interior holiness, not external propriety. There is a world of difference between. "I never stole anything" and "I never wanted to steal". The ninth and tenth commandments were precursors to the whole Christian moral revolution. Coveting is as bad as stealing; lusting as adultery itself. Christ called for such a renewal of our souls that our desires would be good. Then we would be free, for we could do whatever we wished without sinning. As St. Augustine puts it: "Love, and do what you wish."

A corollary to this interior morality is that we can never say "Enough". We can never decide that we are pleasing to God, and we need only maintain the status quo. No, this transformation is a substitution of our earthly desires for God. He is the light that must illuminate our souls until He be all we desire. This will not be fully achieved until Heaven is attained. In this life, we are always in a process: He is infinite, so we can always make progress, and we are so weak that if we cease striving, we retreat. Let us examine our hearts every day, and ask how our deepest desires could be more consonant with one who wishes to love God above every other thing.

Purifying Our Love

When we first hear Jesus' words in the gospel we think of those who have entered religious life and have, literally, left home and the possibility of family, for the sake of the Gospel. We think of missionaries like St. Augustine of Canterbury who was sent by St. Gregory the Great to evangelize England. St. Gregory sent word: "It is better never to undertake any high enterprise than to abandon it once it has started. The greater the labor, the greater will be the glory of your eternal reward." Risk everything for God, and the pay off is worth it, he seems to be saying.

If we compare the reading from Sirach to the Gospel, the message is the same. While the Old Testament author speaks of giving the *first fruits* to the Lord, and tithing, so as to receive a seven-fold return, Jesus Christ calls us to give everything and expect a hundred fold return. We can never give enough to the Lord. We must love the goods that God gives us, people included, only because we love God and see God in them. This is Charity as we learn in the Catechism: Charity is to love God above all things, and to love our neighbor for God's sake. To achieve this detachment is not easy and feels very much like giving up wife, brothers, land for my sake and the sake of the Gospel. The result however, is to purify our love of all selfishness. Thus we love creation and family more, and still we are free to give them up when the giver of every good gift takes them back, as He always does.

This enables us to give back something to God, as the first reading said, with a *cheerful face*.

Loving Others for Christ's Sake

The love John is talking about is Charity, friendship with God. And because we love God, we love what He loves: his creation, ourselves and our neighbors. If we love anyone for any other reason, this does not increase our friendship with God; it can even distance us from Him. But to love as much as God loves, is not easy. In fact it is impossible for us. Love, according to the Gospel demands what is beyond man's ability to give. [No purely human will can decide to leave family and friends to take care of the poor in Calcutta. It is impossible, naturally speaking.] It is possible only as a gift of God, who heals, restores, and transforms the human heart by His grace (*Veritatis Splendor*). It is as we saw in the Gospel yesterday: God commands the impossible: "you feed the five thousand" and then He gives us the ability to do it.

However, this proposal of the most high — to be *as He is, so are we in the world* — is frightening. When Christ draws near with His New Law of love we recoil in fear like the Apostles. "I can't do without *that*," we say. "I wouldn't be happy or fulfilled or free or mature if I didn't do such and such." That burden is to heavy, that person too awful, that demand of the Church too difficult. We fail in generosity and courage a thousand times a day because we forget that Christ brings His grace. He has established a friendship between God and us that enables us to love like God. *Be not afraid, it is I.* Let us trust Him, and like the Apostles, let us be astounded by His power at work in us.

Love is Self Sacrifice

This seems like a passage of the gospel that everybody in the world could agree to, that he who loves his neighbor has fulfilled the law. That love never does anything wrong to the neighbor, hence love is the fulfillment of the law. Everyone in the world, you would think, could agree to that. Everybody admires love, we even have it on our postage stamps, but the reason why this seems so agreeable is that there's an equivocation on the word, love. Most people tend to think of love as what we are attracted to naturally, but love in the New Testament is really that which we are not attracted to, it's sacrifice, it's self-giving. Love is not a feeling, but love is self donation, sacrifice. It's a decision to give oneself to others. And this appears very clearly in Our Lord Jesus' words in the gospel, that to follow Him along the way of love means to be willing to turn away from everything that you naturally love; father, mother, brother, sister, even one's very self.

Self denial is what really shows that we love. So the conclusion, *none of you can be my disciple if he does not renounce all of his possessions.* Not everyone is called to be a Franciscan and have no possessions whatsoever. But yet, everyone is called to be willing to give them up should service and love of Our Lord require it. This is truly the new commandment of love. Not to love in the way everyone has loved since the very beginning, not even to love the way the Jewish people did, to love one another as you love yourself, but what makes it a new commandment is what Christ said, to *love one another as I have loved you.* In other words, to be willing to make that decision to sacrifice everything for the beloved, to carry a cross for them. This should explain how people make mistakes in the moral life, the most obvious one, Euthanasia. They think that they have love in their hearts when they decide on mercy killing, cutting short someone else's life because they see the pain. So they break the law, thinking that they love. Why? Because the love that they're talking about is not real love, but just a feeling. That doesn't guide us, rather the decision to give ourselves no matter what the cost, that sort of love will fulfill the law. That's the sort of love of which Our Lord said, *If you love Me, keep My commandments.*

The only way to know if we have real love, because again, it's not a feeling, is if we keep His commandments. So we must make this very concrete. We have to realize if we're going to grow in love, we have to be making very concrete steps, practical steps that can be seen, decisions to love Him more. Guided by our feeling, we will not know if we are growing in love. This is extremely important for those who pray, for all who make daily meditations, sitting in the Lord's presence trying to increase their love for Him. You will not know if you're growing in love for Him by the way you feel. On the contrary, you may feel a million miles away from Him and, in fact, be loving Him very much. And what is the test? If your prayer ends in a very concrete resolution, how can I do something today to change my life slightly more to be a little more like the Lord Jesus, pick up my cross a little more today and follow in His footsteps. A very concrete way of showing you love the Lord, though you may not feel that you love the Lord any more.

Love One Another

John tells us, *Beloved, love one another.* This advice, this commandment, which is repeated by others in various ways, is one that we have to hear many many times over. We don't often hear it because it seems too obvious to tell each other, "Let us love one another." But in all the major Christian communities that I've known, schools, families, parishes, so on, this simple commandment, and the most essential for us Christians, isn't followed enough, preached enough, or practiced enough. Too often we think of our search for holiness in a very self centered way, really, as a sort of self improvement, making myself more humble, more disciplined, more recollected, or some other virtue, rather than realizing that our perfection will come as a by-product of focusing on the other and loving them. It's very easy to overlook this commandment because, very often, we get along so well with the others with whom we work. We can enjoy their company, we can cooperate well with them, we can be very civil and polite, we can serve them, depend on them, admire them, but all without really loving. So, we have to always remind ourselves to *love* one another and *every* person that the Lord gives to us. It's the great key to holiness. It's the only road to holiness. It's the narrow way, also the shortcut, the fulfillment of the law, the only requirement of the new commandment.

To love one another is to see in each person the good that the Lord Jesus sees in them, the great inestimable value that makes sense of that Psalm, *What is man that Thou art mindful of him?* Something so good in each person that God cared about it enough to die to preserve it. We have to see past all the defenses that people put up, all of the crutches they have, all the superficialities which can make people so annoying or difficult. We have to see past to their soul, just their soul, naked before God, totally nothing without Him, totally depending on Him, needing Him for everything. We have to especially see them, imagine them, with their hidden sufferings, which is what God sees so much and why He loves to go out to them, and heal them. We have to see in them a great potential, the great beauty of what they could be made by grace, raised up to great perfection, the unique reflection of God's beauty that each soul is meant to be. So, we have to meditate upon these things or imagine them in each of our neighbors, especially in the ones that are difficult, so as to love one another. And of course, we must ask God for help.

To Love As Christ Loves

In the first reading from Paul, He tells his people, *of all those virtues put on love which binds all other virtues together and makes them perfect.* And in the gospel itself, which is from the beatitudes of

St. Luke, the Lord explains what He means by love. One almost doesn't want to comment on it, it's the most exalted teaching of our religion. It's what it's founded on, love. We have to be very careful. As St. Francis de Sales said, "Love, the word we vilify so much." We use the word a lot but we don't often mean love in the sense that Our Lord means here. How opposite the human understanding of love is. People who are lovable are usually the ones that are the most attractive, charming, nice to us, as the Lord points out, those are the ones we're drawn to love. So we can very easily think that we're loving people. But the saints show us the opposite really. St. Peter Claver, whose feast we celebrate today, for instance. Who did He love? It was the slaves getting off the boats down in South America at the end of the seventeenth century, the people who were the most unlovable, the most despised, the most ignorant, the most unpleasant. Imagine, getting off the boat after three months at sea, diseased and smelly. People wouldn't want to get near them, yet he came close to them, he loved them, kissed them, he washed them and healed them. He said, "I am the slave of the slaves forever."

Another saint, Claude de la Colombiere, from roughly the same period comments on Our Lord's words, "I often ponder with joy and admiration, the extreme care Jesus took to urge us to love others. In the Gospel we read that He commanded it above all things. *Love one another as I have loved you...By this all men shall know that you are my disciples, if you have love for one another. (Jn. 13:34, 35)* Another time He tells us that no reason, either interest or of honor allows us to hate another. He will not acknowledge us and He ranks us with pagans and infidels if we do not love our enemies, if we will not pray for them and serve them when occasion offers... My God, how sweet and humane this commandment. How worthy of the goodness and the wisdom of God. It is but reasonable that men that have the same nature, the same Father, men who are obliged to live together, who are fellow travelers, and who are to be together for all eternity in Heaven, should begin to love each other here and should render each other mutual services such as they would wish themselves to receive."

God's Special Love

One of the ways of seeing the radical newness of the Gospel is in the teaching on wealth and poverty. Almost overnight, Jesus Christ turned poverty from a curse into a good. It had been a sign of God's displeasure; now, the poor were blessed, the object of God's special love. How are we to live in a world that has homeless people and starving people when we know the story of Dives and Lazarus, in which the rich man was punished for nothing else but *having good things* while Lazarus had none? Nor can we forget that Jesus did not qualify his command given to all his disciples: *Sell your possessions and give alms. (Lk. 12.33)* We must strive to be *rich in God (Lk. 12.21)*, to have our thoughts on *Heavenly things and not things of the earth.*

We are all placed by God into a certain state of life. While all Christians must live the virtue of poverty of spirit, there must be Christians in every strata of society. There have been many holy kings and queens, but they lived among luxury without coveting it. Many would have fled to convents if they could but they were Christians where they were put. We must be content with the lot we are given. Our test is always: how sad would we be if we lost something? Where your treasure is, there is your heart. This is Poverty in spirit which allows even the rich to be humble of heart. As the Psalmist recommends: *If riches increase, set not your heart on them. (Ps. 62.10).* We must not ask "Can I afford this or that?" but "Do we need this or that? Could this money be used for God's glory in some other way?" The only time when the rule for a Christian is not simplicity and utility, is when we are honoring God. Then, even St. Francis of Assisi spared no expense: "Above everything else, I want this most holy Sacrament to be honored and venerated and reserved in places which are richly ornamented."

Even though the Church defends private property as a right in human society, there is a prior order in which we are not the absolute owners of what we have. If someone needs what I have, he has a right to it, even if it has my name on it. In certain cases, what we may consider charity, we owe in justice. Not only does God have a right to all things, but He is in control of them all. *The Lord makes poor and makes rich; He brings low, He also exalts (1 Sam 2.7).* Storing up riches to guard against misfortune can turn very quickly from prudent administration of family resources to a lack of trust in God's providence. We must meditate upon the Lord's words: *O men of little faith! Do not seek what you are to eat and what you are to drink, nor be of anxious mind... your Father knows that you need them. Instead, seek his Kingdom, and these things shall be yours as well. (Lk. 12.22)*

God will take care of us, but He will not keep us from hurting. Indeed, this is what we need to do if we are to follow Him, who for our sakes, though He was rich, made Himself poor. In the words of the *Imitation of Christ* "nudus nudum Iesum sequi", we must be naked to follow the naked Jesus. Mother Teresa tells all people: "Give until it hurts". That is the only measure of how much to give, because then one is thinking in terms of love. Then one can see clearly. "Without suffering, there is no love".

The Widow's Mite

St. Paulinus of Nola was born the son of a noble family of Bordeaux in the middle of the fourth century. With his wife's agreement, he had decided to give away his fortune and join the newest movement in the church — building houses for monks. Of this poor widow, St. Paulinus wrote: "Call to mind the widow who forgot herself in her concern for the poor, and, thinking only of the life to come, gave away all her means of subsistence, as the Judge Himself bears witness. Others, He says, have given of their superfluous wealth; but she, possessed of only two small coins and more needy perhaps than many of the poor — though in spiritual riches she surpassed all the wealthy — she thought only of the world to come, and had such a longing for heavenly treasure that she gave away, all at once, whatever she had that was derived from the earth and destined to return there."

This freedom and joy are perpetual characteristics of saints. Do you know the same joy of giving to some degree? This is what Christ wants to teach us: He is not giving us a new burden to carry when He speaks of generosity, but He is trying to free us up for the joy of the Christian virtue of poverty of spirit. Obviously we are not all called to give away every penny we own so that we must beg our food, as the widow must have done. In fact, in the ordinary plan of God, we are morally bound to keep enough money to take care of our needs and the needs of those who depend upon us. This means not only food and board, but whatever is necessary to lead a becoming manner of life in the state of life in which we find ourselves. What is more than this, is surplus, and should be given away.

However, it won't be easy to decide exactly what is surplus or what is not. The necessities of those in our care will require responsible financial planning for the future; Jesus is not saying that no one can have a savings account! St. Paul provides a justification for this when he says: *Let the thief no longer steal, but rather let him labor, doing honest work with his hands, so that he may be able to give to those in need. (Eph 4.28)* Still, Jesus does wish for grace to elevate our natural prudence to a reliance on Divine Providence that is not foolhardy, but may appear so to those without faith. The important thing is that we view, however much money we have — as well as time, property, talents, etc, — as belonging to God. *What have you*

that you have not received? asks St. Paul. If we are genuinely convinced that what we have stewardship of, belongs to God for His use,
it is so much easier to decide what portion of God's money He wants
me to keep and what portion He wants me to distribute. Certainly, the
test for whether or not one is giving out of one's surplus only or whether
one has arrived at the point of giving out of one's subsistence is simple:
does it hurt? That is the test. Mother Teresa did not want people's excess
money, but would say "Give until it hurts". That is pleasing to God.

This is important because what has value is not the amount of
dollars but the amount of love that they represent. The widow's mite
was of far greater value than the great sums deposited by others because she obviously had greater love. It was the fervor of her charity
that made her gift so valuable. And this was shown by her lack of self-
concern. Charity really comes from God; that is what gives a truly
charitable gift it's power to do much more good than its material value
is capable of doing. Just as the widow of Zarephath's flour and oil was
multiplied by God on account of her love, so the value of the widow's
two coins was multiplied by God on account of her love.

Living the spirit of poverty is daring, it's exhilarating — like
trusting a parachute. It is depending totally on God, that He will not
let someone like the widow come to harm. It is a way of living that
Christians have been drawn to from the beginning. As Paul says of the
Macedonians: *For they gave according to their means, as I can testify,
and beyond their means, of their own free will, begging us earnestly
for the favor of taking part in the relief of the saints (2 Cor 3-4)* Once
again, the Lord's point is not for us to feel guilty that we are not giving as much as great saints, past and present. Rather, let us begin to
see our possessions, time, etc., as belonging exclusively to God. Let
us meditate upon the totality of the Gift of Christ — *offered once to
take away the sins of many* — and seek every day to make greater sacrifices. We will be growing in love and so also in the desire to "give til
it hurts" in many ways. In that context, in prayerful union of hearts
with Christ Jesus, we will be able to judge what is prudent in God's
eyes, what He is asking of us, and what is the path to greater joy.

Why the Poor Look So Sweet

Did we ever stop to ask ourselves why the Lord Jesus cured so
frequently on the Sabbath? It's a good question. It had always seemed
to me that He was simply being provocative. As we heard, there are
six other days on which He could have cured. But He didn't. It seems
He almost goes out of His way to cure on the Sabbath. In fact maybe

there's another reason why we often see Him cure on the Sabbath. Not because He wanted to provoke, but simply because He encountered people on the Sabbath, perhaps around the synagogue. That's where He saw these sick people and He wasn't going to wait to heal them on another day. He viewed it as an emergency, as a case of urgency, to go out and help the people He ran into, as if an animal had fallen into a ditch and needed to be rescued. As soon as the Lord saw someone in need He was not going to delay until another day. This is a beautiful insight into the Lord's heart and we see this in the hearts of the saints, that they had an overpowering attraction for people in need and they went to them to help them at once. Of course there is no better example than St. Martin de Porres.

Cardinal Cushing, writing about him, says, "If he had any fault, it was this, that he could not resist the urge to undertake any good work which could lend itself as capable of accomplishment." He could not resist helping those around him, he was drawn to the poor, he found an attraction in them. An attraction to those we are normally repelled by, that is. This reminded me of something my brother once said before I was born. My Mother always tells the story of how when she was at the grocery store once and they were at the checkout counter he saw a woman ahead of them who he thought was a poor old woman buying a can of soup or something. He whispered to my mother, "Mom, why is it that the poor look so sweet?" What an insight for a boy. First of all to notice that there were people in need, not only to notice that, but to find them sweet and beautiful, attractive.

This is what the Church means by preferential option for the poor, not just that we have a duty to help them first, but that we're drawn to help them first. Maybe this is another way of looking at Our Lord's words, *The poor we will always have with us*, not simply because we'll never solve the problem, but because we need to have them always with us. The poor people in need, the sick, the suffering, the handicapped, are the beautiful things in life that attract us, and teach us to love. So let us give thanks for this plan of God and so many friends of God, these people in need. Let us realize that, serving them, is our greatest honor because, in fact, they have this great mission in life, to be such beautiful signs of people who are like Christ, carrying their Cross in various ways. Let us ask the Lord then for hearts like St. Martin de Porres.

Works of Mercy

The Lord, in the Gospel passage we have here, is announcing to the world that He is the Messiah, that He is the one who was sent to fulfill all of these signs of the Messiah, preaching the Good News to the poor, liberty to captives and so on. Later on, when John the Baptist is in jail and wants to make sure that Jesus is in fact the One sent by God, He sends two people to ask Him, *Are you the One or are we to wait for another?* And Christ gives the same answer and says, *Go tell John what you have seen and heard, that the lame are walking, that the blind are seeing, that the dead are being raised, and that the Good News is being preached to the poor.* All these things really are works of mercy. Of course Our Lord, to show His power did them in a marvelous way, bringing miraculous cures to the sick and so on, but Christians are to be identified in basically the same way. Filled with the same Spirit of God, we're supposed to, likewise, help the sick and the blind, the poor and the prisoners, and do all these works of mercy and love that St. John tells us we must.

We must love our brother. He who hates his brother can't possibly love God. And Jesus said, This is how to identify Christians. They'll know that you are my disciples by your love. In a very similar way that we identified the Messiah by His love, so also people will identify us as Christ's disciples, by our love. Very often we are doing these works of mercy without realizing it and that can be, not a good thing. The other day, for instance I happened to have to go visit one of our parishioners who's temporarily in jail. I had a list of things to do. I went and did them all. Then, later that night when I was doing my prayers, it just so happened that the Gospel passage came up where the Lord said, when I was in jail, did you visit Me? Whatever you did for the least of my brothers, that you did to Me. I realized I was doing what the Lord asked, I was visiting the Lord in jail but I hadn't realized. That's not a good thing, because then we could begin to do these very important works automatically, without putting all our heart into it and without really seeing Christ Jesus there and without perhaps the right intention. We all have to be aware of the opportunities to do good that God gives us every day, which we might be doing, but we should do it now with conscientiousness, with awareness, with gratitude, with more perfection, with great prayer for God's help and so on.

This should be remembered by those who live in a family, mothers especially. All day long they're doing works of mercy. They're feeding the hungry, they're teaching the ignorant, taking care of the sick, they're clothing the baby. They're doing the works of mercy all day long, but it can be so automatic that maybe some mothers don't notice it. So we mustn't do that, but rather every morning, offer to God our day, in general, and then in particular, try to be aware; Here I am, doing a work of mercy. Here I am clothing one of Christ's needy ones. Here's a little one that I'm taking care of so I'm taking care of Our Lord and so I'm being a true Christian, and a follower of the Messiah. So let us ask Our Lord for His help in living as He did.

Good Works

In one of the other accounts of this multiplication of the loaves and fishes, the disciples add, when they say we have only five loaves and two fish, *but what are they among so many?* An Italian Bishop comments on that, "We anxiously ask ourselves the same question in almost the same words, every time we try to do a good deed. We cannot do everything, we cannot help everyone." In other words, what are our meager resources among so much need? He goes on to say that when we do some good, we always feel empty inside afterwards, as if we haven't done very much. "When we do good, we are never satisfied, goodness is infinite like God, the more we do the more there is to do and we never get it done. Goodness means a very great un-slacking effort, hence the disappointment we always feel when we have done something good."

This is a problem that has a solution. Namely, to do all that we do in union with the Lord Jesus Christ. In fact, have Him doing the good in us. Quoting the *Imitation of Christ,* "He rises easily who is carried by the grace of God." We have to remember that it's not the quantity of what we do, it's not the degree to which we overcome all the evil around us, that pleases God, but rather that we do it united to God, and do only what He's asking of us. St. John of the Cross says, "Think not that pleasing God lies so much in doing a great deal as in doing it with good will, without possessiveness and human respect." Very important is that, 'without possessiveness,' because that means you're aware that it's not any of our doing that is going to please the Lord, but rather His grace at work in us that pleases Him. It's what He does in us that He rewards with Eternal Life. Then we begin to understand things like the Lord saying, if you have but the tiniest mustard seed of faith, nothing will be impossible to you. Then we have the sense that not only can we do what's required of us, but we can do all things. St. Teresa of Avila once said, "Teresa can do nothing alone, Teresa can do less than nothing, but Teresa and God can do anything." So let us face these and all of our challenges with true Christian hope.

Others First

In the time of Jesus, lepers and Samaritans were both looked down upon. But Jesus showed his followers that they must love them both in this gospel. We hear from the first reading *The Lord of all shows no partiality, nor does He fear greatness, because He Himself made the great as well as the small and He provides for all alike.* So the Lord God shows no partiality. But there's more that we might add, because on the surface of it, that's something everybody really aspires to; to treat everyone equally.

So Jesus must be teaching us more. And indeed He is. We are not just to treat one another equally, but rather treat everyone else as if they are better than we. Imagine a society where everyone treated others not as equals but as betters. Very, very different. That's what we're called to do. There was a Spanish nobleman who went on to become a Cardinal of the Church, who wrote, "That others may be loved more than I, Jesus, grant me the grace to desire it. That others may be esteemed more than I, Jesus, grant me the grace to desire it. That in the opinion of the world, others may increase and I may decrease. That others may be chosen and I may be passed by, that others may be praised and I unnoticed, Jesus, grant me the grace to desire it. That others may be preferred to me in everything. That others may become holier than I, provided I may become as holy as I should. Jesus, grant me the grace to desire it."

Encouraging Others

We know that human beings often have a tendency to ignore the good in others and focus on the bad, which is what the Gospel was about yesterday, seeing the splinter in the neighbor's eye. It's also a tendency, and a bad one, to see the good and ignore the bad, or it can be, because that might be settling for our neighbor's being mediocre when , in fact, we can help them, help them on the road to being perfect. Because Christ sees the good in us and loves us, for that very reason, He also points out what is lacking. In this case it was this man's attachment to his goods, so He said, *If you would be perfect, go and sell what you possess...*

So let us remember, that is how the Lord looks at us. He sees the good and He sees the bad, very much as the Son of Man speaks to the churches in Revelation, *I know your deeds, your labor, and your patient endurance. I know you cannot tolerate wicked men. You are patient. You do not become discouraged. I hold this against you, however: You have turned aside from your early love.* First He points out the good and then the bad. *I know you hold fast to My name, and have not denied the faith you have in Me, nevertheless, I hold a few matters against you...,* then a list of them, and likewise to the other churches.

So, the Lord Jesus desires our perfection, because He desires our love, because He loves us. We might apply to ourselves what the Holy Father says of the family, "Family, become what you are." In other words, "Christians, become what you are." You are called, by nature, to be perfect, to be holy. Yet it is a lifetime of work. Let us now continue the holy Mass, asking the Lord to perfect us with His Grace.

Christ Our Breastplate

Today is of course, St. Patrick's day. Of all the things he is famous for, perhaps the most beautiful is his prayer, the Breastplate of St. Patrick. "Christ before me, Christ behind me, Christ within me" and so on. Christ protects his disciples, leading them safely through this life.

In the Gospel we see Christ doing just that: protecting a woman in great distress. There is an enormous difference between his action and that of Daniel. Daniel intervenes so that *innocent blood was spared that day*. Christ on the other hand knows that the woman before Him is guilty of her sin but saves her anyway. Daniel protected Susanna from injustice; Christ is protecting this woman from justice without mercy. Christ's message transforms our view of salvation. By nature, we are all sinners — no one can throw a stone. We must wash in his innocent blood that God did not spare on Good Friday. He gives us the grace of conversion, the ability to *go and sin no more*. He becomes our Breastplate and sure defense.

The Annunciation

The Annunciation

The mystery of our Redemption, achieved in the sight of all Jerusalem, had already begun in a very secret place, the womb of the Virgin. For, from the moment of his Incarnation *(CCC 606)*, the Son embraced the will of his Father which is to *unite all things in Him, things in Heaven and things on earth. (Eph 1.10)*. This unification began by the assumption of human nature by God, and it is not complete until divine nature is shared by man when we *acquire possession of our inheritance to the praise of his glory (Eph 1.14)*.

The success of God's plan depends upon obedience: primarily, the perfect obedience of the human will of Christ. *Lo, I have come to do your will.* But it will not be accomplished without our cooperation. As

St. Augustine said: "God created you without you, but He will not redeem you without you." The Blessed Virgin speaks in the name of the whole human race when she cooperates in this salvific plan: *Be it done unto me according to your word.* We must echo her words, follow her example, so that we and those whose lives we touch may likewise share in the salvation willed by God for all people.

There is, however, a difficulty felt by all people who strive to be good: the difficulty of discerning what is God's will. How indeed can we do it, if we do not know what it is? How often we might wish for an angel Gabriel to tell us God's will, so that we might do it! It is clear enough that we must follow the Commandments, but how do we know God's will in the many complicated situations of everyday living? I am sure that you know the usual ways to develop a delicate conscience by which to perceive God's will: spiritual counsel, examinations of conscience, confession. I suggest to you an element often overlooked: prayer. For us the "angel" who will guide us is the Holy Spirit Himself through his Gift of Wisdom. He gives this gift to those who pray for it, and this *enlightens the eyes of our hearts (Eph 1.18)* so that we can have *insight into the mystery of his will* in matters great and small. Christian tradition imagines that Mary was in prayer when the Angel came to her and the Holy Spirit overshadowed her; certainly, we must be in prayer for the Spirit to overshadow us.

All of Creation Waiting

One of the astonishing things about God's plan of salvation is the degree to which He uses human instruments. For instance, at Cana, at Galilee, it almost seems like the whole schedule of salvation, of Jesus' beginning of public life depends on Mother Mary's request. Even more so right here, the whole project of our salvation, of Christ's taking flesh depends upon the word of this young Jewish girl. St. Bernard makes this point so strongly during a sermon regarding it. For instance he says how the angel awaits an answer. It's time for him to return to God who sent him. "We, too are waiting, O Lady, for your word of compassion. The sentence of condemnation weighs heavily upon us." It goes on to say how not only us but, "all of creation is waiting, tearful Adam with his starving family begs this of you, O Loving Virgin, in their exile from paradise. Abraham begs it. David begs it. All the other holy patriarchs, your ancestors ask it of you as they dwell in the country of the shadow of death. This is what the whole earth waits for, prostrate at your feet, and is right in doing so. For on your word depends comfort for wretched, ransom for the captive, freedom for the condemned, indeed salvation for all the sons of Adam, the whole of your race. Answer quickly, O Virgin, reply in haste to the angel, or rather through the angel to the Lord."

Obviously, grace is such that it guarantees our Blessed Mother giving the correct answer, "Yes". She did it in freedom, and yet it was absolutely assured. That's not the case with all of the requests that God makes of us. If we ever stop to wonder why, perhaps, we aren't making more progress, why, perhaps, we don't feel more useful to the Lord, it may well be that the Lord and many, many others are waiting for our, "yes" and we're not giving this. This came home to me in a special way when I was answering the call to the priesthood. I realized that a call requires a response and God really does wait for us to respond to the grace, to make the yes, but it does take a human act of the will to say, yes. Not only to make a life decision, but to every single little request that the will of God makes to us throughout the day. As Augustine said, "I fear God asking and not returning." Bernard has almost the same thought, "Open your heart to faith, O Blessed Virgin, your lips to praise, your womb to the Creator. See the Sire of nations at your door knocking to enter. If He should pass by because of your delay, in sorrow you would begin to seek Him afresh, the one whom your soul loves.".

Silence and Recollection

St. John of the Cross tells us: "The Father spoke one Word, which was his Son, and this Word He speaks always in eternal silence, and in silence must it be heard by the soul" Yes, the only way to have communion with Him is by listening. To have this silence, in which to meet God, we must be somewhat solitary. Notice that Jesus took his chosen few "alone by themselves" up the mountain. St. Luke tells us specifically that they went up to pray. At times we find ourselves alone, but these moments of solitude, that could be a burden or a danger, can be turned into special invitations from Christ such as He made to his three favorite disciples.

How can we make the most of the few moments of silence and prayer in our day? It's not possible to change gears from frenetic activism to recollection and peace. So, while we go about our work we must take care to guard a certain interior solitude. That is our first duty, for without this communion with God, we cannot communicate Him to others. Thus, we must watch what we say and what we hear. The two go together. A gossip always loves to hear gossip. Someone who lives amidst noise makes noise for others. Both what goes into our heads and what goes out, is of varying degrees of value. Conversations, and what we hear and see, can be downright nasty, or simply frivolous, or useful, or holy and constructive. We must be constantly aware of where on this continuum words fall, whether they be spoken by us or heard by us. The saints are very stern about this matter, not hesitating to call useless speech at least a venial sin. St. John of the Cross gives a few reasons, saying: "Joy in hearing useless things gives direct rise to distraction of the imagination, gossiping, envy, uncertain judgments, and wandering thoughts, from which flow many other pernicious kinds of harm." Did not Our Lord tell us that we would be held to account for every useless word?

When the mystery of the Incarnation was revealed before them, words were useless; Peter knew not what to say. We must listen to the Word directly in prayer. Multiplying our words in prayer is a hindrance to hearing Christ. It is a result of our tendency to speak too much outside of prayer. The Blessed Virgin spoke little. She had to ponder in her heart. Even Mary, in order to know her Son, had to be a woman of silence, the contemplative *par excellence*. Perhaps as Lent approaches we could consider a form of asceticism that is much more pleasing to God than giving up some sort of food. It is not what goes into the mouth that we must give up, but what comes out. Frivolous talk, talk without thinking first if it will benefit my brother or glorify the Lord. And, the complement to this asceticism, which is a prerequisite for it, is to seek silence. We can give up listening to the radio, or movies, or talking with friends when we might, at least during Lent, try to be alone with the Alone. In this way we will "cultivate and deepen our relationship with the living figure of Jesus Christ," living now in glory, transfigured forever but still accessible to those who seek.

River of Grace

Grace, according the fathers, is what is signified by *made in God's likeness*. Grace enables us to act like Children of God, and without it His ways are onerous. That's when we begin making excuses like the people in the Gospel, substituting human tradition for Divine Commands. We try to make the demands of the beatitudes less demanding. We try to make God's will do-able without His help. This leads to moral imperfection and sin.

Lent, which begins tomorrow, is the time to grow in grace. Let us take the hint of Providence and make Mary a major part of our Easter preparation. She has showed her motherly concern for the physically ill members of her Son's body, and she will care for their souls. She wants them to be shining bright images and likenesses of her Divine Son. Just as she opened up that spring of water in France to heal bodies, so also she has a river of grace to heal our souls. As Lent progresses we should meditate on what that river of grace is: the flow of blood from the side of Christ. [Bossuet] *It is his innocent blood which makes us to be inundated with Heavenly graces. And to whom will He give the right to that blood if not to her from whom He drew all his blood.*

Lent

Ash Wednesday

Ashes are an ancient sign of penance for the Jews. They remind us of death. *"Remember, Man, thou art dust and unto dust thou shall return."* Is the Church providing us simply with a *memento mori*? No, there is a promise of life: God can take us again out of dust. Is there anything more opposite to dust than a glorified body? But to receive this promise we must die. *Whoever loses his life will save it, if a grain of wheat does not die... I have been crucified with Christ; it is no longer I who live, but Christ who lives in me; and the life I now live in the flesh I live by faith in the Son of God, who loved me and gave Himself for me. (Gal 2.20) And those who belong to Christ Jesus have crucified the flesh with its passions and desires. (Gal. 5.24)*

The motivation for mortification then is eternal life. If this life is all there is, there would be no point not to enjoy it to the full. It is only as one begins to discover and focus on the life to come that the joys and sorrows of this life are made relative. They have importance, but as signs, as means to reach the life to come. A desire to arrive there more speedily and unhindered is the motive for mortifying our desires. We do not wish to be waylaid, distracted and, God forbid, led off course by the goods of this earth. Eternal life is knowing God and Him whom He has sent, Jesus Christ. Thus the motive of mortification is to one day be joined to Christ. It is love of Him. The reason why we give up what we do is that it might distract us from Him. The more we desire Him, the less we desire what is not Him. Love for Him makes us mortify all our other desires. Our goal is to hasten our union with Him. See how the saints sought this final union! "Muero porque no muero" *to be dissolved and be with Christ.*

The best example of mortification, made into a lifestyle is celibacy. here we see that it is a legitimate good — a great good marriage

— and its attendant joys and pleasures, which is given up. Why? Out of love for Christ. Out of a desire to be more whole-heartedly devoted and focused upon Him and serving Him. It is thus a testimony of eternal life. *Some are those who make themselves eunuchs for the kingdom of Heaven.*

The point of fasting is that "[it] strengthens our spirit as it mortifies our flesh and our sensuality. It raises our soul to God. It gets rid of concupiscence by giving us the strength to overcome and to mortify our passions, and it disposes our heart that it may seek for nothing except to please God in everything" (St. Francis de Sales). Because the motive is love, our goal is to bring our will in union with that of God. The essence of all mortification is the mortification of the will. Anything that goes against one's likes or dislikes. Listening patiently, not speaking about oneself, not listening to music, ... "For whoever seeks God whilst wanting to hold on to his own likes and dislikes, may seek Him day and night, but will never find Him." (St. John of the Cross) We are also trying to overcome inordinate desires to which we tend due to the fall. One saint warns us; "If you have all that is licit, you will soon take what is not licit". *Is this not the fast that I choose: to loose the bonds of wickedness, to undo the thongs of the yoke, to let the oppressed go free, and to bear every yoke? Is it not to share your bread with the hungry, and bring the homeless poor into your house; when you see the naked, to cover Him, and not hide yourself from your own flesh? (Isaiah: 58, 1-12)*

We must not fast so that others may see, because it is our cultural custom, because we wish to lose weight, or even to raise money for charity. But rather for love of God only. Does God care if I eat chocolate or not? He will care very much, if you forgo it out of love. If you say, this is a little present for God. That prevents the trap of not knowing how much mortification to do. How do I measure it? The same way one measures how often to give one's wife flowers... it is making little presents to God, as much and as often as your love for Him moves you until the day you are united with Him. *Then you shall call, and the Lord will answer; you shall cry, and He will say, here I am.*

Purity of Intention

It's always good to see how many people come to Mass on Ash Wednesday, although it is not a holy day of obligation. Yet, people come because it's the beginning of such an extraordinary time in the liturgical year which really encapsulates and emphasizes for us the whole essence of the Christian mystery, the whole passage from death and sin to life in Christ forever. This couldn't be symbolized more powerfully than by Ash Wednesday. Much of the words and images today treat of death. There are the ashes, first of all, reminding us that we shall become ashes. From dust we come and unto dust we shall return. Then there's the talk of mortification. What does mortification mean but to make dead, to die?

Our eyes are fixed on the complete opposite when Easter comes. Then we'll have the return of flowers and bright colors and the talk of life, eternal life. So we have this great contrast, death and life. Mixed in with the idea of death, of course, is the idea of sin. As St. Paul says, *The wages of sin are death.* There is a connection between the very fact that we will die and that we are sinners. As we know from the book of Genesis, death entered the world through the envy of the devil, when he caused us to sin. Otherwise we would not have to undergo death. Likewise when we reach Easter, not only is it a symbol of the natural life around, but it reminds us of the taking away of sin and therefore the granting of eternal life.

As we undertake our penances we should remember that, although it's connected with death, and therefore a reminder of how terrible sin is, penance itself is not supposed to be dreary. As our Lord points out here, we're not supposed to go around looking glum. Rather penance should be viewed as a gift from God. In fact, scripture does tell us that penance is an opportunity of faith that the Lord has given us. In other words it is a gift. He's offering us now the opportunity to die in a little way, in a largely symbolic way, so that we don't have to die for our sins. It's a great, great gift to have the opportunity during our whole life and especially during Lent to die to ourselves, now, so that we can live forever. So this joy, this gratitude for the gift of penance, the opportunity for penance, should underlie our Lenten journey and should somehow show in our faces and in our awareness. The dying that we do during Lent is dying that brings life. It is not senseless suffering, it is in fact a reflection of our Lord's death on the Cross that brought life to the whole world. It's a recurring theme for our Lord that those who give up their life now, will take it up again. That's exactly what we do during Lent. We give up our life in various ways to regain it a hundred fold in eternity.

It strikes everybody as odd that the Church asks us to show the ashes in a very visible way on our foreheads today, the very day that we read that the Lord tells us not perform religious acts that we would see. We're not fundamentalists, of course. But, rather we understand the Lord to be saying, Do what you do, with a pure heart, purity of intention, not for an immediate gain. It is very easy to do penances for some sort of self satisfaction for ourselves, a sense of achievement or worse yet, to lose weight, something like that. So the point of penance is to do it with purity of heart, for the intention of bringing ourselves and the world back to God. The same sentiments should be in our heart that the Lord Jesus had when He died on the cross. So, in other words, love has to underlie all the things that we do. Therefore don't be preoccupied so much with , "Am I doing enough during Lent?" but more, "Are my sacrifices done with enough love?" Very similar would be Mother Teresa's famous statement, that we should do little things with great love. In fact, love is precisely what we're trying to do. We're trying to overcome our egoism. This is what we're putting to death, the old man. The old man with all his desires and selfishness. That's precisely what's supposed to die, to be mortified, during Lent.

Hearts Ready to Seek Him

Lent is a good time to think of sacrifices we can make and *why* we should make them. Our Lord's words in the Gospel can help us, for He speaks about those who hunger and go without good things in this life. His words are difficult to grasp, for He calls such people blessed. Now perhaps one can begin to understand this radical language of our Lord, and why such ways of speaking come naturally to saints. St. Paul exhorts us to *set our minds on what is above.* Cardinal Newman warns us against thinking we are not attached to what we can see: "Be quite sure, he says, that every one of us, even the poorest and the most dull and insensible, is far more attached to this world than he can possibly imagine". Saint John of the Cross is a famous example for emphasizing the need to detach oneself from finite goods to reach eternal ones. "The further you withdraw from earthly things the closer you approach Heavenly things".

Love for God is the key to Christian self-denial: that it is done for the sake of the beloved, so as to fly to Him. That is what makes it a delight, for no one notices burdens born for the sake of a beloved. We have reasons for our self-denial however. Firstly, we must deny ourselves certain comforts or pleasures, even legitimate ones, so as to have hearts that are ready to seek Him, that are not already filled and satisfied. The goal of our self-emptying is to be filled up with God. We must take care, even in the smallest things. A single desire, according to St. Elizabeth of the Trinity, can keep us from Him. "A bird can be chained up just as effectively by a thin golden thread as by a heavy iron chain." Secondly, one tends to give things up as one grows closer to Our Lord so as to be more like Him. After all, He gave up all the glory of Heaven so as to be born into poverty and misery. Further-more, by imitating Him thus, we can participate in His redemption of the world which is brought about by sacrifice. And the third reason why, as people grow holy they tend to give up natural goods, is that, possessing the Lord in some way, even now, they do not crave such joys. They can still enjoy them, but as St. Paul said, having known both want and plenty, he was equally happy with both. He was too con-cerned with his treasure in Heaven which he could already anticipate.

Now the words of Our Lord in the Gospel, in the Beatitudes, be-gin to be very clear indeed. He is not condemning natural goods or of-fering the deprived, cheap consolation. Rather, He is saying that the good things of earth are signs of God's goodness. But they very easily fascinate people so that, when created things pass away, those who love them go with them. On the other hand, those who are willing to give them up *for the sake of the Son of Man*, will be blessed in this life and in the life to come. That is an unexpected paradox: Those who are detached from earthly goods, actually enjoy them more than those who seek them. St. Francis appreciated nature more than anyone ever has, and that is because He loved the Creator so much.

This Lent, let us examine where our hearts are. Are they set on Heaven or on things that will pass? A good place to start may be to examine what we tend to think about when we are alone, what we tend to pray about. While it is good to ask for temporal gifts from God like health, or a job, is that all we turn to God for? Or do we also ask Him to fill us with his Spirit and his virtues? Do we ask for finite goods so as to serve Him better and help spread the Kingdom? St. Paul's words must never leave us: *If we hope in Christ for this world only we are the most wretched of all men*. If, however, we hope in Him for eternal life, blessed shall we be.

Journey of Conversion

Lent is not just pious custom. It is a journey of conversion in the Holy Spirit, encountering God in our life. The desert is not only the place to meet temptation but the place to meet God. The desert is a place of dependence upon God, of meditation and of the essential. The desert journey represents a personal experience of inadequacy before God. Only when we make a "desert" for ourselves, that is soli-tude, emptiness, poverty, through various practices of self-denial will we be able to meet God and acknowledge Him as the most important person in our lives. Lent is not just something Catholics always do. It is a real opportunity. A time for grace. A time for grace which will make us strong for a battle that is otherwise too much for us. A chance to change our lives, to get out of ruts that we are in, which lead us where we don't want to go.

Moses reminded his people that because God freed them they must *bow down in the sight of the Lord our God*. We, too, when we were baptized, were brought out of the house of bondage. Our slavery to sin was ended and our entrance into the promised land of Heaven made possible. This is the reason why we should worship the Lord alone and serve no one beside Him. The devil, to whom we pay allegiance when we sin, wants us back in bondage. So, then, Lent is a time to recall the great dignity that has been given us when we were freed by Christ for a life of holiness. It is a time to remember that we have been chosen and cannot live as ordinary men do. It is a time to renounce the devil who has tried to win us back to worshiping idols.

We may not know exactly where to start to make our Lent fruitful. I suggest that — alone in a "desert" with some sort of fasting and prayer — we try to identify what is our biggest obstacle in our attempt to live like Christ? What is our biggest vice? What is the idol that we worship and would hate to see melted down? Go over the list of the seven capital vices and examine which has the greatest hold on you. Then determine to tear down that idol during the year, beginning in a big way during Lent. If we worked on eliminating just one vice a year, and building up its opposite virtue, we would be perfect in a very short time. Let us say that you decide you are envious, because you see that you are always a bit sad when others succeed, and are noticed, and you are not. Perhaps you even see that you tend to criticize others for this reason, and speak of their faults. Well, then, for you, you must fast and pray for the strength to overcome this. Your greatest sacrifice will be speaking well of others, extolling those people that you envy most.

We must not be discouraged at the necessity of this fight against temptation. It should not depress us. Indeed, it is, in a sense, the reason we were baptized. The fathers saw baptism as induction into an army, with the indelible character as our badge. We were given weapons like the gifts of the Holy Spirit and the virtues of Christ. As St. John Chrysostom says "You did not receive weapons so that you might sit at ease but so that you might fight!". The Church sets the tone for Lent in its prayer on Ash Wednesday: "Grant us, O Lord, to set up the defenses of a Christian army with holy fasting so that — about to fight against spiritual enemies — we may be strengthened by the help of continence." So let us wage war on one of our defects that keep us from the Lord. Then, when Easter comes we will be able to celebrate the new life of Christ in us!

Enemies of the Cross

If we are being called into communion with the totally Other, with God, we must expect a very different life in Heaven. Getting from here to there will not be a smooth transition, but a radical upheaval. To make ourselves Heaven-ready, tinkering, putting on finishing touches will not suffice. We don't need to be improved, but totally radically transformed. That is why we must die: *For whoever would save his life will lose it, and whoever loses his life for my sake will find it. (Mt. 16.25) Put off your old nature which belongs to your former manner of life and is corrupt through deceitful lusts, and be renewed in the spirit of your minds, and put on the new nature, created after the likeness of God in true righteousness and holiness. (Eph 4.22-23)*

The world is the problem. It doesn't want us to look beyond it for our happiness, but to be satisfied here and now. "Any Catholicism is suspect if it does not disturb the one who practices it, if it does not mark him in the eyes of the world, if it does not overwhelm him, if it does not make of his life a passion renewed every day, if it is not difficult and odious for the flesh, if it is not unbearable" (Julien Green, French novelist) The enemies of the cross of Jesus Christ, of whom Paul speaks, are not so much those who wish to attack and kill Christians. The enemies of the Cross are those who wish to woo and seduce Christians by an easy, comfortable, cozy life. They are an insidious enemy, one which seeks to tame and domesticate the message, the *Word of the Cross. (1 Cor. 1.18)*: *For the word of the cross is folly to those who are perishing, but to us who are being saved it is the power of God.* They would empty the cross of its power (*I Cor 1.17), as St. Paul warned the Corinthians. They would secularize Christianity.

Indeed, if you look around you, sad to say, *I say it with tears*, there are a great many Christian denominations, and within the Catholic fold, a great many religious orders, publications, educational institutions, not to mention individuals, that seem Christian enough but they have an insipid, counterfeit aspect. Some people call them, without any intention to demean them: "Catholic-lite". It's Christianity minus the edge, the fire, the secret power to challenge and transform the world. Or shall we say "transfigure"? Fortunately, there is a great army of Christians who are being renewed in mind – isn't that what Lent is all about? Many have truly put on the new man Christ Jesus, and they are working on transfiguring this world. This happens now in a mysterious way, at the cost of much suffering, but when the Lord comes it will be perfected *(GS 39)*, and the price we pay will be nothing in comparison.

Personal Conversion

We must all come to share Simon Peter's sentiments upon truly seeing the Lord Jesus, the holiness of God. Realizing the Incarnation, our response must be, I am a sinful man. Peter said, *depart from me, I am a sinful man*, but no, we must realize that the Lord Jesus came precisely to seek out sinners, He loved sinners, He didn't come to depart from us, but rather to change us, to make us like Himself. This is what conversion really is, turning from our own will, our own way, our own perverse path, turning to do God's will. So it's really all tied up with obedience and here we see at this conversion of Simon Peter, "Lord, at your word, if you say so, Lord, I will lower the nets." It's deciding to do the will of God, and that's a continual thing. Simon Peter's conversion didn't just happen, but throughout the Gospel we see that he's this work in progress, he's continually converting more and more to the Lord, to get to know Him better. There's that time, remember, the Lord rebuked him, *Get behind me, Satan,* because, here again, "you're following, not God's ways, but your own ways." That was another point in his conversion. Then again the Lord said, *I will pray for you, and when you have turned, have converted, strengthen your brothers.* So Peter is a good example of God's continual work, continually changing our will, going against our will in ever smaller and smaller things to do the will of God.

See how beautifully St. Paul described that in the first reading and elsewhere. *I've been praying for you, that you will obtain full knowledge of His will, through perfect wisdom and spiritual insight. Then you will lead a life worthy of the Lord and pleasing to Him in every way.* In another place he says, *Be transformed by the renewal of your mind* so *you will know what is good and pleasing and perfect.* So this is the work that we're doing and a help that the Church has always provided is Spiritual Direction. Spiritual Directors can help people know what God's will is in their daily life. Penance is something that helps us turn our will away from what we want to do to what the Lord wants us to do, especially those penances we don't choose, namely all the difficulties that fall into our life. See them as God's will for you and a way of going against your will, converting yourselves to Him. Finally the third big help in all this is the daily examination of conscience. Let's go over the day. Did I do God's will in all things, how can I be more delicate in my following of His inspirations?

Examination of Conscience

St. Paul mentions how he had been doing so many wrong things. But since he was unaware of it, he was treated mercifully. Namely, he was given the great grace of conversion and light, able to see what he was doing wrong, symbolized by how he was blind for a time, then the scales fell from his eyes and he could see. The Lord also speaks of seeing the wrong doing that we do, how we all have planks in our eyes that we can't see. It's so easy to see the faults of others, so hard to see our own. This is especially clear as we approach death. We do so many things that are wrong in the sight of God, that we don't notice. We need God's mercy in order to share His life.

We fortunately have the opportunity to anticipate that judgment day, so that it is not something to be feared. In fact, the Catechism speaks of the Sacrament of Reconciliation precisely as that, sort of a preview of the judgment day because you come before the Lord with your sins, you confess them, you're judged, mercifully, and sent away in the peace of Christ. This is a beautiful thing. To be able to continually come before the Lord, to be judged, and to have our sins forgiven. This helps us to progress. What is very important for making good confessions, of course, is to really increasingly know ourselves, to know our sins. So the examination of conscience is so important. This is a way to every day have that preview of judgment day. Because every day is a microcosm of our life, and it ends at night and is a reminder of our death. In the prayers of the Church, the liturgy, at night we ask God for a quiet night and a peaceful death. So also that last examination of conscience at the end of the day is a little bit that way, a preview of when we're going to examine our life, at the evening time of life.

So the examination of conscience should never be omitted. St. Ignatius would let his sick Jesuits out of every other duty, except the examination of conscience. No matter how sick they were, they had to examine their conscience. So let us be sure never to avoid it and to do it very well, very carefully. Be sure to spend a nice chunk of time and to make sure it's a prayer, that it's not us trying to examine our life, because, remember, we're blind! That's the problem. We have to ask the Lord, shed your light upon me, make me know. How tricky is my heart! How I deceive myself! We need light. As the psalm says, *Search me O God and know my heart. Try me and know my faults. And see if there be any wicked way in me and lead me in the way everlasting.*

The Prodigal Son

This parable is one of the Holy Father's favorites, which he likes to call the parable of the Merciful Father. In a document on the Sacrament of Reconciliation he makes the following reflections: "This prodigal son is man, every human being: bewitched by the temptation to separate himself from his Father in order to lead his own independent existence; disappointed by the emptiness of the mirage which had fascinated him; alone, dishonored, exploited when he tries to build a world all for himself; sorely tried, even in the depths of his own misery, by the desire to return to communion with his Father. Like the father in the parable, God looks out for the return of his child, embraces him when he arrives and orders the banquet of the new meeting with which the reconciliation is celebrated." *(RP 5)*

It doesn't take a great deal of imagination to see that this parable is the perfect image of the sacrament of reconciliation. In the confessional, the priest awaits the return of prodigal sons and daughters with eager longing. It's so lovely to see a country like Italy where old priests stand beside the confessionals for long hours on the lookout, as in the parable, for a lone figure coming into view with a burden that God alone can remove. Here especially does the terminology "celebrating the sacrament" ring true, for then the priest gets to celebrate the joy of reconciliation between Heavenly Father and new found son, portrayed in the parable. "Only the heart of Christ, who knows the depth of His Father's love, could reveal to us the abyss of His mercy in so simple and beautiful a way."*(CCC 1439)*

How sad it is that this embrace of the merciful Father is not sought out by many today!

There are many, many things we could say to encourage people to return to making monthly confession one of their basic spiritual commitments, just as weekly Mass and daily prayer must be. I will mention three effects: Peace, Joy and Mercy. Like the son in the parable, we often begin to seek forgiveness with imperfect sorrow, for selfish, fearful reasons. Or we are not aware of the full depths of our sins. Only in the graced encounter with Christ in the sacrament do we see ourselves as we truly are; there, our imperfect motives are converted into perfect contrition so that we might merit to hear the words "Your sins have been forgiven, go in peace".

The effect of peace is linked to the second benefit which is Joy. If we lose the sense of sin then we also lose the joy of being saved, and this is the beginning of Heavenly joy. Do you experience the joy of being saved? The deep, abiding joy of belonging to God, of having been bought at a price, of being accepted by the one who said *"All that the Father gives me will come to me; and Him who comes to me I will not cast out. (Jn. 6.37.)*? In this sacrament not only are our sins forgiven, but we are put back in relationship with God and the Church. There is the joy of communion with all that is holy and beautiful and true.

Finally, a third benefit of this sacrament is mercy. Let us not forget the elder brother. Even if he had not left the Father with a break, an obvious mortal sin, he stayed ostensibly close and yet his heart was far from him. He worked at pious practices without fruit or purpose. He was selfish and his pettiness grew. He did not ever check his venial sins but let them grow more numerous until the full extent of his pride and vanity was revealed by his hard attitude toward his brother. We must always humble ourselves before God or we will forget that we are sinners. This is why, if priests are to be merciful confessors, they must be penitents themselves.

In sum then, in this great Sacrament we are made capable of loving. The fruits of this love are peace, joy and mercy. What then are we doing starving for these fruits in the land of egoism? Let us rise up, "come to our senses" and return to the Father again and again, month in and month out, in the Sacrament of Reconcilation.

Prisoner of the Confessional

"The Lord Jesus Christ, physician of our souls and bodies, who forgave the sins of the paralytic and restored his bodily health, has willed that His Church continue in the power of the Holy Spirit His work of Healing and salvation ..." thus speaks the Catechism of the Catholic Church in its introduction to the sacraments of Reconciliation and the Anointing of the Sick, the two sacraments of healing. While it's true that God alone can forgive sins, the Catechism goes on to say, "By virtue of His divine authority, He gives this power to men, exercised in His name."

That's an astonishing thing, that we begin to take for granted because we don't see the effects of this interior healing. But it's a much smaller miracle to cure that paralytic of his paralysis than to heal his soul. It only amazed the crowd and served as a proof because it was visible but in fact the transformation of his soul from sinner to saint was far more beautiful, far more astounding, if only one could see. When we leave the confessional with a smile on our faces, it's just the tiniest reflection of the joy of Heaven over one repentant sinner which we can not see. If only we could see, we would be astounded by what happens at every celebration of the Sacrament of Reconciliation.

Christ not only gave His apostles, and through them bishops and priests of our own day, that same power to forgive, but He also gave them the model of how to forgive.

Firstly in the scene which we just saw, where of course the Lord didn't need to hear the confession, or hear the act of contrition, because He saw their faith and He could read their hearts, but He did give absolution. *Child, your sins are forgiven.* How often the Lord left His apostles that example of how to hear and welcome a sinner and have him go away forgiven. Think of the woman caught in adultery, *Neither do I condemn you, go and do not sin again.* Sometimes He told them to go away and gave them some advice besides. Perhaps the most beautiful case of all that shows that He is the master of the art of arts, of curing the soul, was the woman at the well in John's Gospel. He found her an outcast, bitter and alone, having lived with five men with no intention of leaving the one that she was with. How gently He probed into her soul, offering her the gift of God. *If you knew the gift of God*, He said, and He got her to speak freely and to not be afraid of the 'Man who told me everything I ever did'. Although He was weary from traveling, as St. John relates, yet He gave up His lunch so as to hear her confession. Saying, *My food is to do the will of the Father.* This beautiful episode in Our Lord's life inspired the Holy Father, when he was younger, to write a poem about it. I'm sure it's more beautiful in Polish, but in English, part of it runs like this, "He suffused me without difficulty, burst my shame in me and the thoughts I'd suppressed for so long. As if He had touched a rhythm in my temple, and all of a sudden carried that great exhaustion in me and with such care." So beautiful. The Lord bursting the shame of the sinners and so gently with such care, as if handling a small lamb.

So the Lord Jesus Himself shows us the importance of the Sacrament of Reconciliation, and the Church has never ceased proclaiming likewise, most recently, that this is a pastoral task that is absolutely indispensable. There's no substitute for it, not even receiving Holy Communion. It's true enough as the Council of Trent even taught, that the Eucharist is a remedy to free us from our daily faults and to preserve us from mortal sin, but it's not a remedy for mortal sin. The only ordinary manner for that is the sacrament of confession, which also prepares us to receive well the Holy Eucharist. We can only think with great sadness of the terrible cost in graces lost by reception of the Holy Eucharist, either not prepared at all to receive it, or with very poor preparation. All this could be rectified by frequent reception of the Sacrament of Reconciliation.

If each of us in this parish, made even just one month a five minute confession, which is really just the minimum of what we could imagine the Church means by frequent confession, that would mean that Monsignor, Fr. John and I would have to hear confessions for nine hours a day. Needless to say we're not doing that right now. You may say it's impossible for a priest to hear confessions for nine hours a day. But in fact, the patron saint of parish priests, St. John Vianney, the only priest in the whole history of the world who's held up for parish priests as a model to follow, heard confessions for seventeen hours a day, it's practically the only thing he did. When the Holy Father visited Ars, that town in France, as a seminarian, to make a little pilgrimage to his parish church, He went away with the resolution that he too would be a prisoner of the confessional. This is what priests aspire to! We would love to be kept in the confessional for nine hours a day, even through lunch like our Lord, Jesus. The second reason why it's not that unreasonable even to hear twice that many confessions is that the parish would be so transformed into a completely new sort of place, we'd soon have dozens and dozens of vocations to the priesthood. Soon we'd have lots of help hearing confessions and many of the other problems that priests have to deal with would be cut away at the root, so that we'd have more time.

We all must try, especially during this season of Lent, to rediscover the freedom that comes from having Christ say to get up and walk, just as He said of Lazareth, untie Him. It's not for nothing that when He gave this power to His apostles, He said, it's the power of binding and loosening, it's freedom for your souls. It also can be called the Sacrament of Freedom. One spiritual writer wrote, "Let us not lie there helpless in our sins, but truly take up our bed, having been given the power and the strength to pick up and carry the thing that has been carrying us before." So many people are carried about by their passions and by their bad habits and only through regular confession can one regain control and begin to carry the thing that was carrying us before. God alone can set us free. We may try to rationalize our sins away, but at the end of the day, sin is the great oppressor of the human spirit and only God can set us free. He left us this one sacrament as the ordinary means of doing it. As the Church, at once holy and always in need of purification, we must follow, constantly, the path of penance and renewal. It's an uninterrupted task, punctuated by moments of encounter with Christ Jesus in this Sacrament. If we don't use this Lent to return to the frequent and consistent use of this Sacrament, we never will.

Frequent Confession

I've always felt a little sorry for the Pharisee, it seems he is trying to follow the Lord in holiness. Perhaps he's genuinely pitying a fellow who is, by reputation and by his own account, a public sinner. Yet the Lord detects a terrible case of pride. So we must look at the Pharisee more closely: he is aware that sin exists, that miserly, lying, adulterous people abound, but he cannot see these sins in himself. He is forgetting that these vices have roots in all people. If evil growths of bad deeds did not spring up in his life, it is by the grace of God. We must ever be on guard against their appearance even in incipient and subtle forms. The Pharisee does not investigate humbly, but denies proudly: "I'm not being greedy, just enjoying the good things in life; I'm not dishonest, just clever, savvy" and so on… His conscience has grown dull, his rationalizations ever ready.

No doubt the Pharisee spent much more time excusing and defending himself before God, than he did searching out his hidden sins. He should have listened more to the Psalmist: *But who can discern his errors? Clear thou me from hidden faults. (Ps 19.12)* Perhaps, his faults were hidden to no one but himself. The inconsistency between what a man professes and how he acts can be quite astonishing. He might even have been committing adultery but telling himself, that in his case, his irregular relationship was quite a different matter altogether. There are, in fact, many moral theologians, today, who make a living claiming that one can't pick out a certain category of behavior and proscribe it in every possible case. There might be a case, they insist, where the direct killing of an innocent would **not** be murder, where relations with another woman would not be adultery, and so on. The commandments are reduced to mere approximations, guidelines, contrary to the whole of Tradition and the plain sense of Scripture.

The Publican, on the other hand, confesses his sins, honestly and completely, to God. His request for mercy is still, today, an acceptable "Act of Contrition" suggested for use in the Sacrament of Reconciliation. Because He is genuinely sorry, because he does not try to justify himself, he merits the joy of being given a share in God's **own** righteousness. Every attempt to justify oneself by lowering standards or blaming circumstances, by redescribing one's actions or focusing only on ones intentions, inevitably fails. God sees through such attempts to exalt ourselves, to save ourselves. He regards them scornfully, as he does the Pharisee in the story. St. Paul would say that such people are enemies of the Cross, who would *empty it of its power*.

Only the Cross, that is, Christ's righteousness alone, can save us. It was St. Paul's confidence in Christ, not in himself that enabled Paul to speak so hopefully of the "crown of righteousness" that he expected after his impending death. He knew himself to be a sinner as he had confessed on many occasions, as to Timothy, but he knew in whom he had hoped: *The saying is sure and worthy of full acceptance, that Christ Jesus came into the world to save sinners. And I am the foremost of sinners; but I received mercy for this reason, that in me, as the foremost, Jesus Christ might display his perfect patience for an example to those who were to believe in Him for eternal life. (I Tim 1.15-17)*

Now, if we apply this to ourselves, we will want to run to God often to receive his forgiveness in Christ Jesus. Indeed, the measure of a person's humility and resistance to self-righteousness is the frequency that a person has recourse to the sacrament of penance. There is no doubt that "confessing to God directly" leads very quickly to the stance of the Pharisee – head held high, very few sins in sight. But the Lord knows that for us to really face up to and acknowledge our sins, it helps tremendously to have to admit them to another person. That is why auricular confession, individual vocal confession, is so humbling – even when it is anonymous. That is one reason why it is a rare person who confesses frequently – because humility is rare. There is also a lot of ignorance about its necessity — as "the ordinary way of obtaining forgiveness of serious sins committed after baptism". In other words, one cannot miss Mass for no reason, tell a big lie, watch a bad movie, etc., and then come up to Communion without passing through the confessional. We must remember the tax collector, who was not presumptuous like that. Moreover, the sacrament is necessary, not only for reestablishing our friendship with Christ, but for advancing in holiness. It is with good reason that the Holy Father confesses weekly, as did Mother Teresa.

No one must ever be afraid to come to confession. The encounter is with Jesus Christ Himself (the priest is just an interpreter, or instrument that God has chosen to use to receive the confession and to communicate the grace of forgiveness). Jesus is genuinely, completely sinless, it is true, but He is not for all that like the Pharisee, who thinks purity is a reason to despise everyone else. On the contrary, Jesus, sinless though He was, took the part of sinners. He sought them out, He befriended and defended them, He saw the good that was left in them. He identified Himself with them, taking his part with the accursed, dying upon a cross. He is drawn to us, because we are sinners, as a merciful child is drawn to a bird, **because** it has a broken wing. He loves us.

Why don't we all turn again and seek the true face of God which is shown to us in the confessional. The merciful, gentle holy face of God which endured buffets and spitting and a crown of thorns for us, to win us a crown of righteousness. Let us thank God, **not** for making us better than other men, but for making Himself similar to us in our wretchedness. For that reason only can we hold our head up high!

Striving to Open Our Hearts

The early Christians feared no one but God. They "spoke out boldly in the name of Jesus" heedless of the dangers which this boldness brought, and yet, we read, "they walked in the fear of the Lord". This is no servile fear but an anxiety that all serious people, aware of God's holiness and our frailty, feel. The Pope notes, however, that this salutary concern must not become detached from trust and confidence. Therefore the Apostle restores hope: "Beloved, if our hearts do not condemn us, we have confidence in God" *(1 Jn 3:21). God is greater than our hearts*, however set against Him they may be. He can purify them. *Where sin abounds grace abounds all the more.* He can enlarge them. *Widen my heart that I might run in the way of your commands.* He can turn them to the good, without violating our freedom. *I will take out of your flesh the heart of stone and give you a heart of flesh. (Ezek. 36.26)*

What is a heart of stone? A hardened heart, to which Christ so often refers, and with such sadness? A hardened heart is the heart of a person who does not admit their fault. He can no longer see it. It is the opposite of a broken heart, a contrite heart, which is a beautiful heart most esteemed by God. The contrite heart the Messiah takes great care not to injure; it's the lost lamb on his shoulders, bleeding and hungry; it is the bruised reed he will not break; the smoldering wick he will not quench. How blinded can we become? There are seemingly no limits to our potential for hypocrisy and incoherence, our ability to profess a faith with the lips that we deny with our deeds the rest of the week. Sometimes, astonishing examples of hypocrisy can serve as warnings to us, to take care lest we fall. We must never cease striving, therefore, to open up our heart to Christ: Let Him *shine on* you, so that you *may be transformed by the renewal of your mind, that you may prove what is the will of God, what is good and acceptable and perfect. (Rom. 12.2)* For "it is the 'heart' converted to the Lord and to the love of what is good which is really the source of *true* judgments of conscience" *(VS 64)*

Christ wishes us to be in Him and Him in us. He wishes his grace to elevate and motivate us so that we can truly *love one another as I*

(Jesus) *have loved you.* We must be able to say, one day, *it is no longer I who live but Christ who lives in me.* Christ who loves through me. The moral life is all about insertion, incorporation in Christ. We must be branches upon Him, the vine. The sap that gives us life is Grace. Without it we can merit no eternal reward for ourselves or another; we can do nothing of lasting value. We must remain in Him, by never sinning, and we must unite ourselves ever more to Him through prayer, the sacraments and lives of faithful service. Our hearts must be identified with the Sacred Heart of Jesus. We must learn to desire what Christ desires. Those who keep God's commands receive whatever they ask, not so much because God rewards them for their fidelity, but because they only desire what God wants to give them. Thus Augustine: "Can a person, dwelling in Christ, desire anything out of harmony with Christ? The very fact that people dwell in their Savior, must mean that they have no desire that is opposed to their salvation." This is the work of prayer — daily, persevering, humble dialogue with God. Lord, make our hearts like Yours!

Admitting Our Faults

If the gospel, with its endless history changing store of mysterious truths, could be summed up in one sentence, it might be this: "The Gospel is the revelation in Jesus Christ of God's mercy to sinners" *(CCC1846).* The Word made flesh is the "sum total of revelation" so it is no mistake that His name means "God saves": *You shall call his name Jesus, for He will save his people from their sins.* To receive his mercy, we must admit our faults. *"If we say we have no sin, we deceive ourselves, and the truth is not in us. If we confess our sins, He is faithful and just, and will forgive our sins and cleanse us from all unrighteousness."* We must admit our faults, but to admit them, we must know them. To do its work, grace must [first]uncover sin so as to convert our hearts... Like a physician who probes the wound before treating it, God, by his Word and by his Spirit, casts a living light on sin *(1848).* Thus, John the Baptist prepared the way for the grace of Jesus Christ, by beginning the process of self-examination and conversion. Though painful, this cleansing brings joy in time. Therefore, the Lord said of John, [he] *was a burning and shining lamp, and you rejoiced for a while in his light. But the testimony which I have is greater than that of John. (Jn.6.35)* For, Jesus Christ is the rising sun of justice itself. *"I am the Light of the world" "The light shines in the darkness, and the darkness has not overcome it... the true light that enlightens every man was coming into the world"*

The joy of conversion, of being made clean in the blood of Christ, is a joy that our world lacks because it tends not to admit its need of mercy. "The great sin of our century is the loss of the sense of sin" *(Pius XII)*. There is no enemy of joy like sin. *Love does not rejoice in what is wrong but love rejoices with the truth.* We might want to assume that anyone who comes to a penance service is coming to lay open their heart, but we must not be presumptuous. *The heart is deceitful above all things and desperately corrupt; who can understand it? I the Lord search the mind and try the heart.* So the Psalmist prays: *Preserve me, Lord, from hidden faults.* And St. Paul did not trust his clean conscience, but awaited the judgment of the Lord in salutary *fear and trembling.* It is not always easy to see one's sinfulness; part of this inability is God's mercy; He does not let us see how filthy our souls are, for the discouragement would be insufferable. But part of it is our sins themselves, which keep us from seeing us as we truly are.

Our first reaction is probably to think that sins we are unaware of, are not to be worried about. Can we be responsible for what we are ignorant of? We must be careful to distinguish between invincible ignorance and ignoring what we know or should know. Pius XII had strong words on this subject: "The first and most serious stigma of our age is its knowledge which renders inexcusable its outrage against the Divine Law... the possibility or presumption of ignorance, concerning norms which govern relations between creatures and Creator should no longer find a place — nor, for that matter, the excuse founded upon this possibility which might lessen guilt".

If you think you only need an oil-change, ask yourself if you are not one of the many Catholics in need of a spiritual overhaul. Indeed, it is not uncommon to find Catholics, practicing Catholics, who have made a compromise with sin, yet feel no burden of it. Of course, many plead ignorance, but St. Paul told us that what the law requires is written upon the heart. Let us beware then of complacency. Is not so much of the lack of interest in religion, caused by persons who fear, in their heart of hearts, that if they actually delved into the Catechism they would find that they need to do a lot more than they bargained for, to make straight the paths for the Lord? Or perhaps they have despaired that there are definitive, objective answers to the question, "What good must I do to inherit eternal life?" The journey to eternal life, the narrow path which we must make straight, is the road of conversion.

Another area in which we need the light of Christ, is not merely to show us what we have done wrong, but to show us how much it hurts our relationship with the Lord. One must beware of assuming that common sins like speaking ill of others, lying, skipping Mass, habitual sins, and indiscriminate use of the media are venial sins. They may be, but we must be very careful not to take them lightly for that reason. They can slip over the line by desensitizing us to the will of God. We must strive against them with all our might, with practical, concrete, determined programs of reform united with concerted prayer. We cannot imagine that such sins are simply the price of living in the world. Take, for instance, the use of the media. One cannot go to movies very much without agreeing to see and hear much evil, evil which will make one unable to see and hear the truth of one's state of soul. When one makes rationalizations, one is not genuinely ignorant: moral lethargy, obtuseness, and culpable insensitivity expressed by the biblical term "hardness of heart" is at work. Christian, beware. The Lord does not lower his standards for Christians, when society lowers its standards for itself. *It is now the hour for you to wake from sleep, for our salvation is closer than when we first accepted the faith. The night is far spent; the day draws near. Let us cast off deeds of darkness and put on the armor of light. (Rom. 13.11-12).*

There are many good souls who do make every genuine effort to avoid deliberate sin, even venial. They, however, like all of us, often experience the difficulty of not knowing what to say in confession. It is a grace to have one's faults and imperfections shown one by God. Do not be distressed if you cannot see them. Look especially for omissions. Perhaps I commit no sin by actions, but there may be a great deal of good you leave undone: kind words, smiles, apostolic initiatives, letters, prayers and so on. Know that you can always confess a sin that has already been forgiven, if necessary, to gain the grace of the sacrament. So often, we confess things that bother us, not things that offend God. If we confess that we are impatient, or that we don't keep the house in order, it may well be that we are merely expressing our desire for a calm life and an ordered house. God's will, on the other hand, may be to keep you humble, struggling with these things, and keep you from the vanity of having them all mastered. He may be much more concerned with your lack of prayer, or omissions of charity.

A habit of daily examinations of conscience will help you develop a more sensitive conscience so that you can see the many ways that you do offend the Lord. *For the just man falls seven times a day.* (a lot). Frequent confession will also give you a more delicate conscience. One and all, then, regardless of how blind we are, let us acknowledge our blindness before the Lord, and ask for His Light. *I am the light of the world; He who follows me will not walk in darkness, but will have the light of life.(Jn. 8.12)*

The Price of Redemption

This story which Our Lord tells us is frightening, for the king seems to fly from one extreme to the other. First, He exceeds our expectations by generously pardoning all of the debt, when he was only asked for an extension. But when he discovers his servant's maltreatment of his subordinate, the king goes so far as to hand the wicked servant over to the "torturers," as the original Greek has it. Then come the words which make every faithful heart run cold: *So also will my Heavenly Father do to every one of you, (if you do not forgive your brother from your heart)*. Our Lord shows us that both, God's mercy and His justice, exceed our understanding.

As we gather together to consider how we have offended Divine Justice, and to plead for His infinite mercy, we should ponder these great attributes of God: justice and mercy. I wish to propose a key to help see into these mysteries. The key is a good look at sin. We tend to think of sin from our perspective only. We allow ourselves to grow used to sin, telling ourselves that it is an inevitable part of life. Then we fail to be horrified by sin, as indeed our entire generation has. For this reason, Pius XII said that "the greatest sin of our day is the loss of the sense of sin." Only if we see it in all its ugliness will we understand the decisive response of Divine Justice and the reason why Our Lord paid such a price to redeem us. For He did not simply "write off" our sins as a bank does bad loans; they are not merely debts that God could forget about. Rather, *God put forward [Jesus Christ] as an expiation by his blood. God in his divine forbearance had passed over our former sins*, but this divine forbearance was only in view of the sacrifice of Jesus that God foresaw. He knew that Jesus would be handed over to the torturers on our behalf.

When we sin, it is as if we take a step into a deep well; the step we can take, but to get up again from the bottom is beyond our power. Three things happen when we sin, known as stain, corruption, and debt; all of them are beyond our ability to fix. The stain refers to the loss of grace that immediately follows mortal sin. Our soul, made beautiful by grace in baptism, when we *put on Christ*, gets sullied. We participated in the very nature of God, and obviously, once lost, only God can return it to us. The second loss, corruption, refers to the damage that our fall, down the well of sin, does to our own nature. Just as saints have greater ease in seeing the will of God and doing it, so in the contrary sense, if we sin, we increase the obscurity of our minds that keeps us from seeing good and evil. Worse, we harden our hearts so that it is easier to sin in the future. Only God can heal our natures so that our mind and hearts can be subject to the Lord and able to keep all our emotions and desires subject to our mind. Finally, the debt of sin. Because we offend an infinitely great Lord this, too, is infinite and beyond our ability to pay. Who can pay the ransom for their soul, then? No one, of course, but *we are justified by his grace as a gift, through the redemption which is in Christ Jesus, whom God put forward as an expiation by his blood, to be received by faith.*

Our consideration of the terrible effects of sin, shows us why Christ, so mercifully, died for us. We were helpless, and He took pity on us. This effect of sin, which we see every time we look at a crucifix, shows us the true malice of sin and moves us to conversion. The trouble with the wicked servant in the gospel was that he was not truly sorry when he asked the Lord for mercy. This he manifested by his unwillingness to forgive others. For if we truly consider our sins and the terrible toll they have taken upon our Savior, we will not see the faults of others. We will not imagine that anyone could be so great a sinner as us. We will only be concerned to see that we do not offend our Majesty again, as St. Teresa of Avila used to say: "I'd rather be cut up into a thousand pieces than commit a deliberate venial sin". Moreover, we will rush to imitate the Lord's mercy to others if we truly believe that He has been merciful to us. Therefore, we must acknowledge our sins in all their ugliness. That is the key to seeing God's mercy in Christ, and to avoiding his strict justice that will one day be shown in Christ.

Converting Our hearts

Jeramiah gives us one of the most memorable lines of the prophets, "More tortuous than all else is the human heart, beyond remedy, who can understand it?" The Psalms speak of the human heart, the interior of man, as an abyss. Not even we, ourselves can really know where we stand or how our heart is, what we do that is right, what we do that is wrong. But Our Lord can. Here the prophet speaks of judgment, because the Lord will probe the heart to reward or punish. Of course the goal is to have the Lord probe our mind and heart before we come to that time. Confession is described in the Catechism as a precursor, as a foretaste, as a trial run, coming before the Lord to have Him probe our heart here and now. In the opening antiphon we asked the Lord to test our heart, to see if we're walking in the way of vanity and make us go instead on the path of life everlasting. The Lord alone can do this. John's gospel especially talks of the Lord Jesus as knowing what is in the heart of man. He alone can, not only know what is in our hearts, but also reform them.

We see how hard it is for our hearts to be reformed by the gospel here. Even if someone should rise from the dead and tell us that we are going in the wrong direction, very likely we wouldn't pay attention to him. Our opening prayer speaks of unwavering love of Truth. So often our erroneous ways are so engrained that we assume it is part of our nature. Lent is surely a time to make good use of our examination of conscience, in asking the Lord to illumine us so that we can truly see what in us needs to be changed.

Lenten Renewal

There are many new converts to the faith, but the people who, in a sense, most need to hear the message of conversion, of renewal are the cradle Catholics because they don't often think that they are in need of renewal. They, too, can and must have a major turning point in their life. The word in Greek for this conversion is metanoia, literally a new mind, a change of mind. We see this in the life of the great saints, many of them born Catholic, had such a great turning point, Ignatius, for instance, and Francis. They may have lived bad lives before, worldly lives anyway, but also there are those that were very holy. St. Therese of Lisieux, for instance, had a major turning point, that she speaks of in her *Story of a Soul*. Teresa of Avila, also, even after reaching the convent, had a major turning point in her life.

Everyone must experience the renewal of their mind, a major change of heart that makes them more fervent, more consistent, more radically devoted as a disciple of the Lord. Indeed, if everyone can and must experience a metanoia, a conversion, then we can also say everyone can and must experience more than one. We must be continually turning toward the Lord. Since He is an infinite mystery, we can always approach Him without arriving, we can always drink without exhausting Him, we can always learn without comprehending Him. That's why, by Divine Providence, Lent comes around every single year. We must have a genuine, real, demanding and life-changing Lent every year. It's very easy to say this in theory, I'm sure we'll all agree. Yes, we have to improve. It's also easy to fail to grasp the urgency of it and also to be immediately discouraged. It seems impossible to improve much, we bring the same old sins to confession every time, aren't we human after all?

It's true, we are human, but the fragility of the flesh, is precisely the old vessel that needs to be replaced. Our humanity needs to be replaced, if the grace of Christ is not to be lost. Paul says we have this treasure in earthen vessels. That is, we receive the grace of Christ into our very fragile nature, into this old man with all his egotism and tendency to turn inward, and to choose self over grace. It's our nature, our fallen nature, and on our own there is a limit to the amount of progress that we can make. Christ must remove our old wine skin so He can fill us up. God will renew us, if we do what is our part. If we strive with all of our strength, no matter how little we have, but with all of our strength, to eliminate our defects, to do penance, to grow in virtue, to learn to pray. Then He will begin to purify us of what we cannot do on our own. The gifts of the Holy Spirit are given to us as remedies for these defects which we could not fix on our own. They were given to us at Baptism, but perhaps they're as yet unopened, unless we learn to pray. So we must not be content with what is naturally good. To be a true disciple of Christ, to fall upon the way of the Cross, to become holy like Him, to be radically renewed, is a participation in Divine Nature and, not indeed, our own doing.

Why does God desire to make us so beautiful like Himself? He Himself tells us in the Gospel we just heard, that's why He calls Himself the Bridegroom. He desires to make us beautiful so as to unite us to Him, so as to take us to live with Him in Heaven. We must realize, He has not chosen us because we are beautiful or faithful, or good already. We are not. He's chosen us because He pities us and as the prophet says, He's led us out into the desert, to make us beautiful again. That's the purpose of all the desert times of our lives, all the adversities, all our sufferings. He's taking what is old and frail in us and changing us to make us young and beautiful, so that we'll be ready for the wedding banquet that is in Heaven. That's what Paul says to the Ephesians, "Christ loved the Church and gave Himself up for her that He might sanctify her, having cleansed her by the washing of water and the Word, that He might present the Church to Himself in splendor without spot or wrinkle, or any such thing. That she may be holy and without blemish."

That's why the Church and every member of her, is called the spouse of Christ. In this amazing love story that is salvation history, our Divine Lover died for us, that we can live forever, happily ever after with Him. What would have been a romantic tragedy, turned out by divine intervention, which is the Resurrection, into the happiest drama imaginable. St. Paul adds, "I feel a divine jealousy for you, for I betrothed you to Christ, to present you as a pure bride to her one husband." We were betrothed to the Lord Jesus in Baptism when He gave us those gifts, to make us beautiful for the wedding. Gifts which we must open.

A measure of our desire for union with God, is our manner of reception of the Holy Eucharist. This is the preview of the wedding feast of Heaven, where we are invited to have Communion with our Divine Spouse. His Precious Blood is truly the new wine which so often pours out of our fragile, old riddled souls since we have made no efforts to make them new, dispose them to receive so great a gift. This is why the *Imitation of Christ,* one of the greatest Spiritual books we have, writes, "Yet it is much to be lamented, pitied, that we should be so lukewarm and negligent, as not to be drawn with greater affection to the receiving of Christ in Whom consists all the hope and merits of those that shall be saved. So many esteem so lightly this saving mystery which rejoices Heaven and preserves the whole world. O the blindness and hardness of the heart of man that doesn't more highly prize so unspeakable a gift and from daily use (or weekly use) falls into a disregard of it." So let us thank the Lord this Lent and ask Him to renew our souls. He can do what we can not, we must simply do all we can, and He will do the rest.

Don't Look Back

Last week we heard Our Lord say, *If anyone wants to be a follower of mine, let him renounce himself and take up his cross every day and follow me* (Lk. 9.18-24). Today, three would-be disciples promise that they will follow Him, but they seem to intuit the renunciations that it will involve, and they begin to excuse themselves. How familiar this is to us, too. In prayer it is easy to say to the Lord, *I will follow you wherever you go,* but when the first trial comes... The gospel is replete with examples of enthusiasm without follow-through: the seed that falls on the path, sprouts quickly but has no roots; the many disciples in John, chapter 6, who turn back saying, *This is a hard teaching, who can bear it;* Peter, who promises to die rather than betray Jesus, on the very night that he denies Him three times.

The only people who cannot relate to this gospel are those who have never even started out after Jesus, who have never even had the grace of desiring to follow in His footsteps. But for every soul that, impelled by the example of Christ's death for us, has had a burst of generosity and a desire to suffer with Him, that soul has also experienced the dread feeling that one is unable to follow, unable to ever arrive with St. Paul at the exclamation *I have fought the fight, I have finished the race.* Too easily we become discouraged and feel that we have only our own energy to carry us.

The first step to take as a willing disciple, who will stop making excuses, is to eliminate all serious sin from one's life. We cannot be content with a lax attitude towards sin, counting on the Lord's mercy in confession. God will provide the grace to take every step closer to Him but one must begin with a daily meditation before a crucifix. The one who does this will be guaranteed to get out of his rut of sin, unless he gives up the prayer first. We must remember that while God requires a great effort, He always supplies what we cannot provide. *We are not tempted beyond our strength.* We must, as the old saying goes, "work as if everything depended upon us, and hope as if everything depended upon God." He will provide the help we need, but not so much as to keep us from difficulty. God does not give "extra" grace. When St. Paul prayed to God to be delivered of a certain difficulty, the response came, *My grace is enough for you.* But it is just enough. We, too, must sometimes experience what Jesus experienced upon the cross, a sense of abandonment: *My God, my God, why have you forsaken me?* But, of course, the Father was with his Son, more than ever, at that moment, and He is supporting us in our trials as well.

After one eliminates major sin, one can be tempted to settle at a plateau, a spiritual rut. Many people, perhaps most, lead this kind of spiritual life. I see it very often in old people that I visit: they pray the same prayers and seem to have the same understanding that they did in grade school. In a way this is touching, but in a way it is sad. If, in the last seventy years they learned so much about so many things, why did they not learn more about Christ, about prayer? There is, moreover, a greater danger than simple stagnation. In a recent interview, Cardinal Ratzinger speaking of the health of the Church as a whole, states, "Faith is in jeopardy everywhere, and that belongs to its nature." The Church always seems to be struggling, she has been persecuted in every age. What he says of the Church as a whole, is true of the faith of an individual as well: it is its nature to be in jeopardy. One cannot leave it unattended, one cannot cease to strive, one cannot relax, or one finds one has slid backwards. It is like an airplane: if it is not moving ahead, it is dropping like a rock.

Thus we must fight mediocrity with all our forces. Mediocrity literally means "half-way up the hill." We have begun to climb the Holy Mountain of the Lord and we will not reach our goal until we die. Let us not stop half-way up. If the Lord leaves us time on this earth, it is because we have progress to make. Remember, too, that the degree of charity we have achieved at our death is frozen, as it were; that level determines your degree of eternal happiness. It's worth making an effort now. Besides, as one begins to make progress after Jesus, the succeeding steps get, in a sense, easier and easier. Soon, love, true love of God above all things, will fill the soul of the disciple making him strong to meet and overcome whatever temptation, obstacle, or difficulty lies ahead. Remember that true love never delays: But "the lover flies, runs and exults: He is free and is not held back. ... Love feels no weight; it makes light of suffering; it attempts more than it is able; of impossibility it takes no account, because love considers all things possible..." *(Imit. of Christ)*

Let us draw inspiration from Our Lord. *He left us an example that we might follow in his footsteps.* St. Hilary relates that "Christ hastened to carry out [the Father's] wishes with regard to His passion...He had a great longing to eat the Passover with his disciples, and He celebrated the paschal meal in haste. He had an intense desire to drink the cup of His passion, for He said: *Shall I not drink the cup which my Father has given me?* When the search party came to arrest Him and asked which man was Jesus, He stepped forward of his own accord. He asked for the sour wine which He knew He was destined to drink, and having drunk it, and achieved His great purpose, He said: *It is accomplished*, thus expressing his joy at obtaining his heart's desire."

The disciple is not greater than the Master. Let us not shrink from effort, from desolation, but attack any bad habit and make real progress in our spiritual life.

Remaining Faithful

God has been faithful to us from the first moment of our existence: *The Lord called me before I was born, from my mother's womb He pronounced my name (Is. 49) .. from my mother's womb you have been my help...* The Lord goes even further: *Can a woman forget her sucking child, that she should have no compassion on the son of her womb? Even if these may forget, yet I will not forget you. Behold, I have carved you on the palms of my hands.* Carved us on the palms of his hands? When did God show such faithful love to us, except when He, in the person of Jesus Christ, was nailed to the cross. Since then, St. Paul tells us, *Nothing can separate us from the love of Christ,* says St. Paul. He means that Christ will not let go of us and nothing is strong enough to break His grasp of us. We can, of course, separate ourselves from His friendship, but even then, He will ever remain faithful *[2 Tim, 2.13] if we are faithless, He remains faithful — for He cannot deny Himself.*. We see this illustrated in the disciples. We see three today in the Gospel. They had all been with Him from the beginning. Jesus selected the ones that He wanted, made them his closest companions and collaborators — and see how differently they reacted to his love.

John, the disciple Jesus loved most, responded to Christ's love with total dedication; he was not afraid to stand beneath the cross with Mary on Good Friday. It seems that he was so enthusiastic to spread the Gospel that he never married, but preached and prayed until he was an old man. Then he merited a great vision of Heaven, so holy had he become.

Judas loved money more than his Master, more than truth and goodness; He sells Jesus to the authorities for thirty pieces of silver. Moreover, he will not trust in the goodness of the Lord, so he does not repent, but despairs instead. He is a tragic case. Jesus tells us, *It would have been better if he had never been born*, but with sadness, because right up to the end, Jesus had called him *"Friend"*.

Peter is in between; he falters; he fears the cost of following Jesus in good times and in bad. Late Thursday night, concerned for his comfort, while Jesus is being maltreated, he warms himself beside a fire where the servants of the high priest are chatting. Worried only about himself, he denies Jesus three times. But, of course, deep down, Peter loves the Lord, and so he quickly repents and turns to *strengthen his brothers*. He preaches bravely, gets jailed and beaten. St. Paul tells us that he was tempted still to preach an easy message to some, and there is a tradition that he was afraid when it seemed he would be killed in Rome. The story goes that Jesus appeared to him as he was fleeing, saying, "Where are you going?" and he returned to die, valiantly, on Vatican hill.

We see clearly that God is faithful, but people are sometimes faithful in return and sometimes not. Usually we are unfaithful either because we are selfish, as Judas was, or when we fear what others will say or do to us, as Peter was. Thinking only of ourselves, can make us easily ignore the will of Christ. All during Lent, we have given up things to overcome our tendency to selfishness and make us freer to run faster after Christ, wherever He might lead us. The other obstacle to our faithful response to God is fearing what others may say or do to us. [2Tim 3.12] *Indeed all who desire to live a godly life in Christ Jesus will be persecuted*. We must set our eyes on the Lord and do his will. I have always remembered a girl from my grade school. She was not even in my class. She would pray grace before meals when none of the other children would. I was worried that people might make fun of what I had brought to eat, and she was willing to publicly pray! Moreover, she belonged to a minority, she might have wished especially to fit in, and yet she prayed because God wanted it. And, look, thirty years later, when she has forgotten that she ever did that act of faithfulness, people she doesn't even know are still admiring her courage.

True Christians, faithful Christians, don't care too much about their own needs, but the needs of others. And they don't care what other people might say or do to them. In short, we are not afraid of the cross. In fact, we welcome it, and then a curious thing happens, just the opposite of what we might have supposed. We don't die, but we actually thrive, and get happier and stronger. That is why the Second Vatican Council makes the following curious statement: "The Church itself also recognizes that it has benefitted and is still benefitting from the opposition of its enemies and persecutors" *(GS 44)*. When one Christian is killed, it always seems ten rise to take his place. Speaking of martyrs, the Holy Father's comments: "Their blood is the seed of new Christians, the seed of reconciliation, of hope." Our Lord's death was supremely fruitful in this regard; from the blood of His cross watering the earth, there bloomed up the Church in every part of the world.

And, so, as we live the next few days in the company of our Lord, following Him in His footsteps to Calvary, let us promise Him to be ever faithful. We will follow the example of St. Peter, and especially of John the Evangelist, the disciple whom Jesus loved. We will do what is right, knowing full well that, at first, it will make us stick out. We will do it anyway in the spirit of martyrs, in the spirit of Christ Himself. At first, the cross seems to divide: some become persecutors and some persecuted. But then we will see how all those who wish to be faithful to God will rally round. By His cross, Christ united the world in a "universal brotherhood". He tore down the wall that separated different races, classes, and nations, making one family under God. As He said: When *I am lifted up, I will draw all men to myself.*

Sharing in Christ's Baptism

The end of Our Lord's public ministry has a curious connection with the beginning, his Baptism, which was itself a sort of prediction of the great emptying Himself of his glory by which He was to return, with a ransomed people, to the glory that was His before. When the mother of James and John asks for her sons to share in his glory, Christ asks: *Are you able to drink the cup that I am to drink?* In Mark, He adds *or be baptized with the baptism with which I am baptized?* Christ is referring to his passion, as his baptism, as He does in another place: *I have a baptism to be baptized with and how I am distressed until it be accomplished.*

We, too, have asked for a place in God's kingdom, or, like Mother Zebedee, our mothers and fathers asked God to give us a place in his kingdom when they brought us to be baptized. But did they know what they were asking? Did they know that they were also asking for us to drink from the cup of suffering that our Lord drank of? Did they know that our baptism means sharing in the baptism that came at the end of Christ's life, His Passion? Indeed, if baptism by water has any power to save it gets it from the cross. That is why baptism by blood, sharing as a martyr in Christ's death, is equally efficacious. The blood and water flowing from Christ's pierced side were seen as the opening of the first and universal baptismal font. "See where you are baptized," says St. Ambrose, "see where Baptism comes from, if not from the cross of Christ, from His death. There is the whole mystery: He died for you. In Him you are redeemed, in Him you are saved."

The Church tells us that the water symbolizes both the eternal life we receive and the mystery of the cross by which we receive it *(CCC 1220).* In Baptism we share in Christ's death, its merits are applied to us. *We are baptized into his death ... so we too might walk in newness of life (Rom. 6.4)* But, as Christ implies in today's gospel, this process is more painful than being splashed with warm water. It means that we must share in Christ's priesthood, his making of Himself an offering to the Father. We, too, must make of ourselves a sacrifice, living, holy, and pleasing to God *(Rm 12.1)* We do this by participation in the sacraments, prayer and thanksgiving, the witness of a holy life, abnegation, and active charity *(LG 10).* In general, we are obligated to strive for holiness, knowing that this only comes with great effort and suffering, spiritual and physical. We must ask for it, as the mother of John and James did, but we must work for it, too.

Love of the Cross

Our Lord's disciples will have to carry the Cross to follow in His footsteps. This is the reason why so few people really convert to the Lord, or why His disciples, in name, so rarely follow Him with all of their hearts, because of the Cross. It just so happens that today, the Church offers in the Liturgy of the Hours, one of the most beautiful passages of one of the greatest books, the *Confessions of St. Augustine,* where he talks about his conversion and how late it came because of the price of the Cross. "Late have I loved You, O Beauty ever ancient ever new, late have I loved You. You were within me, but I was outside and it was there that I searched for You. In my unloveliness I plunged into lovely things which You created, You were with me but I was not with You. Created things kept me from You and if they had not been in You, they would not have been at all. You called, You shouted, and You broke through my deafness. You flashed, You shone, and You dispelled my blindness. You breathed your fragrance on me, I drew in breath and now I pant for You. I have tasted You, now I hunger and thirst for more."

Then quoting Job, he goes on to speak of the Cross. "Is not the life of man upon earth a trial? Who would want troubles and difficulties? You command us to endure them, not to love them. No person loves what he endures, though he may love the act of enduring. For even if he is happy to endure his own burdens, he still would prefer that the burden not be his. I long for prosperity in times of adversity, but I fear adversity when times are good. Yet, what middle ground is there between these two extremes where the life of man would be other than trial?"

What a great insight he gave us there, that no person loves what he endures, but he may love the act of enduring. The Lord doesn't ask us to love the Cross, but He does ask us to love bearing the Cross out of love for Him. He concludes, "All my hope lies in Your great goodness."

Hoping Perfectly in Grace

Once again Peter says many beautiful things, and in particular, *Set all your hope on the gift He conferred on you, on grace.* In another translation, *Hope perfectly in grace.* Grace, remember, is a gift higher even than the angelic nature. Into these matters angels long to search. Peter goes on to say, *Become holy in every aspect of your conduct after the likeness of the Holy One Himself. Be holy yourselves as God is holy.*

If we're to see grace as our only strength in this life, there's an obstacle, which is to find strength in other things, in other comforts. If you think of the word, comfort, what it really means is a strengthener, something that gives strength. We get through life, through lots of little comforts, anything little, like a warm sweater or a cup of tea. These are things that comfort us, that strengthen us through the day. All kinds of physical comforts, psychological comforts, support of other people, financial security, all these things are things that strengthen us in our passage through life.

All these are good, all of them are necessary. They should be valued and seen as a gift of God, seen as sent by Him to get us through life. On the other hand, we can find all our strength in them and they can become an obstacle to hoping perfectly in grace. Our comfort comes from God, who is called in revelation the Comforter. That's one translation for the Paraclete, the one who really must give us comfort.

So to some degree we have to be ready to leave aside all these other comforts. We should never be afraid of weakness in this life, because when we are weak, that's when we're able to feel the strength of the Lord. That's when we're able to really hope perfectly in grace, when we're not afraid of weakness, but see it as something we embrace willingly. We have to leave everything, as Peter said, *We left everything to follow You, Lord*. We have to be willing to feel empty, especially during Lent when we remember, that's what Jesus came to do, to empty Himself as He died on the Cross.

Of course we have to keep many of the comforts in our life, so what the Lord really asks us is to be willing to leave everything, to have everything just put on the block, so that the Lord can take it if He likes. Remember, He didn't ask everybody that He met to leave everything that they had and follow Him. There's the example for instance of the demoniac that's healed who said, "Lord, I want to follow you now." The Lord didn't invite Him, He said, "no, go back to your family, your people, and tell them all I've done for you." Likewise, He doesn't ask everybody to leave family and friends, He doesn't ask everybody to have a terrible illness, He doesn't ask everybody to give up these things, but He does ask everybody to be willing to give it all up. During Lent we can show our willingness by giving up some of our comforts.

Light of Christ's Face

Do you believe in the Son of Man? Who is He Lord... What marvelous openess of heart. It merits the reply: *you are looking at Him.* The once-blind man bowed down and worshiped. A moment of personal revelation of Christ to an individual soul. Have we all encountered Christ in this personal way, face to face, giving us the unshakeable conviction that He must be the Lord of our lives? St. Paul said, *You were in darkness once but now you are light in the Lord.* We Christians have been enlightened by Christ at our Baptism, wherefore it is called "illumination". "Healing the wounds of sin, the Holy Spirit renews us interiorly through a spiritual transformation. He enlightens and strengthens us to live as 'children of light' through 'all that is good and right and true'" *(CCC 1695)*. The tragedy of the Pharisees is not that they were blind, but that they refused to be enlightened by Christ. They refused to admit their blindness, but said *We see.*

Christ is constantly following after us, knocking on the doors of our hearts, whether we have plunged back into the darkness of sin or whether we are simply living a mediocre life. We can always be further enlightened by Him. Therefore, the Church reminds us constantly, and certainly every Lent, that we must never cease striving to open up our heart to Christ: Let Him *shine on* you, *so that you may be transformed by the renewal of your mind, that you may prove what is the will of God, what is good and acceptable and perfect. (Rom. 12.2)*

We can always grow in our relationship with Christ. He can always make further personal revelations to us about who He is and who His Father is. As St. Paul tells us: *it is the God who said, "Let light shine out of darkness," who has shone in our hearts to give the light of the knowledge of the glory of God in the face of Christ. (2 Cor 4.6)* The mystery of God and the way of salvation are visible on the face of Jesus Christ, the Holy Face. He who dwells in inaccessible light became the light of the world visible for all who have eyes to see. As a result, we who have looked upon Christ, become light to others as He Himself tells us *You are the light of the world.* And Paul: *shine like stars in the midst of this wicked generation.*

Especially during Lent, let us seek the face of Christ. First, we can find it in scripture, where "the face of the Nazarnene emerges with a solid historical foundation". The details presented by the gospel will nourish our prayer, where in meditative silence we gaze upon Him in love, according to the words of the Song of Songs: *O my dove, in the clefts of the rock in the covert of the cliff, let me see your face, let me hear your voice, for your voice is sweet, and your face is comely. (Cant. 2.14)* Secondly, in Lent let us seek his face by walking after Him on the road of self denial. Even a little fasting or sacrifice will bring to mind the same face, suffering for us, with no comeliness in it, but covered with bruises and blood. Finally, let us seek his face in the poor, lonely and sad by performing readily and cheerfully good works and almsgiving. This is Lent: prayer, fasting and good works. Seeking thus the face of Christ will prepare us for the sight of the face of Jesus, Risen from the dead – first in faith at Easter and one day in Heaven, when we see Him face to face, the object of our gaze for all eternity.

Holy Face

Nothing ever was, ever will be, more attractive than the face of Our Lord Jesus Christ. Especially Christ crucified, Christ who loved me and gave Himself up for me. That holy face, which the leper was granted to see, which He left on the veil of Veronica is also the face the centurion saw crucified and converted him and made him say, *Truly this was the Son of God.* St. Paul says that its on the face of Christ that the light of the knowledge of the glory of God is made visible. It's a noble, humble, wise, brave face. We in our prayer, and in our meditation have to seek out His face. Just as the psalmist says, *Thou has said, 'Seek ye my face. My heart says to thee, Thy face Lord do I seek.* The more we look to Him the more we'll want to follow Him and imitate Him. Then we'll be able to say with St. Paul that great line, *Be imitators of me as I am of Christ.*

An analogy that's often used by spiritual writers is that of a magnet. We're drawn to Christ and then we want to imitate Him. We especially meet, and get to know and learn to imitate Christ in the Holy Eucharist. In fact the rite of ordination contains the line, the most famous part of it, "Imitate what you handle." The priest is reminded on that great day that the Holy Eucharist that he holds in his hand is what he must imitate in his life. Christ is truly present in the Blessed Sacrament, just as He was in Galilee, and we can imitate His example. So silent, so meek, so gentle, and most of all so full of self sacrifice out of love of us. More over, it's only in receiving this great sacrament, also called the sacrament of love, that we're given the ability to imitate Christ Jesus, to imitate His love. It's not possible to live the Christian life, which Jesus summed up as, *love one another as I have loved you,'* without receiving Holy Communion. First we have to love like Christ, only then can we go and love others.

So we're attracted to Christ, attracted to imitate Christ, but there's more, we can only imitate Him if we're transformed into Him. One of the most famous books of spiritual writing is called the *Imitation of Christ.* Within our century another extremely famous book is called *Transformation in Christ,* because on our own we cannot imitate Him, it's too great an example to follow. This holy food we receive in Holy Communion is not like any other food because it does not become part of us, we become part of it. Regular bread that we eat is transformed into the cells of our body, but in this sacrament when we eat the body of Christ Jesus, He is not transformed into us but we into Him, into members of His Body. St. Catherine of Sienna once wrote how He touched the lives of lepers, "For us You have made a cavern in your open side, where we might have refuge in the face of our enemies and in this cavern we have come to know your charity. There we have found the bath in which we have washed our soul's face clean of the leprosy of sin." The leper has his body cleansed on the outside, but we, through the washing of Baptism and the receiving of the Holy Eucharist, are cleansed on the inside.

This is how we are capable of imitating Christ in our exterior actions because He makes us like Him interiorly by grace. We're changed in the depths of our souls. We're configured to Christ in Baptism and

He leaves an indelible mark on our soul so that *it's no longer I who lives,* says St. Paul, *but Christ who lives in me.* So the moral change in us is preceded by this change in our being. We have to be transformed into Him and then Christ is seen by the whole world. The Holy Father said in his Lenten message for this year, "Thus, through charity, Christians make visible God's love for man revealed through Christ and makes manifest Christ's presence in the world to the close of the age. For Christians, charity is not just a gesture or an ideal but is so to speak the prolongation of the presence of Christ who gives Himself."

That's the end of this beautiful mystery. That we're attracted to Christ, we desire to imitate Him, He gives us the power by transforming us into Him, and then we're made so beautiful, the image of God is so restored in us, that we can attract people. People are attracted to us by our good example. We must always remember that the leprosy of sin, which is contagious indeed, is not half as contagious as the beauty of goodness, of charity, of the image of Christ which is supposed to shine on all of our faces. So let us pray that God will transform us, so that we can transform the world.

Holy Week

The Passion

The Church has been reenacting Our Lord's triumphal entrance into Jerusalem for centuries. It was clear to all that Our Lord's mission was coming to a climax; the prophecies were being fulfilled; his "hour" was clearly at hand. Now the Messiah, the true King of Israel was entering the Holy City. They cried out "Hosanna to the Son of David". Christ, who had previously refused to be proclaimed King, who had fled when they tried to crown Him, accepts the title. The hour has come, for all to be made known.

Jesus Christ bears the new law of love, not inscribed in stone, but in his Sacred Heart. His Heart is called, in the Litany, "Tabernacle of the Most High, Holy Temple of God" for it is the resting place of this new commandment of love which He is to share with his disciples over the Last Supper. The Heart of Jesus, so full of love for us, is to be rent by a lance, even as the curtain guarding the Holy of Holies will be torn. In that same moment, the temple of Heaven is also opened; the gates of Paradise, closed since the dawn of human history, will admit the brothers and sisters of Jesus Christ. His entry into Jerusalem amid so much joy, must remind us of the entry of all the elect into the

Heavenly Jerusalem; He has preceded us gloriously, but all those who follow Him on the way of the Cross, will follow also into glory. Yet, for a time, the Heart of Jesus must still grieve. Before He comes to the gates of Jerusalem, He pauses on a hill overlooking the city to weep. The Heart of Jesus grieves at the thought of all those who will not rejoice, who will not welcome Him. He knows all hearts of every time and place; He can see us and our infidelities and He weeps. He certainly does not weep for Himself but for us, as He will tell the women of Jerusalem: *Weep not for me, but for your children.*

He foresees the change that will come over the people more suddenly than a tropical storm. St. Bernard describes it: "How different the cries 'Away with Him, away with Him, crucify Him.' and then 'Blessed is He who comes in the name of the Lord, hosanna in the highest!' How different the cries are that now are calling Him 'King of Israel' and then in a few days time will be saying, 'We have no king but Caesar!' What a contrast between the green branches and the cross, between the flowers and the thorns! Before they were offering their own clothes for Him to walk upon, and so soon they are stripping Him of His and casting lots for them". Soon they will mock the Kingship they now acclaim: *He is the King of Israel; let Him come down now from the cross, and we will believe in Him (Mt. 27.42).*

My brothers and sisters, we, too, have been fickle, fair-weather friends. We have often used *the same mouth* for *blessing and cursing. My brethren, this ought not to be so. Does a spring pour forth from the same opening fresh water and brackish? (Jas.3.10)* We might say the same of all our faculties: will we use our imaginations now to meditate upon the life of the Lord and at another time to dwell on evil thoughts? Will we use our ears both to listen sympathetically and then to soak up gossip, calumny, blasphemy?

We have yet another week left. A week to look at oneself long and hard. Use whatever time you can to prepare your heart to receive graces of conversion, to continue the task of putting to death the old-man so that the new and perfect man, Jesus Christ, can live within you. Identify a tendency, a habit, an attitude that you wish to nail to the cross this year. It is said, truly, that if we eliminate one vice a year, we will soon be holy men. Then, come Easter, we can truly rejoice at our real share in the power of Christ's resurrection over sin and death, and when the Eternal Easter comes, we will have in our hands the palms of victory and on our lips the Heavenly hymn: *Holy, holy, holy Lord God of power and might, Heaven and earth are full of your glory, hosanna in the highest, blessed is He who comes in the name of the Lord, hosanna in the highest.*

Hearts of Stone

Today is Palm Sunday, also celebrated as Passion Sunday. It is the day that we read the "passion", the account of Christ's suffering and death. To them [Christ] presented Himself alive after his passion by many proofs... a transliteration of the Greek and Latin word to *suffer*. *Patior, passus*. The word has come to mean emotion, since when we feel strongly about something, we suffer bodily changes. Not surprisingly, we also describe the most fervent love as "passionate" because it makes us suffer, *I am sick with love. (Cant. 2.5)*. We are willing to suffer a great deal for the object of true love; this is passionate love. Christ showed his love for us by suffering. *For God so loved the world that He gave his only Son,(Jn. 3.16)*. *God shows his love for us in that while we were yet sinners Christ died for us. (Rom. 5.8)*.

What hearts of stone those people had — to see the Lord, shown to the crowd in hopes that his pitiful condition would make the crowd relent; yet this did not move them. It was a futile attempt, *for [Pilate] knew that it was out of envy that they had delivered Him up*. Hearts of stone. We, too, have them do we not? "O wounds that wound stony hearts, and set frozen minds on fire!" (St. Bonaventure). When we meditate upon the Passion we melt our hearts, we learn to love. Paul of the Cross "It is very good and holy to consider the Passion of our Lord and to meditate on it, for by this sacred path we reach union with God. In this most holy school we learn true wisdom, for it was there that all the saints learned it". We have learned of God's infinite love for us by his willingness to die for us. Shall we expect Him to take our word that we love Him back, without willingness to die for Him? St. Peter professed his love three times to the Lord, but the Lord demanded proof, by predicting Peter's crucifixion: *You will stretch out you hands, and another will gird you and carry you where you do not wish to go. (Jn. 21.18)*

Also we participate in Christ's cross by self denial. "Try to make yourself worthy of God's favors by always seeking to refuse nature what it demands both interiorly and exteriorly. Do not be self-willed, but try on the contrary always to do what others wish rather than what you yourself wish, even in indifferent things. Thus you will find that Our Lord is close to you and that your hardness of heart will melt away." (St. Claude de la Colombiere) We cannot claim to love the Lord, or even to want to love Him, if we do not wish to sacrifice. The Lord knows the human heart well. He knows that we must overcome self-love before we can love Him. In this life, there is no genuine love without suffering. "Be a friend of the passion of Christ". *ad lucem per crucem.* (St. John of the Cross) Also St. Gregory Nazianzen: "I will say more: we must sacrifice ourselves to God, each day and in everything we do, accepting all that happens to us for the sake of the Word, imitating his passion by our sufferings, and honoring his blood by shedding our own. We must be ready to be crucified." Love transforms what seems like death into life.

He Gave Himself for Me

We have all heard stories of people who gave their lives that another might live. These are rare cases. Imagine how grateful the person saved would be, how he would be the first to revere the memory of his benefactor. I dare say every moment of one's life would be transformed since none of them would have been possible without that unexpected, unmerited, and – on a human level – inexplicable sacrifice. It would be so much easier to appreciate life, and to live without pettiness and superficiality, inspired by one's new lease on life to give more generously of oneself.

Of course, people in this situation are not really so rare, after all. We are all in that boat. Christ, *the Son of God, ... loved me and gave Himself for me. (Gal. 2.24)* And, yes, in Paul's life this realization totally transformed him: *it is no longer I who live, but Christ who lives in me; and the life I now live in the flesh I live by faith in the Son of God, who loved me and gave Himself for me.* Perhaps we could define a saint as someone who knows, not intellectually but existentially, not with the lips but the heart, that Jesus Christ died for me! Yes, we *are not [our] own;* but have been *bought with a price. (I Cor.6.20)* And what a price! Why are we so loathe to recognize this truth with all its ramifications? Why are we unmoved by this news, which is the heart of the Good News? That namely, *God so loved the world that He gave his only Son, that whoever believes in Him should not perish but have eternal life. (Jn 3.16)* The answer is simple enough. It means admitting that we were in danger in the first place, that we needed a Savior, that we caused the death of the Just One. While Paul admits that *perhaps for a good man one will dare even to die*, this is not why Christ died; but rather *while we were yet sinners Christ died for us. (Rom. 5.7,8)*

We must recognize ourselves in the apostles saying, "Is it I?", in Judas who did betray Him and in the crowd calling for Christ's crucifixion. We must see ourselves in the good thief asking for a place in his Kingdom, and in the soldier who pierced his side if we are to hear Him praying for us "Father, forgive them for they know not what they do." Let us then continue our penance this Holy Week, so that our Easter joy, the celebration of Christ's triumph, may be deep and full and true.

Power over Death

Christ was about to institute the New Passover as the Lamb of God. Now we too only have a few days until this Passover is complete and we celebrate Christ's Resurrection on Easter morning. This is very little time and like all people who know that they are about to die within days, Our Lord sees everything in this perspective. So the perfume that's poured out upon Him has that special significance for Him, "She has done this to prepare Me for burial." People, in our experience, often hold onto life near the end, not so much because they love life, but because they fear death. Martin Luther King once said, "You are never really free while you are afraid to die."

Our Lord is certainly not afraid to die, He knows He's come for this. *No one takes my life from Me, but I lay it down of My own accord.* Our Holy Father pointed to Our Lord on His way to Jerusalem as an example of supreme freedom, "The crucified Christ reveals the authentic meaning of freedom, He lives it freely in the total gift of Himself and calls His disciples to share in His freedom." Christ gives so great a reason to be free in the face of death because He knows that, while He is to lay down His life, He has the power to take it up again. He has shown that power over life and death by raising Lazareth from the dead. And so great is His power over death that He will enable us also to take up our lives after we die too, as the letter to the Hebrews tells us. "Christ through death, destroyed Him who has the power of death (that is the devil) and He delivered all those who, through fear of death, were subject to life long bondage."

Let us accompany Our Lord during these last few days of Holy Week, these last few days of His life among us, certain that He will repay all of our acts of love, all of our self-giving, all of our attempts to die to self with a share in eternal life.

Embracing the Cross

Today's reading from the prophet Isaiah with the description of the suffering servant, "I gave my back to those who beat me, my cheek to those who plucked my beard," and so on, was the preparation for Jesus' announcement that He was the Holy One sent by God to be rejected, to suffer greatly and to be killed. St. Peter refuses to believe that it could be necessary or even permissible by God that the just, and especially the Chosen , the Holy One of God should have to suffer. But Jesus' response is firm. He rebuked Peter, *Get behind Me, Satan, for you are not on the side of God but of men.* Perhaps there's some self interest in Peter's eagerness to find some other way than suffering to redeem the world. Maybe he anticipated what Jesus was going to say next. *If any man would come after Me, let him deny himself, take up his cross and follow Me.* Yes, Peter will be told that he must be led where he would rather not go, after the Resurrection that's how Jesus foretold his death, and of Paul too, Christ would say that He, Himself would show Paul all that he had to suffer for His Name's sake. Almost all the Apostles were martyrs and so were the first thirty popes. And is there any saint, from apostolic times down to present day, who did not have to prove his love for God through heroic self sacrifice? There isn't. Suffering is the only anvil, the only crucible in which human beings can be made holy. Why is that? Because, as St. John of the Cross tells us, the way of perfection requires denying one's own will so as to conform it to God's will, and this is what suffering is, things that we don't want. Love of God consists in this, doing His will, obeying His commandments and any other clear manifestation of His will, no matter what the cost.

As a result, any other religion or any version of Christianity that proposes a life of virtue or way to salvation without suffering, is a sham, and any morality that says the Commandments are mere ideals, so they hold in the majority of cases but not in the really hard ones, is a false morality, foreign to Christ and His Church. You can always tell the authentic gospel preaching when, like St. Paul, it seems to know nothing except Jesus Christ and Him Crucified. Unfortunately though, what Paul calls, 'the Word of the Cross' is rather rare. Many don't wish to speak too much of this aspect of Christianity, central though it may be, for fear of driving people away. "If we make the demands too harsh we will surely lose them to more upbeat churches," people say. That may be true, but only if we tell people half the story. That we must all suffer is half the story. That Christ gives us the power to more than conquer, as Paul says, is the other half. Let us not forget where evil comes from. God does not make death and He does not delight in the death of the living. It was through the devil's envy that death entered the world. God's almighty providence does not allow the devil, or wicked men or disease or any other evil, to act except in accord with His great purposes. It would be to no end to allow evil simply so as to restore things again as good as new. God permits evil in order to draw forth some greater good, for there is nothing to prevent human natures from being raised up to something even greater, even after sin, says the great St. Thomas. Or in St. Paul's words, *Where sin abounds, grace abounds all the more*! Christ's inexpressible grace gave us blessings **better** than those that had been taken away. Which is the reason each Easter we sing 'O happy fall that gained for us so great a Redeemer!'

So we have nothing to fear from any sort of evil, we fear God and need fear nothing or no one else. This is why, if we take another look at the lives of the saints, it's not all suffering, it's not all gloomy, but it's rather an uplifting story. Christ came to their aid with supernatural strength so that they could endure all things. With Paul they could boast from the Cross of Our Lord, rejoicing to have been counted worthy to suffer for the Name, certain that even the cruelest agony was but a slight momentary affliction, preparing us for an eternal weight of Glory beyond all comparison. Indeed, as the Song of Songs says, *Love is as strong as death*. And God who is Love, who created life in the first place, is not threatened by death. His Son knew that no one could take His life from Him, but He came to lay it down willingly. This act of self donation is what perfects us as human beings because we're made for love. Because Christ was united to every human being by the Incarnation, His self-giving to the Father was redemptive for all mankind, and all those who participate in His sacrifice can likewise be united to God the Father in the Son's gift of Himself, thus they can be saved.

Love is not only as strong as death, but stronger. It allows those who suffer to so anticipate the joys of God's reward for loving self sacrifice that suffering can be, amazing as it sounds, the road to joy, even in this life. So we read of martyrs astonishing their torturers, not only by their peaceful resignation but even by their lightheartedness, by their singing of hymns and telling of jokes. And mystics, who have only arrived at such a high level of union with God through terrible suffering, tell us that they wouldn't have it any other way. St. John of the Cross, for instance, laments the many who are scandalized by the cross, for in it spiritual delights are found. But the Cross is none the less a scandal. *We preach Christ crucified*, says Paul, *a stumbling block to the Jews and folly to the Gentiles. But to those who are called, Jews and Greeks alike, Christ is the power of God and the wisdom of God.*

Yes, let us remember that God is wise and all-powerful when we are suffering. There is no reason to rebel or complain, become disturbed or distraught for, as Cardinal Newman said, "He knows what He is about." Knowing so much about suffering from his own life, the

Holy Father says, "In the person of Jesus Christ, God plumbed the depths of human suffering, and in so doing it has been linked to love, to that Love that creates good and draws good out of suffering, just as the supreme good of the redemption of the world was drawn from the Cross of Christ and from that Cross constantly takes a beginning."

Holy Way of the Cross

If any man would come after me, let Him renounce Himself and take up his cross every day and follow me. Are there any words spoken by Our Lord that are less understood than these? "The doctrine of the Cross, *a scandal for the Jews and a folly for the Gentiles (I Cor 1.23)* is that which men understand the least" (says Lammenais, a famous French preacher of the last century).

Are there any words that are more necessary to understand than these? The same Lammenais points out that our salvation depends upon coming to appreciate and assimilate this doctrine. "Heaven had been separated from the earth; the cross has united them; and it is from the foot of the cross that everyone who goes to Heaven departs" But of those who understand Christ's teaching that *He who wants to save his life will lose it, but He who loses his life for my sake will save it*, of those few who accept it, even fewer practice it. St. John of the Cross refers to this lamentable fact saying: "I think it is possible to affirm that the more necessary the doctrine the less it is practiced by spiritual persons." How common it is for people to speak of the importance of self-sacrifice, but "in practice, people fear, complain, excuse themselves and shrink as soon as there is a question of suffering" (*Triumph through the Cross*)

The Holy Way of the Cross opened up by Christ, the difficult way through the narrow gate that leads to life, is not overcrowded, but, in his own words, *those who find it are few. (Mt. 7.14)* Therefore, we must consider for a few moments this sacred doctrine so that we will love it and put it into practice. First of all, observe that crosses in this life are inevitable. The question is not whether one can go through life without suffering, but whether one will accept it out of love. Will one suffer with Christ so as to share also in his glory, or will one grumble against God in this life like those do who are punished for ever? But there are yet better reasons to wish to run to pick up our Cross, even as Our Savior did His, with an ardent Heart from the moment of His Incarnation. We are wise to suffer anything in this life, because the sufferings of this age are nothing in comparison to the reward that they obtain for us. "With reason you should willingly suffer a little for

Christ, when many suffer greater things for the world" *(Imitation)* And this little suffering, united to the unique Sacrifice of Christ, is capable of conquering every obstacle. The Cross is the best weapon, the most terrible object to demons, the swiftest cure for the malady of mankind. "If there were anything better or more useful for the salvation of men than suffering, Christ surely would have shown it by word and example" *(Imitation)*

Now nothing that I have said so far is too mysterious. But a marvelous thing happens when one willingly accepts a cross. It becomes, in Christ's words, a sweet yoke and a light burden. (*cf. Mt. 11.30*) In fact, "if you carry the Cross willingly, it will carry you to the goal you seek, namely to the end of all suffering, but that is not in this life" *(Imitation)* "The cross [becomes] a supporting staff and greatly lightens and eases the journey" *(AMC II, 7, 7)* Now this is strange. We call those things that seem opposed to our good "crosses" and yet, by the power of Christ to renew all things, our very crosses bring us to our greatest good. The very things that our nature abhors and flees — pain, humiliation, rejection — become, when accepted out of love of Christ, sweet. The joy from "a single tear shed at the feet of Jesus is a thousand times more delicious than all the pleasures of the age" (Lamm) Saints begin to desire nothing so much as to share in Christ's passion. And Our Lord does oblige them, giving to generous souls, as His greatest gift, sufferings far above the lot of ordinary men in this valley of tears. "When you will have reached the point that tribulation is sweet to you and pleases you for the sake of Christ, then consider that all is well with you, because you have found paradise on earth." (*Imitation*)

Is it any wonder that a doctrine that is so counter-intuitive and so opposed to our nature is misunderstood, rejected, ignored, denied? It is a doctrine that only makes sense to people of faith who live by grace. People who realize that Love that is worthy of the name wishes to sacrifice for the beloved. True love wishes to die for the beloved without losing the beloved, a paradoxical desire that is only possible in the context of eternal life. This sort of love, which comes from God, which is God, was perfectly revealed by Christ's death on the Cross. The doctrine of the Cross, of self-denial, is the doctrine of true love, that is why it is called by St. John of the Cross, "the one thing necessary" "the root and sum of all the virtues". (*AMC, II, 7.8*)

It is a long road of daily work to approach this point. "The journey [to Christian perfection] does not consist in consolations, delights, and spiritual feelings but in the living death of the cross, sensory and spiritual, interior and exterior" (*AMC, II, 7.11*). We must not be discouraged! Remember that those who have progressed so gloriously far along it, who prayed for the grace "not to die, but to suffer" (Mary Mag. de Pazzi) all began at the same stage we are. It is a matter of setting our will to seek, beginning with small things, at least some of the time, what we do not like. Our Lord emphasized that those who follow Him must pick up their cross *every day*. For us, too, every day will include dozens of inconveniences, sorrows and setbacks that we can use to take little steps forward on the Holy Way of the Cross. Be not like those who "are content with a certain degree of virtue, perseverance in prayer, and mortification, but never achieve the nakedness, poverty, selflessness or spiritual purity about which the Lord counsels us here" (*AMC II, 7*). We cannot stop along the road, but must press on, leaning against "the cross, which is our consolation, as it is our strength" (Lamm). The secret is in Who died upon that first Cross, and how great was His Love. Sharing in it, we are made invincible conquerors of sin and death. *In all these things we are more than conquerors in Him who loved us, Christ Jesus. (Rom 8)*

⊘oly Thursday

Gift of Self

Christ washes His disciples feet, and tells them to do likewise. We naturally think that He's giving us an example of service, and telling us to serve others. His action can be interpreted as a rather dramatic exhortation to be thoughtful, helpful, and humble. But it is more. Much more. If we remember that when Christ speaks of being a servant, He's thinking of the Suffering Servant, the one who came *to serve and not to be served but to lay down his life as a ransom for many*, we begin to approach the meaning of His action.

The whole evening was, as the Holy Father commented during his recent visit to the Upper Room, "charged with mystery". The Evangelist gives an obvious sign that this action is not a teaching technique but a major revelation, for only *knowing that the Father had given all things into his hands, and that He had come from God and was going to God,* only then did Christ rise *from supper,* lay *aside his garments, and* gird *Himself with a towel.* What Lord are you showing us that requires you to call to mind your divine origin, mission and destiny? What are you asking us to take part in?

"We must never cease meditating anew on the mystery of that night" the Holy Father tells us. "These are the hours of the great battle between the love which gives itself without reserve and the *mysterium iniquitatis* [the mystery of evil]..." Christ was girding Himself for this battle when He took up the towel. He was not cleansing us of dirt but of the uncleanness of sin which is a betrayal of our Lord.

Christ is about to speak, for the next four chapters about the hidden life of God, about his Father with whom He is one and about the Holy Spirit, the spirit of truth that He and the Father will send. He is revealing the essence of God's inner life which, as John Himself will tell us in his letter, is love: *God is love*. And this love is made manifest by Christ's action, so symbolic of his entire mission as Incarnate Savior: "In Christ, God has 'stripped Himself', and has taken on 'the form of a slave' even to the utter abasement of the Cross." (ibid, 4). Oh, indeed, He will next be stripped to be scourged, and then finally, stripped to be nailed to the Cross. He knows what it means to "lay aside his garments".

And what else does He do that night, something so much at the heart of the early Church, and of the Church in every age, that John does not even allude to it? He institutes the sacrament of the Eucharist. Another sacred action whose meaning is never to be exhausted: "How can we not return ever anew to this mystery — says the Holy Father — which contains the entire life of the Church?" At every Mass we proclaim it to be *the* mystery of faith, for any understanding of the Holy Eucharist, presupposes the revelation of the Trinity and the Incarnation. For, Jesus was about to sacrifice his life on the Cross in "a total gift of Himself" *(VS 85)* to the Father, in loving obedience, for our sake. His gift of self does not end on the Cross, but continues, or is re-presented, at every Mass so that we too, in receiving communion, can be enabled to make a similar saving gift of self.

No matter how much natural man admires altruism, he cannot make a gift of himself without this encounter with God, "God, who comes to meet him through His Eternal Son". What a lesson to learn and to take to heart! Where do we encounter Him more intimately and powerfully than in the Holy Eucharist, the sacrament of God's infinite love for humanity? If you receive well, says St. Augustine, you become what you receive. If we receive well, we, too, can follow the example left by Christ. *For to this you have been called, because Christ also suffered for you, leaving you an example, that you should follow in his steps [I Ptr. 2.21]*

This is the freedom for which Christ has set us free — free to walk the way of the Cross, to tread the narrow path out of the Egypt of our passions, our egoism, our sensuality, our pride, we now passover to the Promised Land of holiness. "He sealed our souls with his own

Spirit, and the members of our body with his own blood" (Melito of Sardis). Let us not, like the Israelites, keep hankering after the delicacies we ate in the times of our servitude. Christ reveals that authentic freedom is a capacity for realizing the truth of God's plan...even when that plan includes the Cross (*FC 6*). The total acceptance of God's will is the act proper to a free man. Who, then, was ever more free than the He who laid down his life for the sheep, saying "No one takes it from me, but I lay it down". It is only in denying ourselves that we are affirmed, and in emptying ourselves that we are fulfilled. Here, where no one would think to look for it, is the fruit of abiding joy, growing on the Cross, which has become the tree of life. Follow me, says the Lord, in a radical acceptance of God's will, nailing your own desires to the cross, and though *you have sorrow now,... your hearts will rejoice, and no one will take your joy from you.*

Good Friday

Merciful Love

The Lord burdened Him with the sins of us all... The Lord has been pleased to crush Him with suffering. Do we ever stop to marvel at these words? Obviously the death of Christ was not caused directly by God, but by men — Pilate, the Chief Priests, Judas — but still we must say with St. Peter: *This Jesus [was] delivered up according to the definite plan and foreknowledge of God (Acts 2.23)*. The Liturgy of the Church is clearer yet, even blunt: "God, you wished that your Son should submit for us to the yoke of the Cross so that you might expel from us the power of the enemy..." You *wished* that your Son should submit... The love that the Father has for the Son from all eternity goes beyond our describing, beyond our imagining. And yet, mystery of mysteries, the Father *so loved the world that He gave his only Son, that whoever believes in Him should not perish but have eternal life (Jn. 3.16)*. God *did not spare his only Son* but *made Him sin who knew no sin, so that in Him we might become the righteousness of God (2Cor 5.21)*

Were it not the Father's plan, how could it have unfolded with such stupefying beauty? Everything fits into place: the very cause of our predicament, a tree, the tree in the Garden of Eden, becomes, in the tree of the Cross, the source of salvation. Were it not arranged by God how could it be that *Christ died for our sins, in accordance with the Scriptures (1 Cor 15.3)*? Indeed, the whole Old Testament speaks of Christ and the events of these three days: "In Abel [Christ] was slain, in Isaac bound, in Jacob exiled, in Joseph sold, in Moses exposed to die. He was sacrificed in the Passover lamb, persecuted in David, dishonored in the prophets." (*Melito of Sardis*)

Everything written about me, says Christ on the way to Emmaus, *in the law of Moses and the prophets and the psalms must be fulfilled* (*Lk. 24.44*); and yet He carried out his Father's will freely and willingly. At any point He could have said 'enough': *Do you think that I cannot appeal to my Father, and He will at once send me more than twelve legions of angels?* (*Mt. 26.53*) Yet, He vigorously rebuked anyone who tried to dissuade Him, as Peter did, from persevering: *Shall I not drink the cup which the Father has given me?*(*Jn. 18.11*) *And what shall I say, Father, save me from this hour? No, for this purpose I have come to this hour.* (*Jn. 12.27*)

Christ Himself recognized from the beginning why He had come. He said, on coming into the world, '*Lo, I have come to do your will, O God*'. Already at age twelve, He was intent on being about his Father's business. "The desire to embrace his Father's plan of redeeming love inspired Jesus' whole life, for his redemptive passion was the very reason for his Incarnation" (*CCC 607*). He foretold his upcoming death many times; He looked forward earnestly to his "baptism". While moved by love of us, He did everything ultimately for the Father: *The Father loves me, because I lay down my life* (*Jn. 10.17*).

Christ, by his burning love that, from the Cross, lights up all of human history, banishing the powers of darkness, reveals God the Father as love, as merciful love. He revealed God as omnipotent love; love that is stronger than sin, stronger than death, love that cannot be overcome by any force: not by *death, nor life, nor angels, nor principalities, nor things present, nor things to come, nor powers, nor height, nor depth, nor anything else in all creation* (*Rom 8.38-9*), and yet, which can be rejected definitively by any man, even by a child. My brothers and sisters, let us not reject the love of the Father that comes to us in Christ Jesus Our Lord. Christ has gone so far as to beg, *Behold, I stand at the door and knock* (*Rev. 3.20*). The Father has gone so far as to "invite man to have 'mercy' on his only Son, the Crucified One". (*DM 8.3*)

How will we have mercy on Him? Three ways. Firstly, by avoiding all sin. Citing the letter to the Hebrews, the Church tells us that "Since our sins made the Lord Christ suffer the torment of the Cross, those who plunge themselves into disorders and crimes crucify the Son of God anew in their hearts (for He is in them) and hold Him up to contempt" (*Rom. Cat, CCC 598, Heb. 6.6*) Secondly, we must have mercy on the Crucified Lord by seeking to help all the members of the Body of Christ who are now suffering: the lonely, the sad, the confused, the poor, the handicapped... Finally, we have mercy on Him when we enthusiastically, bravely and generously help Him bear His Cross by accepting all manner of contradiction, frustration, humiliation that comes into our lives. Let us *make up in [our] flesh what is lacking in Christ's afflictions (Col.1.24)*. We must remember that our lives, no less that Christ's, have been planned by Divine Providence. Every difficulty that comes our way has been measured and timed by the Father who demands much of those that He wishes to make *perfect through suffering (Heb. 2)*. They come to us from his merciful love. Let us see his loving hand behind them, and, when we accept them, we become, like Christ, "radical revelations of mercy" to a world so in need.

Mystery of the Cross

There is an ancient hymn we sing this day which speaks of the mystery of the cross. *Fulget mysterium crucis.* the mystery of the cross shining. Nothing could seem less mysterious or resplendent than the cross – what hidden treasures, what great surprises could be contained in crude, naked wood used to torture criminals? The mystery contained in the cross is so great that Cardinal Newman hesitated to speak of it. This great holy doctor feared that words would obscure this shining, glorious mystery.

May God help us to learn something of the mystery of the Cross. To us it is all darkness. Emptiness – like this Church without its ornaments or flowers. Sadness. Ugliness. Bitterness. "Why" is the question on all lips. On Christ's: Why have you abandoned Me? On Peter's: Why should the Messiah have to die? On those of every generation that has followed: How could the greatest injustice ever – the agonizing death of a perfect man — right the wrongs of history? Yes, the key to the overturning of Satan's reign of hate was Christ's show of love. *Love is stronger than death*. This gift of Himself on the cross is what was pleasing to the Father, not his agony. There was no easier way, since, after the fall, love and suffering are inextricably bound. This mystery of the cross must not remain hidden from the world. We must make it known. We pray for it to be better known every year, for it is by faith in the Crucified that we are saved.

We can make it known by living lives where the inevitable sacrifice, the inevitable cross, is not feared but greeted with supernatural fortitude. This is the sign to unbelievers that our Gospel is true. When the martyrs went to the torturers without fear, that made the Romans think. But in our day too: when doctors see mothers joyfully accept a handicapped child, that makes them think. When classmates see a child endure mockery for the truth and good, that makes them think. We can conquer the world by our faith that the cross is not death to us, but the tree of life. So let us who are Christians not be afraid of anything, for though we feel abandoned upon our crosses, *we are more than conquerors through Him who loved us.* We seek no glory or consolation in things that pass away. With Paul we say, *far be it from me to glory except in the cross of our Lord Jesus Christ, by which the world has been crucified to me, and I to the world. (Gal. 6.14)*

This is a mysterious, dark truth indeed. From the beginning, the cross we preach — Christ crucified — is *a stumbling block to Jews and folly to Gentiles, (1 Cor 1.23).* Yet it is a mystery that contains all the answers to the meaning of life and history, the path to freedom joy fulfillment and hope. Let us decide with St. Paul *to know nothing ... except Jesus Christ and Him crucified. ... a secret and hidden wisdom of God, which God decreed before the ages for our glorification. (I Cor).*

Easter

The First Easter Morning

When Christ died, the world was wrapped in darkness. There was an earthquake and all of nature seemed to mourn its Creator. As Joseph and Nicodemus carried that Sacred Body to the tomb and the two Marys stayed behind, imagine how for them blooming flowers or singing birds would have seemed a mockery, and totally out of place. Well, forty hours later, on Easter morning, the contrary is true. The good news of Christ's resurrection is good news for every man, woman and child on the face of the earth, and for all creation too. Doesn't a rainy Easter day seem odd? How much odder a tearful face. Thus, the angels' first words to Mary Magdalen, and Christ's also: "Woman, why are you weeping?".

How can anyone weep on Easter Day? Or for that matter on any day after the first Easter, or are we capable of forgetting what has happened? Indeed, it is not even a mere historical event that could fade in collective memory over time; rather, Christ's rising transcends history: it is as immediate and fresh today as on that first day. Eternity and time have touched. God has intervened in a dramatic way. As the

Exsutet sung last night proclaims: "The power of this holy night dispels all evil, washes guilt away, restores lost innocence, brings mourners joy; it casts out hatred, brings peace, and humbles earthly pride." It has, in short, made all things new, and there should not be any more cause for sorrow. But we know that we will be sad again, even before the next Easter. Only in Heaven, the eternal Easter, will *every tear be wiped away.* Now we live in a mysterious mixture of joy and sorrow; the duel between death and life has been won by Life but the fight – mysteriously – continues in us, the Body of Christ. Our Head won redemption on the first Good Friday, yet, somehow, as St. Paul said (*Col 1.24*), we must *make up in [our] flesh what is lacking* in that complete, indeed, superabundant sacrifice *for the sake of the body the Church.*.

So, we live a mystery: we *have been raised with Christ (Col. 3.14)* and yet we still suffer, bear crosses, *are slaughtered for his sake all the day long (Rom 8)* But the power of the resurrection is not empty; it gives our sufferings a new light: *we do not grieve as others do, who have no hope.* Indeed, as the power of the Resurrection grows in us, our sufferings seem ever smaller. In the saints we not only can see the glory of the resurrection reflected, but shining marvelously! St. Ignatius, for instance, confided to a friend that He could not imagine any event that could disturb his peace and joy. Likewise, St. Therese of Lisieux was so far from being daunted by pain that she could say "suffering has become my Heaven here below". She still suffered, but she was raised with Christ, and hidden with Him in the Heavenly places. We must work, every day, in prayer and meditation, study and sacrifice, to see all things and especially our Crosses in the light of the Risen Christ.

St. Paul said, *For [Christ's] sake I have suffered the loss of all things, and count them as refuse, ... that I may know Him and the power of his resurrection,. (Phil. 3:8-11)* This Easter season let us make some resolution, pay some price to take a step in our "walking in newness of life". Then we will know the only permanent joy in life, the joy that no one can take from us, the joy of knowing that Christ's victory is our victory. Temptation, addiction, sensuality, bad habits, apathy, superficiality, depression, fear, hatred – all of it, then, flies like darkness before the rising Sun that is Christ Jesus risen from the dead.

Joy of Easter

There is, of course, no joy like the joy of the Church today. She is one with the Blessed Virgin Mary who experienced first, in the wee hours of Easter morning, the joy of seeing her Son alive. Her joy goes beyond that of holding her Son on Christmas morning; it goes beyond even the natural joy of having a dead son come back to life, for Christ has not *returned* to life, but has entered into the glorious life of Heaven body and soul. He promised Mary to join Him soon in her Assumption, and we, too, have been promised.

Easter is the greatest feast of the Church year. In fact, it is so great, so mysterious and powerful and astounding, that it's too much for us. It is Christmas that everyone loves so naturally. Everyone can appreciate the human beauty of the birth of Christ. At Easter, it is opposite: the human element escapes us: Mary Magdalen is told not to hold the Lord and the disciples do not recognize their friend. Our reaction still tends to be one of amazement rather than spontaneous joy. Still, if we are to capture for ourselves the authentic Christian spirit, we must learn to rejoice at the news "He is Risen!". The apostles didn't care if they were beaten or killed or ridiculed just so that they could bear witness to this truth: *we cannot be silent about what we have seen and heard.* They bore witness to a historical fact, that the tomb was empty and the Lord alive. But, more than that, they bore witness to a mystery: the Man they crucified was also God and could not be held bound by death. We call this a mystery because it cannot be fully grasped. It is accessible only to those who have the gift of faith.

The Resurrection of Christ must be a truth that changes us, too. Even though we still live our natural life, we possess that new and glorious life of His. *If then you have been raised with Christ, seek the things that are above, where Christ is, seated at the right hand of God. (Col. 3.1)* We are in some sense already in Heaven, participating in the Eternal Easter, especially through the sacred Liturgy, *hidden with Christ in God.* Let this show on our faces. Let it be the light in our hearts that can never be conquered or even shaken by life's vicissitudes. We are Christians — we bless when cursed, we're are rich in poverty, serene in adversity, — we can do many things that the world considers contrary to nature. We live by a moral code that they say is not possible. We can do this because of this mystery, because we have grasped by faith what does indeed go beyond natural power. *We were buried therefore with Him by baptism into death, so that as Christ was raised from the dead by the glory of the Father, we too might walk in newness of life. (Rom. 6.4)*

Let us walk, let us run, in newness of life. Our very lives, transformed by Christ, gloriously triumphant over sin and death, will witness, even without words, to the truth of the Resurrection. No obstacle is too much for us, since Christ has blown away the greatest burden — death — as though it were morning mist. No temptation, no sorrow, no loss, no setback, nothing is too much for us — we have the life of Christ in us. At Christmas He came to share our life, our nature; at Easter, we share his life, his nature. Christ is truly risen, alleluia.

New Life Within Us

"The Prince of Life who died reigns immortal" as the Easter sequence tells us. The logic of our world, has been wholly overturned in one glorious night. Worldly logic is a logic of fear: death is all powerful. The worst evil is suffering and death and anything should be allowed to avoid it. Christ's logic is different: love is triumphant. The worst evil is infidelity to God and anything should be endured to avoid it. We cannot live by His logic as long as we are afraid to die; Christ came to *deliver all those who through fear of death were subject to lifelong bondage [Heb. 2.15];* He freed us for lives of dignity, nobility, and heroism.

When the disciples first learned that Christ had defeated death, they were amazed, of course, and rejoiced, but they still did not understand what it meant for them. Only after fifty days, with the help of the Holy Spirit, on Pentecost did the full truth begin to dawn upon them: Christ not only conquered sin and death, but He has given that power to us! We, too, have fifty days of Easter celebration to meditate upon the victory of Christ so that it will penetrate our hearts and change us completely. No longer must we live by a logic that is based upon the fear of suffering and death. When we were baptized, we put that old nature to death. *We know that our old self was crucified with Him,* says St. Paul, *so... we might no longer be enslaved to sin.* Now we can *Put on the new nature, created after the likeness of God in true righteousness and holiness. [Eph. 4]*

The old man has died, a new creature has been born in us. To paraphrase a Vietnamese Bishop, Van Thuan, who learned much about the Christian mysteries in his years of confinement by the Communists: Christ's cry of abandonment on the Cross summed up the cry of all humanity separated from God (sinful humanity)[and it] becomes... the cry of a "new creation," of a new birth occurring, our birth into children of God. Those who are born again by baptism are collectively called the Church, and the Church, the spouse of Christ was born from his wounded side, from the side of the New Adam, as He slept in death upon the cross. Christ died and Christians were born. This is the secret of the new birth: The Prince of Life dwells in those who are in a state of grace — *it is no longer I who lives but Christ who lives in me*; Since "Baptism radically configures the faithful to Christ in the Paschal Mystery of death and resurrection", we can even say with St. Augustine: "for we have become not only Christians, but Christ. Marvel and rejoice: we have become Christ!".

This life of holiness is to be preserved at all costs. That is why the sign of genuine Christians is the refusal to sin no matter what the price... loss of freedom, or friends, loss of work, money or health, even loss of life itself. "It is always possible," writes John Paul II, "that man... can be hindered from doing certain good actions; but he can never be hindered from **not** doing certain actions, especially if he is prepared to die rather than to do evil." *(VS 52)* To be ready to make such sacrifices we must constantly increase Christ's life in us. If we receive well, we become what we receive, other Christs. (St. Aug.) The early Christians received the Eucharist every day precisely because martyrdom was a daily threat. John Paul II has also asked us to open our eyes to the 'new martyrs.' "A century like ours, where there has been so much comfort, so much attachment to life, so much fear of losing it, has also been a century of Christian martyrdom. The martyrs have been among us. What is more, they are the strength of the Church today and of the century that is beginning." Martyrs are the great witness to the transforming power of the resurrection in ordinary lives.

But we must not only be ready to die a martyr's death but to live a martyr's life. *While we live we are always being given up to death for Jesus' sake, so that the life of Jesus may be manifested in our mortal flesh.* We must learn to suffer every contradiction, great or small, with joy. United to Christ, conqueror on the cross, there will be in us a resilience, an unassailable power come what may:. *We are afflicted in every way, but not crushed; perplexed, but not driven to despair; persecuted, but not forsaken; struck down, but not destroyed; always carrying in the body the death of Jesus, so that the life of Jesus may also be manifested in our bodies.* This is not will power, but rather *the transcendent power* [of the Risen Christ] *belong[ing] to God and not to us.*

Why Are You Weeping?

"Woman, why are you weeping?" This is a question that should be asked of all Christians, all Christians who grieve at one time or another in their life. Why are you grieving, why do you live as if Christ were not alive? The Lord asked His disciples on the road to Emmaeus the same kind of question, this time a little more sternly, "Why are you so hard of heart, so slow to believe?" Was it not necessary for Christ to suffer and so enter into His glory? So why are we weeping, why are we discouraged? The reason we are discouraged is that we aren't seeing, aren't recognizing the happiness set before us, just as Mary did not recognize the Lord standing before her, so we seek happiness where it isn't, in sin. We grieve about things we shouldn't. When people die early and go to Heaven, if they've lived a good life, why should we grieve? Why should we worry when things do not turn out our way? Is not God all powerful?

One of the great religious leaders of our time, Fr. Marcel Maciel, founder of a religious congregation, tells us it's not so very hard to be happy in this life. Every time we find we are sad, we must ask ourselves, 'Why am I sad?' "Really, it's very easy to be happy," he writes. "They don't seem to notice that happiness is within the grasp of each one of us, in accepting or not accepting Christ. Christ, the risen Christ, stands before each and every one of us, needing only to be recognized for us to be happy." All these things grieve us; death, our past sins, some tragedy that we're going through. So many look back, saying, 'Wouldn't it be better if that never happened, or if this weren't happening,' instead of looking forward to the good that God means to bring out of every evil, by His omnipotent hand. The resurrection tells us that from the greatest evil that ever was, God brought out the greatest good that ever was." So why should we ever weep over our problems?

Christian Joy

This translation says that they went away from the tomb half overjoyed, half fearful, but, in fact, they were mostly overjoyed. *They went away with fear and great joy!* You have to remember the angel had just told them not to fear, but still they had fear in them. Soon after, they meet Jesus and again He tells them, "Do not fear." Their fear had gone down and when they see Jesus their fear, perhaps, disappears altogether. We should be pondering what it is that joy is during this joyful season. Joy, first of all, is specifically human and, in fact, intimately Christian. It's a gift, a gift that comes through contact with God and especially through Christ Jesus.

Most people we know are not joyful because they're fearful, because fear has some hold on them, anxiety, insecurity, self consciousness, some sort of fear that comes from distance from God. If one's truly united to God, then one's not afraid of anything. They fear God and nothing else, and so one's full of joy. That's why Easter is a time of joy par excellance, because the Christian is fearful of nothing, not the worst tortures, not the greatest terrors, nothing can over come God and the gifts, the graces, that come to us through Christ Jesus. So He fulfills His promise on Easter morning, *I will give you a joy that no one can take from you*. Nothing can take it from us, not even suffering. Indeed, Christian joy somehow increases with suffering, almost as if suffering proves that we're so united with God that nothing can keep us apart.

Joy is particularly characteristic of the Christian religion, and that's why it's a sign of heretical versions of Christianity where their joy disappears. They somehow think that joy isn't Christian when , in fact, it's what Christianity is all about. St. Thomas Aquinas goes so far as to say, very memorably, "Everyone who wants to make progress in the spiritual life needs to have joy." That's something that we should remember every single day, and should be part of our examination of conscience at night, 'Were we joyful?' "Everyone who wants to make progress in the spiritual life needs to have joy!" And everyone who wants to help others lead the Christian life needs to have joy. What is more important in the work of evangelization than being joyful? It's more infectious than anything, it's what's more attractive than anything, and it's what's characteristic of a true Christian. To increase our joy, then, we must not only accept our crosses without fear, embrace them, but also since it's a gift, ask the Lord to increase our joy, and ask through the Blessed Virgin Mary and invoke her as the 'Cause of our Joy'.

Faith

Healing our Wounds of Unbelief

St. Gregory the Great, commenting on this famous episode, said, "Do you really believe it was by chance that this chosen disciple was absent, then came and heard, heard and doubted, doubted and touched, touched and believed. It was not by chance but in God's providence. In a marvelous way God's mercy arranged that this believing disciple, touching the wounds of his Master's body, should heal our wounds of unbelief. This brief encounter has done more for our faith than for the faith of the other disciples." One way we can see that is in the tremendous transformation that took place in Thomas, going from a doubter to great apostle, going out to all the world to preach the good news, most likely as far as India where many Indians are called 'Thomas Christians'.

We need to follow his example. We need not fear perhaps so much doubting our faith, positive doubts that he had, that refusal of his will, I will not believe unless such and such. That may not be so much the danger for us, but rather having a faith that is in some way dormant, some way not as dynamic, strong, growing, or real as it ought to be, but simply a dry, intellectual, and somewhat sterile faith. We have to remember that faith is more than just the intellectual be-lief plus good will. It was Thomas who said to the other disciples, *let's go down and die with Him, when* Jesus was going up to Jerusalem. That wasn't enough to keep him strong. We need the essential grace of faith. It's described here by the Holy Father, "Faith in it's deepest essence is the openness of the human heart to the gift, to God's self-communication in the Holy Spirit."

So how is it that we will keep that openness of the human heart? How we would do that is not really just an act of will on our part. We have to first of all ask for it, ask for it, all the time. Lord, increase my faith. Also the apostles asked that, *Lord, increase our faith.* It's a very important prayer of petition, especially when we begin to pray. And this is the second thing, to pray, mental prayer, to meditate upon the humanity of Christ. Thomas touched the body of Christ, he had to ex-perience the humanity of Christ as the Way. Remember how Thomas had asked the Lord, *We do not know where you are going Lord, we do not know the way.* And the Lord responded, *I am the Way.* It is our faith that leads us down this way that is the humanity of Christ, that helps us see in this man, *my Lord and my God* and the only bridge to God, to holiness. Our mental prayer is always a deepening of our rela-tionship and understanding of Jesus Christ the Man. This is the faith, because He is the fullness of God's self communication in the Holy Spirit. So we're open to Him. Thirdly, study. Although study of itself won't give us the grace of faith, it certainly disposes us and helps de-velop the seeds of faith that God gives us. So every day should in-clude some study of our faith, some spiritual reading, something of that sort. Let us ask the Lord today for this gift of increased faith and do all we can, in our power, to make it grow.

Inflaming Our Hearts

We hoped that it was He that should have redeemed Israel. By this remark, the two disciples reveal that they are already growing tepid in their faith. As St. Gregory the Great said: "[He seemed a stranger to them] for He was as yet a stranger to faith in their hearts". Christ refrained from showing Himself so as not to deprive them of the merit of believing, but rather "He inflamed their hearts in faith before allowing them to see" Him, finally, in the mystery of faith, the Eucharist (St. John of Cross). The faith of the two disciples was weak because it was not founded upon Christ Jesus. They had not made Him the bedrock of their faith; He was not the fullness of revelation of the Father, towards which every aspect of religion was oriented. They thought Jesus Christ was simply a teacher who could be stopped and killed, not the Lord of History who gave up his life according to *the deliberate intention and foreknowledge of God.*

In fact, there can be no genuine spirituality, not only without God, but without Jesus Christ. We, Christians, must beware, lest, like the two disciples on the way to Emmaus, our faith is not solidly founded upon the rock of the Person of Jesus Christ, true God and true Man. Perhaps, we do not cling to the *useless way of life [our] ancestors handed down* to us, but perhaps we are infected by the useless ways of life that surround us. Let us not be shy of striving for mystical prayer, but shy of methods that do not go explicitly through the humanity of Christ, the Son of God. "...contemplation is not a privilege reserved to the few; on the contrary, in parishes, in communities and movements there is a need to foster a spirituality clearly oriented to contemplation of the fundamental truths of faith: the mysteries of the Trinity, the Incarnation of the Word, the Redemption of humanity, and the other great saving works of God." These must be the objects of our prayer that make our hearts burn with love of God and desire to serve Him.

Mystery of Faith

Today's readings are brimming with paradoxes. Zechariah tells us that the king of Israel will ride to triumph in meekness, on the back of the foal of an ass. Our Lord tells us that to find rest we must take his yoke upon us. And Paul, fully aware that He preached a wisdom that seemed folly, boldly proclaims: *if you live according to the flesh you will die, but if by the Spirit you put to death the deeds of the body, you will live.* Paradoxes are everywhere in Scripture, especially in St. Paul who said when *I am weak, then I am strong.*

Religion must speak the language of paradox because it tells us of a reality that surpasses our ability to comprehend. That is why we speak so often of "mystery." At every Mass, at the most solemn moment, we proclaim "the mystery of our faith". We mean that all of these realities are partially visible and comprehensible, fully reason-able, and yet that they surpass our understanding. We would know nothing of them if God had not revealed them, and we will only fully understand when we see Him *face to face*. Acknowledging mystery does not end investigation, but keeps it open. It does not say that our reason has no place whatever, but that it has no place to rest. We must never say "Now I understand", for speaking of the divinity, Augustine says, "If you comprehend, it is not God".

Heresies are nothing but the removal of mystery, the emphasizing of one truth — Christ's humanity, our freedom, whatever — at the ex-pense of another truth that appears irreconcilable — Christ's divinity, God's grace, etc.. For this reason, St. Thomas More says: "It is a shorter thing and sooner done, to write heresies than to answer them". That is why heresies always come in pairs — rationalism and fideism, for instance — with the true faith in the midst. This is far from saying that the truth is "middle of the road", a compromise — no, the truth is a mystery, it is an extreme, it is of another order. Understanding this helps to forward dialogue. We can see that the truth cannot be attained by pressuring, compromising or poll-taking but by following the Spirit of Truth with humble fidelity. It is the world, that has no con-cept of the Church as mystery, that describes it in purely sociological terms, as divided into liberals and conservatives. A true man of the Church will transcend these labels..

Indeed, our natural world is filled with mystery for those who have eyes to see, like children. Wonder is the beginning of philosophy, an essential element of being human, and Chesterton pointed out that, in our own day: "We have no lack of wonders but of wonder" itself. Because nature is mysterious, the more science discovers, the more fascinating and the more baffling does nature appear. This should, of course, produce humility in modern man, but the contrary is often true. As St. Augustine tells us, we are prepared by natural mysteries to accept supernatural mysteries of the faith. This closing off to mystery leads soon to a rejection of religion. This produces the most terrible emptiness, boredom, of all. Thus, Nietzche lamented, "Against bore-dom even the gods themselves struggle in vain". When one rejects Christianity, this life becomes, among other things, intensely boring. Peter was so right when he said that without Christ, *to whom would we go*.

The Church, thanks to her faith, knows natural reality profoundly; she does not sell it short, because she knows that natural things have been created and they therefore share in the mystery of God. She speaks therefore, of the mystery of life, of death, the mystery of sin, and the mystery of man. All of these realities, exceed our ability to comprehend them. The Church is "an expert in humanity" because she knows the mystery that illumines natural mysteries and the mystery of man, in particular; that is Christ. As the Second Vatican Council said, "it is only in the mystery of the Word made flesh that the mystery of man truly becomes clear... Christ... fully reveals man to himself and brings to light his most high calling."

How then shall we grasp this truth? These mysteries? How shall we learn to thirst for it? We must humble ourselves. It is marvelous to see how "little ones" lap up the faith, but catechism is not just for children. Since these truths surpass reason, we must do more than study, we must contemplate them. We must never forget that the ability to appreciate the faith is a gift. Our Lord tells us, *"I thank thee, Father, Lord of Heaven and earth, that thou hast hidden these things from the wise and understanding and revealed them to babes; yea, Father, for such was thy gracious will."* Let us then ask, humbly, for the gift of faith, for it is beyond our natural capacity. Eternal God, the mystery of mysteries, You who are the deepest reality, God, who comes to us as Jesus Christ, who is Truth and Light, illumine our minds and our worlds today!

Divine Mercy

Divine Mercy Sunday

Understanding Mercy is so important for understanding God. "It is precisely because there is sin in the world... that God, who 'is love' cannot reveal Himself otherwise than as mercy. God's omnipotence is most clearly seen in his mercy (*Coll. XXVI*) because merciful love is powerful: it raises up one who is in need, re-creating, restoring, transforming. Merciful love is the most beautiful, the most God-like sort. It is the most Christian; it is peculiarly Christian. The world is used to loving those who are lovable, but mercy loves those who are not so lovable, precisely insofar as they are not lovable. Precisely because there is a value missing that needs to be restored, because there is a potential good that needs to be actualized. This is the love for the hungry, homeless, sick (the corporal works of mercy) or — the spiritual works of mercy — for the ignorant, confused, sorrowing, and especially for the sinner. The sinner is the person most in need of mercy, most needing to be pitied, as he suffers from the worst defect possible, loss of friendship with God. Christ has identified Himself with all those who need mercy even with sinners, so that God, the source of all mercy, has also become the term or object of mercy.

Many of these works of mercy are included in the raising of a child: clothing the naked, feeding the hungry, instructing the ignorant. It is a real work of mercy, a having pity on Christ in need. The response to pity, another word for mercy, is piety. In Latin, and for a long time in English, pity and piety were the same word. That is why the attitude of a child to a parent, who has from his most defenseless years had pity on him, is described as filial piety. So also our attitude of grateful reverence towards God, which we call piety, is because He has had pity, mercy, on us. He found us bereft of grace, hungry for truth, imprisoned by sin and has made us free children and heirs to eternal life.

Divine Mercy Sunday is an ideal day to celebrate the mercy of God, and to renew our call for mercy which is at the heart of piety. Early in this century a Polish nun, St. Faustina, received many visions of Our Lord similar to the revelations of the Sacred Heart to St. Margaret Mary Alacoque several centuries ago. In both cases, Our Lord expressed His great desire to have mercy on all men, but requested that many people pray and make reparation asking for His mercy. "For the sake of his sorrowful passion, have mercy on us and the whole world".

It is not easy to ask for mercy. It means admitting that we are in need, that we are miserable. It requires great humility. God is drawn to us like a magnet by our needs, when we admit that we need Him, when we cry out to Him. Our age is one that is fiercely independent, even of God. It lacks humility, piety and, as a result, it lacks pity. Only when we experience God's mercy can we show mercy to others. Now, while all Christians accept the idea that God is merciful, not all like the idea that we must ask Him to have mercy on us or that we can be intercessors, mediators, asking for His mercy for others. Why should we have to ask God to have mercy on us? If He is infinite in mercy, what is the point? The greatness of his mercy is shown by its contrast with justice. He has willed to distribute the riches of his mercy in the manner He wills, namely, by granting us the great dignity of participating in our restoration. God allows His mercy to be limited by our degree of correspondence. To those who ask for more mercy, more is shown.

Finally, wishing to unite all men in one great effort to help each other, God holds back his mercy until it is asked for by third parties, by intercessors. Now this idea is odious to many, especially, non-Catholics, but it is an inescapable part of Christian tradition. The Blessed Virgin, invoked as "Mother of Mercy", is the intercessor *par excellence*. The Holy Father's Lenten letter ended with the words:

"May Mary intercede with God, that there may be a fresh outpouring of Divine Mercy". On this, Divine Mercy Sunday, let us learn to ask the Lord for mercy, for ourselves and for the whole world. "O my Jesus, forgive us our sins and save us from the fires of Hell; bring all souls to Heaven especially those in most need of thy mercy"

God Makes All Things New Again

Like all people living in time, we long with nostalgia for things in their pristine state, and dread their inevitable corruption. But God promised to make all things new again: *a new heavens and a new earth*. It's a constant promise made by God, from the lips of Isaiah – *see, I am doing something new* – to the triumphant cry of Christ risen from the dead: *And He who sat upon the throne said, "Behold, I make all things new." (Rev. 21.5)* The ability to make things new again, even better than the original creation is a prerogative of God. God Himself is ever new – He never ages for He is eternal. Moreover, because He is infinite, we will never cease seeing new insights of his beauty and magnificence; for all eternity we will never be bored. when we say that God is immutable, unchanging, this is not to say that He lacks life, but rather, that He is so alive that He does not lose any of his perfection, but is always new.

He is also the source of renewal in creation. Only things that are in contact with God get a share of His ever new-ness. Thus the Church, the Bride of Christ, is, after two thousand years, no less young and beautiful than she was at first. Indeed, if anything she gets "newer" in that she approaches the day when she will shine in *splendor, without spot or wrinkle or any such thing, ...holy and without blemish" (Eph. 5)* That is why her teaching office is likened to *the householder* mentioned by Christ *who brings out of his treasure what is old and what is new (Mt. 13.52)* In other words, we are always discovering new depth and new ways of presenting the timeless, unchanging deposit of faith revealed by Christ. Without ever speaking novelties, the Church's teaching is always fresh.

Now not only the Church as a whole but each one of us, her members, is in contact with God. We have his divine life, *new life of the Spirit* (Rom. 7.6), which is God's undying life within us by grace. As St. Paul says: *if any one is in Christ, he is a new creation;*(2 Cor 5.17); we have *put on the new nature, created after the likeness of God in true righteousness and holiness.* (Eph. 4.24) We *walk in newness of life* (Gal.6.4), following *a new commandment* (I Jn.), destined to sing *a new song* of praise to God forevermore. That is why as we mature in the Christian life, we become like children – more innocent, more joyful, more simple, more vigorous and full of life. What makes people old spiritually, is sin. It is chiefly in mercy that God makes us new. Mercy, we must note, is much more than ignoring or forgetting sin. On the contrary, it is essential to Mercy that Justice be done, that our sin be recognized. Significantly, Christ tells those He cures "to sin no more". He does not fall into the trap of false mercy so prevalent to-day which has no power to renew us. *If we say that we have no sin, we are liars, and the truth is not in us.*

It can be the greatest act of charity to help someone to admit their sin. Mercy, again, does not deny or ignore the sin; it overwhelms it with love. The merciful God, because He is all powerful says to the sinner: "I still love you no matter how heinous your crime, because I have the power to take the good still left in you and make it increase. I can make you new again. I can even bring good out of the evil you have done. It is all a part of my Providence. Together, we can make up for any sin. This is the power of the blood of Christ: to make all things new, back in order, beautiful, harmonious again." Mercy is not weakness or wimpiness, passivity or leniency; it is strength. That is why it is in virtue of God's omnipotence, his power to bring good out of evil, that He can be merciful: the Church prays "Father, you show your almighty power in your mercy and forgiveness..." Because even our sins are part of God's Providence, that is, they can bring Him glory by being the occasion for the exercise of his Almighty Mercy, we should never be despondent about our past. St. Paul, who knows what being renewed by Grace means, gives us a good example of this in the second letter. A persecutor of Christ, and enemy of the faith... after he came into contact with Christ, he was able to "forget what lies behind" and strive for ever greater heights of holiness. God made his sinful life redound to the glory of God. Thus useless breast beating was replaced by humble thanksgiving.

Thus, while we are called to be always repentant for our sins, and even to grow in sorrow for them, it is a sadness without vexation, discouragement, dread, or embarrassment. As St. Augustine – a great sinner himself at one time – put it: "The penitent should ever grieve and rejoice at his grief". It is a bitterness suffused with love which produces the sweetness of an incomparable consolation. For we know that grace abounds more than sin, that our sins fit – like the treachery of Joseph's brothers – into a greater plan of God that cannot be ruined, and that we ourselves are called to be made new. Here on earth to some degree and perfectly in Heaven for the praise and glory of the God of mercy.

Preferential Option for Sinners

I think it's a fact of experience that mothers don't love all their children equally, but that they especially love those that are in some way suffering, handicapped, or sad. Whether it's true of natural mothers or not, it's certainly true of the Church, Holy Mother Church. She has a special love for certain members of the Church and this is sometimes called Her preferential option. One usually only hears of the Church's preferential option for the poor, and indeed, the poor is one of those groups. But there are several others; the sick, children, the ignorant or unbelievers, and especially the fifth and most important group, sinners. The Church has a special love, a special preferential option for sinners. And we see that in the example of the saints. This bishop, Charles Borremeo, loved the poor. He used to travel on foot to be with them, and, I'm sure, many of the sick he met along the way. He loved to teach, he was a great teacher and writer, he helped the ignorant and, of course, most of all, his heart went out to sinners.

Obviously in this, the Church is doing nothing but following the example of the Lord Jesus, who also cared especially for the poor, the sick, children and sinners. He loved sinners most of all. That, in a way, is why He loved so much the poor and the sick. Those are almost images of the greater illness, the greater mishap of sin. And when He showed his love for children, it was especially to see that they were never scandalized, that they would come to Him without obstacles. But it's for sinners that He came. He came for this purpose as the great Doctor of Souls. Not for those who were already healed, but for all the rest. And if we wish to imitate Him, we must, not only, not judge sinners, but we must love sinners, more than anyone else. We must love them so much that they also are attracted to us. It should strike us as amazing that tax collectors and sinners were all gathering around Jesus, to hear Him. They were attracted to Him. Would that all sinners were attracted to us, that we loved them so much that they wanted to come to us and be with us and learn about Jesus from us.

Fear of the Lord

The message of the readings couldn't be more clear, we have that terrible warning by St. Paul to the Romans, the psalm reminding us that the Lord rewards man according to his works, and then the Gospel, Our Lord telling the people of the times, the Pharisees and lawyers to beware, "Woe to you, alas and woe." And in fact, we should often stop to think about the judgment, there is good reason to con-

sider it and, in the proper sense, to fear it. The fact that the consequences are eternal, and we also know from Our Lord's own words
how severe, how very precise is His judgment, every idle word we
will have to render judgment for. How great is our tendency to self de-
ception! *Preserve me O Lord from hidden faults,* the psalmist says and
in many other places the scripture says the same thing, that many consciences are deceiving themselves and many have much to fear on
that day.

One must understand all this, when St. Paul talks of wrath and
fury. We could get the wrong impression of God and of His judgment.
In fact those terms which are applied to God merely are the subjective
experience that the sinner would experience on that day. Everybody
comes before Love, itself. The Holy Father in talking about God who
judges, reminds us that this God is above all, Love, not just mercy, but
love. Not just the father of the prodigal son, but the Father who gave
His Only Son, so whoever believes in Him might not perish, but have
eternal life. It's this loving God that everybody comes before. So
there's a mystery, because those who come before Him without love
in their hearts, their experience is of something they absolutely must
flee. They cry out, *Mountains fall on us, hills cover us!!* Even though
they are before Love itself. There's a famous poem by Cardinal
Newman called the 'Dream of Gerontius'. It's the story of a soul who
comes before the judgment seat of God. This is a just soul, but one
who needed purifying. Those who go to Purgatory can't stand to be in
the presence of Love when they're not yet perfect and especially those
who are not in the state of grace, they couldn't stand to be in the presence of God. But it's always Love, God is always Love... "We'll be
judged at the evening of our life on love," says St. John of the Cross.

This is what gives proper character to this fear. We should be
most afraid of hurting this most loving God. And the more we live our
life in love for Him, the more that fear is transformed into a proper
fear of a son for his father. "This perfect love," St. James says, "casts
out all fear." Finally Cardinal Shaunborn says, "And when we begin,
with rising alarm, to gain a sense of our unworthiness, when our own
heart condemns us, then fleeing from the judgment, God's infinite
love tells us, God is greater than our hearts."

Sin Against the Holy Spirit

There's so many things that could be mentioned here, but the sin
against the Holy Spirit is the one perhaps that disturbs or confuses
people most of all. There's two principle confusions here. First of all

that there's a sin that we could commit that God could not forgive, that would be an incorrect understanding of this passage. Or that there's something special about the Holy Spirit that He's somehow greater or holier than the other two persons of the Blessed Trinity, so that if you said something against Him that it would be somehow worse than if you said something against the Son or the Father. Neither of those interpretations of this passage would be correct. Nonetheless Our Lord said in all three gospels, "Whoever blasphemes against the Holy Spirit will never be forgiven." So what does the Lord mean?

Over the history of Christian tradition, St. Augustine and St. Thomas and others have come up with various explanations of what this might be. They came up with several lists of certain sins that this might be; initial impenitence, obduracy of sin, presumption, rejection of a known truth, envy of the grace of others and final impenitence. These six things, tradition says, is what the Lord means by the sin against the Holy Spirit. How's that? Because all of these strike against the very springs of forgiveness. They involve rejection of the graces and gifts by which the Spirit calls us to mercy. Again it will be the whole Trinity which draws man to Him, but this is attributed to the Holy Spirit in His work of converting hearts. And if one has made his heart hard against the Holy Spirit, has rejected the Lord's mercy in some way, one of these ways, that obduracy, that rejection of truth even if one knows it, then one is making one's salvation extremely difficult and for that reason the Lord says that this sin will not be forgiven. In other words you're rejecting the Lord's mercy.

The Holy Father repeats this in another way in his encyclical on the Holy Spirit. "Blasphemy against the Holy Spirit, then, is the sin committed by the person who claims to have a right to persist in evil, in any sin at all, and who thus rejects redemption. One closes oneself up in sin thus making impossible ones conversion and consequently the remission of sins which one considers not essential or not important for ones life."

So it's not that there's any sin that the Lord cannot forgive and it's not that we should give up hope on anybody, as long as someone is alive, there is reason to hope. What the Lord is saying is that people of their own free will can harden their hearts against the Lord, so that His mercy, that He wants to have on them, can be rejected, making forgiveness impossible. For that reason we must emphasize over and over, God's desire to have mercy on us so that we never despair. In other words all this is despair, thinking that it's hopeless to go to God for mercy, He can't have mercy on me. That's why this votive Mass.

To remind ourselves as the Lord did by giving us Mother Mary, that He so much wants to have mercy on us. Remember how St. Margaret Mary Aloque had those visions of the Sacred Heart of Jesus. Again the Lord finding every way He can to say, "I want to have mercy on you, there is no sin too great for me to pardon." This is a message we all need deep is our hearts, that needs to reach the rest of the world as well.

Margaret Mary's spiritual director has beautiful words to say about how we should have great confidence in God and in His mercy. For instance he says this, "Do you know what I should do if I were as near having to render my account as they tell me you are?" He's writing to someone who is about to die. "I would excite my confidence by remembering the number and gravity of my sins. It shows a confidence really worthy of God if, far from being discouraged at the sight of her faults, she strengthens herself, on the contrary, by the thought of the goodness of her Creator. It seems to me that confidence which rests on innocence and purity of life does not give such great glory to God." Isn't that beautiful? "Pray that my faults, however grave and frequent will never make me despair of His goodness. That in my opinion would be the greatest evil that could befall anyone." That would be the sin against the Holy Spirit. "When we can protect ourselves against that evil, there is no other which could not turn out to our good and from which we could not easily draw great advantage."(St. Claude de Colombiere)

Pentecost

Holy Spirit, Source of Unity

Ever since the construction of the Tower of Babel, mankind has been seeking to regain its lost unity. But the pursuit of the brotherhood of man will continue to elude anyone who does not remember this great lesson of Babel: the division among men followed an affront to God. Only insofar as communion is reestablished with God, will men also live together in peace and harmony. Who restored this friendship between God and Man if not Jesus Christ, the one Mediator between God and Man? As a result, we are *all one in Christ Jesus (Gal.3.28) For He is our peace, who has made us both one, and has broken down the dividing wall of hostility, ..., that He might create in Himself one new man in place of the two, so making peace, and might reconcile us both to God in one body through the cross, thereby bringing the hostility to an end. And He came and preached peace to you who were far off and peace to those who were near; for through Him we both have access in one Spirit to the Father.[Eph 2.14]*

The Church was first manifested when, at the sound of the Spirit, representatives from every nation under the Heavens, *gathered together* outside the Upper Room. The family unity that all men seek with one another is not only given to us in the Church, but given in an unexpectedly noble way. We have a unity that is supernaturally strong for it is a share in the unity of the three persons of the Holy Trinity. Christ prayed that we might be one, even as He and the Father are one. The Holy Spirit is the eternal love, which binds the Father to the Son so closely, that Christ would say *the Father and I are one*; this Holy Spirit poured out upon the apostles "builds, animates and sanctifies the Church" *(CCC 747)* rendering Her "the sacrament of the Holy Trinity's communion with men". That is to say, just as the soul keeps all the members of a body in a living, acting unity, so also the Holy Spirit is the "soul" of the Mystical Body of Christ, the Church.

The same marvel that was worked on Pentecost, that natives of a variety of countries should all of a sudden find themselves communicating, one in heart and mind, has never ceased being worked over the ages. We see this marvelous diversity at the highest level of the Church: men from African, Indian, the United States, France, Germany, Poland, often representing countries that have long standing feuds between them, come together speaking the same language of faith hope and love. Who can fail to see in such ecclesiastical gatherings a sort of echo of the first Pentecost? The Church alone can transcend the babble which begun at Babel, with the Word of God, the message of salvation, which finds a hearing in every heart that the Holy Spirit has visited beforehand to prepare a welcome there.

There is a temptation to seek a sort of unity that is not really worthy of the name, an unstable, superficial sort of unity that comes from overlooking significant differences. This has become a sort of new religion in our culture, whose only commandment is toleration. Our only commandment is love, and a prerequisite of love is respect for the truth. By holding fast to what is true, though it often seems that we are only perpetuating arguments and resentments, we are actually preserving the only basis upon which to build a genuine and lasting communion of heart and soul. This is why the Holy Spirit, who is "the supreme source of unity" *(Dom Viv 2)* is also the Spirit of Truth, promised to lead us into all truth. Unity in the world, as in the Church, is not to be found by averting our eyes from our disagreements, but in converting our hearts to Him who is Truth.

We must remember that the cells of the Body of Christ are Christian families. Think how strong our parish would be if every family that made it up was progressing in love, growing closer to each other every day, refusing to be content with peaceful coexistence! We must beg the Lord to build up this unity. And finally we must heed the Apostle, every day, especially in the little Church that is the family: *I therefore, a prisoner for the Lord, beg you to lead a life worthy of the calling to which you have been called, with all lowliness and meekness, with patience, forbearing one another in love, eager to maintain the unity of the Spirit in the bond of peace. (Eph. 4)*

Fire of the Holy Spirit

Today is the birthday of the Church. Even though every Christian is a citizen of **two** fatherlands – one earthly and the other spiritual – we aren't very "patriotic" about the latter. Many of us would, and some of us have, risked our lives in defense of this nation; but are we all willing to take risks and make sacrifices for our faith? Frequently as history demonstrates Christians have been put to death precisely because their duty to the Church was seen as contrasting with the duty owed their earthly nation: just think of the Roman martyrs, St. Thomas More, or the Cristeros in Mexico. I think especially of the late great Cardinal Kung of China, whose fidelity to Rome could not be dampened by thirty years of hard labor.

Very often, as these examples show, there is a spirit in earthly nations, not unrelated to the evil spirit, "the Prince of this world", a spirit which is indeed in opposition to the Spirit of God. As John Paul II has written: "Against the spirit of the world, the Church takes up anew each day a struggle that is none other than *the struggle for the world's soul*". Yes, the Church, which from the earliest days has been called "the soul of the world", cannot perform that role of enlightening and enlivening the world, if she herself is not informed by the Holy Spirit. We must acquire burning hearts — if we are to light up world. Remember, **that** is what Christ came to do: *I have come to cast fire upon the earth; and would that it were already kindled. (Lk 12.49)* On Pentecost, Christ's mission became ours. St. Catherine of Sienna said of Christians, "if you are what you ought to be, you will set the world on fire!"

More than any other people, we Americans have idealized our nation. That's not necessarily bad — at all, but it would be if it leads us to forget either our failings **or** the fact that there **is** a nation with a truly "manifest destiny," a nation that has the mission to save the world and is realizing this ideal; this is the other nation to which we belong, whose passport is a baptism certificate and whose chief executive is called His Holiness. Yes, the Church of God, led by the Spirit, does have an irrepressible dynamism leading it into all truth. She alone has the God-given mission to spread to all nations, not to make trading partners of them or to teach them all about free elections, but to conquer them for Christ, and bring them into the kingdom of God. The timetable is uncertain, the progress reports are depressing, but the victory is ultimately assured.

On Pentecost we must renew our commitment to Christ and his Church. The manner in which the Church began gives us a clue to the manner of its renewal. The Holy Spirit came down over each of the disciples gathered in the upper room. The Church cannot be renewed without the renewal of each of the "living stones" that make her up. The kingdom of God must extend within us, if it is to spread beyond us. The Holy Spirit is constantly at work in the Church, renewing and rejuvenating her, and the Church, by that same Spirit, is renewing the face of the earth. We must cooperate, however, by praying to the Holy Spirit every day, as the Apostles had been doing, gathered around Mary. Did not Christ say that the Heavenly Father would never fail to give the Holy Spirit to those who ask? And how desperately we need Him if we cannot say "Lord" nor *know how to pray as we ought* without his gentle guidance!

Come Holy Spirit…

Mansions of the Spirit

Do not let your hearts be troubled. Our Lord comforts his disciples before His departure, by promising to send them His Holy Spirit. … *it is to your advantage that I go away, for if I do not go away, the Counselor will not come to you; but if I go, I will send Him to you. (Jn. 16.7)* The gift of the Spirit is essentially love, divine charity. *The love of God has been poured into our hearts through the Holy Spirit which has been given to us (Rom. 5.5).* Out of love, God became Man and, in so doing, united Himself with every man. Out of love, He sends his Spirit into the hearts of believers to unite them to God more closely. By fidelity to his commands, by walking according to the Spirit, we are called to increase that union. This is the path of sanctification which leads to a union with God which can be ineffable even in this life, the prelude to union with God that is Heaven.

We are temples of the Holy Spirit. God, desiring to be one with us, comes to dwell in our souls. *If a man loves me, He will keep my word, and my Father will love Him, and we will come to Him and* make our home with Him. *(Jn. 14.23)* Our souls are described by the great mystic, St. Teresa of Avila, as a succession of "mansions" through which we progress to find God at the center — assuming of course, a soul is in the state of grace. It is the spirit of love that guides us in the difficult path of seeking God. According to St. John of the Cross: "... love is the inclination, strength, and power for the soul in making its way to God, for love unites it with God. The more degrees of love it has, the more deeply it enters into God and centers itself in Him... A stronger love is a more unitive love, and we can understand in this manner the many mansions the Son of God declared were in his Father's house" *(Liv. Fl. of Love, n.13)* For indeed, if our soul has various dwelling-places in which God dwells, God is also our home, towards which we tend. The degree of union attained on earth will determine the dwelling place we will have for all eternity. "In the evening of life we will be judged on love."(St. John of the Cross)

Striving to Live According to the Spirit

There is a whole system that has developed over the centuries of the Church, examining the revelation of God in Scripture and Tradition, a system of Spiritual Theology. All sorts of terms with which of course St. Paul was not familiar, and most people aren't, but it's truly beautiful to begin to examine and also to see that what St. Paul was living and describing was simply systematized and made clear by the Christians who had followed him. When he speaks of *'not being debtors to the flesh, not living according to the flesh, but striving to live according to the Spirit,'* this is what we call asceticism, all of our efforts to pull away from what our senses naturally tend to so as to focus more on the Lord and of things of the spirit. Then this line where he says, *'all of you who are led by the spirit of God are sons of God,'* is taken as a clear Scriptural sign of how the Spirit of God leads Christians through the gifts of the Holy Spirit, and this is the beginning of the Mystical Theology, where our work is less important, the ascetical work; and the work of the Spirit, the Mystical work takes over.

Those gifts of the Holy Spirit of course are seven, one of them is also implied here the gift of fear. Because, he tells us, we don't have the spirit of slavery, that servile fear where we're afraid of God but we're His children and we cry out, Abba, which means in Aramaic, Dad. We have that sort of fear, that gift of fear, that we love the Lord so much that we would never want to offend Him and being separated from Him is our greatest fear. It's the gift of fear that we should ask the Holy Spirit to give us, to make us true children, true children of the Father. It will have this effect, it will give us a more lively sense of His great majesty, the Majesty of God and the ability to adore Him profoundly in Spirit and in Truth. It will give us a genuine horror of sin and a greater contrition for all of the times we have offended our Father. It will help us be extremely vigilant over even small things, with a more delicate conscience and then again it will detach us from all creation which is of course where St. Paul started, with that detachment from the things of this earth.

St. Augustine was thinking of this also when he commented upon this Gospel. The woman who was incapable of looking up to Heaven but for eighteen years had been looking down to the earth is a symbol of those who have their heart set on this world. The result is that terrible spiritual blindness which the Pharisees manifested. Let us ask the Lord to give us this gift, stir up this gift of fear in all of us, filial fear, for a Father who has been so good to us.

The Spiritual Life

The Spiritual Life

We have this reading from St. Paul where He is explaining to the people of Corinth the great need for preparation to receive, well, this Sacrament of Holy Eucharist. Apparently some people still had a desire to join in with the pagan rituals, those idolatrous meals that had been popular before the Christian people came. And he says, no, you mustn't. You mustn't pretend that you can go to that sort of an event and also to Holy Mass. He says, *Is not the cup of blessing we bless a share in the Blood of Christ?* You have to realize what you are receiving, in order to receive it well. So from the earliest times, the order of Mass has begun with a frank acknowledgment of our unworthiness, a little examination of conscience, and then asking the Lord for forgiveness. But we have to admit that something strange happens, or can happen, which is, we can do all this, we can hear the words of the Lord, as in the Gospel He says, *Many are those who Hear my words, but do not put them into practice.* We can hear the words of the Lord and not really be changed, and we can even receive this Precious Blood of Christ and eat His body and still not be changed. How many people are there, who've heard all the Lord's words and who've frequently received His Body and Blood, and yet really don't seem changed? Indeed wouldn't someone be transformed, one would almost think, immediately, into a saint if they really and truly received the Body and Blood of the Lord! But we know that's not so, that there are these obstacles in us.

St. John of the Cross talks about this. "God gives many souls the talent and grace for advancing in the spiritual life, holiness, and should they desire to make the effort they would arrive at this high state. And so it is sad that people continue in their lowly method of Communion with God because they do not want, or know how, to advance and because they receive no direction on breaking away from the methods of beginners." Many times he, and other spiritual writers lament that God desires everyone to be a saint and He gives us everything we need in these powerful sacraments, and yet, so many people just don't seem to advance very far. How sad. But perhaps we get a little bit of a hint on what we must do by looking at the rest of what Our Lord said this morning. He said that any man that hears His words and puts them into practice is like someone who is building a house and knows how to build a house. He builds that house with a deep foundation laid upon rock. In another place He talks about those who are building. He says they have the foresight to see that they have enough materials to finish the job. We can see that this is the perfect analogy to the spiritual life.

It's just like building a house, one needs to be very practical, one needs to have a plan, one needs to get advice from those who have built good houses before. Reading the lives of the saints, talking to holy people, people who can teach you and being docile to what they say. One has to realize that one has a goal that one's setting out to achieve, so one has to even set up a schedule, as a builder might. When do I want to achieve this goal? When do I want to achieve that goal? And be accountable to oneself. Am I making progress? Or have someone else to whom one is accountable which is what spiritual directors are. One has to also think about the means to achieving various goals, for attaining this virtue. What will I do in order to become more humble? Well maybe for the next month or two I will try not interrupting people at meals, whatever. Whatever one might do, that's a sign of not being humble. One has to make this sort of plan , revise it frequently, to make it even more effective, and follow it with self discipline, with perseverance. Again like workers building a house, they don't go out to build when ever they feel like it and then they stop working when ever they don't feel like it. They have a schedule and they know they have to persevere if they are going to reach their goal. They have to work hard even when they don't feel like it.

So perhaps if we ask the Lord for the grace of a new attitude in our approach to the spiritual life, a practical attitude and one that is very determined, then we will be able to take full advantage of the graces He gives us, especially at every single Mass.

Growth in the Spiritual Life

This gospel passage where the Lord says that to those who have, more will be given, those who have not, will lose even the little they think they have, is another example of the Heavenly Father's sort of justice that surprises us. Remember the parable of the workers in the vineyard who were all paid the same for having done different work, and the other parable where the talents that are taken away from the one, who buried his, and are given to the one who had the most. Why does it surprise us that the one who has the most is always given more in the Gospel? This we have to understand. What the Lord is trying to express to us, or one reason for it, is that growth is a gift and doesn't follow some sort of natural law of growth, rather, it's completely an effect of the meeting of two freedoms, the freedom of God and our freedom. So according to this spiritual law of love, it's meant to grow and to grow quickly. Growth in spiritual life should be an acceleration, the closer one gets, the more one has, the more one wants. We're always in motion in the spiritual life, we're always accelerating in one direction or another. This is how one must think of it. It's like gravity, when things fall, they fall faster the closer they are to the huge mass to which they are attracted. The closer we get to God, the more quickly we're attracted toward Him, and likewise, we can go in the opposite direction.

We have to think of ourselves according to that image of the holy people in desert leaving Egypt. We're caught between two realities, Egypt, which draws us away from God, and the promised land, union with God. We know we can't stay in the middle in the desert, we're hurrying toward one or the other. We must therefore examine our spiritual lives constantly. Have we fallen into a routine, have we become content or complacent with just a certain level of spiritual life? Do we pray the same way we always have? Do we have the same interests we always have? Do we have the same sins in confession we've always had? Are we stagnant? This is a very common phrase among spiritual writers, 'if you make no progress you are regressing.' You must constantly be drawn in love, accelerating towards the Lord.

So remembering this, that this is the law of spiritual growth, a beautiful result is that growth doesn't happen at a very boring slow pace, but the Lord is willing to give quickly and can bring people to Him very quickly. As St. Teresa of Avila said, " 'Who is more fond than You of giving when there is someone open to receive.' As a result we wrongly suppose that we must measure our progress by the years in which we have practiced prayer, and it even seems, put a measure on Him who gives his gifts without any measure, when He so desires. He can give more to one in half a year than to another in many years. This is something I have seen so clearly in many persons that I'm amazed how we can even stop to consider it." So let us replenish our hope in the spiritual life, in the fact that the Lord does want us to be saints, and that He's only waiting for a generous heart.

Spiritual Life for the Young

This memorial in honor of St. Aloysius affords us an opportunity to see many lessons about the spiritual life. The first is that the Lord doesn't Hesitate to call children to holiness. St. Aloysius, who is now the patron saint of youth, was only ten when he vowed himself to a life of celibacy and virginity. He continued to grow in holiness throughout his youth, entering the Jesuits at the earliest possible age. Another little lesson is that saints come in groups and that we don't become holy, or get to Heaven, alone, but that we help one another. When he was twelve, he received his first Holy Communion from the hands of St. Charles Borromeo and later on in his life, St. Robert Bellarmine was his spiritual director. We also see the importance of the Holy Eucharist, which was the cornerstone of his spiritual life.

The Lord prescribes for us in this reading, which we usually read on this first day of Lent, those three great ways of honoring Him, of fasting, of prayer and of almsgiving. We see in St. Aloysius great examples of those. Although he was from a noble family, he immediately gave up his inheritance, as quickly as he could, to his brother, to become poor. In fact, loving those who were poor and sick during the plague was how he lost his life at the age of twenty three. We see in him a great example of penance. Despite his great innocence, he lived a very mortified life, and all the more so when he joined the Jesuits.

Finally, his great example of prayer. He was a great mystic and apparently at the oddest times, even during mealtimes, he would fall into ecstasies, so much did he love the Lord. In one of his last letters to his mother, one gets an idea of how great a mystic he was when writes to her, "The Divine Goodness, most honored lady, is a fathomless and shoreless ocean, and I confess that, when I plunge my mind into thought of this, it is carried away by the immensity and feels quite lost and bewildered there. In return for my short and feeble labors, God is calling me to eternal rest. His voice from Heaven invites

me to the infinite bliss I've sought so languidly and promises me this
reward for the tears I have so seldom shed."

That gives us an idea of how to sum up his life. It's that of someone who's in a hurry to get to Heaven. He writes again, "I write all
this with one desire, that you and all my family may consider my departure a joy and favor, and that you may especially speed, with a
mother's blessing, my passage across the waters 'til I reach the shore
to which all hopes belong. He died, as many saints have, with the
name of Jesus on his lips.

Vigilance

The Jewish people had a beautiful custom included in their marriage
ceremonies. After the wedding, the bridegroom would lead the bride
from the father's house in procession, accompanied by lit torches, to his
own house. There, apparently, some virgins, bridesmaids, would be waiting to greet them. All would go in to the couple's new home for a
great celebration. Our Lord saw this as a perfect image of His mission. He came down from his home in Heaven to creation to seek a
bride, namely the Church. The Church is the Spouse of Christ as are
all of its members not just those vowed to virginity. "Christ is the
bridegroom of all holy souls; as St. Paul says: *I have espoused you to
one husband that I may present you as a chaste bride to Christ*. Christ
is taking us up to Heaven, which is our true home forever, to live united
to Him. That is why He often refers to Heaven as the marriage feast of
the Lamb, and "blessed are those who are called to his supper".

In the early Church, the Christians thought that the world would
soon end. They began to be worried that some were dying before
Christ's return. St. Paul is reassuring them, telling them that the Lord
will come for us in one of two ways: either by our own deaths or by
the end of time. The same advice: *Stay awake, for you know neither
the day nor the hour*, applies equally well to our death or the end of
the world; as a result of both, we come face to face with the Son of
Man. In either case, meeting Christ means being judged; when we
die, we are judged at once (the particular judgment); at the end of
time there is the general judgment.

The message of our Lord is simple then: see to it that you are
ready, that you are in a state of friendship with Christ at that hour.
Then you can enter the wedding feast; you will be ready, with your
wedding garment on, as Christ puts it in another parable, so that the
host will not throw you out, but perhaps even say, *Friend, go up
higher*. It is, therefore, out of his great love for us, his great desire to

see us confirmed forever in the joy of union with Him, that Jesus tells us, as a mother guarding Her chicks: beware! St. Paul, who imitated his Divine Master so closely, speaks in the same terms as he takes leave of the infant church of Ephesus: *I know that after my departure fierce wolves will come in among you, not sparing the flock; and from among your own selves will arise men speaking perverse things, to draw away the disciples after them. Therefore be alert, remembering that for three years I did not cease night or day to admonish every one with tears. (Act. 20.29-31)* The Church's pastors have never ceased to repeat the warning. "Vigilance and custody of self in whatever age is necessary to all" (St. Bruno)

Of what are we to be vigilant? We are to be vigilant because temptations to sin are not always obvious. In fact, if we are good, faithful people it is not easy for us to all of a sudden break our friendship with God. The devil, of course, knows this; that is why he is a deceiver, a liar from the beginning. As St. John of the Cross says: "It should be noted that among the many wiles of the devil for deceiving spiritual persons, the most common is deceiving them under the appearance of good rather than of evil, for the devil already knows that they will scarcely choose a recognized evil. Thus you should always be suspicious of what appears good ... To do the right thing, and be safe in such a matter, you ought to take proper counsel." The great danger is not that we will fall all of a sudden, but that we will begin to take false steps in small matters. It is little infidelities that begin to dull our consciences so that we are set up for a big fall. He who is faithful in little matters will be faithful in big ones.

Persons living in the world must be vigilant lest they fall into the same fate as can, it is said, happen to a frog. Thrown into a pot of boiling water, the frog can jump out at once before He is scalded. But if a frog is put into a pot of tepid water and the heat is slowly turned up, he will gradually get tired and slow and eventually succumb. We are surrounded in our culture by bad examples, by blasphemies, by false logic, and wrong opinions. We are assaulted by images that pull us away from decency and purity, sounds that rob us of peace and recollection. It can seem that the Lord's will is impossible just an ideal and that if I do better than most, I am alright. One can begin to give in on "small matters". One begins to stop patrolling the borders of one's soul: one looks and listens and even agrees to things that Christians should oppose with all their might, but always it begins in small matters at first. "It won't do any harm."

We must vigorously then, take a stand in small matters. We must realize that venial sins are actually very important, very important to keep out of our life, for they begin to hurt our relationship with the Lord and set us up for a complete break. What we must do then is every day examine our consciences before we go to sleep to check up, have I slipped at all? I should be growing in the love of the Lord. And accompanying your examination of conscience every day should be frequent confession. With a daily examination of conscience, one realizes that there's many things, many venial faults that one wants to confess to the Lord. One begins to develop a very delicate conscience, one that's fully alive, fully alert, fully awake. Let us therefore, ask the Lord Jesus to purify our consciences and move our hearts to love Him so much that we will hate even the smallest offenses to Him.

Conquering Our Passions

Keep oneself unstained by the world. Anyone who has made the perilous journey through adolescence knows how hard it is to arrive at adulthood with one's baptismal grace intact, white and beautiful. Yet, this according to St. James is a necessary condition for practicing a *religion* that is *pure and undefiled before God and the Father.* The psalmist sings: *My heart and flesh sing for joy to the living God.*

Passions are neither morally good or evil in themselves. Only free will determines our moral standing, while our passions are moved by various stimuli beyond our direct control. We have not necessarily sinned, simply because we feel a passion. Anyone who has lost his temper knows that it happened in one of these two ways: either he willingly gave into the temptation of a mood or an annoying event, so as to experience the desired sensation of "venting, letting off steam", or he failed to place obstacles in the way of mounting passion, for example, leaving the room and counting to ten. Our will should ensure that our passions are "disciplined by right reason illumined by faith." Struggling with our passions is a long and arduous process that makes up a good part of the spiritual life. We must conquer our passions, not by extinguishing them, heaven forbid, but by ordering them. Saints are not less passionate for being saints, but they have learned, through a process of continual mortification of their passions, to re-train them to desire what is truly good. Then their passions help them to be passionately in love with God — moved heart and soul with pity for the poor, with courage for spreading the Gospel, with fear of the slightest sin whatever. Indeed, they need their passions, for as Pascal said: "Nothing great is accomplished without passion".

Keep yourself unstained by the world. How hard it is to do this in our world especially! And yet how necessary if we are to save our souls. After listing much the same sins as Jesus did, St. Paul adds: *I warn you, as I warned you before, that those who do such things shall not inherit the kingdom of God.* No wonder that from the earliest days, Christians have fled the world, interpreting in the most practical way, St. Peter's injunction: *"Save yourselves from this crooked generation." (Acts. 2.40)* But of course most Christians are not called to flee literally to deserts and monasteries. Nonetheless, you must learn to make your homes and your hearts sanctuaries — that is holy places and places of refuge — where your soul can live and breathe far from the poisonous atmosphere of the world with its exaltation of all that drives the passions crazy: money, fame, pleasure, power and so forth. This indeed will cost you, dearly. St. Paul continues his warning to the Galatians thus: *Those who belong to Christ Jesus have crucified the flesh with its passions and desires.*

Remember this the next time you go to the cinema. Know what is in a movie and then calmly, allow your reason to work, illumined by faith through the light of the scripture; ask yourself, "Should a Christian witness those scenes, hear those sounds? Is it good for the soul? A help to the growth of the word planted there? or a hindrance? when we Catholics begin to ask these questions, we will begin to *shine like lights in the world.* St. Paul enjoins us: *Do all things without grumbling or questioning, that you may be blameless and innocent, children of God without blemish in the midst of a crooked and perverse generation, among whom you shine as lights in the world, holding fast the word of life, (Phil. 2.15).*

Supernatural Prudence

Our Lord proposes two examples of situations in which prudence is required. It is a virtue desired by all men as it enables us to achieve our goals. It is known as the "charioteer of the virtues" because it is needed to direct all the others. Someone seeking to be generous, for instance, cannot find the right balance between giving too much, or too little, in a given situation without prudence. We must not confuse prudence with the conscience. The conscience judges what is right or wrong in a specific case, but it is prudence that makes us want to choose it. Great imprudence makes people act without informing their conscience, so that they do not realize how grave their situation.

So Our Lord taught us with his parable that we must be prudent. If we wish to accomplish a great thing, such as being his disciple, and following Him to eternal glory, we must, like the builder or the king, sit down and figure out if we are employing the necessary means. It does not suffice to have a vague desire to follow Him, to have a good intention; what we need is to put that desire into effect, and to do that, we need prudence. If we really want to be Christ's disciples, not in word but in deed, we must take certain measures. What does Christ demand? What virtues do I lack, what are my stumbling points? How will I make a structured program to overcome them? We must be like a king planning a battle. *Heaven is taken by force*, said our Lord, *and the violent bear it away*. Those who think we will reach our goal without figuring out the means are imprudent.

Prudence is not something we are born with. It can be acquired and perfected by daily effort to act prudently. One must make the effort to reflect, discern, analyze circumstances in the light of faith. Many Catholics are prudent in worldly matters, but we must be, more so, in matters of faith. To get to a goal that is so high above us, we need more than the natural virtue of prudence. We need to know God's will in each circumstance of life, but the problem, as St. Paul tells us, is: *Who can know the mind of God? Or who has been his counselor?* He continues, however, *Be transformed by the renewal of your mind that you may prove what is the will of God, what is good and acceptable and perfect.(Rom. 12.2)* To determine the means to reach a supernatural goal, we need to have a prudence that is elevated by grace.

Christ gave three conditions for discipleship which natural prudence would consider imprudent: to turn from family, embrace the cross and renounce your possessions. He is presenting to us the means one would choose to unite oneself to Him if one had supernatural prudence to a heroic degree. To develop prudence, we must remember our Goal. The only reason for doing anything is that it will contribute to my eternal welfare and that of others, and so glorify God. Sit down, reflect, learn, study, seek advice, pray to find out the will of God. Beware of false prudence: either worldly prudence that does not have the proper goal, or craftiness that does not choose honest means, or excessive worry which comes from egotism. As people progress in knowing and following God's will, they also activate the Gift of Counsel, one of the seven gifts of the Holy Spirit received at Baptism. With the Gift of Counsel we can know God's will, even in extremely difficult moments, when we must act quickly. It enables God's holy ones to choose rightly with peace and serenity.

These heavenly gifts which give us true insight into God's will are the fruit of union with Christ. Jesus Christ knew what was the will of God and was able to carry it out. He was therefore, supremely prudent. He knew God's plan and adopted every means necessary to in-

augurate the Kingdom and secure the salvation of those the Father entrusted to Him. It is in Christ that Paul makes so bold as to say that we
can know the mind of God. *Who has known the mind of the Lord so as
to instruct Him?* We do, Paul, instructs us, for *We have the mind of
Christ. (I cor. 2.16)*

Fidelity

The Church opens for our meditation, the story of two sons of
Abraham, two of the Jewish people who were so faithful to the Lord
that they are a good example, not only to their nation, but to the whole
Church for all time. Both were faithful to the commitments they had
made. We also have to make sure that we are faithful to the commitments we have undertaken. What's the good of promising God something, if we can't come through on it? Remember the Lord's example
of the two sons, the one who promises and doesn't come through on
it, is worse than the one who repented. We have to be sure that we're
faithful to the extent that others will even think us crazy. Even if
people don't see our fidelity in small things, we have to be faithful because God sees. God sees everything no matter how small.

In our striving to be more faithful we should remember what the
Lord said just this Sunday, "well done, good and faithful servant, you
have been faithful in small things, I will put you over big things now."
It's important for us to be faithful in very small things. We can't just
be roughly honest, we have to be sure not even to tell the smallest
white lies. It's not good enough to avoid making cruel remarks, we
have make sure our jokes don't have a tinge of criticism in them. It's
not good enough to be generally abandoned to the will of our Father,
but we have to see that we don't complain either. We have to set no
limits to our fidelity. And of course this takes a very strong will, and
the constant strengthening of our will.

Here are some examples of what one can do every day to
strengthen one's will. Daily we can perfect these qualities, for instance, by not backtracking on our resolutions, by finishing what we
start, paying special attention to details, always working with order
and foresight, not getting carried away by the spur of the moment, doing everything with determination, never procrastinating. Demanding
that extra effort from ourselves in the small but significant things of
life, like organization and punctuality, frugal use of our time, dedicat-
ing ourselves to study, work and prayer. Actually every human activity
is an occasion to fortify our will. The opposite is also true, by doing
things lazily and carelessly our will grows weak. Let us strive every

day to strengthen our will, to serve our Lord perfectly after the example of His Son.

Small Things

Nobody is perhaps comfortable with the image of God as an exacting judge who will make people pay all of their debts unto the last penny. Though He is merciful, saying, just make amends before it is too late, He does present Himself as demanding that exacting judgment unto the last penny. This is how He was interpreted by St. John of the Cross, in his most famous poem, The Spiritual Canticle. The bride, in that poem, knows of 'the thousand other benefits by which she has been obligated to God from before the time of her birth and that a good part of her life has vanished and she must render an account for everything, of the beginning of her life as well as the later part, unto the last penny when God will search Jerusalem with lighted candles. We've all been late and the day is far spent remembering such evil and harm.' So that would be an authentic interpretation, that the Lord, while not being narrow minded, while not caring about what really is small, nonetheless, He does have a care for our every act, everything we do. For everything that we do, we will render an account, but this shouldn't, as it might tend to at first glance, make us think of God as somehow unloving or harsh, but quite the contrary.

There's two ways in which this shows us that God is truly a loving God. The first is that, that tendency to be indignant at the idea of a God who should care about minutia, about little things, about what some human creature might say in a conversation with a neighbor, that the almighty God should care about those things, that indignation, is not really respect for God but quite the contrary. It is a return to the sort of god that is not the Christian God. A god that is high above everything, every human concern, untouchable, unchangeable, that sort of god is not the Trinity. Rather the true God is closer to us than we are to ourselves. God who is with us. God who, indeed, can care about even these smallest things, because He is infinite. So we must put away that idea of a false grandeur of God — a god who is too superior to deal with us. Rather we must realize that the God, that Christ revealed, is one who is so close to us that our smallest act is important to Him.

The second reason that this reveals God's great love is that He said, *unless your holiness surpasses that of the scribes and Pharisee's you shall not enter the kingdom of God.* In other words it makes a very big difference how holy you are. Of course, being infinite, He could overlook these things. He could not care, but because He loves us, and wants to have communion with us, He wants us to be perfect. It's because He wants us to be perfect, that He is going to care about even the smallest things, as He said in another place, *for every idle word you will have to render an account.* He wants to have a relationship of love with us and love has to do with total openness. Every aspect of our soul at some point, here or hereafter after will have to be purified before can be united to Him. So let us remember this. This is why the Lord is so exacting with us, because He loves us so very much.

Human Respect

The Lord, full of grief, is talking to people who can not accept Him and the number one obstacle which He points out is, what we might call, human respect. How can people like you believe when *you accept praise from one another but do not seek the glory that comes from the one God.* You accept glory from men, you care what they say, but you really don't care what God thinks of you. This human respect is also called worldly fear, caring what other people, especially wicked people, think and not what the Lord and His servants think about you. But really, just caring what people, in so far as they're human, think of us. This is a great obstacle to the spiritual life. The Lord Himself says, *Fear not those who can kill the body…*fear not what any human power does to you, fear only God Himself. Yet it's so much part of our nature, we have to continually be examining ourselves on this point.

We have to desire only the praise that comes from God, we must seek true humility. It means the kind of glory that's completely undeserved. We have to place ourselves before God and realize that our whole entire worth lies in the price that was paid for our salvation. We were bought with a price, totally undeserved. That is the only thing we should glory in, glory in the cross of Christ Jesus. We have to see that our entire worth and value is wrapped up in what Christ did on the cross, and what others say about us, doesn't matter at all.

I'll just read you a paragraph from St. John of the Cross on this point. "The soul possessing the Spirit of love glories rather in beholding that she has achieved this worth in loving, and lost all things of the world. So she says, 'You will say that I am lost.' Few spiritual persons reach such daring and determination. Some relax in this way and are considered far advanced, but they never lose themselves entirely in some matters, whether worldly or natural, and never execute works for Christ with perfection, and nakedness of spirit. They think about what others will say or how their works will appear. If these persons are not lost to themselves in their works, they cannot declare, 'You will say that I am lost.' They are still ashamed to confess Christ before others by their works. Because of their human respect, they do not live entirely for Christ, stricken by love." As we meditate on the Cross of Christ, let's put human respect even more to death within ourselves.

Mortification

The Lord is not saying that He doesn't want people to make sacrifices, but that He does not want sacrifices that are devoid of charity, that are not animated by love, that do not have that steadfast love or mercy included in them. In fact, far from not wanting sacrifices, the Lord does ask for them, and indeed that call is being renewed in our Church in our day. If you read the full text of the third secret of Fatima there was an apocalyptic vision which included an angel flying above the world saying, "Penance, penance, penance." So at any rate, we must not ignore the call for penance.

Mortification isn't just moderation, but actually genuine self denial, not just giving up things that are bad for us, as many do during Lent, but rather giving up things that are good, making a genuine sacrifice by giving up a good thing. Mortification can be both exterior, which we call corporal, or interior. And so there are as many sorts of self denial as there are passions that incline our will. So you can deny yourself food, or TV, or speaking out, interrupting someone, sleep, or any kind of comfort, listening to music or any little thing that we're inclined to do, one could deny oneself.

St. John Chrysostom wrote, regarding the difference between those interior or exterior ones, "Many people do not find giving up food or drink or a soft bed too difficult, but bearing an insult or wrong or hurtful words, (interior mortification) this is something to be borne, not by many, but by few." So, in fact, those can be more difficult, those hidden ones. It's true that the best mortifications are those chosen by God, ie. the accepting of His Will, abandoning ourselves to Providence, performing perfectly the duties of our state in life, cheerfully conversing with a boring or annoying person who comes our way. But we mustn't only wait for mortifications, or choose the interior ones only, because we prepare for the harder things in life, that God chooses for us, by systematically and perseveringly forming our wills, by choosing small voluntary sacrifices, both the interior and the exterior. We can't forget the exterior, corporal, although they are very out of vogue today. As one saint said, "He who performs only interior mortification will soon perform no mortification at all." But remember, what we just heard in the Gospel, when we're denying ourselves something good, it must be done in moderation, for the sake of the greater good, love of God.

This love of God is what moderates our sacrifices. It's the rule that shows us how much to give up. And it's why, we shouldn't feel bad, or shouldn't even try to imitate the great sacrifices we might read about in the lives of the Saints. They had this great level of love that told them what to do for the Lord, if we tried to imitate them, it would be pure pride, we don't have yet their level of love. For us little disciples, let us be content with little sacrifices, made with all of our love, consistently, joyfully, serenely. As St. John of the Cross said, "Deny your desires and you will find what your heart longs for." (namely the Lord Jesus).

Detachment from All Things

We all have the same question in our hearts that the rich young man did, that there must be something more, even if we keep the commandments. We all have that sense, as we know explicitly from revelation, that we're made for union with God, that God is perfect and we can't be with Him unless we're perfect. So indeed we have to become perfect, as Jesus said, *Become ye perfect as your Heavenly Father is perfect.* So this invitation to seek perfection is for all of us, as the Holy Father writes, "This vocation to perfect love is not restricted to a small group of individuals, the invitation to go sell your possessions and give to the poor, and the promise, *you will have treasure in Heaven,* are meant for everyone because they bring out the full meaning of the commandment of love for neighbor such as the invitation which follows, *Come follow Me.*" It's necessary for all of us to go beyond the minimum, and that's what this invitation from the Lord signifies. Of course it's not the case that everyone will literally sell all their possessions, but it is the case that one must be detached from them and live in complete, as possible, conformity to the Lord Jesus Christ, with the Perfect Man. To be perfect we must be conformed to Him.

Now what did Christ do, His love was expressed by emptying Himself, by becoming a man. For God that was a great emptying. Yet He continued to empty Himself to death, to death on a cross. So everyone who wants to follow in His footsteps must become poor in that sense, detached from every appetite without exception. In fact, St. John of the Cross makes the point that not only is it necessary to be detached from all our appetites so as to reach the final stage of perfection, but to even start, to even make any step toward spiritual progress. He sums up with a little formula for how to make quick progress down the way of perfection. "Endeavor to be inclined always, not to the easiest, but to the most difficult; not to the most delightful, but to the most distasteful; not to the most gratifying, but to the less pleasant; not to what means rest for you, but to hard work; not to the most consoling, but to the unconsoling; not to the most, but to the least; not to the highest and most precious, but to the lowest most despised; not to wanting something, but to wanting nothing; do not go out looking for the best of temporal things, but for the worst, and for Christ. Desire to enter into complete nakedness, emptiness and poverty in everything in the world." Let us ask the Lord for that grace, even if we live in palaces, to be completely detached from everything in this world.

Crumbs from the Table

We learn from the gospel that for those who would approach the Lord, the path is difficult. As we know, scripture can mean many different things, all of them true. St. John of the Cross gives an interpretation of this gospel as regards our spiritual life, but to understand it, one has to remember how much appetites need be mortified, in order to find the Lord. So St. John of the Cross writes, for instance, "Oh, if spiritual persons knew how much spiritual good in abundance they lose, by not trying to raise their appetites above childish things, for in God, or in the state of perfection all appetites cease. The road that is an assent to God necessarily demands an habitual effort to renounce and mortify the appetites. The sooner this mortification is achieved the sooner the soul reaches God, but until the appetite is eliminated, one will not arrive, no matter how much virtue is practiced. For one will be failing to acquire perfect virtue, which lies in keeping the soul empty, naked and purified of every appetite. The reason is, that those who love something together with God, undoubtedly make little of God, for they weigh in the balance with God, an object far distant from God."

Keeping in mind this doctrine, so characteristic of St. John, he interprets the gospel. "This is why our Lord said to St. Matthew, *It is unbecoming to take the children's bread and give it to the dogs.* All those who dispose themselves for the pure reception of God's Spirit through the denial of their appetites in creatures, our Lord compares to children of God. Those who feed their appetites on creatures, He compares to the dogs. It is the privilege of children to eat at table with their Father and from His dish, which is to share in His Spirit, but the dogs must eat the crumbs that fall from the table. Our lesson here is that, all creatures are like crumbs that have fallen from God's table. Those who go about feeding on creatures, then, are rightly designated as dogs and are deprived of the children's bread, because they refuse to rise from the crumbs of creatures to the un-created Spirit of their Father. This is precisely why they wander about hungry as dogs. The crumbs serve more to wet their appetites then to satisfy their hunger and if they are not filled, they will murmur, this is the characteristic of those with appetites, they are always dissatisfied and driven like someone who is hungry."

This is a difficult but obviously true way of looking at the spiritual life. We only make progress in the spiritual life, in so far as we, little by little, detach ourselves from all things, even good things, even family members, everything, loving them yes, but only out of love for God, and knowing that Our Lord may well deprive us of them. In conclusion, the only appetite God permits and wants in His dwelling place, is the desire for the perfect fulfillment of His law and the carrying of the cross of Christ.

Seeking God in Solitude

St. Bruno is one of the great monumental figures of Christian history. Today's Gospel is rather appropriate because the Lord is speaking of judgment. It was indeed an awareness, a correct fear of judgment that made Bruno leave the world, made him pursue God so avidly. He feared the day of judgment much more than he feared the Cross and a life of penance. He was afraid, as few people are, but many should be, that one can race through life, especially such a successful life as he had, without really being sure that one is going in the right direction. Much better to withdraw from the world and make sure one's on the right tract. So, Bruno made his goal to "seek God insidiously, to find God promptly, and to possess God fully."

This is what God has planned for each of us. There's such a beautiful dialogue between God and Job, where God says how much higher and greater He is that any human being. But that doesn't mean that the Lord doesn't want to enter into friendship, communion, intimate discourse with each and every one of us. He does. So Bruno was raised up to the skies and indeed did come to possess God fully. He became a great saint. He understood the joys of the hard life he had chosen, as he said to his brothers, "How greatly the solitude and silence of the hermitage contribute to the benefit and joy of those who love it. Only those who've experienced it can know it."

We today have an opportunity to experience a little bit of that flying from the world and sinking ourselves into solitude and dialogue with God. The world as we know is in great flux and God doesn't change. The only way to come to God, to come into union with Him, is to withdraw, according to our state in life, from all that change and all that noise that makes up life. These great men and women of prayer came to identify silence and God almost, because God seems to speak only in silence and it seems that only in silence could they learn anything of God. That's true for us as well. We have to be aware of that even though we live in the world.

Some things that we might think about, practically, that might be intruding on our attempt to build a relationship with God are of course radio and television. Not the judicious choice of certain programs, but the ongoing noise that those means of communication can be. It is a very sad thing if you work in an environment where the radio is on all the time or the poor people in the nursing homes whose televisions are on all the time. With that noise, it is impossible to come to speak to God and to have a habit of union with God. So we should beware of that and likewise idle chit chat, that can go on all day too. Activism. Even if we're doing good things and things that seem necessary, being busy is incompatible with the life of dialogue with God. Those three are exterior silence.

Internal silence is very important too. What's going on inside your soul? Is one overly curious about, either the affairs of the world, or especially the affairs of our neighbor? Minding one's own business is absolutely essential to growing in union with God. Quieting one's imagination and one's memory, all these things that come back we have to not give in to them but turn away from them. Then of course worry, learning to trust the Lord and therefore not having to worry about things ourselves. We can take advantage of the moments of silence that we have, if we're ever left alone. Thank God for it and use that moment to draw closer to Him. Try as much as possible to have some time in the early morning before things are noisy and difficult. Then especially if a retreat day comes your way, take advantage of that time as an invitation from the Lord for you to draw close to Him. I'll just close with a quote by Pascal, one of the more famous things that he said, "I have discovered that all human evil comes from this, man's being unable to sit still in a room." So if we quiet ourselves enough so that we love to sit alone in a room, because we are not alone, we're with God, we'll find our life much improved.

Duty

The Centurion certainly understood obedience and duty as he made clear. He didn't take liberties with the Lord, having Him come to his house, but rather he felt it was not his place to have the Lord there, and he was true to what he considered his place, his duty. Also the man we are honoring today, St. John Chrysostom was a man of duty. It wasn't his will to ever be Patriarch of Constantinople, he was a monk, and yet when he had to take on that responsibility, he was faithful to it. He taught the truth, no matter what the cost. He was exiled twice and during those exiles, which included great hardships, forced marches in cold weather, he died. Almost one could say, a martyr for being a confessor of the faith, and true to his duty.

In the Church's liturgy, for the feast of pastors, they quote this line from proverbs, "Many men are said to be merciful, but how often do we find one who is faithful to his duties." This is what is esteemed in the Church's pastors, but not only in them. St. Paul in the first reading asks us to pray for Kings and men in authority. They are the ones with the greatest responsibilities, but all of us of course have duties.

St. Claude de Colombiere, a famous Spiritual Director, now a saint, spoke these words about the duties we all have, "The good order of things in the world depends upon the fidelity with which one performs the duties of his state in life. All disorder originates in negligence upon this point. What a grand thing it would be if everyone acquitted himself of his duties. It is perhaps the thing that is most neglected, even among pious people, indeed probably more often among those, than among others. A man who neglects the duties of his state is a discordant voice in the harmony of the world, no matter what else he does. Those who are faithful to all other duties, often neglect these. Those who do not omit them, perform them negligently, or through human motives, or self interest, and this is not fulfilling their duties. Sins of omission on this point are easily committed, hardly noticed, and consequently reparation is rarely made."

So when we make our examination of conscience, this is a good place to begin, with sins of omission and especially by examining what it is our state in life requires. What are our duties and do we perform them with great love?

Fidelity to Duty

Today the Lord is talking about the fidelity to duty that he expects
of his disciples. It's not that he's asking for great things or extraordinary things. The example that he uses is simple fidelity to duty, just
what is expected of a servant or of a steward. As he said in another
place that when we're done our work we should say: We're simply
useless servants who have done what we were asked to do . But the
important thing is being faithful to these little requests of the Lord
with constancy. He said again, in another place, *Those who are faithful in little, will be faithful in much.* And this, I think, is the secret. Often great saints didn't seem great at all to their contemporaries. What
struck me in an interview with some of the nuns that Mother Teresa
had been with before she began her order, they thought she was an ordinary nun. Or in many other cases, St. Therese of Lisieux, even, although her sisters began to realize how extraordinary she was, if you
recount her life to anybody they think, "What did she do that's unusual?" But it was this fidelity to the small things that God asked of
her.

In the Liturgy of the Hours for the feast of Pastors there's a line
that says: There are many who are merciful but who will be found
who is faithful? And this is the difficult thing, to be faithful to our
daily duty, every day, and every minute of every day. In fact, it's
rightly said that to be a saint we do not need to do different things. We
have to do the things that we do differently. In other words, out of love
of God. If you stop to think about it, we tend to do, or very easily can
do, all we do, either for ourselves or because others expect it of us, or
out of routine or because we don't seem to have any choice in the matter. Once we've made a life choice, for instance, to get married, or become a priest, then so many of our duties just seem as if we have no
choice in the matter. So we just do them almost automatically or
sometimes out of a natural love, and that's not bad, but this won't
make one a saint. Every single thing one does, one must do out of
love of God.

So, if we wish to be saints, let us not only begin the day with a
morning offering, but also try to make every day, and every duty
throughout the day, something that we do with a ever more personal
and total surrender to the will of God, out of love for Him. Often if
we're having a difficult day, this is very important to remember: I
don't have to look ahead to what comes after. I just have to look at the
next duty and do that for God because God asks it of me, with all of
my heart and all of my strength. Just one last thing, I was reminded of

a saint, he's not been declared a saint, yet, but very likely he will be, whose life consisted in being a Cistertian peeling vegetables and wrapping chocolates, who said in a very beautiful way, "God could have sent me out to convert all the pagan nations but it's a greater thing, it's a more glorious thing for God if I do this simple thing with love of God than to do those great tasks with less love of God." And so it is for our lives too.

The One Thing Necessary

In the first reading we have a wonderful example of doing penance, the fasting and the lamenting, the sack cloth and ashes and so on. As we know, in the lives of the saints, penance is often a major factor in their life and in their sanctification. For all of us it plays a role, nonetheless, extraordinary acts shouldn't ordinarily be necessary to please Our Lord. Very often, when we desire to become saints, we start looking for extraordinary things and we start thinking that God's will is so very hard to figure out.

The truth of the matter is that all we need, is right in front of us. We saw that yesterday, for instance. The lawyer came up to Our Lord and asked Him what one must do to gain everlasting life. He knew the answer already. He gave the answer himself and Jesus said, "You answered correctly. Do it and you will live." But the problem was, he wasn't really doing it. He wasn't really loving his neighbor with all his heart. And so Our Lord had to teach him with the story of the Samaritan. Do what you have to do much more radically. We see this in the story of Martha and Mary too. Martha trying to go out of her way to do great things for the Lord, and if she'd only sat down in front of Him, and focused upon Him, that was the only thing necessary. The sort of obvious thing that was right there in front of her all the time, to just love the Lord rather than trying to please Him some other way.

The Cure of Ars, St. John Vianney, who was, of course, a great lover of penance, nonetheless, he says, when telling people how to be saints, "Serving God changes nothing in all that we have to do, on the contrary, we simply do better, all the things we must do."

Now We Shall Work

Our Lord's life, the great mission and the trust that the Father had placed in Him, clearly, in so far as He was a man, a human being, is a work, a mission. He did not come to do His will, but the will of the Father who sent Him. Just as the Father is always awake and active, so also was the Lord, constantly at work as well. My Father is at work until now and I will work as well. Of course throughout the Gospel, He never spared Himself anything, praying throughout the night, going from village to village, preaching without rest and so on and so on. So, we also, have to work. A Christian is someone who has to work, work hard. Not only at the work they have to do, but also at spreading the Gospel message. The last thing a Christian would be is a lazy person. There's nothing more common among the saints than the expression, "I have no time to rest here, Heaven is when we shall rest." Here on earth is where we shall work. St. John of the Cross puts it very strongly, "How is it that you relax so fearlessly, when you must appear before God and render an account of the least word and thought?"

On the other hand though, we must remember that rest is something Our Lord did command us, so as to regain our strength. Sunday, of course, is to rest. He tells His disciples to come apart and rest with me a while. We have to remember that recreation and relaxation is also important in the spiritual life, but always in that context of God's will for us so that we can serve Him with renewed strength. Another thing we have remember when we think of work, it's not the same as activism, constant work is not the same as a frenzy of activity. John of the Cross also said, "Let's not think that pleasing God lies so much in doing a great deal as in doing it with good will, without possessiveness or human respect." So let us try to follow Our Lord's example in true service of our Heavenly Father.

Sacred Heart

Devotion to the Sacred Heart

Of all days, this is a day for great joy in our hearts. We celebrate during this whole year the incarnation, the great mystery that God became man out of love for us, so that He could take on human flesh so that He could die for us. This is essentially the mystery that we celebrate here, the Sacred heart of Jesus. To be precise, we really and truly are referring to His physical human Heart which began to beat in the womb of the Blessed Virgin Mary so soon, as we now know, after the moment of Incarnation and which Pius XII tells us still lives and beats in His risen body in Heaven and also in the great mystery of the Eucharist. We can and must adore His physical heart, in virtue of the fact, that there is only one person in Christ Jesus, one divine person, but His human nature belongs to that divine person. Just as we say that when Jesus wept, God wept, so also this human heart belongs to God.

So what is this devotion? Briefly as possible, it's recalling the great love of Jesus Christ for sinful man, and responding to that love as best we can. Symbolized in the physical heart of Jesus is a three-fold love; that divine inter-Trinitarian love, His supernatural love, and His sensitive love that is also shared in by our human physical hearts. We must, not only recall His love for us, but remember that His love is often unrequited and spurned by sinful man so we make reparation also for the offenses against it. Paul VI says, "Everything depends…" What strong language! "Everything depends upon rightly adoring and making amends to Christ Jesus especially in the most Sacred Mystery of the Eucharist." This has been done traditionally through the making of the nine first Fridays, the Act of Consecration, making reparation, and enthroning the Sacred Heart in our homes. Let us endeavor to do all of these things to stir up in our hearts true devotion to the Heart of Jesus through contemplating His loving Heart and contrasting that to ours, and to the world's, so often hard and cold hearts, saying, Lord make our hearts more like Yours.

Christ's Mystical Marriage

The Sacred Heart of Our Lord, his physical heart, is the symbol of His love for us. For Christ, as for us, the heart plays a role in our sensible loves, and it is the symbol of our spiritual love, our will transformed by grace. But for Christ, his Sacred Heart was also the mirror of his infinite divine love for us, as the *fullness of the Godhead… dwells in [Christ] bodily. (Col. 2.9)* Since this love surpasses and encompasses all forms of human love, they are all used to describe it. As all fatherhood on earth takes its name from God's fatherhood, so also all motherly love, all married love, and so on are images of Divine Love which exceeds them all.

The image of married love is particularly apt for us today. When we look at the image over the tabernacle we see portrayed the reality described in the Gospel. *A Lamb standing, as though it had been slain* (Ap 5.6) It was on the Cross that the Lamb of God was slain. The last wound He received pierced his heart, and out flowed blood and water. St. John sees in this event great mystical significance. The sacraments of the Church poured forth from the Heart of Jesus, and with them, the Church itself was given life. It did not escape the notice of the Church Fathers that Adam fell into a deep sleep and his side was opened, and Eve his wife was brought forth. Likewise, the New Adam sleeps the sleep of death, and his side is opened, too. From the side of Christ, from his Heart came the Church which is rightly called, the Bride of Christ.

Christ had come down from Heaven precisely for this, to solder an exclusive and unending covenant, a marriage, with all mankind. The union began in his person, in the wedding of human and divine nature in the Incarnation. But it was only "through the shedding of His blood [that Christ] contracted a mystical marriage with the Church" (Haurietis Aquas, Pius XII). "Through charity He suffered for the Church who was to be united to Him as His spouse" (ST, Supp, 42, 1, 3). Only in Heaven will *the wedding feast of the Lamb [have] come* (*Ap 19.7*), and will the loving union sought by the Sacred Heart be secure. This love was and is for each of us, for *Christ loved me and gave Himself up for me* (*Gal 2.20*). Let us take the responsibility to recall with gratitude the marriage contract, the exclusive covenant of love, that the Sacred Heart forged on Good Friday. That is why every first Friday of the month we recall His love as a wedding anniversary of sorts.

To Know Christ Jesus

Our Lord once said, *This is eternal life, to know Thee, the only true God and Jesus Christ whom Thou hast sent.* We understand that by the gift of faith, we have the gift of eternal life here on earth, namely true knowledge, true knowledge of God through Jesus Christ. We have to everyday deepen that faith, explore that faith, ask that that virtue grow, that our knowledge of Him grow more true and more certain with every passing day so that we'll be ready to step right into eternal life. There's many people who think they know the Lord but, in fact, they don't know the Lord.

Blaise Pascal said a curious thing once, "Knowing God without knowing our wretchedness leads to pride. Knowing our wretchedness without knowing God leads to despair. Knowing Jesus Christ strikes the balance, because in Him we find both God and our own wretchedness." Many people err by stressing that He is man, but He is also God, and they forget all these glorious truths about Him. That all things were made through Him, for instance, that He will return in glory. So we have to meditate on His Divinity often. We must also remember to meditate on His humanity; that He thought with a human mind, that He acted with a human will, that He loved us with a human heart and that He wept and so forth. Only when we keep these two opposites in mind, then, by the grace of God, we will know Our Lord.

Christ Our Hero

All heroes have a few characteristics in common. Firstly, a hero *sees a value and assumes responsibility* to secure it; something is at stake and he's not going to sit by while it's lost. Also, the hero is *generous, willing to endure something*: danger, discomfort, ridicule to save that good. Finally, he acts *without any desire for personal gain* – like the Lone Ranger who did not even stick around to be thanked.

Those may not be all the characteristics of a hero, but they suffice to help us identify the greatest Hero of all time, who is: Jesus Christ the Lord. From his throne in Heaven He watched as humanity slid into corruption. He knew that men had no claim at all to be saved, and yet He saw the value, the potential left in us, and He refused to stand by. *I have come to cast fire on the earth, and how I wish it were blazing already.* Cold and dark, miserable and doomed was world He found, but lit up by truth and burning with love was the world when He left it. But like every genuine Heroic act, this was not to be accomplished by a snap of the fingers. No, He would have to undergo "a baptism", which is to say, a wrenching experience – like being plunged into a river – so as to make all things new, not Himself but the world for whom He labored. This "baptism" was His Passion, where He would be submerged under the flood of insults, covered with the sins of mankind, and bathed in his own precious Blood. *They surround me like a flood all day long; they close in upon me together* (*Ps. 88.17*) So He *endured the cross, despising its shame* voluntarily. Why did He undergo this great act of Heroism when He was supremely happy from all eternity? Only out of love, pure selfless love – love for us, yes, but love firstly and essentially for his Heavenly Father to whom He presents the elect as a sort of gift. Christ is the consummate Hero; He towers above all the mythical heroes and yet He is also gentle — so approachable, so humble. His divine personality causes us to marvel without ceasing. This is what we must do in our meditative prayer: get to know and love this Person, our Hero!

Still, the wonders of the Christian teaching on salvation contain a surprising twist. We are also called to cooperate in salvation, to share in the heroic work of apostles. Thus the author of the letter to the Hebrews exhorts us to look at all the great heroic figures who have gone before us – *the great cloud of witnesses*. What courage we can draw from them who, by the grace of God, were made strong and brave and wise beyond any natural bound. Weak and sinful though they were, they *kept their eyes fixed on Jesus, the leader and prefecture of faith*. Then they were enabled to *run the race, to fight the good fight*. They overcame savage princes, masses of ignorance and indifference, heat and hunger, resisting often *to the point of shedding blood*. To be a saint one must practice Heroic virtues.

The letter to the Hebrews encourages us to persevere, because the work of a hero is not easy. How often we feel like poor Jeremiah! As He sank into the mud, in the dark, ignored by all, and ready to die, those promises of the Lord must have seemed like cruel lies. Everybody knows what it is like to be stuck like Jeremiah: in a habit of sin, or a cycle of addiction. Stuck in a depression, or a relationship that defies fixing, in poverty or inability to believe. Indeed, every one of us is presently stuck in some difficulty which requires us, at every moment, to cry out to our Hero. Come, Lord, make haste to help me! *I sink in deep mire, where there is no foothold; I have come into deep waters, and the flood sweeps over me. (Ps. 69.2)*

The help of the Lord never seems to come fast enough, yet it comes, and it comes with abundance. *Part your Heavens, O Lord, and come down; touch the mountains, so that they smoke. (Ps. 144.5) I have waited, waited for the Lord, and He stooped toward me.* The Lord always hears the cry of the poor and always answers. Sometimes, however, we are calling out to be preserved from the job of the hero. In other words, we are calling from our Cross, for the Heavenly Father to rescue us, instead of calling for grace to persevere in the work of a Christian, which is a hero's work. See God's hand in all things – in humiliations, in losses, in sorrows and afflictions – every cistern that we fall into can – if we are courageous – be turned into a mountain, a Calvary, on which we do the work of saving, we who are so in need of a Savior ourselves.

This Tremendous Lover

This passage from this letter of St. Paul is surely one of the more striking, more beautiful expressions of Paul's tremendous love, making it very clear that this new Christian should be treated with great dignity. What tremendous love for this person that everyone else in society was treating as a slave. It's easy to see that St. Paul is calling himself here an ambassador of Christ. This makes us think that he is showing us how God loves us. In another place he says, 'Imitate me, as I imitate Christ.'

So God's love for us is just exactly like this, totally unexpected, undeserved love of someone free for someone who is a slave. Someone who is so infinitely worthy of dignity, lowering himself, to love someone who isn't worthy of such dignity. This is our relationship with God, and it's important to remember it when we pray. Our prayer should be nothing but this relationship of love for someone that we have no reason to deserve that He should love us. So this is what should make prayer such a beautiful experience. It's always strange to me to hear people say they forgot their prayers, as if it was some monotonous, boring duty. It mustn't be that way. This should be your favorite time of day when you get to spend quality time with this Great Lover, who we have no reason to expect to love us but He does. This is the Son of Man who will light up the sky at His coming, yet He chose to suffer and die for us. So to spend some time with Him in intimate communion is our greatest privilege and something we should look forward to every single day and of course give a good chunk of our day to.

St. Gertrude wrote great words about the love of God, "Ah, wake up O soul, how long will you sleep? Hear the words I announce to you. Above the heavens there is a King who is held by desire for you, He loves you with His whole heart and He loves beyond measure. He Himself loves you so mercifully, and He Himself cherishes you so faithfully that for your sake He humbly gave up His kingdom. Seeking you, He endured being seized as a thief. He loves you so heartily, cherishes you so vigorously and jealously, envelopes you so powerfully, that for you He cheerfully surrendered His flower-like body to death. This is He, who washed you with His blood, who through His death set you free. How long will He wait for you to love Him in return?"

Divine Spouse of Our Soul

The liturgy recently presented this reading to us on a Sunday according to Mark who gave us an additional detail regarding the woman who had the hemorrhage, that she was trembling and afraid to admit that she was the one who touched Jesus.

What a wonderful image we have then, of how we, too, are unworthy to touch the Lord, to have contact with His Sacred Humanity. Yet what does He do? He doesn't only allow us to touch Him but He says rather, that He wants us to become united to Him, to become one flesh with Him, in fact to be His Spouse. He uses this imagery as in the Old Testament all the time, He is the Bridegroom who has come to seek out us, the bride, and has come to purify us to make us worthy of Him. Hosea uses that bridegroom imagery after a long passage saying how unworthy Israel was, having gone off to play the harlot. But now the Lord will return and make her faithful again. She shall be able call Me, my husband, and I will espouse thy fidelity and ye shall know the Lord.

This shows our Lord's great condescension, His great love for us, He not only uses that spousal imagery for the whole Church, which is called the Bride of Christ, but for each and every soul. This is especially obvious or clear for those who are consecrated. Those who have chosen the life of virginity or celibacy, can more easily see how their spouse is the Lord, but this is true of every single soul. This is clear if you read the lives of the mystics, (and everyone is called to be a mystic) the final stage of which is loving union. The imagery that they all use is of engagement to the bride and then the end of the spiritual life, especially in Heaven will be in loving union with the Lord.

The Holy Eucharist

The Bread of Life

In any time or place, but certainly in Palestine, where food was scarce and famines frequent, a man who could produce bread, literally, from scratch, could lead the nation. Thus *they were about to come and take Him by force to make Him king (Jn. 6.15)*. But the Lord did not come to be a populist Messiah, filling our material needs. He escaped from these admirers of his, rebuking them later when they found Him: *Truly, truly, I say to you, you seek me, not because you saw signs, but because you ate your fill of the loaves.(Jn 6.26)*. Unlike the kingdom of man which seeks to be built upon prosperity and plenty, *the kingdom of God*, says St. Paul, *is not food and drink but righteousness and peace and joy in the Holy Spirit (Rom. 14.17)*

Perhaps the Lord has many followers today, too, many people who call themselves Christian, who seek the Lord only for help with this present life. We haven't progressed very far over the most short-sighted of the Old Testament figures, if we think that a long life free of suffering is a sign of God's favor. *If for this life only we have hoped in Christ, we are of all men most to be pitied. (I Cor. 15.19)* God knows what we need before we ask it; He will not give us a stone when we ask for bread; but we are not likely to always want what we really need. Certainly, God wishes to give us also temporal gifts. He knows that we need bread in order to live; John tells us that it was Christ Himself who thought of the people's hunger. Our insistence that there are needs which far excel those of the body does not mean that we are indifferent to these material needs, especially when we find them in our brothers and sisters. Indeed, the opposite is true. The more concerned we are for the ultimate welfare of a person, the more solicitous we become of even their smallest problem as well. Thus, the Church does not ignore the fact that many in the world are hungry for bread made of grain.

Nonetheless, the Church seeks to fill a greater hunger than this. "[M]an, especially modern man, is so hungry: hungry for truth, justice, love, peace, beauty; but, above all, hungry for God." "There is a famine on earth, 'not a famine of bread, nor a thirst for water, but of hearing the words of the Lord.' *(CCC 2835.)*" The bread that we need is the Word of God, because *"Man shall not live by bread alone, but by every word that proceeds from the mouth of God"* (*Mt 4:4; cf. Dt 8:3*). But if the Bread we need is the Word of God, spoken through the prophets and apostles, it is especially the Word, Himself, spoken by the Father in eternal silence: *In the beginning was the Word, and the Word was with God, and the Word was God. ... And the Word became flesh and dwelt among us, full of grace and truth; we have beheld his glory, glory as of the only Son from the Father.*

Yes, the Heavenly Father, gives us the true bread! He will not deprive us of what our souls really long for, if only we will open them up. He gave us this true bread when He sent us His only Son. *I am the bread come down from Heaven*, He exclaimed, not long after performing this miracle which prepared the way for his discourse on the Bread of Life. Yes, there in Capernaum, with *the Passover, the feast of the Jews, at hand*, Christ spoke of what He would accomplish at the next Passover feast, that is during the Last Supper. Then He would make the same gestures, the same lifting of his eyes to Heaven and giving thanks, and He would distribute the bread to his disciples. They, in turn, performing this rite in memory of Him, would give the Eucharist to the people of God, divided into groups, dioceses and parishes. This bread would bring us not just an extension of life on earth, but eternal life, whence St. Ireneaus calls it "the medicine of immortality". Christ calls it "real food and real drink" promising that *a man may eat of it and not die. I am the living bread which came down from Heaven; if any one eats of this bread, He will live for ever; and the bread which I shall give for the life of the world is my flesh." (Jn. 6. 50-51)*

Most people, however, are undernourished on spiritual food; they do not know that a lack of God in their life is the cause of the emptiness in their lives, the source of their languor. Even most who ask God for their daily bread, do not realize how hungry they really are for God,. Many people have filled up their spiritual hunger with junk food, and have forgotten their need of King to supply for them. In this vein, St. Paul chided the Corinthians: *Already you are filled! Already you have become rich! Without us you have become kings! (I Cor. 4.8)* Put another way, many of us who believe are content with a thin rule of spirituality, which perhaps keeps our souls alive (in a state of grace perhaps) but no more. Therefore, we need to be reminded by St. Augustine, "We must hunger for God!" Yes, we *must be hungry for God*! We must have an insatiable appetite for the things of God. Christianity is an opulent banquet of grace and truth, of beauty and power; we can feed our souls by reading books, good books of which there have been more written by the saints and doctors and great minds of Christianity than you could read in a thousand lifetimes. We can feed our souls by receiving the sacraments again, and again. We can feed our souls by contact with other Christians. Most importantly, however, we can feed our souls by prayer — by meditation or mental prayer, conversing with the Father about the Son in the Holy Spirit.

Then as we fill up our souls on the "daily bread" which God offers us through the Catholic Church, we can accept the challenge of Jesus Christ; referring to the hordes of people who have less access to grace and truth than we, He says: *You give them something to eat.* The Apostles were stunned and dismayed. "It's an impossible task". Yet, when they assumed their places as pastors, they set about feeding the world by breaking open the bread of scripture and the bread which is the Eucharist.

Trusting in God, and strengthened by his gift, we will be able to do more than we hoped or imagined in the apostolate. We will have left-overs, grace in superabundance. Lord, give us this Bread always, which will unite us one to another and to you, which will strengthen our souls to live the demands of Christian life, which will be our fore-taste of eternity.

The Holy Sacrifice of the Mass

In this short excerpt from Jesus' "Bread of Life" discourse, He mentions the idea of "life" — eternal life, drawing life from Me, living forever, and so on — almost a dozen times. He is telling us *most solemnly* how we can live forever: only by eating his body and drinking his blood. But what is it about Holy Communion that makes it the source of eternal life? Part of the answer is that Christ the Savior is truly present in the Eucharist, but there is more. There is an intimate connection, better to say — an identity — between the Sacrifice of Christ on the Cross which won for us eternal life, and the Mass which gives us this eternal life-giving bread.

The Early Church fathers knew this, for which reason they saw the blood flowing from the side of Christ as an image of the Eucharist. Christian art often shows angels hovering with chalices about the Crucifix catching the Precious Blood pouring out for us. The substance in the chalice at Mass, which tastes like wine, is this identical blood from the side of Christ. Other fathers said that the Eucharistic bread was "baked" in the Passion of our Lord on the Cross. He, the bread of life come down from Heaven at every Mass, was sent by the Father for one reason: to offer Himself *as a ransom for many.*

This offering of Jesus Christ to His Father, this self-immolation out of love for the sake of mankind, happened two thousand years ago on Calvary, but, in the mysteries of the liturgy, it is truly present and actual to us in our own day, yet in an invisible, hidden, hence we say "sacramental," way. Christ came *to cast fire upon the earth,* and how He wished that it were burning already. In that statement He expressed the fire of his charity, showed his burning zeal and revealed his Sacred Heart enflamed with love; this is the fire that devoured Christ Jesus and which raises the offering at every Mass up to God. Likewise, the words "sacrifice", "offering," "victim" etc. are found throughout the Eucharistic prayers. We pray "that my sacrifice and yours may be acceptable to God, the Almighty father." We must take notice when we hear these terms, and think with love of the Lord on the cross! Jesus does not suffer again nor die again, for He is glorious in Heaven. But He continues to offer Himself, *Christ Jesus,* says St. Paul, *who died, yes, who was raised from the dead, who is at the right hand of God, ... intercedes for us (Rom 8).*

Although the priest alone confects the Eucharist, the faithful offer with Him their own spiritual sacrifices, represented by the bread and wine which is carried up in procession. A sacrifice is the "voluntary surrender of something precious to God". It is not necessarily the surrender of your life (as a martyr), but every precious thing you surrender is a sort of death to self. The procession symbolizes the offering of all of our hardships, sorrows, temptations, disappointments — all of our daily crosses in union with the Cross of Christ. From that union, all of these difficulties are endowed with meaning and purpose. From the charity of Christ in which we share when , under the influence of grace, we generously accept these crosses out of love of God, they become lighter; we are given strength and even joy. Finally, these sorrows are given value, the power to help redeem the world: *I rejoice in my sufferings for your sake, and in my flesh I complete what is lacking in Christ's afflictions for the sake of his body, that is, the church, (Col. 1.24)* St. Paul, when He says "what is lacking", means that Christ has willed us to share in his work of redemption, but only as participants who can do nothing without Him who alone has saved the world.

We are to offer ourselves along with Christ — how marvelous, but how sobering! No wonder we ask pardon lest we offer anything that is evil. But the Mass is designed by God to perfect us; He knows we're not already there. From its fruits, we are drawn closer to God as are those who have died, especially those for whom the Mass is offered, and all creation is restored to the Creator.

Let us prepare now to receive the Lord by standing in faith beside his Cross, offering ourselves as Mary did herself, and then receiving the host as if it were the first time, the last time, the only time that we could receive Him. Let us see in the Host the Lord who died for us, who is present now beside the Father interceding for us, and whom we shall, God willing, one day see face to face in glory. All this, thanks to the great mystery of our Faith, the Holy Eucharist.

The Real Presence of Christ

After feeding the five thousand and walking on water, Jesus explained at length that He was the bread of life, and eating his flesh is the condition for being raised up on the last day. Many of his disciples left Him saying "This is a hard saying" but Peter stood firm "You, Lord, have the words of eternal life". Let's make it our goal to understand better, or rather, to appreciate even without clear understanding, but with a more certain faith, the mystery of the Eucharist. Read this sixth chapter of John's gospel tonight. A careful reading of these few pages cannot leave us unchanged. Ask the Holy Spirit to enlighten you, *for they shall be taught by God.*

The three main aspects of this Sacrament, which is "the source and summit" of the Christian life, are intimately connected; for instance, the Church instructs us that: "When the faithful adore Christ present in the sacrament, they should remember that this *presence* derives from the *Sacrifice* and is directed toward both sacramental and spiritual *communion*." (Instrctn) But today we speak only of "presence". God is present to all things as their cause, holding them in being. He is also present, in a vastly superior way, in those people who are justified by grace; this is the indwelling of the Trinity in our souls. Jesus Christ, who is the Second Person of the Trinity inseparable from the Father and the Spirit, is present to us in both these ways as well. However, when He took flesh, in the womb of the Virgin, He alone became present, by means of the body He assumed, in a determinate time and place. God became locally present. Thus, He is called "Emmanuel": God with us. Now when we say that He ascended into Heaven and took his seat at the right hand of the Father, we mean that that unique resurrected body is not found locally anymore anywhere on earth. How then could He promise that He would be with us always, as God-Man, even until the end of time? He left a means by which He could, really, truly, and substantially (Trent) stay with us, while remaining forever on his throne as King of Heaven. This means is the Holy Eucharist.

Certainly the Lord Jesus is really with us in various ways. For instance, He is present in the Church as she performs works of mercy; as the Word of God is read and preached; in the Shepherds who govern the People of God; in all the sacraments which are actions of Christ, and especially, He is present in His Church as she offers in His name the Sacrifice of the Mass. (cf. Mys. Fid., 41-48) Indeed, when ever the Church acts, when ever even two or three are gathered in his name, Christ is present among us. Yet, says Paul VI, "there is yet another manner in which Christ is present in His Church, a manner which surpasses all the others; His presence in the sacrament of the Eucharist... the reason is clear; it contains Christ Himself". For this reason, to designate this presence in the fullest sense of the word, which is also the source of all the other presence's (Hidden Manna 271), we call this presence of Christ in the Most Blessed Sacrament "the Real Presence."

The Eucharist, indeed every host and every part of a host, is identical with the Jesus who "was born of the Virgin and, offered up for the salvation of the world, hung upon the cross and now sits at the right hand of the Father" (Greg. VII, for Berengar of Tours). Thus, while He is not locally present, lacking the visible appearances of his body, He is truly present. Thus, rightly, do we adore Him in our Churches, bending the knee before the Eucharist in fitting homage to the Lord. This teaching is essential, for the life of the Church. Since all of our life derives from Christ, from contact with his body, a failure to appreciate and live this doctrine cuts at the root of the Church. The Church is dying on the vine in not a few countries, and this mass "apostasy" follows a loss of faith in the "mystery of faith" which is the Holy Eucharist. Yet, the real measure of the faith is: how many Catholics come to visit the Blessed Sacrament outside of Mass? If it is truly Jesus Christ, body, blood, soul and divinity, dwelling among us still, He must be visited. Again Paul VI, "In the course of a day the faithful should not omit to visit the Blessed Sacrament...Such visits are a proof of gratitude, an expression of love, an acknowledgment of the Lord's presence." If He is present to us, we must not be absent from Him!

We take for granted the infinite treasure that is ours as Catholics. Most people, and not just Catholics, know that someone is present in a Catholic Church when that red light is lit, while an empty Protestant church or a synagogue or mosque is simply empty. This presence attracts people — like the Jewish man I met once in New York who always loved to sit in Catholic churches and finally at the age of fifty converted; or there is the more famous example of Saint Elisabeth Ann Seton. Well, we all need to be converted, every day, by sitting in the presence of the Lord. We must sit at his feet like Mary for a few minutes. Moreover, we all need His strength. How jealously have imprisoned priests — like the late great Cardinal Kung of China — guarded small particles of the host so that, in solitary confinement, they were not alone! They derived superhuman strength from contact with the Lord; we all need that strength to win the battles for chastity, humility, patience. This is not an easy teaching. But, Lord, we believe, we take our position behind Peter and say with him: *You, Lord, have the words of eternal life.*

The Feast of Corpus Christi

This feast of Corpus Christi began 700 years ago. Pope Urban IV, a French pope was called from the Patriarchy of Jerusalem to lead the Church from exile in Orvieto and Viterbo. To Urban, we owe the phrase "real presence." "Christ is present, whole and entire in his physical 'reality', corporally present". (Mys. Fid).

That is an amazing claim. It is one of the principle differences between Catholics and other Christians. Often, the realization that Christ is present in the Eucharist is what brings Protestants to seek full communion. This was the case with the first American born saint: Elizabeth Ann Seton. More recently, it was the case with Supreme Court Justice Clarence Thomas, who, after years of alienation from the Church returned, after a discussion with a priest. Thomas had pointed out many real problems with the Church, but all his objections were overcome by the priest's simple statement: "True, but we still have the Eucharist". Just as the Lord Jesus, the carpenter's son, was recognized only by those who had faith, so also He is present among us, but only for those with faith. This is no creation of the Middle Ages, indeed, the doctrine of the Real Presence was never in need of a defense until the middle ages! It is the obvious meaning of the Lord's words and of Paul's.

Much has been said about Catholics who do not believe in the Real Presence of Christ in the Eucharist. But an even greater problem is the many who believe, but do not believe enough. Why? Because, intellectual assent is not God's objective, communion is. One soul who takes full advantage of this sacrament can give God more glory than ninety-nine who believe but have cold hearts. In this sacrament, we have the privilege of Mary. She was the first to hold in her arms the infant Jesus, the body, blood, soul and divinity of Jesus Christ. For this immense privilege, priests have their hands consecrated with chrism and before every Mass, two washings, one material, one symbolic are prescribed. For the priest holds the body of Christ at the moment of sacrifice, just as Joseph of Arimethea was allowed to do, taking Him down from the Cross. Further, we hold the body of the Risen Christ. We are allowed to touch the flesh of the Risen Lord as doubting Thomas was invited to do. "Ave Verum Corpus, natum ex Maria Virgine, Hail true Body, born of Mary Virgin, which truly suffered and was immolated on the Cross for Man, whose side, pierced, poured forth water and blood. Be for us a foretaste (of glory) at the moment of death." (St. Thomas Aquinas + Mozart)

If you believe that you are coming to meet the King of Heaven, to draw near and embrace Him, come prepared. Dress properly, clean your hands, talk in whispers, come early, stay late and adore at other times (get keys, sit on stoop). If it is true, that Christ is present in our Church — body, blood, soul and divinity — we must act accordingly. We must not leave Him alone. When Christ walked in Galilee, He was always mobbed. But is He not here "corporally present", still able to listen to our cares, still able to speak to our hearts? Can we not be with Him, even if we cannot see Him? Stop in as you drive by. It will soon be a habit that you cannot live without.

Christ does not only want to be adored but united to us through communion. *Remain in me and I in Him... participation in the body of the Lord.* It is awesome enough for us to be invited into his Presence, but to become one body with Him? We should tremble. Receive Him worthily. Cleanse not only your hands but your hearts. Make use of the great sacrament of confession so that the Merciful Father can prepare your soul to receive Christ, even as He prepared the soul of the Blessed Virgin for her altogether unique union with Him. We must reorient ourselves to be focussed upon His Presence. As the bride of Christ, invited to union with Him, we must come to meet Him as *a bride adorned for Her spouse.* Does any sin make us so unfit as sins of the flesh? *The body is not made for immorality but for the Lord, and the Lord for the body... Do you not know that your bodies are members of Christ? ... But He who is united to the Lord becomes one spirit with Him. Shun immorality. Every other sin which a man commits is outside the body; but the immoral man sins against his own body... So glorify God in your body. (I Cor. 6, 13.15.17.20).*

Jesus Christ portrays Himself as the Bridegroom and the Church as the bride to emphasize that his goal is loving union with us. Just as marriage consists of a mutual gift of self, so He has given Himself to us: first in the Incarnation and death on the Cross, then in this august Sacrament, and the final time will be as our reward in Heaven. (cf. *Transiturus*) He is the model bridegroom, who gives Himself, who would willingly lay down his life for his bride. *Husbands love your wives, as Christ loved the Church and gave Himself up for Her, that He might sanctify Her, having cleansed Her by the washing of water and the word... [Husbands should love their wives as their own bodies]. For no man hates his own flesh, but nourishes it and cherishes it, as Christ does the Church, because we are members of his body. (Eph. 5, 25.26.28.29)*

The Apostles, when they saw the Lord, rejoiced. Similarly, we should rejoice on account of the Eucharist, because it means that Christ is here with us. With us, moreover, so as to live in us. We seek to be *dissolved and be with Christ.* The goal of life is union with God and in receiving Holy Communion, we come as close to Heaven on earth as is possible. Alas, alas, for the sins, the ignorance, the blindness that keeps us from rejoicing! See how Urban IV rejoiced: He hoped that "devout throngs of the faithful might gather lovingly ... and rise up and rejoice in songs of praise. Then let the hearts and votive offerings of all mouths and lips break forth in hymns of saving joy; then let faith sing, hope dance, charity exult, devotion applaud, the choir be jubilant, and purity delight. Then let each one with willing spirit and prompt will come together, laudably fulfilling his duties, celebrating the solemnity of so great a feast." (*Transiturus*)

Giving All for the Beloved

Come without paying and without cost, exclaims the prophet. The saying is true that "the best things in life are free". The best things must be free, for whatever we can afford is finite. But our soul is infinite. It was made for immortality, for eternity, for God. It cannot be satisfied with created goods, but is "restless until it rests" in God. (Augustine)

Therefore, whatever will quench our soul must be free. Can anyone pay the price of their soul? *What should a man give in return for his life? (Mt. 16.26)* Buy it back, redeem it? [Ps.89.48] *Who can de-liver his soul from the power of Sheol?* [Selah] No, the beatitude that we hope for was paid for at a great price (*I Cor. 6.20*) *You are not your own; you were bought with a price* namely, by Christ's death on the cross. He bought happiness for us at the greatest possible price. *Though He was rich, He became poor* divesting Himself of every-thing in an act of total generosity. So all is gift, the Lord has paid for everything. So all we need is faith in Jesus Christ as Our Lord and Savior, sit back and wait for glory? Not quite. Anyone who knows the Christian life, knows that it will cost one. *Through many trials...* but whenever He asks for a sacrifice, He gives us the grace to make it. Remember, He has to give it, for, alone we can merit nothing: *apart from Me you can do nothing*.

Yet when we are asked for our token payment, we get very pru-dent and worldly wise. We begin to make excuses. We are so small, so poor, and the demands of the Christian life are so great. There even arises the temptation to compromise and falsify the standard of good and evil. "It is quite human for the sinner to acknowledge his weak-ness and to ask mercy for his failings [warns the Holy Father]; what is unacceptable is the attitude of one who makes his own weakness the criterion of the truth about the good, so that He can feel self-justified, without even the need to have recourse to God and his mercy". (VS 104) The Lord used all five loaves and both fish to feed the crowd, though He could have done with one or even none. He wants our con-tribution and He wants to use all we can give. *He who sows sparingly will reap sparingly, and He who sows bountifully will reap bounti-fully. (2 Cor. 9.6)*

The key to understanding the Gospel message on generosity is to realize that Christ is not asking us for a lot but for all. Moreover, if Christ will only be satisfied with total generosity, we cannot speak only of money. All of our time is His. All of our energy is His. All of our relationships are His. All of our comfort is His. We must turn it all over to Him. Each and every act of our day must be only for Him, to please Him alone. *Love the Lord your God with your whole heart, your whole mind, and all your strength...* So this is a curious sort of free gift: it requires us to pay with all that we have and are! Such are the laws of the Kingdom of Heaven. God gives everything to us; we give everything back,... It is the law of love. Love is always extreme, a total, unconditional, irrevocable self-gift. That's what marriage is an image of, but every Christian must give themselves to God that way. That is to begin to live the life of the Kingdom of Heaven here on earth, to establish it, to live the nature of the Church which is to be

Spouse of Christ, willing to give everything for her beloved, Christ, who gave Himself up for her on the cross. "This King doesn't give Himself but to those who give themselves entirely to Him" (Way of Perf.) To be a contemplative, to reach transforming union, one must sacrifice all!

The Multiplication of the loaves foretells the Mass, just as Mass foretells the Wedding Banquet of Heaven. But the Mass is more than a symbol of the union that will exist between Christ and his spouse, the Church. It brings it about. It is here that we experience His generosity to us, His total gift of self, not only dying in sacrifice, but giving Himself to us as food, coming to dwell in us, body and soul and divinity. It is here that we are given the ability to be totally generous in return. We become what we receive, if we receive well. Just as Christ gave them bread lest, dismissing them hungry, they should faint on the way, so also He gives us this bread from Heaven lest we faint on the way to Heaven. In the words of Jerome: "In danger are they who, without celestial bread, hasten to arrive at their desired resting place."

It is primarily through the Eucharist that the contradiction of a free gift that costs us so much is resolved. when we receive this bread, we receive Christ, and He lives in us. *I have been crucified with Christ; it is no longer I who live, but Christ who lives in me; and the life I now live in the flesh I live by faith in the Son of God, who loved me and gave Himself for me. [Gal. 2.20]* He lives in us, He fights for us, He sees that no opposition will separate us from Him. No suffering is too great, no temptation too strong, if only we remain true to Him and to receiving Holy Communion worthily.

Preparing to Receive Our Lord

Remember how the Lord was invited to the Pharisee's home and he does not make Him welcome. Whereas remember the other case of the Centurion, he says, "Lord, I am not worthy to receive You under my roof." That is used at every Mass as the model we use to prepare ourselves for Communion. Many saints have commented on this need to prepare ourselves well. St. Claude de Colombiere, cites the purity of Mary, who was so pure, she was worthy to receive the Lord into her womb. "In Holy Communion we receive the same Jesus Christ that Mary bore for nine months in her womb. What is our purity? What care do we take to prepare our soul? O my God," he promises, "I will so try to prepare my heart that You may take pleasure and delight in it and so that I may not place any obstacle to the immense graces I shall receive if I purify myself and realize what great good I shall lose if I do not do so." Those simple desires are, no doubt, what made him the saint that he is.

Here St. John of the Cross gives us another reason to prepare ourselves, "How joyful would a man become if he were to be told, 'the king is coming to your house and shows you his favor.' I believe that you would not be able to sleep or eat at all. You would be constantly thinking about preparations for the royal visit. Brothers and sisters, I say to you on behalf of the Lord God, that He wants to come into your soul and establish His kingdom of peace." So our preparation should be joyful and full of expectation.

You see it's a favorite theme, here from the *Imitation of Christ.* These words he puts into our Lord's mouth, "I am the lover of purity and the giver of all holiness. I seek a pure heart and there is the place of my rest. Make ready for Me a large upper room, furnished, and I will eat the Pasch with thee, together with my disciples. Thou would have Me come to thee and remain with thee, purge out the old leaven and make clean the habitation of My Heart. Shut out the whole world and all kinds of vices, sit like a sparrow solitary on the housetop and think of thy excesses in the bitterness of thy soul. For every lover preparest the best and fairest room for his dearly beloved and hereby is known the affection of him that entertains his beloved."

The Transfiguration

The Transfiguration of Our Lord

The Transfiguration of the Lord was an event of such significance that the Church lays it before us twice a year. Although every event in the life of Christ is a mystery that can be endlessly contemplated, this one, in particular, is an abyss for us. Peter *hardly knew what to say* when he saw Heaven literally open before them, and neither do we, when we hear his account of it. There *on the holy mountain,* as he describes it in his second letter, he was an *eyewitness to Christ's exaltation.* The glorious light, the voice of God, the transfigured body, the communing with saints of every age — this was truly a glimpse of Heaven.

Peter, James and John needed this privileged view so that they could endure the scandal to come. These were the three who would, in forty days, be Christ's companions in the Garden of Gethsemane, when the Father who had thundered *"This is my beloved Son"* would retreat in silence, seeming to abandon Him; when the body which could light up Heaven and earth with its splendor was crumpled and sweating blood, *sorrowful unto death*; when the *God of all consolation* begged to be comforted by a few angels and three sleepy apostles. Forty days after the Transfiguration is Good Friday; likewise forty days from today we will have the feast of the Triumph of the Cross; this feast prepares us, reminding us that the scandal of the cross was temporary; better yet, it was truly a triumph!

But this glimpse of glory does not just prepare us for Christ's suffering, but for our own. If you visit a nursing home occasionally, you cannot but be impressed by the inexorable decline of our physical nature as time goes on: our body, ordinarily a fair instrument for contact with others becomes a sort of prison; what once glowed with health and beauty, now wastes away; what once not only got us around but ran, played and danced, now cannot turn over in bed. The reality of our life on earth is that we are all headed towards Calvary, but there is a power at work in a faithful Christian soul which can enable us to look forward to this future with the same serene confidence that Christ did as He spoke with Elijah and Moses about his impending departure. That power is grace.

Grace is a gift of God, a supernatural but created quality that inheres in our souls, sanctifying them, and making them like God. We are, as Peter put it in that second letter of his, *"called to [God's] own glory and excellence.. to become partakers in the divine nature"*. Now we remain humans, but the image of God, disfigured by sin, is restored in us and the "likeness of God" is returned to us. What the Father said of Christ *"this is my beloved Son,"* He says of every person in a state of grace, in an analogous way: *See what love the Father has given us, that we should be called children of God; and so we are. (I John 3.1)* Grace is best described as "the beginning of eternal glory in us"; yes, *you were buried with Him in baptism, in which you were also raised with Him through faith in the working of God, who raised [Christ] from the dead.(Col.2.12)*

But why do we not see this transformation that has taken place at the baptism of each one of us? Why can't we tell a Christian as he walks down the street? Where is his halo? Part of the reason is that not very many people have developed this life of grace in them. Many baptized Christians may have lost the gift; others may not have nourished it with prayer, sacraments, and good works. But even saints can look very ordinary on the outside; to some degree the problem is that we are not very adept at noticing holiness. Incidentally, this is not the case with devils: "The devils fear a soul united to God as they do God Himself.. They dare not even look at her" (St. John of Cross). Contrariwise, if we could see a soul in grace, mystics tell us, we would want to worship her, so beautiful is the sight.

But the fact remains that in this life, to mortal eyes, *it does not yet appear what we shall be, but we know that when [Christ] appears we shall be like Him (1 Jn 3.4)* In fact, what we can see, the body, only appears to become ever more vanquished by the effects of sin, by suffering, age, immobility, breakdown. But listen to the apostle: *So we do not lose heart. Though our outer nature is wasting away, our inner nature is being renewed every day. [2 Cor 4.16]* Our definitive transfiguration will only come after our Calvary: when "*we all, with unveiled face, behold the glory of the Lord, being changed [transfigured] into his likeness from one degree of glory to another.*" Grace is at work in us already, but it is only the beginning of eternal glory, the promise, the down payment. Let us remember always, when we want to know what our bodies will be like, the glorious figure of Christ Jesus, resplendent upon the Holy Mountain or, in a more muted fashion, meeting his disciples after his rising from the dead. Like Him we will be unable to suffer again. *He will wipe away every tear from their eyes, and death shall be no more, neither shall there be mourning nor crying nor pain any more, for the former things have passed away* (*Rev. 21.4*)

All this awaits us, too. Our body needs to be transfigured so as not to be an obstacle to the soul's soaring up to union with God. This dignity for the flesh is only made possible by the fact that God Himself assumed flesh. This act of the Incarnation — the uniting of carnal, fleshly, bodily nature to the divine nature — is what we celebrate. If we stop and think just for a moment, we will see that it truly is cause for celebration. *It is good that we are here*, Lord, basking in your glory. "The fact that the eternal God has entered into perishable flesh.. . imprints the stamp of eternity upon the flesh" our flesh, too. Think of that the next time that you look at yourself with sadness: whether it be a small matter — when one might think vain thoughts like "if only I weighed five pounds less," or whether it be a big matter — as when , for instance, you are seeing your body, or that of a loved one become crippled, twisted, amputated, or emaciated. These bodies are made for glory, they are going to become dazzling, too, on God's holy mountain, reflecting the splendor of the Word made Flesh for all eternity.

The Assumption

"The Immaculate Mother of God, Mary ever Virgin, when the course of her earthly life was finished, was taken body and soul into the glory of Heaven" (Mun. Deus). In these simple terms, Pius XII irrevocably confirmed this most ancient tradition of the Church to be true and revealed by God. Let us consider one aspect of its significance: what it tells us about Heaven. Close on the Heels of World War II, at the mid-point of a century of demonic rebellion and hatred, Pius XII raised a beacon of hope. "In the Virgin, risen with Christ, the Church... already has realized the consummation of its mystery. In this first member, ... the Church has attained Her goal, Her rest, and Her fulfillment — bodily presence with Christ forever" (Laurentin). Looking to the Blessed Virgin Mary, we have a preview of what St. Paul foretells, when Christ hands over the Kingdom to God destroying *the last enemy*, death itself. Then all those *who believed that the promises of the Lord would be fulfilled* will enjoy, body and soul, the fullness of life forever.

It is worth reflecting on the fact that our communion with God through Christ is renewed through a bodily action: partaking of the Most Holy Eucharist. Our bodies are called to be united to God in this life and the next. We say that Heaven is not a place in our universe, but bodies, real flesh-and-blood bodies are there. Heaven is not just a state of mind. The great privilege of Mother Mary that we celebrate today is that she is already there with her body. At the end of time, after the resurrection on the last day, the bodies of all the just will join Jesus and Mary's.

So, Heaven is a communion of the whole person, body and soul, with God. What more does the feast tell us? Pius XII did not settle the debate concerning whether or not Mother Mary experienced death before being taken into glory. We will not examine it here. Yet, the very possibility that Mary could have passed from this life to Heaven without the intermediary step of dying helps us to see that this life is supposed to be lived as a beginning to the life of Heaven. Faith is nothing but the precursor of the unveiled vision of God; it's the beginning of eternal life. Charity is the bond of communion with God and the just in Heaven. We are to begin to develop these virtues now, thus establishing our place in Heaven and making earth just a bit more heavenly, by our faith and love, in the process.

Christ tells us to have our heart set on our treasure in Heaven, and Paul tells us to keep our mind on things that are above, things which we can even now anticipate: "*God, who is rich in mercy, out of the great love with which He loved us, even when we were dead through our trespasses, made us alive together with Christ (by grace you have been saved), and raised us up with Him, and made us sit with Him in the heavenly places in Christ Jesus, (Eph. 2.4-7)*" The Church is the "seed and beginning of the Kingdom of God" and the Kingdom of God is Heaven; so the Church, this Catholic Church which people take so much for granted, is really "Heaven on earth".

Life on earth, in this Church, is filled with true joy, the reflected rays of Heaven, to the degree that one is holy, advanced in the ways of faith, hope and charity. One particularly advanced soul, St. Teresa of Avila, serves to illustrate what we have said. She often felt so drawn towards Heaven, that, even though it is not up in the clouds, she experienced the extraordinary phenomenon of elevation, literally being lifted into the air during her prayer. Heaven is communion with God in Christ, communion of body and soul to be begun even now. It is also only for the pure of heart. It's no coincidence that the only two bodies in Heaven, now, are those ever virgin and immaculate ones of Mary and Her Son, Jesus. How jealously we must guard the purity of our bodies and minds in view of our great hope of resurrection, of being joined to God and the saints. *And God raised the Lord, and will also raise us up by his power*...said Paul... *Do you not know that your bodies are members of Christ?... So glorify God in your bodies. (I Cor 6)* This is why this virtue of chastity reminds us of Heaven. Truly chaste people seem like angels, and everybody is drawn to them.

So it is ironic: the more people think of Heaven as a state of mind, the more they tend to think that one can take lightly now what one does with one's body; the more we remember that our body, too, has a place prepared for it in Heaven, the more we will live now in angelic chastity. May the glorious and ever-virgin Mary help us with her prayers!

Triumph of the Cross

The Exaltation of the Cross

We're so blessed to have this beautiful feast. That beautiful song *Lift High the Cross* expresses so much what's in any Christian's heart, but especially Catholics, I think, can understand participation in the cross. It's a great mystery, what we celebrate today, this mystery of our redemption. St. Louis de Monfort wrote a beautiful book on the Lord Jesus, *Love of Eternal Wisdom,* which has a whole chapter on the cross and it begins with this sentence, "The cross is to my belief the greatest secret of the King, the greatest mystery of Eternal Wisdom."

Let's make a prayer of petition to the Holy Spirit because truly this is a secret and a mystery, St. Paul calls it 'a hidden mystery,' when He speaks to the Colossians. "This is the mystery hidden for ages and generations but now made manifest to His saints." Let us ask the Lord to send His Holy Spirit upon us to enlighten us. Help us Lord to understand this topic, which perplexes human beings more than any other, suffering, how it is and why it is, that there is suffering and that somehow suffering can answer all the problems of mankind? You sent Your Son precisely to suffer, as we read in that opening prayer. "You willed that Your Son should die upon a cross." It's a mystery. We ask You Lord to reveal some part of it to us, so that we can serve You, and can make this mystery efficacious for all the men, women and children that Your Son died for. We ask this through Christ our Lord.

Let me read a little more of those opening pages of St. Louis de Monfort, "Oh how distant and how different are the thoughts and ways of Eternal Wisdom from those of man, even the most wise. This great God wishes to redeem the world, cast out and shackle the demons to close Hell and open Heaven to man, and to render infinite glory to His Eternal Father. Such is His purpose, His arduous task, His great enterprise. What means would be chosen by the Divine Wisdom, whose knowledge reaches from end to end and orders all things sweetly. His arm is mighty and, in a thrice, He can destroy all that is opposed to Him and create whatever He wills. By one word of His mouth He can annihilate and create. He has but to will to do all things. But His love gives the law to His power. He wishes to become incarnate in order to convince man of His friendship. He wishes to come down upon earth in order make man ascend into Heaven. So be it. It would appear that this Incarnate Wisdom will come glorious and triumphant, accompanied by millions and millions of angels, or at least millions and millions of chosen men. With these armies, He will come, with majesty, not poor, not dishonorable, not low, not weak. He will crush all His enemies and win the hearts of men by His charms, His favors, His honors, riches, nothing less than all that.

But O the wonder! He perceives a thing which is a scandal and a stumbling block to the Jews, an object of foolishness to the gentiles. He sees a piece of vile, contemptible wood, which is being used to humiliate and torture the most wicked and most unfortunate of men. It's called a gibbet, a gallows, a cross. He looks upon this cross. He takes delight in it, He loves it, and chooses it above all that is great and resplendent in Heaven and on earth. He chooses it to be the instrument of His conquests, the adornment of His majesty, the riches and delight of His empire, the friend and spouse of His heart. Lo! The depths of the wisdom and knowledge of God, how amazing His choice! How deep and incomprehensible His way of acting and judging, but how ineffable His love of the cross!"

That beautiful chapter gives us some indication of the great mystery that is before us and helps us understand, how it was, that it was a scandal to those whom He came to save. Again Paul tells us, *For He has made known to us in all wisdom and insight the mystery of His will, according to His purpose which He set forth in Christ as a plan for the fullness of time, to unite all things in Him in Heaven and on earth.* This is what Christ came to do. This is also the mission of His Church, to unite all things in Heaven and on earth with God, who created them. It is also our mission, every Christian's mission. To help bring about the full effect of this redemption, wrought by Christ. How did Christ do it? He did it by the cross. When *I am lifted up, I will draw all men to myself.* We might ask, why did Christ die on the cross? We've always taken it for granted that it was necessary. In fact the first book that was written on the subject by St. Anselm assumed this, that it was necessary. But when we stop to think about it, it wasn't at all. Because Christ was God and Man, everything He did had infinite value. Even a sigh, a drop of His blood, could have redeemed the whole world. So there is this mystery. Why He should go so far as to die on the cross?

A British Benedictine, writes this paragraph to explain why Christ died on the cross, "To make shine more and more in the eyes of the world, the immense love which the Son had for the Father. *So the world might know that I love the Father...* and the ineffable charity of this same Son toward us, *there is no greater love than this, to lay ones life down for a friend.* So as to make us grasp, by a more vivid and sensible manner how infinite is the Divine Holiness and how profound the evil of sin... For all these reasons, the Eternal Father claimed as expiation for the crimes of the human race, all the sufferings, the passion and the death of His Divine Son. Such manner that the satisfaction was not received until, when from upon the cross, Jesus, with a dying voice pronounced, *'It is finished.'* "

The operative word in all of that was 'love'. It was to show everybody how much Jesus loved the Father, and to show everybody, to convince the world, how much He loves us. For this, Christ went through all that He did. Love is the only explanation for the cross, the only explanation for that mysterious choice that St. Louis was describing. Love is also going to be the only answer to that problem of suffering. Why we must suffer? This is one of the greatest scandals that there is, that there's suffering in the world, that the all good, all powerful God should allow evil in the world, scandalizes people. It's a major reason why people don't believe in God, why they separate themselves from God. Likewise if we can provide for them the answer for why there's suffering in the world, which we can do, then they would beat a path to our door. Everybody would come to the Catholic Church if they realized that the Catholic Church has the answer of how to transform suffering into something beautiful.

We mustn't forget that this is the feast of the Triumph of the Cross. There was a great triumph here! It's true that there is no love in this life, in this broken world, without suffering. This is how we have to show our love, we know that, even ourselves. People realize you love them when you make a sacrifice for them. It's also true that this love is stronger than death, as we read in Holy Scripture. So we see that this is what this feast is really celebrating, that the love of God is stronger than all evil, stronger than the devil, stronger than sin, stronger than death itself.

You might have noticed something unusual, curious, in the vespers prayers. One of the antiphons said, 'We worship you, O Cross!' or 'We adore you, O Cross!' Also on Good Friday when the Deacon carries the cross down the aisle, He invites everyone to adore the cross, Come let us worship the cross. And it's the cross, it doesn't have a Corpus on it, it is the cross that we are adoring. Which is an amazing thing! As we know, adoration is owed only to God, not even to the Blessed Virgin Mary. This is a beautiful thing because it shows how united to it the Lord is, as St. Louis says, "He even made the cross His spouse." He accepted everything the Heavenly Father asked of Him, He didn't accept it grudgingly but He really made it a part of Him. So just as we adore His flesh, which is created, because of the union with His Divinity, so we adore the cross. Just as His body was the instrument of our salvation, so also was the cross.

This glorious cross was discovered in the year 320 by St. Helena and this is one of the things this feast commemorates, her finding of the cross. Six years earlier that cross had enabled her son to transform lower Europe into an entire Christian Country. Everyone knows how he saw a vision of the cross in the sky as a sign, 'you will conquer.' The cross is going to enable us to conquer the world for Christ in the manner Christ wants it conquered, not with weapons, but rather the only weapon, the cross, the love which is willing to sacrifice. This, in fact, will win the world over.

We not only adore the cross, we glory in the cross. The antiphon at Mass is a quote from St. Paul saying, *'We glory in the cross.'* The cross united to Christ, likewise, is a share in His Glory. One can think of it perhaps as His throne. It was at the end of His life, when He was most reduced, most laid low, during His passion, that His Kingship, His ability to conquer was shining out the most strongly. You remem-

ber, especially in St. John that this was brought out, how He enters
Jerusalem for the first time as a King. For the first time He shows
Himself as a King, as the Messiah. They sing Hosanna, Son of David,
to Him. This is what He is accused of, the charge brought against
Him. Pilate questions Him, 'Are you the King of the Jews?' He answers, *'My Kingdom is not of this world, if it were my followers would
come to save Me.'* Then Pilate goes out and says to the crowd, 'Will
you have me release to you the King of the Jews?' Then He is taken
away and a crown of thorns is made for Him and they say, 'All hail
King of the Jews.' He is robed in purple, then Pilate brings Him out
and says to the Jews again, 'Here is your King.'

There is a truth here obviously, that God is communicating to the
world. "Shall I crucify your King?" he asks them. Then he sends Him
down the way of the cross, which has been called in tradition the royal
way of the cross, it's a famous chapter in the book, *The Imitation of
Christ*, the Royal Way of the Cross. There, over the throne on which
the King is placed, He puts the proclamation, Jesus of Nazareth, King
of the Jews. Here, in suffering the death of slaves (it was not allowed
for others to die that death, so dreadful and cursed was it), He shows
Himself to be King. He shows us that He wants a new way of conquering the world. So began the beautiful history of the Catholic
Church, trampling over the world without seeming triumphant.

Think, for instance, of Maximillian Kolbe, how the Nazi's
thought he was destroyed. But he wasn't. Just a short time after he
died, the Holy Father visited his cell. The Nazis were all gone, their
empire destroyed, but Maximillian Kolbe was being raised to the al-
tars. There's many cases of the small and the humble who embarrass
the great and the mighty. But it's in living this new kind of leadership
that Our Lord had spoken to Peter about, 'No longer will you lord it
over people, I have a different way of leading them.' This also must be
the way we lead the world to salvation, by attracting them, by living
the Cross. We have to see the cross as the key element of our
apostolate. It is the tree that bears fruit for God, the cross. As Paul
said, 'We have to be willing to make up in our flesh what is lacking in
Christ's afflictions, for the sake of His Body, that is the Church.

The Lord, of course, accomplishing everything Himself, nonetheless, allows us to participate in His redeeming work. This means participating in His sufferings as well, but we also participate in His
glory. This is, as I mentioned, with no intention of demeaning other's
love for the Lord, this is something that is particularly Catholic. I
know that from my own family. My Grandmother, who was an Anglican, in her last moments, wasn't able to suffer it with peace and with

joy. She had no understanding and had never been taught this idea of offering it up in union with our Lord's cross. It will bear great fruit, and not only that, you will be given the grace to carry on, be the sufferings great or be they small. We can unite them to the cross of Christ and that makes it easier. It doesn't make the suffering less, but it makes us able to endure because of the triumph of the cross. So we mustn't be afraid of the cross, participating in it.

Cardinal Newman, as you know, began as an Anglican and became a Catholic. He made a little comment to this effect, that Christ's cross is not just something that was done for us and we view from the outside, but we have to participate in it. He wrote, "Christ's cross does not justify by being looked at, but by being applied, not by merely being held by faith, but by being actually set up within us and that, not by our act, but by God's invisible grace. The cross must be brought home to us, not in word, but in power, and this is the work of the Spirit." Bringing the cross home to us, even loving it, like a spouse. There's so many who talk of the cross, these spiritual writers say, but how many really live it, really appreciate it?

In our own life we might first begin by the sort of cross that is required to conquer our passions. If we're going to conquer the world, we must first conquer our passions. This idea of doing violence to one's own natural likes, natural tendencies or inclinations. This is the first place where we find the cross. This is why the *Imitation of Christ* says, "Everywhere you go you find the cross, because everywhere you go you take yourself with you." St. Dominic says, "The man who governs his passions is master of the world. We must either command them or be enslaved by them. It is better to be the hammer than the anvil." We can begin here by occasionally denying ourselves some legitimate pleasures, making little penances, little sacrifices for God and in so doing we will be training our passions. We'll gain governance of ourselves and that way we'll be able to lead the world to Christ, no other way. To accept the cross means to desire God's will alone. To crucify the passions and desires, as St. Paul says, so that one can be willingly led where he otherwise wouldn't want to go. This is how Christ described St. Peter's upcoming crucifixion. And so besides seeing that we aren't dragged around by what we desire, we have to also see that we aren't kept under control by what we fear.

We mustn't fear anything. In this regard, St. John Chrysostom spoke so beautifully as he anticipated his upcoming exile. He was trying to console his people before that should happen. "Waters have risen and severe storms are upon us, but we do not fear drowning for we stand firmly upon a rock. Let the sea rage, it cannot break the rock, let the waters rise, they cannot sink the boat of Jesus. What are we to fear? Death? Life to me means Christ and death is gain. Exile? The earth and it's fullness belong to the Lord. Confiscation of our goods? We brought nothing into this world and we shall surely take nothing from it. I have only contempt for the world's dress. I find it's blessings laughable, I have no fear of poverty, no desire for love, I am not afraid of death, nor do I long to live, except for Your good. I concentrate therefore on the present situation, I urge you my friends to have confidence." So it was, even though he was being expelled by the emperor, he's the one who was conquering. There was no trace of fear in him.

Finally then, when we have control of our passions, when we desire nothing and fear nothing, (and of course this is the whole process of the spiritual life, not gained in a day), we have conquered the world, in the sense, that it will be attracted to us. Then we begin to attract people to us, the way Christ attracted the world. '*WhenI am lifted up, I will draw all men to myself.*' This is sharing in what John Paul II calls, the Lord Jesus' 'kingly service.' We are all called to share in it.

It's precisely the principle of Kingly Service that imposes on each one of us, every person in the Church, in imitation of Christ's example, the duty to demand of oneself exactly what we have been called to. What we have personally obliged ourselves to, by God's grace, in order to respond to our vocation. Our vocation, which is a singular unique and unrepeatable grace from God to each and every member of the Church, is going to be exactly what Christ's mission was, to bring together all things, to unite them to His Heavenly Father or to spread this great mystery of the cross and the power of the cross throughout all the world. This is what it means to be a king, to be willing to also be a servant. When one's a servant, it means a suffering servant. But we mustn't fear. This is to give ourselves, to give ourselves fully, unreservedly to God and to our neighbor. So it's love. In fact, that is at the heart of this whole call. It's love, that comes from God, that will enable us to triumph.

I'll just close with these few words from the *Imitation of Christ* which emphasize that we can only do this with the love that comes from God. "This is not man's power but the grace that comes from Christ that can and does effect such great things in frail flesh — that what it naturally rejects and shuns, even this, through fervor of spirit, it now embraces and loves. To bear the cross, to love the cross, to chastise the body, to bring it under subjection, to fly from honors, to be willing to suffer reproaches, to despise oneself, to wish to be despised, to bear all adversities and losses and to desire no prosperity in this world, are not according to man's natural inclinations. If thou look upon thyself, thou canst do nothing of this by self, but if thou confide in the Lord, strength will be given thee from Heaven and the world and the flesh shall be made subject to thee. Neither shall thou fear thine enemy, the devil, if thou be armed with faith and signed with the cross of Christ."

Sorrows of Mary

For a few days, in the middle of the Fall, the Church asks us to almost go through Lent again, the preparation for Our Lord's suffering, death and Resurrection. And so forty days from yesterday was the feast of the Transfiguration, where the Lord foresaw His upcoming death. Then after forty days we came to yesterday, the feast of the Holy Cross reminding us of Good Friday, the Lord dying on the Cross. Then on Holy Saturday we often think of Mary, how she was left behind, Mary, Mother of God. And so it is today in this mirror of Lent that we have this feast of Our Lady of Sorrows. We remember this during Lent when we come to the Stations of the Cross and we sing that song, *Stabat Mater.* Stabat Mater dolorosa, Juxta crucem lacrymosa... That famous song which the Church sings also today means Standing by Her Son, was His mother weeping. And of course it comes from the gospel we just heard, near the cross of Jesus, there stood His mother.

It should strike us as rather amazing, that even though she was overwhelmed with sorrows, she'd be standing. That she'd be standing and not crumpled up with sorrow. That doesn't show that she wasn't suffering, but rather that she was fully taking part in Her Son's suffering. In fact we can call her a martyr, and even the Queen of Martyrs. The Church has always shown how she participates in the sufferings of her Son. Sometimes we see a statue of swords in Mother Mary's heart, seven swords, because if we look through the gospel, there were seven things in particular that made the Blessed Virgin Mary sad, seven sorrows. It was no accident that she was there, no accident that she was standing and taking part. And why was it that the Lord, my God, who arranges all things, why was it that He had the Mother of Jesus suffer like that? Why couldn't she have been taken away early, like St. Joseph, so she didn't have to see it all?

The reason is that the Lord asks us, all of us, to share in the sufferings of His Son. It's a mysterious thing, the Church says of the Saints, through Christ, with Him, and in Him. The Saints lay before the Father the merits, through Christ Jesus, the one mediator between

God and man, they have won on earth while completing in their flesh what was lacking in the suffering of Christ. The Lord Jesus won salvation for us all by Himself, but He allows us to share in it, to share in His suffering and so also to share in His glory. And Mother Mary shared in that to the fullest, so much so, that the second Vatican Council could even call her a Mediatrix. She was a mediator in Her Son. It went on to say, "It must be understood to neither diminish nor add to the dignity and efficacy of Christ the one Mediator." It remains true that, not only Mother Mary, not only the Saints, but all of us are called to suffer. We have a vocation to suffer with Christ. when Saint Paul was converted, one of the things the Lord God said to Annanias about him was this, "*I the Lord, myself, will show him how much he has to suffer for my name.*"

The Lord has planned out from all eternity, how much He wants each of us to participate in His Son's mission of dying on the Cross. All of us, carrying our cross after the example of Jesus. Really, it's not something we fear at all, it's a sign of the Lord's great love for us, because who did He love most of all? His Mother. And He gave Her the biggest share of all in His suffering. In fact, St. Teresa of Avila, who had a sense of humor, once when she was suffering a great deal, said, "Lord, if this is the way You treat Your friends, no wonder You have so few of them."

One of the things that anyone that has gone to Catholic Schools has had to learn, is the simple expression, 'offer it up.' What that means is that, whenever we have a little suffering in our life, for instance a rainy day, perhaps we can't go out, or perhaps we get cold and wet. Whatever suffering comes into your life, you have to know that the Lord is giving it to you as an invitation to share in His Son's suffering for the good of the world. So with Him, you offer it up. You say, 'Lord, I accept this suffering, I accept this thing I don't like, I accept the insult someone just gave me. I offer it up in union with Christ's suffering.' And you can do so much for the good of the world, just as Mother Mary did so much beside the cross.

Remember also where we are now, we're at the Holy Sacrifice of the Mass, as it's called, because at every Mass, the Lord's sacrifice on Calvary is here again. We're witnesses, and just like Mother Mary, here we are standing beside the cross, witnessing the Lord's death for us. So here also, bring all the difficulties, all the sufferings, all the sadness, all the loneliness, whatever, bring them and offer them, offer them with the Lord, with the sacrifice at this Mass. Offer them to God and know they will share in that great efficacy of Our Lord's own sacrifice. I'll just close with a quote from a Cardinal who suffered a great deal at the hands of the Communists. When he finally got out of prison, he went to Rome and spoke to a number of bishops, "We must work for the Kingdom of God, that is a great thing. We must pray for the Kingdom, that is more important still. We must suffer for the kingdom, with the crucified Christ, that is everything." When he said that, all the other bishops stood up and applauded, so moved at the example of this man who suffered so courageously in union with Our Lord.

Our Lady of Sorrows

Stabat mater dolorosa iuxta crucem lacrimosa. Thus begins the famous sequence that describes what we celebrate today: Our Lady of Sorrows. What a striking image: a mother in tears looks at her dying son. As the sequence continues: could any one not weep upon seeing the Mother of Christ in such great torment?

Mary's sorrow is not merely an accidental detain of the drama being played out on Calvary. It was her vocation, an essential part of God's plan. Some thirty years earlier, Simeon, without knowing how a spear would one day pierce the side of the babe in her arms, while his mother looked on, had predicted that *a sword will pierce through your own soul also.* Doubtless, Mary did not understand the fullness of her vocation at that moment, but, as was her custom, she stored it in her heart and pondered upon it. Perhaps she understood better the call when she returned to the Temple twelve years later to find her son teaching the doctors of the Law. She must have noted then, for the first time, that Jesus' fidelity to his Father's will would wound her heart as well as his own.

Her sorrows had a purpose and that purpose is clearly that they contribute to her Son's mission, the salvation of the world. Mary, by the unimaginable sorrows she experienced, played to the full, this mysterious role, by which the Body of Christ suffers along with its Divine Head. It is on account of Her Divine Maternity, that Mary has a share in Christ's mediation, that is unlike that of the other saints. Her distinctive role is intimately linked with the fact that she was the necessary condition, by God's disposition, for Christ's own mediation. Indeed, it was she who gave flesh to the Word, providing Him with a human nature united to the divine so that, in Leo the Great's words, "He could die in one nature and not in the other." It was her own flesh and blood that she looked upon, suffering on the Cross.

Unique as the Blessed Virgin's mediation is, we are all called to imitate her example. She followed the grace of her divine maternity with "complete openness to the Person of Christ: to his whole work, to his whole mission" (Red. Mater*)*. This we can strive to do also. Here at the Holy Sacrifice of the Mass, we, too, stand beside the Cross and beside the Mother of Christ. Let us ask her to show us how to make our lives, in some way, a filling up of the suffering needed to save the world, redeemed by Christ. She who, as Mother of God, enabled the Lord Jesus to be the one mediator between God and man, will enable us to share in his mediation.

The Seven Last Words

"...[T]He Blessed Virgin advanced in her pilgrimage of faith, and faithfully persevered in her union with her Son unto the cross, where she stood, in keeping with the divine plan, grieving exceedingly with her only begotten Son, uniting herself with a maternal heart with His sacrifice, and lovingly consenting to the immolation of this Victim which she herself had brought forth. Finally, she was given by the same Christ Jesus, dying on the cross, as a mother to His disciple with these words: "Woman, behold thy son"." In this manner did the Council Fathers at the Second Vatican Council describe the scene that we are to ponder. It was a scene that was not the product of chance circumstance but choreographed by Divine Providence. Artists have loved to depict the Crucified One, flanked by his mother and the disciple whom Jesus loved, because the Divine Artist arranged it first.

This climactic moment of His Son's life was planned by the Father, but it was also, even if unbeknownst to them, the highpoint of the story of Mary's life and John's life from the beginning. Her 'yes' in reply to the Angel Gabriel, loyally complying with the word of the angel, was a 'yes' to the whole plan of God for her extending through this moment; thus she stood in generous obedience, with *fiat mihi* as the only phrase on her lips, without wavering beneath the cross, taking her part in the sacrifice which has saved our race. She only had hints of what was to come, as when she pondered for instance the prophecy of Simeon — that a sword would pierce her own soul too – without comprehending; or when she was separated from the boy Christ for three harrowing days; yet her assent was always total. John likewise could not have predicted what was in store for him when he put down the fishing nets that he was washing with James, said good bye to Zebedee and followed the Lamb of God. Nonetheless, his 'yes' included acceptance of whatever God would ask. Jesus once asked him:, *"Are you able to drink the cup that I am to drink?"* James and John *said to Him, "We are able."* They did not know what they were asking, that the Master Himself would wish the cup to pass by Him, but they sensed that He would give them the strength, and He did.

Jesus Christ, great Teacher, teach us what this scene means to us! It's clear from your manner of speaking: saying *Behold!* not once but twice, that you are revealing something to us. It is not simply that you are allowing us a glimpse of your tender human heart, full of love for your mother and your best friend. No, in you, since you are God and man, the most human of actions contains a mystery, a revelation of your divinity and your plan of salvation. Help us, Lord, to understand some small part of the mystery, by pondering in our hearts, a few of these words which come to us through John.

Firstly, you again call your mother "Woman". You were not speaking in a forced way, but in a natural way, a way natural to you, Lord. Even in your extremist need, you were thinking only of completing your mission; thus you did not accept the tears of the women of Jerusalem, but told them to weep for themselves and their children, for those who needed to be saved. For many men, especially as they die, the word "mother" is on their lips. Even though you were fully human and had told us that you were troubled, that your soul was sorrowful, even unto death, you did not look to your mother for comfort. You asked your apostles to watch with you to be your support, but you did not look to Mary, as your mother, when you needed a mother most. No, as the Psalmist says of you, *I looked for pity, but there was none; and for a comforter, but I found none. (Ps. 69.21)* No, you did not wish Mary to be with you, to comfort you, indeed, many saints have said that the sight of your mother's face, so full of pain, was your greatest suffering.

No, the Mother of God was not by the Cross, to lessen its cruelty. Can we forget that she had hurried her Son towards this moment at Cana, by encouraging Him to begin his public life? Even if we could forget, the title "Woman" reminds us: *"O woman, what have you to do with me? My hour has not yet come."* She is solely concerned with the will of God, and that is why Jesus loves her. Did you not mean this, Lord, when someone called out *"Blessed is the womb that bore you, and the breasts that you sucked!"* and you replied *"Blessed rather are those who hear the word of God and keep it!"* St. Robert Bellarmine goes so far as to say that despite the breaking of her own heart, "even if she had been able, she would not have hindered the crucifixion, since she knew that all these sufferings were being inflicted on her Son according to *'the determinate council and fore-knowledge of God' (Acts. 2.23)*".

What kind of woman is this, more manly than any man we know? Dr. Pierre Barbet, a surgeon at the hospital of St. Joseph in Paris, had seen much gore and frightful sights in his life. Nonetheless, after studying in depth and describing for the world in his book — *A Doctor at Calvary* — the pains suffered by Our Lord, this man was left unable — even 1900 years after the fact — to make the devotional way of the Cross! What supernatural fortitude was not required for the Victim's mother to watch what Dr. Barbet only imagined and to remain standing, *standing by the cross of Jesus*!

The degree of the agony which the divine economy demanded of the Son tells us something about the justice of God and the gravity of sin. The crucifix speaks both of the severity of God's justice and the liberality of his mercy. John must be aware, even if only in some shadowy way, that he is the only sinner in the threesome. Mary had been moved from the beginning of her life to that state at which some great mystic souls eventually approach where, as St. John of the Cross describes it, "God alone moves these souls towards those works that are in harmony with His will and ordinance and they cannot be moved towards others". Jesus, of course, was incapable of sin, not by the gift of grace, but by nature; the union of his humanity and divinity allowed Him to be like us in all things but sin. John, however, is a sinner, and he knows it: *If we say we have not sinned*, he would write, *his word is not in us*. He was aware that Christ was suffering because of him, that, as Paul would say, *Christ loved me and gave Himself up for me*, and that any further personal sin would be to *crucify the Son of God on their own account and hold Him up to contempt. (Heb.6.6.).* We identify with John, who is, in a way, Everyman. Lest he be overwhelmed by the sight of what his sinfulness has done, lest he become terrified or despairing , Christ gives him Mary, as an advocate; who better to help one who fears falling *into the hands of the living God* than the Mother of God herself?

Thus, two forms of prayer to God have developed reflecting the double mystery of his justice and mercy, which are inscrutably but undeniably present simultaneously. When we make bold to pray to God directly, even calling Him "Father", "we proclaim his goodness and mercy", but our prayers to Him through intercessors, especially Mary, show "holy humility which springs from self-knowledge [namely of our sinfulness]... [and] proclaim[s] His greatness and omnipotence, and the reverence which we owe Him". (St. Francis de Sales).

This job of encouraging, defending, nurturing our new life in Christ, which is sometimes just a flickering flame that the Messiah does not want quenched, is the job of a Mother. If we are to become like little children, we need one. Thus Christ has made good upon his promise, *I will not leave you orphans*. Indeed He fulfilled this promise primarily on Pentecost by sending us the Holy Spirit, for the Spirit would cement our divine adoption and enable us to call out to God as "Abba — Father" *(Rom. 8)*. Still, even sooner, Christ took care that we would have a mother, His own. His only and greatest possession, and He gave her to us!

What qualifies the Blessed Virgin for such a role? "In a wholly singular way she cooperated by her obedience, faith, hope and burning charity in the work of the Savior in restoring supernatural life to souls. For this reason she is a mother to us in the order of grace" *(LG 61)* The Fathers of the Church saw her mission, in our regard, flowing from her obedience especially; St. Ireneaus, for instance, says she "being obedient, became the cause of salvation for herself and for the whole human race". She was called by them, the New Eve, the mother all living in the order of grace. Their common refrain: "death through Eve, life through Mary". Thus for St. Ephrem she became: "Queen of all, ... mother of orphans, the redeemer of captives, the joy of the sick and the star of safety for all". We did not merit her maternal solicitude; rather it is because we are alone in our egoism, captive to our passions, sick with sin and in danger of falling away, that we need a mother.

Thus Mary, Mother of God, mother of the Perfect Man, Jesus Christ, becomes also the mother of the New Man, reformed to reflect the face of the Crucified Christ. We cannot explain, but must only enter in silence into this fact: the death of the New Adam was the birth of the New Man in each one of us who believe. "The Cross is the cradle of the New Man" said our present Holy Father, John Paul II; once we have crucified the desires of the flesh, nailing them to the cross — through voluntary self-denial — grace can regenerate us to walk in newness of life. The Blessed Virgin is there for us, like a mother, to help us with our first steps. We fall indeed into many sins, but she helps us to get up and learn finally to walk in truth.

Here again, we perceive the extent of the power of God at work in Mary's heart. What human heart could, by any natural power of love, however refined, see her son dying in such a manner and instantly turn lovingly towards one of the sinners who caused his death? She knows that Christ died for her, too, but she never added to his sorrows by any action of her own. But Mary accepts her new son and in Him all the legions of sinners who cry out to her day and night "Pray for us sinners now and at the hour of our death!". Perhaps she was moved to her immense love of sinners by hearing Christ's words: *Father, forgive them...* What a great thing it is to have such an Advocate when we reach our final battle against sin and death. Just as she stood by

Christ, she will stand by anyone else who calls upon her in their agony. Around the turn of the last millennium, St. Anselm said in this regard: "I consider it a great sign of predestination for any one to have had the favor granted him of frequently thinking of Mary".

Mary is a gift from God that is mysterious and challenging, a gift that comes with a responsibility, a gift that is not always easy to accept or receive, to take into the house of our spiritual lives. We must pray with the liturgy that we be worthy sons of so noble a mother. We must remember what sort of Mother she was to Jesus: she encouraged Him to walk the way to Calvary, to love to the end; she did not pamper Him. In the words of the Council again: "Let the faithful remember moreover that true devotion consists neither in sterile or transitory affection, nor in a certain vain credulity, but proceeds from true faith, by which we are led to recognize the excellence of the Mother of God, and we are moved to a filial love towards our mother and to the imitation of Her virtues" *(LG 67)*.

This is the authentic, simple, deep, noble devotion which magnifies the Lord and speeds us along the narrow path to union with Him. This is the sort of devotion behind the oldest prayer to Mary yet discovered by archeologists, the *Sub tuum prasidium*, with which we may close our reflection:

... We fly to your patronage, O holy Mother of God.
Despise not our petitions in our necessities, but deliver us
from all dangers.
O ever-glorious and blessed Virgin, AMEN.

Humility and Charity

Charity and Holiness

The fact that it's first Friday and the feast of St. Therese of Lisieux reminds us of the connection or the identity between charity and holiness. If you just think of the Sacred Heart. Sacred, the Lord Jesus, infinite in holiness and then the whole point of His revealing His heart, infinite in love. Charity and holiness, one in the same thing. "Charity," the Catechism tells us, "is the soul of holiness, to which all are called, it governs, shapes and perfects all means of sanctification." And in fact what sanctifies us, what makes its members holy, the Catechism tells us, "it's because Christ, the Son of God, who alone is holy, loved the Church, as His bride, giving Himself up for Her." It's precisely, the love of the Holy One, uniting Himself to us, that enables us to be holy. What is holiness but union with God through love, and doing His will.

The Catechism chooses this very passage from St. Therese: "Love appeared to me to be the hinge for my vocation. If the Church was a body composed of different members, it couldn't lack the noblest of all; it must have a heart, and a heart burning with love. And I realized that this love alone was the true motive force which enabled the other members of the Church to act; if it ceased to function, the Apostles would forget to preach the gospel, the Martyrs would refuse to shed their blood. Love, in fact, is the vocation which includes all others; it's a universe of its own, comprising all time and space-it's eternal! I have found my vocation in the bosom of Mother Church, I will be love."

Humility of Little Children

Humility is unique among all the Christian virtues. This virtue, so closely allied to the new commandment of charity, is essential for our relationship with God. So we must understand this virtue. Our Lord sought to explain it to us by calling a child into the midst of his disciples and saying: *Truly, I say to you, unless you turn and become like children, you will never enter the kingdom of Heaven. Whoever humbles himself like this child, he is the greatest in the kingdom of Heaven.* Now what is it about children that makes them examples of humility? It is not that they have already developed this great virtue, no, but something about being a child is itself illustrative of the humble spirit. Perhaps, we can get at a large part of this quality by noting that children are always dependent. They are always unabashedly in need – in need of being held, comforted, clothed, instructed, protected, transported. To be a child, even on Tax forms, is to be "dependent". This is the humble attitude.

Consider also the people that Our Lord recommended to his host to invite to his parties: *the poor, the crippled, the lame, the blind.* Perhaps, no small part of the precious value of these people in God's sight is that they are also, by the circumstances in which Divine Providence has placed them, more likely to be humble. They, too, may not have developed this great virtue, but they are more likely to develop it, since they must rely on others. It is a great training in humility, especially for an adult, to be unable to provide for himself, to be unable to tie one's shoes, or to feed oneself, or move from one place to another. In these external respects, these persons are being returned to the dependent state of children, but – if they learn humility from this

– they become the most honored guests, not just of a wise host, but at the Heavenly banquet, too.

Love means being always present to someone who needs you, and it implies becoming needy of the other in turn. Love means becoming "codependent" in a good sense. How typical of lovers is the expression "I can't live without so and so". In other words, one must be humble, dependent, to love and be loved. Likewise, in our relationship with God, we will not grow in our friendship with Him until we admit, "I cannot live without you" "I need you" – that is humility, the foundation of prayer. We must believe Jesus when He tells us: *Without me you can do nothing.* Intellectually it may be easy enough to assent to the proposition that we need God, but it is a job to have this truth sink in, and permeate our way of being and acting. We live in a world that acts as if God does not exist: as if there were no Creator, no Lawgiver, no Judge. It is quite difficult to admit that all the good we do is His gift, and the wrong we do is our fault.

There is another place we can look for models of holiness besides the little, weak, poor, and suffering of this world. Surprisingly, it is in the opposite direction: the great. The truly great are necessarily humble, for the truly great are made great by God who does not exalt any but the humble. Thus Sirach rightly said: *Humble yourself the more, the greater you are, and you will find favor with God.* We can, therefore, find abundant examples of humility in the saints. Take St. Therese, for example, whom St. Pius X called the greatest saint of modern times. She understood humility: "I see myself as I am in the eyes of God: a poor little thing, nothing at all." Yet, this didn't mean that she was oblivious to her tremendous abilities and achievements. Rather she says: "In fact, I can now rejoice in [my gifts], referring to God whatever good there is in me since He has willed to place it there." Here again we see the aspect of humility as dependence; all the good we can achieve is from God. Or as Therese also said: "Tout est grace".

As high above St. Therese's virtue as the stars are over the earth is that of the Blessed Virgin Mary. She is capable of being such a vessel of grace, "full of grace", because she was totally empty, humble, open to God. Thus she sang at the Visitation: *My soul magnifies the Lord, and my spirit rejoices in God my Savior, for He has regarded the low estate of his handmaiden.* It is also to be noted in Mary's example that humility brings joy. Contrariwise, the desire to puff ourselves up leads to envy which is a sort of sadness at the gifts of others. But there is yet a greater model of humility: the one who said: *Learn from me who am meek and humble of heart. (Mt. 11.29)* Christ Himself said that all of the wisdom He spoke, He heard from his Father, and that all of his actions were done in strict obedience, even unto death. No one was ever, or could ever be, greater or more humble than Christ Jesus.

So then, let us work for humility. It must not remain a vague wish, but it must be the concrete object of a definite plan. Let us meditate upon the models we have been given. Examine your conscience daily. Pray the Litany of Humility. Thank God for all of His gifts when you do well; don't shy away from compliments but attribute it all to God's help and the help of others. Use the occasions of your falls into sin as opportunities to admit that "without Him I can do nothing". Become not despondent but remember also that "in Him I can do all things". Humility is strength, confidence, joy, success. It is union with God now and forever.

Love is Self Abasement

Have you ever wished for something but were too afraid to will the means to attain it? There once was a little French girl who cried all the time. She'd been miserable since losing her mother, ten years earlier at the age of four. She wished to grow up but could not tear herself away from the childish things that gave her security. One day, on Christmas day, she was given the means to do so. She tells us that this was the turning point in her path to becoming a great saint. That little girl was St. Thérèse of Lisieux.

James and John were not timid little girls; they were the "Sons of Thunder." Still, they wished for something that they were too weak to attain. Our Lord warns them: *you do not know what you are asking. Can you drink the cup I shall drink or be baptized with the baptism with which I shall be baptized?* We want the goal: we want to be good, even holy. But are we ready to undertake the means? Our Lord made clear by His life that the only route to exaltation takes a detour through humiliation. That is why He closes today's Gospel by saying that the Son of Man, perfect and innocent as He was, came *to serve and to give his life in ransom for many.* He is referring explicitly to the first reading in which Isaiah describes the coming Messiah as a "suffering servant" Christ is that suffering servant of Yahweh. Our Lord explains to his two disciples that they, too, must become "suffering servants": they must share in his chalice of agony and serve the needs of all. Surely, James and John wavered a bit before they replied *"We can"* to Our Lord's question. Like us, they were attached to sensuality and pride, for which reason the idea of suffering service repelled them. They had not realized that they were asking for a high place in a

Heavenly kingdom whose law is love, not power. As St. Thérèse says "Love is to abase oneself". This was her rule, and as Christ promised, she was exalted in Heaven and on earth. She was proclaimed a Doctor of the Church, one of the saints who were so filled with the wisdom of the Holy Spirit that they have enlightened the world with their insights into the revealed Word.

Thérèse longed to be abased, lowered, reduced for love of Christ. That is why her "longing for martyrdom was powerful and unsettling". Yet, see that the martyrdom that God asked of her was, first of all, interior, and in small things; Her martyrdom began on that Christmas night in 1886. We, too, must tread the same path of continual self-abasement in love if we are to be exalted in Heaven. Not only must we tread it, but we have begun already when we were baptized. *Do you not know that all of us who have been baptized into Christ Jesus were baptized into his death? (Rom 6.4)* We were *buried with Him in baptism (Col 2.12)*, St. Paul tells us. We have been baptized with the baptism of Christ. When we share in this sacrificial meal, we share in his cup of suffering. Artists have often depicted angels hovering about Christ on the cross filling up chalices for us with blood gushing from Christ's wounds as from fountains. Here, the Lord gives us the strength to humble ourselves as He twice humbled Himself: when He came down from Heavenly glory to take up our flesh, and when He allowed that flesh to be nailed to the cross.

This abasement of the Son of God transformed the world. As another doctor of the Church has put it: "Before the Incarnation and self-abasement of Christ, the whole world was in a state of ruin and decay, but when He humbled Himself, He lifted up the world" (St. John Chrysostom). This good news is for the whole world, for God wishes *all men to be saved and to come to the knowledge of the truth.* [This truth is that] *there is one God, and there is one mediator between God and men, the man Christ Jesus, who gave Himself as a ransom for all (1 Tim 2.4-5).* Is it not amazing that St. Thérèse is a patroness of the Missions when she did all her work from the anonymity of the cloister? Not if we remember how Christ saved the world: through the love that is self-abasement. He does not need our strength, our talents our intelligence; rather, He needs our weakness, our humility, our anonymity.

Consequently, let us think twice before we pray for God to remove some suffering in our life. Perhaps that illness is God's answer to an earlier prayer that we had made for the conversion of some soul. We prayed and did not know what we were asking for. Now, will we be able to share our Lord's cup of suffering? With James and John, we answer "Yes, Lord, we can!"

Embracing our Littleness

John Neuman was, of course, a great saint. He was born in Bohemia which for us is the Czech Republic. Imagine what it would be like coming to be a missionary in the United States back then. He was ordained a priest in 1839, but he came before he was ordained a priest, just a seminarian. He didn't know English, and there was no way of getting back. He didn't really know what to expect, he didn't even have the permission to be ordained a priest, but he trusted in God and ended up, of course, doing great things. Besides joining the Redemptorists, being a great missionary, founding various churches, and eventually becoming bishop of Philadelphia. He's also responsible for the Catholic school system and the Baltimore Catechism. So much good did he do!

We have to ask ourselves, how did he do so much good and how we can also make sure we do the good we are supposed to do? Often we feel that we really can't do any good at all, but from John's gospel we get a clue of how we can be as effective, for we know that St. Nathaniel also ended up being a great saint too. But how did he start out? Really, not very wonderfully, he sounded like rather a rude young man, saying, "How can anything good come from Nazareth?" Even when He meets Jesus, he's not at all impressed but again rather rudely says, "How do you know me?" So he didn't start off very auspiciously, and neither do we. We have many, many defects and we often feel, how small I am, how very, very un-useful. So we don't undertake to do much for the Lord, sometimes. But look at the Lord, He doesn't even pay attention to the defects, but rather looks at Nathaniel's good qualities and says, "Ah this is a real Israelite," he will be useful. He says, "I saw you under the fig tree, from far away, from before you were even born, I've been observing you, I've been watching you, I've been loving you and I've been preparing you so that you can do this great work for Me." And of course Nathaniel very quickly begins changing, he says, "Ah yes, You must be the Son of God, what they say about you must be true." The Lord says, "You will see much greater things than this, you will do much greater things as well."

Let me suggest two thoughts that can give us confidence to pursue the mission that God has prepared for us. The first is that you can always do a great deal if you're the right person, at the right place, at the right time. St. John Neuman of course could do so much good because there was so much need, and he just happened to be the right person, at the right place. But all of us can be that too if we follow God's inspirations, because He alone knows where we are supposed to be, what exact part of the puzzle He's made us to fit. Perhaps you know the story of a young boy in Holland who saves the whole town by putting his hand in a little hole in the dike. The little boy was able to save the whole town just because he was the right person, at the right place, at the right time. We also can do great things for the Lord if we allow ourselves to be put just where He needs us, at just the right time. You don't have to be great to do that.

The other thought is that; the way the Lord Jesus saved the world was by laying down His life for us, or as St. Paul says, by emptying Himself. So it wasn't really with His great power or His great wisdom that He saved the world. That wasn't really the point that John and Paul wanted make, but it was by making Himself weak that He saved us. We can certainly do that. No matter how small we are, we can always empty ourselves, in fact, the smaller we are to begin with, the easier that is. So if we feel very, very tired, we may think we can't serve the Lord, but all the better for sacrificing ourselves. If we feel very, very stupid, or shy, or anything else, where we think, well that will make me useless, on the contrary, we simply say, Lord I accept my great limitations, I embrace them. In so doing, by being humble like that, we end up doing a great deal for the Lord.

So let us remember those two thoughts, the Lord Jesus knows exactly what we're like and it's exactly that way that He will do great things through us, if we simply embrace all of our littleness and also allow Him to put us where we'll be most useful.

Guardian Angels

Have you noticed that angels seem to be everywhere these days? TV, movies,... books, everywhere. Much talk of angels today is not Christian, but their existence is part of Christian revelation. "If one wishes to get rid of angels, one must radically revise Sacred Scripture itself, and with it the whole history of salvation". Angels are mentioned hundreds of times, from the Annunciation, to the temptation, to Gethsemane, to the Resurrection, to the Ascension, into the Acts of the Apostles.

We need angels. The presence of Christ in us is what they are especially sent to revere, preserve, and increase. That is why God has arranged, according to St. Basil, that "Everyone of the faithful have beside him an angel as tutor and pastor to lead him to life". Strange as it may seem, increasing the presence of Christ in us, growing to full stature, or maturity in Christ, can also be described as becoming like a little child.

We read the same gospel for the feast of St. Theresa of the Child Jesus, made a doctor for her "little way" of spiritual childhood. The secret to growing up to perfect maturity in Christ is also the key to eternal youth. Saints, of whatever age, are both wise beyond their years and young at heart. *Who is of greatest importance in the kingdom of God?* The child. We are told to be child-like: full of wonder, dependent, innocent. The fact that we have been assigned a guardian angel tells us that we are of immense importance. *What is man that thou art mindful of him? You have made him little less than the angels.* We are *fearfully, wonderfully made.* What does that mean: *you have formed my inmost being? knit me together in my mother's womb?*

The angels remind us that there is an invisible creation and that we are part of it. They are pure spirit, immaterial and immortal, able to think and will because they are spirit. We, too, if we think and love, do so because we have a soul, an invisible, immaterial, immortal spirit that has been knit to our flesh and blood in our mother's womb. Our soul was created out of nothing at the moment of our conception. In virtue of this union of soul and body, we are unique creatures, part animal part spiritual being, a "citizen of two worlds."

Purely spiritual beings express best the likeness of God, who is pure spirit, but we too, as possessors of a rational soul, also bear the "indelible image of God". These considerations should fill us with wonder: in virtue of this soul we can be friends with angels and with God. We should look upon others with wonder too. The least admired among us may have the most beautiful soul. *Never despise one of these little ones.* Even the angels, naturally so superior to us, pay homage to souls united to Jesus Christ by grace, as was made clear by Gabriel, addressing the Blessed Virgin with such profound respect: *Hail, full of grace.*

The second characteristic of a child is dependence. This feast of guardian angels reminds us that we cannot get through life alone but need those guardians that Divine Providence has assigned to us. We tend to think we can make it through life on our own, only if our horizon is very limited. If we saw truly where life's pilgrimage was headed — eternity — and how many dangers and pitfalls are on the way, set even by bad angels — then we would realize how much we need help of every kind. As God said to Job, lest he should presume that by his own goodness he could come to Heaven: *Have you comprehended the breadth of the earth? Which is the way to the dwelling place of light? and where is the abode of darkness?* Like Job we must be ready to be silent, humble, obedient and rely upon the guides that God has provided. "Even though we are children" says St. Bernard, "and have a long, a very long and dangerous way to go, with such protectors what have we to fear?" Let us not just accept the help of the angel as a fact, but cooperate by asking for his help every day: "Angel of God, my guardian dear, to whom God's love entrusts me here, ever this day be at my side, to lead and rule and guard and guide."

Our Lord tells us that our guardian angel's chief occupation is to *constantly behold my Heavenly Father's face.* This is the highest manifestation of adoration of God, which is the supreme role of the angels. That is why we join our praises to theirs at every Mass, just before the Holy Holy Holy, we explicitly unite our liturgy to the Heavenly liturgy led by Jesus Christ and his angels. But what did our Lord tell us earlier on in this Gospel about looking on the face of God? *Blessed are the pure of heart for they shall see God.* Purity of heart means a freedom from all the passions and desires that tend to take the place of our desire for God, obscuring our vision of Him. Purity of heart is hard for us, who are also citizens of the animal world, and heirs to a fallen nature besides. So we must struggle to free ourselves from earthly desires and put them under the rule of our reason, of our soul. This is what Paul means by *those who have wives living as though they had none, those who mourn as though they were not mourning, those who rejoice as though they were not rejoicing, and those who buy as though they had no goods, and those who deal with the world as though they had no dealings with it.* And some, with the grace of God, have gone so far as to forgo these natural joys of marriage and possessions altogether so as to live now *like the angels in Heaven* and so be a sign to all of purity of heart, of a heart fixed on Jesus Christ, eyes set on God, desiring to see his face.

We must see to it that our heart remains free, innocent, pure like a child's also. That is why our Lord added the threat: *Whoever receives one such child in my name receives me; but whoever causes one of these little ones who believe in me to sin, it would be better for him to have a great millstone fastened round his neck and to be drowned in the depth of the sea.* Our Guardian Angel reminds us of our need to be like children to enter the Kingdom of God, full of wonder, dependent and innocent. "God, Our Father, in your loving providence send your angels to watch over us. Hear our prayers and defend us always through their protection. Let us share your life with them forever."

Jesus Meek and Humble of heart

If any one wishes to rank first, he must remain the last one of all. Though we all seek to be first, we are embarrassed by that fact. Isn't this embarrassment about our desire for self-promotion a small trace of our original dignity, a distant echo of the peace of mind that our first parents enjoyed before the fall? We know that we should not seek to be ahead of others, and yet we cannot seem to help it. We admire those who seem uninterested by gaining first place, yet we feel unable to imitate them. The letter of James sheds light on this tragic fact about our sinful nature. He locates the source of our friction with others in an internal division, *our inner cravings that make war within our members*, resulting from the fall. We desire to get ahead of others because we lack peace in ourselves. Only the solution of Jesus Christ solves it: *If any one wishes to rank first, he must remain the last one of all and the servant of all.* We must overcome our disordered nature with a supernatural virtue — humility. This is the ingredient that we admire so much in those who do not seek popularity. It is not that they disdain the opinions of others, but that they do not judge themselves worthy of being admired; this very attitude attracts the admiration of all.

Look at the humility of Jesus Christ and you will be filled with admiration. He had everything that would make Him admired — power, beauty, joy, to infinite degrees, and yet He was humble. And it is his humility, not his power, that attracts us: *Come to me for I am meek and lowly of heart.* The bedrock of humility is trust in God; He is the sole source of our every good. Knowing this, firmly, in the depths of one's heart enables one to be humble, and it also enables one to be deprived of every good without losing one's peace. That is how we must defeat the cravings that are at war in our members; that is why we need not seek the approbation of others.

How necessary is it for us to acquire this virtue! An ancient author warns us: "Woe to them who refuse to willingly humble themselves like children; because the low door of the kingdom of Heaven will not permit them to enter." (*Imitation of Christ*) The door of Heaven is low and admits only the lowly of heart. What a beautiful image. What beautiful teachers we have: children. They derive their whole self-worth from their parents. Likewise, we must be happy reflecting on our Heavenly Father, the most wonderful conceivable. May we, humbly, put all our trust in God.

Prayer

The Feast of the Holy Rosary

We have not only a Heavenly Father who gives us good things when we ask, but also a Heavenly Mother who gives us good things when we ask. All of October is dedicated to the Rosary and here on the seventh we have this beautiful feast, Our Lady of the Rosary. And so it's time to review our use of this devotion, and our own dedication to it, to see its importance, and to see if we're praying it well. One of the prophesies of Malachi calls Jesus, the Son of Justice, and it's a sun that's reflected in Mary so that in the first two mysteries you see Mary as the dawn, foretelling our Lord's coming, the Annunciation and the Visitation, and then this light continues on in her as she shines on through the Assumption and then the Crowning in Heaven.

The Rosary is often criticized precisely because it's so repetitive, over, over, and over we say the same prayer. And indeed that could be a problem if we turn it into sort of a mantra which is not at all the idea. But if it's rather, persistence, as we see here Our Lord telling us to pray persistently and perseveringly, than that's a very different thing.

Prayer is work, which has to be continued every single day of our life, so it requires the virtue of perseverance, which is part of the virtue of fortitude. Perseverance is that special virtue that we need to confront that work that will take a long time to accomplish and precisely, that's what prayer is, it's something that we have to be doing every day of our life, it won't be accomplished 'til our dying day. So we need especially the virtue of perseverance. It's a human virtue. I remember in Scottish folklore, one of their most famous heroes was in a cave. He had tried several times to defeat a certain enemy and he'd failed, he'd given up. Then he saw a spider that was making a web and failing, trying over and over again so he decided to try one more time and succeeded.

All people recognize that we need perseverance, but perhaps not all recognize that we need a special grace from God of perseverance in order to persevere in His grace, and especially to persevere in His grace until the end, final perseverance. We need a very special help from God and this is really what were asking when we pray the Rosary. Fifty times a day we ask, "be with us now and at the hour of our death," bring us to Heaven, we ask Mary fifty times a day, every day of our life. So if we do this with meaning, thinking about who we're asking, what we're asking, then it's not mindless repetition at all.

Pray Always

Today is World Mission Sunday. We remember all those men and women missionaries around the world who are carrying out St. Paul's injunction to *preach the word, in season and out of season*, when there are crowds of eager listeners and when they receive only suspicious glances and threats. We can be sure that our support is of great help to them, but certainly it is their own prayer that chiefly sustains them — thousands of miles from familiar persons and places, with Heavy labors and no recognition. They have understood *the necessity of praying always and not giving up.*

How essential it is for us to stop and ponder this teaching today! The issue of whether *the Son of Man will find faith on earth* and whether He will find faith in us, the question of whether we will find our vocation in life or stick to it if we do, the key to whether we will be happy ourselves and make others happy around us, everything, in short, worth hoping for, depends upon our ability to grasp and meet *the necessity of praying always and not giving up.* Most people will say, right off, that it is impossible to pray always, if one also intends to eat and sleep, work and relax a bit too. Prayer, for too many people, is simply one of their duties which they fulfill during the day, or sometimes forget to. It competes with other duties on the same footing, and often gets edged out for lack of time. When we are praying for a specific need, then prayer might become urgent and thus merit a place on the schedule. Most will always keep a vestige of prayer: "I say my morning prayers, three Hail Mary's, and an act of contrition every day". But, this is not the idea; we cannot lift our hands, but for a few moments, and expect like Moses to overcome all the day's evil.

To understand the necessity of praying always we must recall that our soul has a life of its own, as the body has a life of its own. The life of the soul is grace. This life is a sharing, a communion, now imperfect but very real, in the life of God. A spiritual life, then, is a relationship with the Almighty. Prayer is the expression and fuel of this vital, constant relationship. Like a young boy or girl who has fallen head over heels in love, they do not only think of their beloved when they are speaking with them, but at all times. They feel like they have a new energy and purpose, making every activity, however dreary, exciting. This innocent idolizing of the beloved is a small image of what it should be like to "pray always" to God, *worshiping in spirit and truth.* Christians who are faithful to their duties and keep the commandments are in this vital relationship with God whether they are awake or asleep, at work or at rest, talking to a neighbor or directly to God. In so far as we do all of these things for Him, so as to maintain, augment, and express our relationship, we are praying. Unceasing prayer is a constant desire, an effective attitude, a trajectory of life towards perfect union with God, which accounts for all we do and how we do it. All of our activities should issue from prayer and lead to it; we should be active and contemplative at once, prayerful at all times.

Now Christ is, of course, the example *par excellence* of someone who "prayed always". He had as the Catechism tells us "intimate and immediate knowledge … of his Father" (473) This was not only when He went out at night to pray by Himself, but at all times. His whole life was a striving to please God, as He indicated when He said *My food is to do the will of my father*. Likewise, the Blessed Virgin, another exemplar of prayer, is portrayed as *pondering all these things in her heart* – she kept the mysterious plan of God at the center of her soul as she went about her daily routine. She was a woman of prayer, so that prayer defined who she was, not what she was doing at a given moment. Her whole being *exulted in God her Savior*, not just her voice from time to time.

But how do we approach this happy state, so necessary for a holy life, where prayer is the air, the background, the source of our energy and life? We cannot just decree our whole life to be a prayer, but we must transform it bit by bit, day by day. Hence the issue of perseverance, persistence, constancy. We must begin to pray with the express purpose of changing our own will and not God's. We are not trying to get God's attention focused on us, but we are trying to pry our attention off the visible towards Him. All of this will take time and effort. Prayer, daily mental prayer even for fifteen minutes, will be work. Spiritual labor is harder than manual labor or intellectual labor. We must train our attention upon the person of Christ that we see in the Gospels and gently drag it back from inevitable distractions. We must empty our minds of worry and junk, so that God can speak through the words of scripture or his subtle inspirations (usually to do something we're not inclined to do!). We must ask what changes the Lord wants in our life, concretely, every day, then strive to carry them out. Prayer without growth in virtue is talking to yourself; growing in virtue without prayer is impossible. Gradually, our whole life becomes an offering to God: *like living stones be yourselves built into a spiritual house, to be a holy priesthood, to offer spiritual sacrifices acceptable to God through Jesus Christ. (I Pet. 2.5)*

This mental prayer, the point of which, according to St. Teresa of Avila, is not to think much but to love much, is an essential for every Christian. She considers such prayer, which is, remember, a proof of a genuine relationship with God, as necessary for salvation. We must spend some chunks of the day in dialogue with the love of our life. This is necessary to conform our way of thinking and judging, our desires and our aversions to those of Jesus Christ. Then our choices throughout the day will bring us closer to God, and be themselves a source of glory for Him, conformed as they will be to his holy will.

We will praise Him by our whole lives once Christ has reoriented us. Mental prayer will remain a constant in our life, in season and out of season, at home and abroad, we must never give it up. There are no vacations... In times of consolation or desolation, distraction or ecstasy, we must be faithful to praying. We will want to give God the best moments – early in the morning when we are not yet scatter brained, after receiving communion when our beloved is physically close, occasional whole mornings or retreat days. We will grow in love of silence and will lament the constant noise that assails us, young people in particular, effectively drowning out the possibility of praying always.

Doubtless, as one draws closer to God, one will find more time for explicit prayer. One might add the rosary, first of all, and other traditional, communal, scripturally rich forms of prayer (the Angelus, the Lit of Hours). The time set aside will surely grow. One will experience the amazing phenomenon that men and women of prayer accomplish so much more than others, even in the proportion as they give their time generously to prayer. Nonetheless, there are limits to the number of minutes for explicit prayer. Soon enough, progress must be made in improving the quality of the time we give: deepening the intensity of our love, the delicacy of our conscience, the generosity of our resolutions.

The road of prayer is not easy; it is the narrow and difficult road to life. One must pray without losing heart, without giving up. Do not mind if you feel you are speaking to the walls, if you fear urgent matters are getting neglected, if you have given up or failed before. Get help from others to hold your hands up (as Moses did) – a friend you can be accountable to, a prayer group, a spiritual director. Break bad but comfortable habits. Wake up earlier, kneel longer, be silent more. Teach your children to pray, and to pray well. It is the most necessary lesson of all.

Humility in Prayer

This well known parable of the Pharisee and the Publican speaks about the great precondition or prerequisite for approaching God, which is humility. "Humility," says the Catechism, "is the foundation of prayer, 'for man is a beggar before God,' "quoting St. Augustine. We come to receive the gift of prayer, a relationship with God, a constant communication with God. It's His gift to us. We come to Him as a beggar, totally unworthy of even speaking His name. As a result, the petition of the Publican, the tax collector, "O God, be merciful to me, a sinner," in that form, or one like it, is a constant in Christian prayer. A prayer known especially to Eastern Christians called the Jesus Prayer is almost those very words, 'Jesus Christ, Son of God, be merciful to me, a sinner.' when repeated over and over and over it is one of the chief methods of doing meditation and entering into contemplation in a large part of the Church. The Catechism says specifically of the Jesus Prayer, "by it, the heart is open to human wretchedness and to the Saviour's mercy."

We don't ordinarily think of ourselves as wretched. We aren't, in other words, as humble as we ought to be. Often we think that one can confess the major sins that are known to us, and we're fine, God's happy with us. We really don't know our sins. People often don't feel that they have anything they can think of to confess. But then it's a great mistake to think that, therefore, I'm totally acceptable in the sight of God. At that time, and even all the more, we should say this prayer of the Publican, because it's an even worse thing about us that we don't know all of our miseries, we can't enumerate them, to ask forgiveness. All the more consistently we should say, have mercy on me a sinner, because I can't see my miserableness, my wretchedness, compared to the all holy God. It's not a depressing way of thinking oneself but, in fact, it unleashes great joy because we know that God loves us anyway. In fact it's precisely when one makes oneself totally, totally nothing before God, that then God can raise that person up to Himself. God gives grace to the humble so that He can change us. Jesus says, humble yourself then you'll be acceptable in His sight. Then you can offer the sacrifice. Then you can say you've become like little children, the way Jesus insists we must be to enter into the Kingdom of God. A little child before his parents doesn't think he's great, but he's just so pleased that his parents think he's great.

Here's a little story, with which you may be familiar, to show us how far in prayer one can advance if one's humble. There was a man in the parish of the Cure of Ars, St. John Vianney, who is the patron of all parish priests, such a holy man of God Himself. But he, himself was astonished at the depths of prayer of one of his parishioners. This humble peasant would sit in the back of Church and pray for hours on end. The Cure of Ars began to grow curious, how is it that this man seems to have such a deep relationship with God, what's his secret? He asked him what it was he said to God in his prayer. The man said, "I say nothing, I simply look at Him and He looks at me."

This is seen as the epitome of how to pray, how to pray well, recognizing that we're not worthy to be in the presence of God, but one simply rejoices that God wants to look upon us in our lowliness. I'll conclude with a quote from a great teacher of prayer, a French Dominican. He says, "If we love to be nothing, to accept contempt, and not only accept it, but to end by loving it, we shall make great progress in prayer, we shall be loaded with gifts beyond all our desires."

Silence

The saint today, St. Bruno, decided to start a monastery more austere than any that had been before. Although this certain type of monastery is so very very difficult, its members are very busy with things to do and they're full of joy in their hearts. As St. Bruno said, "Only those who have known the silence and the solitude of a hermit's cell, can understand its blessings and its joys."

.In the monasteries, besides the hard labor, they do nothing but pray, that's their main goal, it's to worship God. St. Bruno used to live in the world, back in the year, 1000. He was Chancellor of his diocese and a professor of theology, then he and ten companions obtained a certain stretch of land way out in the country. And there, living in separate cells, with a common church, they founded the Carthusian Order. Poverty, worship, hard manual labor and study were the basis of their rule. There he especially taught them how to pray. And this he learned from the Lord Jesus. The disciples asked the Lord Jesus, "Lord, teach us how to pray." He taught them the Our Father, but He taught them to pray also, by His example. One day Jesus had been praying at a certain place and just like the Carthusians do today, and other monks like them, He had gone out to a lonely place by Himself, up on a mountain, probably cold in the morning, and probably He was hungry, having not eaten. There fasting and praying, out by Himself, He would talk to God. And that's especially how He taught His disciples how to pray and St. Bruno was a great one of them.

Now it may be that we have some Carthusian vocations here, remember, there are orders for women as well who live this kind of life. But it's a very rare and special vocation, that's for sure. But everybody is called to imitate them, in a way, everybody is called to make solitude and silence and prayer, and simplicity and austerity a part of their lives, every Christian anyway, because we're all supposed to follow the Lord in His example. What I would say to you is to begin now in ways that are appropriate to you. First of all, be very aware that the world can not understand how anyone could live that kind of life, live it freely and find the greatest happiness in it. So be aware that the world doesn't understand these mysterious things, as a result they often go in the wrong direction. They often, because they have this inability to understand where happiness is found, they try to find it in other places. They try to crowd God out and don't make room for Him in their hearts.

That's why there's so little silence in our world, why people are so often afraid of being alone. They love company, they love excitement, they love noise, and that's our society. You have to learn to love moments when you are alone. Those are moments when you can especially be with God. St. Bernard who entered another great order was famous for saying, "I'm never less alone than when I am alone, for then I am alone with the Alone." Never less alone than when I am alone, that's when He can be with God. So cherish those moments when you can be alone, those are the times when you can be with God. Be careful not to completely crowd them out of your life. Remember always, that in silence we discover, either, how empty we are, so we're afraid of it, or we discover the place where we can meet the Lord.

The Ways of Prayer

This feast of Saint Martha provides us with a wonderful opportunity to think about prayer. Martha is always contrasted with her sister, Mary, for having favored action, service, to an excess and having failed in her duty to contemplate the Lord. This, of course, can be exaggerated and many, including St. Teresa of Avila, defend Martha and her service. It is true, although she was certainly reprimanded strongly by our Lord and told she was getting distracted with her service and being worried about many things, nonetheless service is a very good thing and the opening prayer commended Martha for her service. When we worry, however, about our loved ones or anything, about the state of our society or whatever we tend to worry and fret about, we have to see that there is some good and some bad in that. It does show that we love these things and yet the fact that it's so easy, so comforting even, to fall into worry, it is a sign that there's self love there too. It's so easy to do and self serving in a way. So it can be an obstacle to our path to holiness by being an obstacle especially to prayer, being worried about many things.

Spiritual guides have always taught that mental prayer is essential for progress in the spiritual life, what we saw Mary doing, gazing upon the Lord, listening to His words, contemplating Him. We have to beware lest activity in our life crowd out that time for mental prayer, or when we're actually trying to pray, when we've set aside the time, letting those worries about our family, our society or ourselves, crowd out our mental prayer. We who have the privilege of being at daily Mass have to be especially vigilant lest the habit of this kind of prayer, praying in common, can sometimes be a substitute for mental prayer, meditation, for going into our room, as our Lord says, locking the door and praying to our Father who sees us in secret. These spiritual guides will tell us that nothing, not even the Holy Sacraments, can substitute for that time of prayer, that separation from life, from haste, from worries and turning to God. This is proved, unfortunately, by the fact that so many daily communicants, so many priests, so many nuns also, don't make progress in holiness really, though they do come and receive the sacraments often. One has to, yes, receive these graces through the sacraments often, but also strive, yearn with all one's heart for the Lord, expressed in daily meditation. So we see that work, activity, can be an obstacle to prayer. I was told recently that the founder of the Boy Scouts, who was a good man, was once told by somebody that they were too busy to pray. He said, "Well, then you're just too busy." If you're too busy to pray, you're too busy doing other things and you have to find that time.

It's also true that in the midst of activity, and most of us are active, not contemplatives, there is a place for prayer. There is the sort of prayer that is compatible with the active life, as well, and it is described by this author here, "The sort of prayer that continues throughout the day and forms a sort of backdrop for each and every one of the day's activities. It is immanently spontaneous, it is a continuing dialogue in the interior of your soul, in which you talk with Christ and share with Him your thoughts and activities, projects and accomplishments, desires and intentions. You offer Him the success of your undertakings, ask Him for light and help to deal with difficult matters. Thank Him for the countless blessings that are constant reminders of His presence, the new day, the sun, a smile from your wife, a hug from your child, a successful venture, etc. The unending succession of daily events forms the topic of this interior conversation which you use to cement your friendship with Christ and try to become more like Him. The soul that loves Christ, not only thinks of Him, but keeps up a continuous conversation with Him and tries to please Him in the midst of, and specifically by means of, his daily activity."

We know that that's true, that we don't only have to separate a certain amount of time during the day for God, but also in the midst of activity. That's also a time for God. We know that's true for the saints have lived it so well. Just think of how active the saints were, how much they accomplished, although they were always in prayer. They had the specific time of the day for the Lord, but then also the rest of their day was lived in union with Him. So let this be our goal, that we can truly be contemplative and then be also truly active for the Lord.

Persistence in Prayer

The Old Testament, especially the psalms are filled with lines like, "How long, Lord, how long?" That idea of waiting for the Lord, longing for justice. The first two readings spoke of that, how the Lord finally came and did justice for the people of Israel, bringing them out of the Red Sea, on an unimpeded road, and into the Promised Land. These are the marvels that the Lord has done. Israel had to wait so long in Egypt, waiting for their deliverance. Also it's similar to the waiting of the prophets, waiting so long for the Son of Man to come, waiting for the Messiah to come in the fullness of time. To us, it seems like long waiting, it seems like God is delayed. But to God all points in time are equal distance from eternity and for Him there was not a delay. We get that sense from the line in the first reading, how He's *rushing down to help us*.

But to us, God's response is always delayed. We have that experience when we pray, every Christian always has. St. Augustine responds to the problem like this, "If God seems at times to be slow in responding, it is because He is preparing a better gift. He will not deny us. We well know that the long awaited gift is all the more precious for the delay in it being granted. Through this asking and seeking, you will be better prepared to receive God's gift when it comes. God withholds what you are not yet ready for. He wants you to have a longing desire for His greater gifts. All of which is to say, pray always and do not lose heart."

There's so much in that for those who pray. That prayer is especially preparing our hearts to receive God's gifts, His gifts which are not always easy to receive. We do not always know what is good for us, so we ask for something which really would not be good for us. The Lord is giving us what we really need, but it takes time for our heart to be made ready to receive it. We should remember also that He knows what we need anyway, before we ask for it, so that it is the asking, itself, that longing, that waiting, without losing hope, that is very meritorious and draws us to God. That time of scanning our hearts so that we may say, '*Thy will be done*,' in truth. All that is the fruit of those long hours of prayer, when we seem to be ignored.

One of the things that we wait for especially is the coming of the Kingdom and our entrance into that Kingdom through death. These are things that Christians should wait for with longing just as the Israelites waited for their deliverance, yet we tend to sort of dread, or wait for with fear. We mustn't do that. We mustn't think of the second coming of our Lord, to which He Himself refers, *'When the Son of Man comes will He find faith on earth?'* We mustn't think of that as a dreaded proposition. Of course it will be the end of the world, but we must think of that as something good, to look forward to, the Lord's coming again. Likewise if we're to meet Him before the second coming, if we're to die before He comes, again we should be looking forward to that with joy! I remember seeing Mother Cabrini's room where she died, near a Church we used to go to. It's a happy place, to visit a place where a saint died. Because one realizes that they went to a much better place, that they couldn't wait to leave this world. So the place where they die is not a sad place, but a happy place.

This week we have another example of that. St. Martin who has his brothers in religion gathered around his bed saying, "Father, why are you deserting us, who will care for us when you are gone? Savage wolves will attack your flock and who will save us from their bite when our shepherd is struck down? We know that you long to be with Christ, but your reward is certain and will not be any less for being delayed. You will do better to show pity for us rather than forsaking us." St. Martin was so full of love that he asked the Lord, "Lord if your people still need me, I'm ready for the task. Your will be done." But it wasn't the Lord's will, it was time for his reward. So He turned to his brothers and said, "Allow me, brothers, to look toward Heaven, rather than at the earth, so that my spirit may set upon the right course when it is time for me to go on my journey to the Lord." So let us pray that our waiting for the day, when we are to be joined with the Lord, will be full of hope and joy. Let us look forward to that day, knowing that we go to the place where we're supposed to be, a much better place. It's a day we should long for every day of our lives.

Perfection through Prayer

St. Teresa of Jesus, as the opening prayer reminds us, shows the Church the way of perfection. One of her most famous works is *The Way of Perfection*. This is what she dedicated her life to. All Christians, as we know, are called to perfection, Christian perfection or holiness. The second Vatican Council of course reaffirmed this and emphasized this. God, of course, calls us all to Heaven, and no one will be in Heaven if they're not perfect. So one must be perfected either in this life or in Purgatory. It's God's plan for us to be perfected here on earth. The way of perfection, the whole Christian life, such as the building up of virtue, is important, but the essential part, the most necessary part is of course prayer. Prayer, which unites us to God, is the means by which we come to know Him and how to please Him in all things.

Prayer is essential to growth in holiness. Real prayer, and yet so little known and so little practiced by Christians. When we say real prayer, we mean the lifting up of the mind and heart to God. It's real union with God, in Christ, through the Holy Spirit. That first reading by St. Paul is so important, that we do not know how to pray as we ought, but it's the Holy Spirit who teaches us. We cannot properly say even Lord without the Holy Spirit, we read in another place. All prayer, even the vocal prayers, will have this character of being true mental prayer, true union with God if we make the effort to make it so. The importance of prayer, St. Teresa underlines it saying, "There is no greater cause of straying from the path of faithful perseverance than letting up of prayer." She says that in many different ways. This prayer, if it's true union with God, is more of a gift of God than anything else. Genuine Christian mysticism has nothing to do with technique, it's always a gift of God and the one who benefits from it, knows himself to be unworthy. It's not so much something we do, as something we open ourselves up to, that God can give it to us. It's always union, lifting up our mind and hearts to God, but in Christ.

This is also a point for which St. Teresa is famous, that Christ must always be the center of our prayer. If you take, for example, Pope John Paul II, he is described as a Carmelite soul. Those who hear him pray, say he groans there in the Chapel, because words can't express the gift of understanding that the Lord's given him. But it's nothing, if not centered on Christ. That's very, very important. True prayer is always going to be centered on the Lord Jesus. As the Pope, when he was in Avila, said in a homily, "Any method of prayer is valid in so far as it is inspired by Christ, and leads to Christ, who is the Way, the Truth and the Life." When we say Christ, we mean the humanity of Christ. In prayer the Gospel is so key to one's meditations, focusing on His humanity, His birth, His being tired, especially His death on the Cross. This is what we have to fill our soul with. St. Teresa teaches us the way to perfection, the way to Heaven, and who is the Way but He who said, I am the Way, and the Truth and the Life. But it's in His humanity, because as God, Jesus is goal, not the way, but as flesh and blood, our Saviour, He is the Way and should always be the center of our prayer.

Mental Prayer

Our Lord Jesus was in constant union with the Father through prayer, a sublime union which we are privileged to glimpse in this ineffable 17th chapter of St. John, known as the Priestly Prayer, of Christ Jesus. There we see His longing for the Father, and His longing to bring us and all of creation into union with Him. We lead all creation to its fulfillment, to the coming of the Kingdom, to the new heavens and new earth, when we strive for union with God, our Heavenly Father. *For the creation waits with eager longing for the revealing of the sons of God...* How do we strive for union with our Father? Through prayer.

The first thing the disciples did upon returning from Mt. Olivet was to pray. *All these with one accord devoted themselves to prayer, together with the women and Mary the mother of Jesus, and with his brothers.(acts 1.14)* To approach the Lord we need Mary; He came to us through her, and we shall not come to Him but through her. They gathered around the Mother of God and the Holy Spirit came upon them. It is true that the Church in our day, and in every day, lives is in a perpetual Pentecost, for the same Spirit comes to us with his sevenfold gifts through the mystery of the sacraments. Nonetheless, it is also true that we live a perpetual waiting for that Spirit, for He has come with his first fruits only. *We know that the whole creation has been groaning in travail together until now; and not only the creation, but we ourselves, who have the first fruits of the Spirit, groan inwardly as we wait for adoption as sons, the redemption of our bodies.*

We are already united to God through faith, hope and charity, yes, but we are still on the way to Him. We grope for Him in darkness still, and it is the Spirit that lights our way. *Likewise the Spirit helps us in our weakness; for we do not know how to pray as we ought, but the Spirit Himself intercedes for us with sighs too deep for words. And He who searches the hearts of men knows what is the mind of the Spirit, because the Spirit intercedes for the saints according to the will of God. (Rom.8.19-27)* The Spirit of Christ prays within us. Our prayer should be more than modeled upon that of Christ, it must be Christ's prayer. We must participate in his eternal intercession for us before his Heavenly father. For true prayer is union with God, and we cannot rise up to Him, but He must carry us into his Presence. It is always a Gift — offered to all. As the Lord says through Ezekiel: I will give you a new heart and put a new spirit within you. *(cf. Ez.36.22-26).* Prayer is not then something that we do, a duty that God requires of us. True prayer can never occur without God's grace. We cannot even say the name of the Lord without the Holy Spirit. Prayer is a mystery. It is an encounter between man and God, the finite and the infinite, time and eternity. It is a real beginning of that union with God which is Heaven. *And this is eternal life, that they know thee the only true God, and Jesus Christ whom thou hast sent.(Jn.17.3)*

Do we know God? *He who says 'I know Him' but disobeys his commandments is a liar, and the truth is not in Him; but whoever keeps his word, in Him truly is the love of God perfected.(Jn.1.4)* It is certain that through prayer, we can obtain favors from God to help us on our pilgrimage to Him. W*hatever you shall ask in my name will be done for you.* Yet the goal of prayer is not to obtain what we desire, but to find and accept what God desires. The Lord is generous, but He really most wants to give us The Gift, his Holy Spirit. *(Lk.11.13) If you then, who are evil, know how to give good gifts to your children, how much more will the Heavenly Father give the Holy Spirit to those who ask Him!"* It is this Spirit who reveals to us the Father, and the Father's will. This same Spirit enables those who pray to know and to embrace the will of the Father, to be generous and joyful. Prayer alone makes possible what Peter enjoins upon us: *rejoice in so far as you share Christ's sufferings... if one suffers as a Christian, let him not be ashamed, but under that name let him glorify God. (I Pet. 4.13-16)* Since the only measure of the quality of prayer is growth in virtue: humility, patience, charity, peace of mind, we must make sure that our prayers end with concrete resolutions of how to serve the Lord better today.

The prayer that we are speaking of is often called "mental prayer". "Mental prayer" according to St. Teresa of Avila, "in my opinion is nothing else than a close sharing between friends; it means taking time frequently to be alone with Him who we know loves us". Most people admit to "not praying enough" but they should be more concerned about not praying well enough. Yes, we must spend time, much time in prayer — it must be as the water which we fish continually seek to jump back into when duties no longer detain us — but we must especially see prayer as work. It is too easy to read beautiful words, to repeat consoling favorite prayers, to ask for this or that. There is a place for this vocal prayer, yet all Christians are called to strive to know God, to seek his Face, to learn His will, to strive for the union, the knowledge of God in which Heaven consists even now. This is work. It takes generosity, perseverance... yet there is no holiness without it, and salvation itself is put into question.

Listen to the words of the Pope and the bishops of America speaking with one voice in their recent synod: "Contemplation is not a privilege reserved to the few; on the contrary, in parishes, in communities and movements there is a need to foster a spirituality clearly oriented to contemplation of the fundamental truths of faith: the mysteries of the Trinity, the Incarnation of the Word, the redemption of humanity, and the other great saving works of God." You may say — how can I ever begin on the path of mediation and contemplation? I'm lucky if I say a few Our Fathers before bed. Well, the Pope urges you to get assistance: "In order to mature spiritually, Christians do well to seek the counsel of the Church's ministers or of other persons expert in the field of spiritual direction, which is a traditional practice in the Church. The Synod Fathers felt that it was necessary to recommend to priests this important ministry". "St. John Vianney likewise endeavored to inculcate upon souls, eager to go forward on the road of perfection, the habit of daily mental prayer, and he taught them how to go about it. To those who felt unable to apply themselves to methodical meditations he simply recommended to think frequently of God."

Take pity upon your souls. "Whoever has grown from infancy to manhood and attained to spiritual maturity possesses the mastery over his passions and the purity that makes it possible for him to receive the glory of the Spirit. He is that perfect dove upon whom the eyes of the bridegroom rest when He says: *One alone is my dove, my perfect one.*" (St. Gregory of Nyssa) Our souls are meant to be like beautiful doves. Make them come out of the shell of egotism and into the light of God every day. See to it that they are nourished by a constant sacramental life, lest they be stunted. See to it that their wings are allowed to flap, cleansed of every sin. Let them fly up above daily concerns and anxieties, seeking gusts of wind from the Holy Spirit. Prayer must lift you and the rest of creation into the presence of God.

Fruits of Prayer

Today we shall continue our reflections on prayer. What the scripture teaches us today may at first seem to contradict what we said on the feast of St. Martha. We said that good works, service, cannot substitute for prayer. But today we shall recognize the role that good works do have in our spiritual life.

Moses came down from the mountain with his face shining. Contact with the Almighty had made him similarly holy. Yet it was not an empty conversation that Moses had had with God. He carried down commandments which show how fundamental is the relationship between what we do and whether we can converse with God as a friend. This is true of our prayer, too. The fruit of it must always be practical. We must come down with a clearer idea of God's commandments and how to fulfill them. This is actually the litmus test of an authentic spirituality. If a "mystic" does not grow in virtue — humility, especially charity, — one can be sure that they are fakers. All the spiritualities that seek an altered state of consciousness but are not actual dialogue with the Almighty, do not change the person into a better one. Great sinners can and do meditate using Eastern methods, but no one who practices authentic mental prayer can persist in sin. It is contact with the Holy One and it must change us or we will give up praying.

Therefore, God's will must be what we seek. Prayer is love. What does our Beloved want? What is His will? The giving up of our own will is a radical proposition pictured in two vivid ways in today's Gospel. The love that Our Lord invites us to is radical: we must be all for Him, totally devoted to Him, or we can have no part in Him. The practice of mental prayer gradually introduces us to Him, to His will, and strengthens us to commit ourselves to Him.

Disposing One's Heart

Prayer is a loving conversation with Love Himself, and it can indeed provide the closest joy to that which shall be ours in Heaven. Still, it is more common, even for great saints, to view prayer as difficult, as a duty. It is a struggle. "From this account [of Jacob wrestling with an unknown figure] the spiritual tradition of the Church has retained the symbol of prayer as a battle of faith and as the triumph of perseverance" *(CCC 2573)*

There are two principle obstacles to prayer, distractions and aridity. By struggling bravely to pray (even against obstacles sent by God) we will begin to attain the goal of prayer, a union with God in thought word and deed in this life which will prepare for eternal union with Him in the next. Then too we will ask for things in accord with His plan, things that will really help us and the world. From Jesus' words in the Gospel, we gather that prayer must be a cooperation with God's plan. A progressive disposing of the heart to do the will of the Father.

Abandonment to Divine Providence

God's Will Be Done

As the liturgy today shows us, God's faithful people have always been asking Him through prayers of petition for His blessings after the great examples in the psalms, "Lord, on the day I called for help,

You answered me." And the Lord Jesus only strengthens our confidence that God will answer any of our prayers. Going so far in the Gospel to say, "Whatever you ask in my name, it will be given to you." But we know also from His own example, that every good prayer of petition is followed by, "But not my will but your will be done." In fact we can say that every good prayer of petition is nothing else than asking that God's will be done. And that's why every good prayer of petition is always answered, because God's will, always will be done. What then is the point of praying? The Lord always knows what we need before we ask Him as Scripture tells us. He only wishes to give us the things that we need in answer to our prayers, with our cooperation, so that we can participate in Divine Providence. The Cure of Ars says, "Won't you agree with me that if we don't receive what we ask God for, it is because we do not pray with faith, with a sufficiently pure heart, with enough trust, or because we do not persevere in prayer as we should. God has never denied, and never will deny anything to those who ask for His graces in the right way." Because these are the graces that He wants to give us, that He's planned to give us from all eternity. He's only asking for us to cooperate.

Very often the trouble is that we don't know our true good. What's actually good for us, we don't want. For that reason St. Augustine says, "Look well on Him who does not give you, when you ask for it, what would not be in your best interest." Whenever our prayers are not answered, most likely we're not asking for what we really need. And what we often really need are crosses in our lives, and these are often what we are precisely asking the Lord to take away. Sometimes, some people even ask the Lord for crosses, along with the grace to bear them, and this is a prayer that is always answered. A beautiful example of a prayer of petition is that of Cardinal Kung who was a great Confessor of the faith in China. He was thirty years in prison, much of it in great suffering and solitary confinement. But before going to prison, when the persecution started, he was leading his diocese in a Marian Year procession and he closed it with armed policemen watching, knowing his arrest was immanent saying, "Holy Mother, we do not ask you for a miracle, we do not beg you to stop the persecutions, but we beg you to support us, who are very weak."

Divine Providence

The liturgy today provides us with two examples of people who trusted in Divine Providence, first of all, Daniel, who wanted to keep the commandments of the Lord and trusted in the Lord. And also this poor widow, who so trusted in the Lord, that she was able to give more than she could even afford, every penny she had to live on. Trust in Divine Providence is very tricky, because how do we know when we have supernatural prudence or whether we get into foolhardiness and tempting God? For us to have this virtue, we have to live it every single day.

This is a short summary from the book, *Abandonment to Divine Providence*: Remember our great principles. "One, that there is nothing so small or trifle, even the falling of a leaf that is not willed or permitted by God. Two, that God is sufficiently wise, good, powerful and merciful that He can turn the most seemingly disastrous event to the good of those who are faithful to calmly accepting all the manifestations of His divine and adorable will. Is there anything more consoling than these two principles, particularly when the repugnancies and revolts of nature, far from depriving us of additional merit, really increase it when we sincerely submit with the higher powers of our soul. And further, that our half involuntary fits of impatience and gloom, are but imperfections and faults, which do not destroy our submission, but only slightly diminish its merit. Remember, it is a great grace from God, not to suffer courageously on a grand scale, but in a small and humble way, thus giving occasion to be small and humble all at once." Trust in Divine Providence, suffering martyrdom in a thousand little ways every day.

Following God's Plan in Our Lives

Our lives are part of a story, a true story, written by God. *He chose us in Him (Christ) before the foundation of the world, that we should be holy and blameless before Him. (Eph. 1.4)* Just as salvation history, the inaugurating and building up of the Kingdom of God in time, has a goal towards which it is inexorably moving and is therefore a story which makes sense, which has an ending and a truly dramatic but ultimately happy one, so also the life of each Christian is a part of that story. We have a role to play in that great drama. Our lives, too, are stories written by God, with a point, a happy ending. We have a nature and if we live according to other rules than those that God has written on our heart, we will not be happy. Likewise, He has a plan for each of us, and if we set other goals we will not be happy. We cannot disrupt the script for the overall story, but we can make our own role a tragedy: Pontius Pilate for example.

Every event that comes into our lives — no matter how small (a leaf falling from a tree) — no matter apparently a result of chance —

and no matter how much a product of free decisions by human agents, cannot come into our lives without the Divine Script Writer having put it there. That is the great consolation. The story definitely involves heartbreaks. It is filled with crosses. Each one is carefully planned by the Author of History, measured out to our capacities and accompanied by sufficient helps to carry it. If we knew all the crosses that are in our personal scripts, we could never get out of bed in the morning. God hides the future from us mercifully, *Therefore do not be anxious about tomorrow, for tomorrow will be anxious for itself. Let the day's own trouble be sufficient for the day. (Mt. 6.34)*

When one embraces crosses, one finds that they had been prepared for them all along. God wrote the story. Our example for a successful life is Christ Jesus. We must embrace willingly, even eagerly, the sufferings of each day. No matter how petty, even if they be just splinters of the cross. If we do not, we not only fail to fight with Christ and to obey our Father, but we diverge from the truth of our lives. If we spend our life fleeing crosses, we do not live the role that fits us. We will be playing the complaining, frightened, bitter, lazy part, instead of the Heroic lead that we are all called to. We are all called to be saints remember. Our only interest must be: What is your will, O God? Like Jesus who came into the world saying: Lo, I have come to do your will, O God!

Trust in God

Today, the Church presents to us a number of witnesses, old and new, beginning with Elijah. He's taken as a precursor of John the Baptist who was known for his zeal in defending the law of the Lord. And St. John Fisher was, in a way, following in John the Baptist's footsteps because he was willing to give his life in defense of this teaching, the inviolability of marriage as did John the Baptist. Of course this is why John Fisher was put to death , not because King Henry disagreed with his theology. But when he wanted to marry a second time, John Fisher would not approve . Most of the other bishops, perhaps all of them in England did. Which is why at his death, Fisher had to say, "Courage has been betrayed by those who should have defended it." But, he was kept strong . He along with Moore, were the great lights of their time.

St. Thomas More's life is better known . He is proof that this level of holiness is obtainable by everybody. He was a layman. He has, in fact, a beautiful letter in the Liturgy of the Hours to his daughter which shows how far he had advanced in life in being abandoned to Divine Providence . "And finally Margaret, I know this well, that without my fault, He (God), will not let me be lost. I shall therefore with good hope commit myself wholly to Him. And if He permits me to perish from my faults, than I shall serve as praise for His justice. But in good faith, Meg, I trust that His tender pity shall keep my poor soul safe and make me commend His mercy. Therefore, my own good daughter, do not let your mind be troubled over anything that shall happen to me in this world. Nothing can come but what God wills and I am very sure that, whatever that be, however bad it may seem, it shall indeed be the best."

Both of them are great saints. But we should just note that it wasn't some great unusual thing, but rather the faithful fulfillment of their daily duties that made them into great saints. We are reminded of this by the Our Father that is presented to us here by our Lord, how we are to pray. Our spiritual life is an ordered plan. It is a routine that we should all adopt into a plan of life, of which the cornerstone would be the simple prayer that the Lord teaches us, not great babbling, but simple prayer, from the heart. St. John Fisher had a very careful plan of life. His house was like a monastery, it is said, very prayerful, very austere, very ordered. To the degree possible, St. Thomas Moore, though he lived in the world, would have done the same. So each one of us should make our lives nothing but a hymn of praise to the Father, but simple. Simple and ordered. Then , hopefully if we are called upon, we will be like Fisher and Moore.

Come and See

A quick look at some of the writings of Elizabeth Ann Seton and one is struck by her constant preoccupation with the next life. For instance, "We are not always to have what we like best in this world, thank Heaven, for if we had, we should forget the other, a place of endless peace. But better days will come, there is another and better world. Afflictions are the steps to Heaven. Eternity, that voice to be everywhere understood, eternity, to love and serve Him only, who is to be loved and eternally served and praised in Heaven."

So, although she lived so many centuries after Andrew and the other disciples, she experienced the Lord Jesus. Through prayer and the power of grace, she came and saw and stayed with Christ and experienced Him as the Messiah and she was filled with that excitement of having been saved and having all of her troubles fixed by Him. She went out and she told her children and everybody else who would listen and invited them too, to Come and See, to come and see. Be with the Lord Jesus and see how He will solve every problem, even now, but then especially and fully when we stay with Him, where He stays forever in Heaven. She drew near to Christ on earth and so it was that she felt the power and passion of dwelling with Christ forever in Heaven. That future bliss illumined all of the sad and difficult parts of her life. So, whenever we're sad, we should think of the Lord Jesus inviting us, Come and see how I can lift your burdens. When ever we're confused, Come and see how I can illumine you with my truth. Whenever we're afraid, Come and see how I have arranged everything to protect you from what is ultimately bad for you.

Just one more word of hers to some of her new sisters. "Be above the vain fears of nature and efforts of your enemies. You are children of eternity. Your immortal crown awaits you and the best of Fathers waits there to reward your duty and love. We may indeed sew here in tears, but you may be sure, there, to reap in joy."

Faith in God's Providence

The first reading tells us of what we are to expect in Heaven. It is a wonderful vision where the painful *things past* are *not remembered or called to mind* and *weeping and crying are not heard*. This is how it shall be in the *new heavens and new earth*, that God will make as our everlasting dwelling place. There as St. Augustine says — summing this up in three words — "We shall behold, we shall love, we shall praise".

Precisely because we shall behold, see God face to face, we will have no need of faith in Heaven. Faith has a role to play on earth when God's glory is hidden from us. Faith is taking God's word that He exists, loves us, is in control of our lives and destinies. If we only believe this when He is performing great prodigies, we really have not faith at all. Then He is showing his power, rather than calling forth our belief. Jesus lamented that *unless you people see signs and wonders, you do not believe*, because the need for such signs is a sign of weak faith or no faith at all.

Faith then, is not believing God exists on a lovely day, when we feel that we live in a paradise already, but rather on a cold, miserable day. Faith is believing in God's love for us when we lack people around to make that love tangible and obvious. Faith is believing in God's providence when our life seems upside down, not when things are working out perfectly. In other words, when life seems very unlike Heaven will be — when we do not see God, we cannot feel his love, and we don't feel like praising Him — that is the time to prove that we have faith. We do not see signs and wonders, Lord, but we do believe.

Suffering in Accord with God's Plan

Everybody has some experience with suffering, more or less, whether it be insults, such as James was describing, tiny inconveniences or real suffering of one sort or another, loss of children or great physical suffering itself. All suffering we know, as we think about it, is as the word in Latin suggests a certain being acted upon, a passivity, something opposed to our self actualization, a being emptied as opposed to being fulfilled, a loss of being. Again some sort of annihilation, a lack of being in control, and something, naturally, for that reason, we resist. And we can see Peter resisting it here. Yet something marvelous happens the instant we accept suffering, the instant that we see that although we might be out of control, God is never out of control.

We must see that we judge by God's standards, saying, "Lord, You must have a plan…You brought all being out of nothing, You can also bring good out of this evil. You can bring being out of this annihilation of myself. You can make me more of a person, even when I feel that I am becoming less and less. The minute we trust God in that way, then the suffering receives meaning and purpose. It becomes the way to freedom, the way of being fulfilled, of discovering who we are, accepting His will.

The Lord asks, "Who do they say that I am?" … Who are we? We discover it only in suffering. Everything we depend upon, everything that gives us strength and identity, and what we think fulfills us, when all that's taken away, be it friends, even someone with cancer, be it our hair, the way we look, when all that's taken away, as the *Imitation* says, "Naked we follow the naked Jesus," then we discover who we are, nothing, nothing before God. St. Catherine was told by Jesus, "You are nothing, and I Am." Then we discover, that although we're nothing on our own, everything we are, is in union with God. In suffering and union with God, we find who we really are and we find joy. The more we suffer with Christ the more strength, mysteriously, we discover. So let's ask the Lord to illumine these great mysteries for us and not let us flee from His plan.

Suffering Afflictions

There's a very strong theme here in the readings, which is that the Lord often appears to be found, or to be staying, on the sidelines in time of difficulty. Likewise in many of the psalms there is the refrain, "Why do you let this happen? How long will you let us be miserable?

Why are you hiding your face, forgetting our woe and oppression?" This is often our experience and very often one prays to God as this leper has, *If you will to do so, you can cure me.* But the Lord doesn't will to intervene, at least not now, at least not the way that we want. Even though, the Lord is moved by pity, always, He may not always move to solve our problems. He very often prefers that we suffer through them, suffer for a time. This is better in the long run. This, of course is the experience of all Christians and certainly all saints.

In the life of St. Anthony, there is a story that He was allowed to be afflicted terribly by the devil, himself. Then, once as he was lying there miserable, but having received a vision from the Lord, he said to Christ, "Where were you, O Good Jesus, oh, where were you? Why did you not come sooner to help me heal my wounds? And the Lord answered him in his vision, "Anthony, I was there, but I waited to see how you would fight. Now because you fought manfully, I shall make your name known over all the earth." And so it is that very often the Lord appears to be hidden or appears to ignore us in our time of need, especially, so that we will be willing to fight with Him and carry a cross with Him.

One spiritual writer, puts it in a beautiful nutshell, "If one wants to be a victim," meaning if one wants to be a willing sufferer along Christ the Lord, "to be a victim is to smile. Smile all the time, with the big sufferings and little." Ask the Lord for that grace, to smile and then one knows one's being a willing victim, to fight manfully beside the Lord.

Preparing to Suffer More

St. Agatha suffered one of the more horrific martyrdom's that I know of. I read about it in a huge old Lives of the Saints that belonged to my great aunt. It said that she was comforted by an angel in just this manner. The angel healed her in her cell *so that she could suffer more* for her Divine Spouse. When we pray for healing, as well we should, we may be healed, also, so that we can offer God another sacrifice.

Perhaps the hardest pastoral task for priests, is also their most common: consoling the suffering. It is difficult because we are called to do more than simply cheer people up. We are not here to make them forget about their troubles, so much as to encourage them to face them, bear them, even embrace them. This is to *comfort* them in the sense of strengthening them to suffer more. This is what the author of the letter to the Hebrews is doing. *You haven't even bled yet*, he

tells them. *You must prepare yourself to suffer more.* This shepherd of
souls says that it is God's way to ask his beloved to suffer and therefore we must not flee it, as nature bids us do, but embrace it as grace
enables us to do.

For those who are suffering, it is difficult to understand why God
allows it. It is a perennial problem for philosophy and even a tricky
problem for some theologies. The holy scripture read today explains it
simply as the chastisement of a Father for his son. Now this seems in-
sufficient if we think of the frightful sufferings that so many people
must endure. What kind of a Father would ask a child to suffer even
bloodshed? The answer was given yesterday. Our Heavenly Father did
ask his Son to *ignore the joy set before Him, despise the shame, and
endure the cross.* Unlike most children who endure punishment un-
willingly, Christ suffered willingly. It was not punishment for Him. It
was chosen out of love and that is why it was given without measure.
Likewise, we, if we suffer out of love, will be given more and more,
because it is not punishment but the only way we have of showing
love.

True Peace

All three of the readings today speak of peace. If we take the
more common translation of Isaiah, it says, *I will spread peace over
Jerusalem like a river...* and the prayer of Paul for us, *peace and
mercy be to all who follow this rule* then of course the Gospel which
speaks of peace a great deal. Now peace, most people would think,
and most dictionaries say, is the absence of war and other hostilities,
freedom from quarrels. But if this is all peace is, it's a non-entity, it's
like darkness, it's an absence of something else, it has no subsistence
of it's own. But then how can it be poured out like a river in this
prophecy. There must be another concept of peace, a fuller one, a very
different one in fact. If there weren't, how could the Prince of Peace,
the Lord Jesus, have said, *Do you think that I come to give peace on
earth, no I tell you, but division.* Then later He indicated that there
was indeed an inadequate, earthly kind of peace when He said, *Peace
I leave with you, My peace I give to you, not as the world gives do I
give to you.*

This worldly view of peace, understood as an absence of conflict,
wishes to eliminate war by eliminating everything worth fighting for.
This new gospel, we could call the gospel of toleration, of anything
and anyone. There is another kind of false peace which would be
achieved by sacrificing the good and the true in ourselves. No more

need to struggle for moral virtue, no more difficult quests for intellectual advancement for truth, but rather find a sort of peace in self indulgence and passivity, a counterfeit kind of peace, a temporary and superficial kind of rest.

So much for the false peace, but what's the kind of peace that Christ Jesus came to give us? What is the permanent and profound kind of rest that is the goal of our religion? It's very central to all we do. If you notice at Mass how often we mention the word, "peace". It's at Mass that the Prince of Peace comes to us with His presence and establishes peace on earth. *He is our Peace,* as Paul says, and He came to give peace especially when He rose from the dead. So many times He greeted them, *Peace be with you."* This was the essence of the gospel that He asked to be preached. So the first words of His disciples were said to be, *Peace to this household.* And notice how different this peace is than mere absence, it's something which could rest on them and if it was rejected, it returned to the apostles. This reality is mysterious indeed, St. Paul poses it, *The peace of God surpasses understanding.*

Why is it mysterious? Because it's a first effect, an aspect of the Kingdom of God, the kingdom of Heaven on earth. Christ came to bring that Heavenly kingdom into contact with our earth to somehow establish it here. This is what they were to preach, the kingdom of God is at hand for you, and this was the peace they were to experience, first of all in their hearts. The God of Peace had established Himself in their hearts,... *and the Peace of Christ ruleth in your hearts.* This is what makes us into new creations that Paul talks about, citizens of that kingdom where peace is perfected, where peace flows like a river. And here on earth, that part of the kingdom that Christ came to establish through His apostles, we have just a seed or beginning of, that kingdom of Heaven. It will only be perfect in the Heavenly kingdom because from there evil has been completely cast out as our Lord said, *I observed Satan falling like lightening from the sky.*

There we will have perfect peace, and what is the image that the Holy Spirit has chosen for that perfect peace? A nursling carried in his mothers arms in that prophecy of Isaiah. And why is the infant who has just finished feeding the perfect example of Heavenly peace? Because He has no other desires whatsoever, total contentment, and this is what Heaven is, to have every conceivable desire of body and soul satisfied. We want nothing more, once we have the fullness of God. This is the perfect image of Peace and we have to begin to experience that peace here on earth. There's many other places in holy scripture where peace is exhorted upon us, and sometimes the very same image is used, such as in this psalm, 131. *I have set my soul upon His peace, like a child quieted at his mother's breast, like a child is quieted even so my soul.* So if we're going to begin to find peace on earth we have to somehow have all our desires quieted like child on the mother's breast.

Now the wrong way to achieve this peace is to go about trying to satisfy all our desires. This leads sometimes to a temporary, illusory peace, but eventually always to frustration and futility. St. Paul teaches us this when he says, *To set the mind on the flesh is death, but to set the mind on the spirit is life and peace.* That's why he boasted that, *the world has been crucified to me and I to the world* or as he put it in another place, *those who belong to Christ have crucified the flesh with its passions and desires.* This is the road to peace. As Isaiah said, *The body will flourish like the grass and the heart will rejoice,* but only in Heaven. And now all the goods and pleasures in this life are only to be indications pointing us toward that Heavenly kingdom, they should never distract us, waylay us, or divert us, from our Heavenly goal, or we will lose all peace here and hereafter.

To make sure that our passions are ordered to our final goal we have to keep them under a strict discipline. God's peace then will be the fruit of a battle, of constant combat. The world's peace is the avoidance of that fight. We must remember that we're not pacifists, and certainly not in the spiritual life which is a constant combat. But our Lord assured us of the victory when He said, *I have said this to you that in Me you may have peace. In the world there are tribulations, but be of good cheer, I have overcome the world.* So we must fight to attain this genuine peace through self denial and asceticism and we must keep it secure in our hearts for it is in the hearts of good people that the kingdom of God exists. The evil one will try to destroy this peace with all his might. This is why he sends temptations, first of all, indeed, to make us sin, but second of all his goal would be to get us upset, to discourage us in this battle, and we must fight this very strongly. St. Francis de Sales for instance says, "Do not lose your inward peace for anything, whatsoever, even if your whole world is upset, do not burden yourself with a host of cares, wishes or longings under any pretext whatever." So if we're to stay on tract for that eternal rest symbolized by the baby on his mother's arms then we must rest even now in our Heavenly Father's hands, in His care, being content with whatever befalls us, knowing that it comes from Him for our good.

The disciples rejoiced when they returned from their mission of spreading the kingdom on earth and subduing the evil spirits but Christ reminded them that they should be rejoicing most of all that their names were written in Heaven, that they were headed for that Heavenly rest. Likewise we too should fight to build up the kingdom of Heaven here on earth, the civilization of love in our homes, our families, our society, but we must remember that Christ didn't come to perfect this world and we shouldn't seek to find our happiness or peace in it, rather all the progress we make is to help us, and others, toward that ultimate goal. Our Lord Jesus has come to teach us what true peace is. He is our Peace, and so as long as we long only for Him than we will find the truest peace here on earth and the guarantee of that river of peace in the life to come.

Grace

Hidden With Christ through Grace

"In Christ, God has raised us up with Him, and has made us sit with Him in the Heavenly places".(St. Anastasius) Another way of putting this mystery of Christ's presence in the world is to say that He is always present, from the time of his first coming to his second, in the Church. He is continually coming to the world through the Church. And so, one can speak of a third coming of Christ: His coming into the hearts of each one of us. *Behold*, He said, *I stand at the door and knock*. In addition to recalling his coming at Bethlehem and looking for his *parousia*, we must be on the lookout for Him "when He comes day after day to stir our consciences" (Pasc. Radbertus) This ninth century author continues, "He comes to us now in order that his future coming may find us prepared... Only if Christ is already living in me and I in Him will it go well with me when He comes in judgment."

The Church asks us to turn our attention to various themes which can be linked by the thread of *grace*. First, we turn to God the Father who adopts us as his sons by sharing his divine nature with us through the gift of grace. We also focus on the theological virtue of Charity, which is the finest work of grace. Grace sanctifies us and the fullness of the Christian life is the perfection of charity. *(LG 40)* We are asked to meditate in a special way on *Mary, full of grace*. For "Grace is *favor*, the *free* and *undeserved* help that God gives us to respond to his call to become children of God, adoptive sons, partakers of the divine nature and of eternal life." *(CCC1996)*. Christ had two natures — divine and human; by grace, we though remaining human, share in his divine nature.

When did Christ first come to our souls to inhabit them, changing them into something holy, if not at baptism? That is when we received grace, sanctifying grace. This grace enables us to perform, literally, superhuman acts. On our own, we cannot perform acts that will merit eternal reward, but with grace — which St. Augustine described as "God working within us, without us" — we can. It is grace that enables saints to draw so many to the faith, to pray so long and so effectively, to write stacks of learned books, to smile beatifically when wracked with bodily ills, even to die at the hands of torturers blessing their enemies.

Only someone in the state of grace lives in God's friendship. A single conscious and willed offense in a serious matter destroys this friendship. One may not feel at all different, but one has crashed from Heaven, where a baptized soul is *hidden with Christ in God* (Col.3.3)) to earth, just as Our Lord said of the devil: *I saw Satan fall from the sky*. This grace that we receive not only grants access to Heaven, but the place we will have there. One can have more grace or less. This divine life in us can be more vigorous, robust, energetic or less; we can be healthier or grow weak. If only we knew how vital it was to see that we were always growing in sanctifying grace! It is so much more important than growing stronger, but see how hard athletes train; it is so much more important than being beautiful, yet see how many people diet while so few will fast!; so much more important than being well off, yet see how hard people work, even when their needs are met; it so much more important than learning or fame or power. The tiniest increase in merit — which is only possible through grace — is of an altogether different order and eternal besides. Let this be our overriding concern.

How does one grow in grace? By prayer, sacraments, and good works. Prayer is not a discharging of a duty so much as a necessity for maintaining this divine life in us. We could survive in a state of grace without prayer as easily as our natural life could survive without air or food. We must draw close to God, and beg Him to take up a greater presence in our souls. The sacraments are the ordinary means for growing in grace. Besides beginning our life of grace at baptism and renewing it with sacramental penance, all the other five sacraments increase grace in us. Finally, living in grace, every good work we do merits an increase in grace as well as a reward in Heaven. Let us long for this great gift of grace. *If you knew the gift of God*! He is coming to meet each one of us by an increase of grace.

Purity of heart

O Lord of hosts, you who test the just, who prove mind and heart... What terrifying words we hear today. The All-holy knows our inmost thoughts and... *Nothing is concealed that will not be revealed, nor secret that will not be known.* St. Paul echoes the point writing to the Churches of Corinth and Rome: *[When]the Lord comes [He] will bring to light the things now hidden in darkness and will disclose the purposes of the heart. (I Cor.4.5)... on that day when , according to my gospel, God judges the secrets of men by Christ Jesus (Rom.2.16).*

The societies of Corinth and Rome were overrun especially by sexual sins. The unruliness of people's thoughts and passions which cause shame and the desire to keep them secret is nowhere more apparent than in this area. Last week the Holy Father made purity of heart the theme of one of his homilies to the Polish people. "The culture of death is determined to destroy purity of heart. One of its strategies is to deliberately create doubt about the value of the human attitude which we call the virtue of chastity... A culture which in this way impairs or even destroys a correct relationship between individuals, is a culture of death, for man cannot live without love". Worse still, failure to keep one's heart pure can lead to eternal death. The Pope reminded his audience that a pure heart is "a condition we need to fulfill, in order to encounter God, to know Him and to be united to Him". Did not the Lord say *Blessed are the pure of heart, for they shall see God?* And St. Paul again leaves no room for doubt, heading his list of "works of the flesh" with *immorality, impurity, licentiousness* and concluding *I warn you, as I warned you before, that those who do such things shall not inherit the kingdom of God (Gal 5.21).* Indeed "nothing" writes St. Thomas Aquinas "leads more quickly to contempt of God" or leads one further from Him (cf. St. Alph. Lig.).

But let us lift up our eyes and our hearts to the wonderful possibilities of grace! Did not St. Paul hasten to add: *But the gift is not like the transgression? The gracious gift of the one man Jesus Christ* overflows for many, lifting them up and over the pull of concupiscence into the glorious *freedom of the sons of God. For freedom Christ has set us free!* It may be, as St. Augustine noted, that in the realm of lust "The combat is common and the victory rare", but sufficient grace is given to all to win this battle. How glorious that victory is! Is there anything more beautiful than those persons who live in our climate of filth while maintaining (even if they had to regain it at some point) their child-like innocence? They *shine like stars*, giving us a glimpse of heavenly love.

To attain purity of heart requires two principles, principles given by our Lord: *Watch and pray that you enter not into temptation, the spirit is willing but the flesh is weak (Mt. 26.41)*. Watch is the first principle. Be on guard against temptations, however slight and ubiquitous they may seem, and flee them at once. Trust the Lord that one can be happy without dubious sorts of entertainment; indeed, one can only really be happy without them. To eliminate them, to stay clear of even "borderline" areas requires a radical lifestyle choice. But the Lord Jesus Christ is radical. *I say to you that every one who looks at a woman lustfully has already committed adultery with her in his heart. If your right eye causes you to sin, pluck it out and throw it away; it is better that you lose one of you members than that your whole body be thrown into Hell. (Mt. 5.28-29)*. We could add that it is better to enter life without a TV or Internet, than to go with all these things into Hell.

Remember that in this area, every offense involves grave matter. In other words, although all lying is wrong, tiny lies, "white" lies are not mortal sins. Or, although all theft is wrong, stealing a paper clip is not much of a sin. But in the realm of impurity, every willfully entertained disordered desire extinguishes the life of grace in the soul. This is because persons are involved, and persons can never be treated as objects, but as sisters and brothers in Christ. Besides, anyone who flees temptations when they are small, will gain the victory, never encountering temptations that are too great for him.

The second principle: Pray. Watch and pray, said the Lord. Purity is a gift from God. Wise old Solomon knew this: *And as I knew that I could not otherwise be continent, except God gave it... I went to the Lord and besought Him.(Wis.8.21)* The struggle for purity is not a psychological battle, but a spiritual one. We need the help of the angels and saints, especially St. Joseph. Put holy images in your house, on your TV, on your computer. Take them, and holy water on your business trips. Pray especially to the Blessed Virgin: "Mother most pure", "Mother most chaste", "Mother inviolate", "Mother undefiled". She will obtain for all of us a heart which is pure, full of genuine love for God and neighbor.

Chastity

We see in this Gospel how they praise God for giving such authority to men, which is a sort of echo of when the Lord tells us to do all of our works so that *'people will see your good works and give glory to God.'* In other words, we too, can cause people to praise God by living in such a way that it's clear that it is the grace of God at work in us. In no virtue is this more clear than in the virtue of chastity. Because of our fallen nature, we are so weak in that area that we cannot keep the dictates of the natural law without the help of grace. Then especially when people go so far as to live consecrated chastity, virginity for the kingdom of Heaven, what a stunning witness that is, because it's clearly only possible through the grace of God.

Today we have this great saint, Saint Maria Goretti, to teach us this great lesson. Pius X11 both beatified her in 1947 and then canonized her during the Holy Year in 1950. No doubt he was keenly aware of the attacks under which human dignity was coming because of the changes in western culture against chastity. So in making Maria Goretti a saint and a model for the Church, and in proclaiming Mother Mary's holiness in body and soul, he helped to defend this truth of our faith, this truth about this virtue of chastity and the need of God's grace to be chaste. I'll read several quotes from Pius XII and you'll see how they all turn on this point of the need for God's grace.

Likening St. Maria to St. Agnes, he said, "They both had strong hearts, strong in that supernatural strength, whose germ every Christian receives in Baptism." Later, after lamenting the weakness of so many people who fall into sins of the flesh, he says, "All the more we must admire the strength of pure hearts. It is a mysterious power, it is a strength which out strips the limits of human nature and often enough the limits of ordinary Christian virtue. It is the bond of love for the Divine Spouse." ... "Maria was not guided simply by natural sentiments of reserve, though still very young we can catch a glimpse in her of a deep and intense love for our Divine Redeemer." He goes on to say that this was nourished especially through Holy Communion. "She did not hesitate to travel a long dusty road in mid-summer, under scorching sun, to receive Jesus in Holy Communion. 'I don't know what time tomorrow I will receive Holy Communion,' she said one day. That tomorrow was to come and that Communion, but what a tomorrow and what a Communion! For the very next afternoon of that day on which she spoke those words, she shed her blood to remain faithful to her spouse, a virgin."

After commenting upon the great changes that were taking place in society, in the 1950's, he said, "Such deep and speedy alterations, certainly will bring about most grave consequences to religion and morals of women, therefore it is necessary to strengthen in women those deep personal and supernatural values that shone in our saint. There must be a spirit of faith and modesty, not merely natural modesty and decency, but a carefully cultivated Christian virtue." Then turning to what he said when he canonized her, "At that moment of crisis, she could have spoken to her Redeemer in the words of that classic *The Imitation of Christ*, 'Though tested in faith by a host of misfortunes, I have no fear so long as your grace is with me, it is my strength, stronger than any adversary, that helps me and gives me guidance.' " And later, speaking of parents and of how they raise children, he says that, "Parents can then learn to train them in the Catholic Faith, that when put to the test, God's grace will support them and they will come through undefeated, unscathed and untarnished. With determination and God's help all of us can attain that goal by persistent effort and prayer." He concludes, "So let us all with God's grace strive to reach the goal that the example of the virgin martyr, St. Maria Goretti, sets before us."

So while we would necessarily despair, living in the culture that we do, on our own, with our own strength, rather, looking at our own weakness with God's grace we should be full of hope and so he closes his first talk with a beautiful affirmation of our hope in God's Grace. "Our hope is not in vain, thus we do not hesitate to repeat here the words of the Apostle Paul, *'Where sin abounds, grace abounds all the more!'* Behold the Church, the ranks of those who believe, who pray, who impose heavy sacrifices on themselves, they grow and form, even among the youth. They squarely reject what is against God's will and wisdom. They are restless until they have brought back to Christ and His law their friends and associates who have fallen away from God. They are our comfort and joy.

The Joy of Belonging to God

St. Paul certainly has choice words for those who sin against chastity, here and many other places. What would he say if he had known about television? I don't know. But he says something which tells why Chastity is a virtue that has been so exalted and so spoken of by Christians in particular. He says when he refers to it, no lustful person, in effect an idolater, will enter the kingdom of Heaven. That's so key. In this letter to the Romans he says that those who would not worship the true God, though they could have or should have known Him, instead began to worship animals. He says that God gave them up to their passions and they did all kinds of horrible things.

This is so important, the relationship between chastity and God. In fact, there's a beautiful definition I came upon by a Spanish priest who defines chastity thus. "Chastity is the joy of belonging to God." This is something we must think about a lot because we think about chastity usually only in terms of a virtue that guides our social relationships with others. But in fact, when we meditate on the value of the human person body and soul, it has everything to do with our relationship to God. On the contrary, unchastity is the expression of a empty soul, a soul that does not have God within it. As a result of that there is a constant turning toward the exterior, the superficial, toward self — revelation in inappropriate ways.

There is then such a thing called Spiritual Chastity, which is guarding the soul for God. Spiritual Chastity is related to silence, discretion, humility, modesty, all those particularly Christian virtues. Worship of God comes through having the soul remain a sanctuary, a sanctuary where God dwells, which is kept for God alone in secret. So a spiritually chaste person is one who goes into his room to pray to God in secret, one who doesn't let his right hand know what his left hand is doing and so on. The temple of their soul belongs to God. So let us not forget that phrase, "Chastity is the joy of belonging to God."

Superhuman Tasks

The Apostles are so great and of course the liturgy praises them as the glorious band of Apostles. We remember our Lord's words to them in Revelation, that they would be on twelve thrones, judging the tribes of Israel, that they would be the foundation stones for the New Jerusalem. We think of all the wonderful things they did, the powers that Christ gave them to go out and cast out devils as He did, to heal people, to preach the kingdom so effectively. Think of how they suffered terrible martyrdom's without giving up the faith, and of St. Jude's great letter to be read until the end of time.

So the Apostles, they did so many great things. But then we have to remember how they were just ordinary men. Simon, from a small town in Cana, and Jude Thaddeus, whose name means 'courageous one', but he also, just a normal man of his time. Both of them perhaps cousins of the Lord Jesus. But they were very ordinary men and they remained that way throughout all those wonderful things that they did. This is described by Blessed Jose Escriva, this funny mixture. " *'Do you not yet perceive, or understand,'* Jesus said to them, *'is your heart still blinded?' Though you have eyes you do not see, though you have ears, you do not hear.'* They were not educated, nor were they even very bright, judging from their reaction to the supernatural, when even the most elementary examples and comparisons are beyond their grasp. They turn to their Master and ask, 'Explain the parable to us.' when Jesus uses the metaphor of the yeast of the Pharisees, they think He's reproaching them for not buying bread. So ordinary were the disciples Christ chose that they remain unchanged till the Holy Spirit fills them and they grow into pillars of the Church."

Nevertheless they remain the everyday sort of men, complete with defects and short comings. Of course this applies very well to us, because we are often overwhelmed with the lot that we're given. We come into this life with all sorts of responsibilities and burdens that we didn't choose ourselves and they often seem too much for us, then what the Lord asks us on top, to be apostles ourselves, to bear burdens with joy, to suffer those who oppose us and to love those who oppose us. All these things certainly seem too much for us. They are superhuman tasks in fact, if you think especially of great suffering, of bearing cancer with full resignation, or having to help a very ill or autistic child, or a mother with altzheimers. All these terrible problems and to bear them all with deep resignation and even joy, is certainly a superhuman task and yet we're so human.

The sacraments we receive don't take away that humanity, that ordinariness. They do give us the ability, like the Apostles, to somehow rise up to the task of living a superhuman life. We have to remember, as was the case with them, that Christ chose them for this. *You have not chosen Me, I have chosen you*. Then, like them, we will get to dwell with the Lord, Jesus Christ, get to know Him and live with Him, and speak with Him. And like them, finally Christ is dwelling in us. It is in fact the answer to a question by Jude Thaddeus, in John '14. *Lord, how is it that you will manifest yourself to us, but not to the world.* The Lord revealed this great truth, perhaps the greatest of all, that *the Trinity will come and make our home within you.* We have all of that as well to help us, so always remaining human, we may rise up to our superhuman tasks.

Doing the Impossible

Yesterday the Lord Jesus asked His disciples to do something that was clearly beyond their powers. They saw the huge crowds there, they had practically nothing with them, then He says, *You give them something to eat.* Something impossible to them. Then today we see again the Lord saying, *Come, walk across the water to Me.* Something, perhaps even more impossible for a mere mortal man to do. The Lord does ask us to do the impossible. He's not interested in what we can do with our human natural powers, efforts, but only what we can do with grace, His power. He doesn't hesitate to ask us to do the impossible, many of the things He asks us, people make the mistake to think that they are naturally possible. Take for instance, a holy

Christian marriage, indissoluble until death, with all the challenges of raising a family, chastity in general, certainly chastity for the kingdom of God, all of these are naturally impossible, at least for fallen human nature, but with God all things are possible. We only succeed in all these tasks the Lord gives us, we only can keep all of His commandments, the ten commandments, but also the greatest commandment of love to which the Lord leads us, we can only do this with His power.

Without an intimate relationship with the Christ Jesus, we tend to close down all of our horizons to a human level, to what seems possible, to what seems prudent, and this is a great mistake. The Lord has high ambitions for us, high ambitions for Christians in His Church. So we must keep that relationship with Christ in His horizons. It will be His power within us, but we must not also forget that our cooperation is absolutely necessary. St. John Chrysostom said, "When our cooperation is lacking, God also refuses to help us."

There are two main areas that the Lord is demanding of us this impossible task. It is to conquer two kingdoms, to install the Reign of God in two places, the first is within us, the second is outside of us. The Lord wishes that Christ Jesus, Himself, rule our hearts, be King of our entire person, there be no more dissention and disorder within us. St. Dominic spoke of this, he says, "A man who governs his passions is master of the world, we must either command them, or be enslaved by them, it is better to be the hammer than the anvil." Remember it will only be with God's grace, His power, that we will be able to restore order within ourselves and be able to overcome the disorder that is ours through original sin. St. Dominic points out that it is a prerequisite to also installing the kingdom of God around us and having it spread beyond us, by first having the Lord rule in our hearts.

The second area is of conquering the world around us for the Kingdom of God. We have a beautiful example in St. Dominic. He was a Spaniard but he found himself living in a time of terrible conflict, the heresies of the Waldensians and Albegensians had spread throughout Europe like wildfire. Some people lived a very rigorous and exaggerated spirituality and others thought that if it can't touch our souls, we can do whatever we like with our bodies, and there was terrible immorality, general chaos, reaching the heights of violence. Also the efforts to put it down were terribly violent, burning at the stake and burning whole cities. It was into this terrible situation that St. Dominic arrived with his Bishop. The Bishop went back to Spain to get help, leaving Dominic age twenty-four, practically by himself to fight this battle. One of the first things Dominic did was to found a monastery of cloistered nuns who would support his preaching ministry by their prayers. It shows that he knew that this impossible task of converting Europe would not be possible by himself alone, but with the help of the Lord, he succeeded.

We can't fail to see the similarities between the history of days gone by and history of today. A heresy was at the root of that terrible disregard for the nature of man, likewise today the same terrible disregard for the dignity of human life is at the heart of the culture of death. Just as he was faced with an impossible task, so also are we, just as the Church conquered through it's saints in those days, so also for us, nothing is impossible to you says the Lord Jesus Christ. With faith in Him we can certainly overcome all odds. Did not St. John say this is what overcomes the world, our faith? Not only our faith but our love, St. Dominic preached with great love. Let us work with love for the conversion of these people who are bringing havoc to our faith. Let us ask the Lord then through the intercession of St. Dominic to strengthen our faith and our love and make us bold preachers of the truth about man and about God and to fear not the odds, remember the Lord Jesus, *get a hold of yourselves and I am with you, do not be afraid.*

The Value of a Soul

Both St. James and Our Lord are talking about salvation. We usually say salvation of our souls, and in fact in that short passage the Lord uses four times the word psyche, from which we get the word psychology or the Latin 'anima', soul, translated here as himself or life. The Catechism explains, "In Sacred Scripture the term soul often refers to human life or the entire human person, but the soul also refers to the innermost aspect of man. That which is of greatest value in him, that by which he is most especially in God's image. The soul signifies the spiritual principle in man."

The Lord is trying to show us how incredibly valuable that most valuable part of us is. Because what does it profit a man to gain the whole world and destroy himself, to lose his soul in the process. Even just on a natural plain, the soul is a fabulously valuable thing, the second Vatican Council calls it 'the seed of eternity', it's not like anything else on the face of the earth. Pascal makes a big point of saying how all of creation that can be seen is nothing compared to the value of one single soul. Besides being, by its own nature, the most important thing, also it can be elevated by grace. This makes the soul much more important still and St. Thomas says, "The good of grace in one, is greater than the good of nature in the whole universe."

That's something that can be meditated on a great deal. And to see how startling that can be, we have the same doctrine slightly in reverse put by St. John Neuman. "The Catholic Church holds it better for the sun and moon to drop from heaven, for the earth to fail, and for all the many millions on it to die of starvation in extremest agony, as far as temporal affliction goes, than that one soul, I will not say should be lost, but should commit one single venial sin, should tell one willful untruth, or should steal one poor farthing without excuse." This tells us how valuable a soul is, how infinitely valuable is a soul in grace. Because the soul is something the Lord Jesus assumed to Himself and sanctified. And He gave his life on the cross, not just for all people in general, but for each and every one of us. As St. Paul says, *He gave up His life, He died for me.*

So let us thank the Lord this Friday for the sacrifice made on one Friday long ago. Let's ask Him for the grace to never ever offend Him willfully, even in the smallest matter.

Purification and Sanctity

Feast of All Saints

"We all want to live happily; in the whole human race there is no one who does not assent to this proposition, even before it is fully articulated" (St.Augustine). We all want to be happy. The question is, How? The reason why today is such a joyful feast is because we celebrate the proof that we Christians know how. We're the only ones who do! The saints are proof that in every epoch, in every culture, in every situation — even the most dire and dreadful, happiness is possible. It's always possible. God's power to raise up is greater than any power to cast down: *in all these things we are more than conquerors through Him who loved us* — supervincimus! — *this is what conquers the world — our faith.* The Saints are our proof, living, historical proof, that God's almighty power, which conquered on the Cross, will conquer any obstacle before his followers. So today, we "rejoice in the Lord and keep festival in honor of all the saints. [We] join with the angels in joyful praise to the Son of God" (ent. ant.).

Canonized saints are persons who have been declared infallibly by the Church on earth to be living in Heaven, members of the Church Triumphant. They are happy now as they enjoy the "beatific vision". Yet, they were happy on earth. Yes, this is important. No matter what they endured, they were happy on earth. "A sad saint is a sad saint indeed". They made the Sermon on the Mount their program of life, and they learned that the Lord was giving a program of life by which to achieve "beatitude", become "blessed", even in this life. Did He not say that He came that our joy might be complete; and that we would receive great rewards *in this age* with persecution, and eternal life in the next?(*Mk. 10:30*).

The words of our Lord, which we have just heard, are not hyperbole — a literary device to motivate us; they are not naive overestimation of the capacity of human nature; they are not empty idealism — they are the lights along the path to happiness for each and every person on the face of this earth. Christ knows us — He knows *what is in the heart of man*, but He knows also that *Nothing is impossible with God.* when He called us to *love one another as I* (Christ) *have loved you*, He knew what He was saying. Obviously it is only possible to imitate Christ by his grace. Without Him, we can do nothing. But *I can do all things in Him who strengthens me.* This is the key to our ambition, to our hope. In Him, our Strength, we can hope to conquer every enemy in the battle of life and win for ourselves Heaven at its end: *the Kingdom of Heaven suffers violence,* He said, *and the violent bear it away.* If all the power is from Christ, then our inertia, our weakness, our sinfulness, our denseness — are not excuses. We can become saints too! And, in the lives of the saints, don't we find that they had all of our human faults, and more?

If we **can** become saints, then we **must**. It is not an option. Christ followed this list of the beatitudes with the command: *Be ye perfect as your Heavenly Father is perfect.* The Universal Call to Holiness is a command. As Mother Teresa says — "[becoming a saint] is not the privilege of a few but a simple duty for you and for me". The Second Vatican Council made this call ring out loud and clear to all of the one billion Catholics on this planet: "It is therefore quite clear that all Christians in any state or walk of life are called to the fullness of Christian life and to the perfection of love, ... the holiness of the People of God will grow in fruitful abundance, as is clearly shown in the history of the Church and the life of so many saints." *(LG 40)* Remember — holiness is happiness. We are persons who tend to make ourselves miserable and God commands us to choose to be happy. We will only be happy and holy when we want what God wants. God wants us to be happy; He knows what is good for us better than we do. Only in this context does Christian morality make sense. The commandments allow the happy life to bud; the beatitudes describe it in its full bloom. Only in this context does the problem of suffering have a solution. God will draw good out of evil; He looks to our ultimate good, while we suffer in the present. Every saint suffered with love and generosity — that is their common denominator. Remember, there is no presumption involved in having this ambition — to be happy, to be a great saint. It is God's will for you and for me. In fact, we were all saints once — when we were baptized. The Saints we honor today, according to the Second Vatican Council, simply knew "how, with the help of God, to conserve and perfect during their life the sanctification they received in Baptism" *(LG 40)*.

The first step is to realize the importance of being a saint. This is the reason we exist. One person who reaches the perfection of Christian life gives more glory to God than the conversion of a hundred sinners. There is a great mystery at work here. The good we do goes up more than exponentially with the sanctity, the degree of charity, of the one doing it. The second step is to desire this goal with all one's heart. St. Thomas Aquinas was asked what is necessary to become a saint and he answered with one word: *Velle*. Desire it. Ask for it. Any holiness at all is pure gift. Pray that your heart expand. The third step is to read the lives of the saints to see that it is possible. Only, do not think that the great deeds they achieved are so far beyond you that you cannot be holy. They were found faithful in little, so they were given charge over much. But their holiness began, and largely consisted in, the little things of every day. Do little things with great love. Never say: I might be able to do great things for God if.... No, everything we need to take the biggest step possible towards God is right before us all the time. We must simply make the thousand choices of each day, one thousand YESes to God. Finally, don't wait until you are a saint to be happy. Because, as a wise French writer, said earlier this century: "There is only one reason to be sad: that we are not saints."

All Souls

There is a manner of speaking about the Church, the body of Christ, in its fullest sense, which we have all heard, but probably not recently. This way of expressing the transcendent and mysterious nature of the Church, by dividing it into three neat categories, is very helpful for understanding the Church's liturgical celebrations at the beginning of November. Yesterday, we celebrated All Saints day, which was a time of rejoicing in the triumph, not of canonized saints only, but of the entire "Church Triumphant", all the souls in Heaven. We who did the celebrating have been, in this manner of speaking, called the "Church Militant". Thus the hymn says: "We feebly struggle while they in glory shine". Now today, on All Souls day, we turn our attention to the third part of the Church: those who have finished struggling, but have not yet come into their final reward. The term "Church suffering" indicates all the souls still undergoing purification after passing from this life. Upon first being reminded of the phrase, "the Church suffering", many of us might wince. Present among us are the families of many of our parishioners who died this year, sometimes after long battles with disease or other sufferings. Typically, the loved ones of the deceased, in such cases, will console themselves with the thought – "At least now she is at peace, her suffering over" – and so the thought of a "Church suffering" is difficult to bear.

However, in this, as always, our faith well understood will bring great consolation. We must recall, in the first place, that there is no law that we must pass through Purgatory after death or that our stay will be a long one. Some of those we honor in a special way tonight, especially those who bore an illness bravely, offering their suffering to the Lord in loving acceptance, would no doubt have been more properly honored yesterday – on All Saints Day. But we are right not to canonize our loved ones too quickly, and to presume that the vast majority of us will require a period of passive purification upon leaving this world. Still, there is no reason to shrink from the consideration of Purgatory. Once we unburden ourselves of false concepts and images, we will find that it is an aspect of God's mercy, His Fatherly correction of His children's imperfections. In particular, it is right to say that a soul in Purgatory is "at peace" in this sense: the will of the deceased is entirely in accord with the will of God: "No peace is comparable to that of the souls in Purgatory, except that of the saints in Heaven" (St. Catherine of Genoa). The soul knows that Heaven is guaranteed and agrees that she is not yet ready to enter. In the words of Cardinal Ratzinger: "Purgatory... is the inwardly necessary process of transformation... a constant readiness for reform which marks the forgiven sinner."

In order to embrace the teaching on Purgatory, we must also purify our understanding of suffering. The "great suffering" that the "poor souls" experience is united simultaneously with "great joy" (St. Catherine). They see clearly the purpose of the suffering and the littleness of the price compared to eternal glory. The separation from eternal bliss is experienced as a very great pain, but the assurance of union with God is the source of consolation that we cannot imagine. Only the mystics have come close to experiencing this sort of blessed agony. They find it hard to describe, but they acknowledge that the Dark Nights of the Spiritual Life count as their Purgatory here on earth. Nonetheless, even as a correct understanding of Purgatory should remove our anxiety about it, it should increase our desire to limit souls' time there. It will always be a Plan B, in God's Providence, who wants all souls to come to Heaven and as soon as possible. That is the purpose of this commemoration: to make intercessory prayer, especially the offering of the Sacrifice of the Mass, so that many souls will be enabled to enter very soon into the joys of Heaven.

We should also recall the ways that Christ offers us to avoid Purgatory entirely. First, many have held that one who dies after a great act of charity, most obviously Martyrdom, would go straight to Heaven, in accord with the Scripture: *charity covers a multitude of sins*. This is a reason to accept most generously the manner of death that Providence gives you: a heroic, uncomplaining carrying of the Cross through cancer treatments, for instance, is designed to ready us for Heaven. Secondly, Jesus extends to us, through his Church, the possibility of purifying our souls by acts which communicate to us the merits of His own suffering. Ways of mystically uniting ourselves to his Passion. Thus, the devout reception of the Sacrament of the Sick, can ready the soul, in the view of St. Thomas Aquinas, for immediate entry into Heaven. Likewise, indulgences also complete the sacrament of reconciliation by freeing us from any temporal punishment due our sins. We can also gain indulgences for those who have died. Thirdly, and finally, we can avoid Purgatory, not by any extraordinary act of charity or gift of grace, but by the constant, persevering growth in charity under the influence of grace, by, in other words, heroic fidelity to the spiritual life. We are all called to progressively transform ourselves, ridding ourselves of venial sin, leading lives of penance and generous self-sacrifice. As mentioned before, it is possible to do our Purgatory on Earth, by answering heartily the "universal call to sanctity".

Let us conclude with the words of the great Cardinal Newman who united his theological acumen to his poetic genius in the *Dream of Gerontius*. In the following section, a person who has just died has learned that he has gained salvation but realizes too that he is not ready for Heaven yet:

"Take me away, and in the lowest deep
There let me be
And there in hope the long night-watches keep,
Told out for me.
There, motionless and happy in my pain,
Lone, not forlorn,
There will I sing my sad perpetual strain,

Until the morn,
There will I sing, and soothe my stricken breast,
Which ne'er can cease
To throb, and pine, and languish, till possest
Of its Sole Peace.
There will I sing my absent Lord and Love
Take me away
That sooner I may rise, and go above,
And see Him in the truth of everlasting day.

Christian Seriousness

All Souls day is an unsurpassed opportunity to speak about what we might call Christian Seriousness. What could be more sobering than turning our attention to that vast array of souls, who have gone before us and who are still not ready to enter Heaven? These were good people, who died in the friendship of Christ, many with the consolation of the Sacraments, some after long service as priests or nuns, but, because, when they had the chance, they didn't strive strenuously enough to purify their souls and grow in charity, they now suffer dreadfully to see their eternal happiness delayed. Certainly, they experience peace and joy, too, knowing that Heaven will be theirs, but what a sobering message they would have for us! "Do not concern yourself with so much junk, my dear descendents — rather focus on the *one thing necessary* — pleasing Jesus, doing God's will. That is all."

The very thought that we have souls – that we are not like the trees or the stars or the creatures of the earth that are here one day and gone the next, but that we are naturally immortal, possessing an indestructible spiritual element – this very thought makes life a serious matter. It gives our choices eternal consequences. In the words of the great Cardinal Newman: "So great a thing is it to understand that we have souls, that the knowing it, taken in connection with its results, is all one with *being serious*, i.e. truly religious. To discern our immortality is necessarily connected with fear and trembling and repentance, in the case of every Christian".

So the great doctor identifies being serious with being truly religious. This requires some commentary. Our first idea of a serious, religious figure is likely to be something like a caricature of a Puritan: dour, gloomy, severe, equating fun with sin, etc. So far is this from an authentic Christian, that it can be considered the opposite: every Saint I know of has had a ready smile, a quick wit, and an indulgent side where others are concerned; true Christians know the value of the created world in God's plan and thus all that is "human", including life's little joys and pleasures, are opportunities for praising God and building up our fellowman.

What is the key to authentic Christian seriousness? It's orienting one's life in light of the great truths, especially the Last Things – Heaven, Hell, Death, Judgment – so that from this perspective everything gets put in its proper place, given its due attention and no more. Such a perspective doesn't crowd out all of life's minor delights – why should it? These are the wildflowers that God has placed along our journey to cheer us up – but it will prevent us from becoming attached to those flowers along the way, so that we never get to our destination, or get there very late.

One reason why we must develop this attitude is that apparently minor and harmless matters can really trip us up. St. John of the Cross makes the famous observation that a bird can be prevented from flying equally effectively by a golden thread as by an iron chain. Even little things, the most fleeting satisfactions or trifling amusements, can draw our will away from God. Consider, for example, how little pleasure one gets from making an insulting but witty remark about someone else – a little laugh, an infintesimal rise in the estimation of people who are no judge of character – and at what price? Hurting our neighbor's reputation or feelings, perhaps weighing down someone who has troubles enough already. And Jesus thinks: *Whatever you have done to the least of my brothers, you have done unto me.* With good reason He warned us that we would be held accountable for every idle word.

There is a reason why the most serious people – the saints – are also the most pleasant to be around. Frivolity gets old fast. People who are trying to find happiness on the way to the One who alone can fill our hearts up, will be forever unsatisfied. They will be restless, envious, tempted to try ever greater thrills to fill up the void, usually ending up bitter, for the futility of turning this valley of tears into a garden of Eden will dawn on them eventually, even if they never admit it. Those who do not expect to find permanent happiness here below, on the other hand, are grateful for life's little joys, which they consider unexpected surprises, not their due. They know that they do not deserve anything but the sort of life Jesus had – poor, misunderstood, ending with a Cross. All our sufferings are a small price for Heaven, so even a full dose of suffering cannot get a serious saint to stop smiling for long.

What can we do to reorient our life? to get serious in a Christian way? It is very simple. One must simply learn to pray. Fifteen minutes of silent reflection, not thinking about ANYTHING except God, His

Only Son Our Lord, the salvation He won for us, Heaven, Hell, the virtues we need to follow Christ on the good path. Fifteen minutes which begins by invoking the Holy Spirit and ends by asking the Blessed Virgin to present the prayer to her Son and help us to keep the good resolution we've made. Fifteen minutes of facing squarely the utter seriousness of being a person with a darkened intellect and a damaged will, contending with unruly passions while living in a world corrupted by the Devil himself, liable to die at any moment and face instantaneously an eternal fork in the road, and having only one hope: a crucified God/Man – fifteen minutes a day would begin to suffuse the remaining hours with a mature outlook, an unearthly wisdom, and an unbreakable confidence that we cannot gain any other way. We will know the stakes involved in life, but also the way to make our victory assured. We will develop that mixture of apparently irreconcilable qualities that characterizes the saint: we'll be fearful but not without hope; mournful, but not without joy; serious but not without fun. And while you're praying, you can put in a word for the poor souls in Purgatory.

Hope in the Resurrection

At times it may seem that death is too powerful for us, but it is not too powerful for Christ. Christ has found a way to be with us when we confront death, so that we may have peace and not fear in our hearts. Death certainly tries to scare us, though. It often involves physical suffering and always brings sorrow and stress. Of course we fear it because what it leads to is so different from our present experience that words could not describe it, nor minds comprehend it. But in addition to all these reasons why death scares us, there is a more fundamental reason yet. God never intended it to happen. He did not create death or will that our bodies should ever lie separated from the soul that gave them life. It is the result of sin, Adam's sin, that we all must die.

But if God's original plan for life was frustrated, his back-up plan, the Redemption, can not be frustrated. *The Father who has life sent me*, we just heard Christ proclaim. *I am the living bread come down from Heaven .... for the life of the world.* It is about this plan, this great wonderful plan of salvation to which we are called to take part in, that I wish to talk to you about this morning. What a consolation that fact must be for all of us! For that plan of redemption I mentioned, with which we are all so familiar, did not end when the Son of God who died for us, rose from the dead and ascended into Heaven. He also arranged for the eternal life that He had merited for us, to reach us. After Baptism, the main source of that life is the Eucharist. We eat the Body of Christ and so become members of his Mystical Body; likewise we share in the immortal life of that body: *so the man who feeds on me will have life because of me.* In a world that seeks in vain for medications to prolong life indefinitely, the Eucharist is called with reason "the immortality drug, the antidote to death".

The fact that we have tasted this holy food must give us great joy. But we can say more. The Lord is so merciful that He does not only wish to visit our hearts the bare minimum, but He wishes to return again and again increasing and perfecting His life in us. He wants us to begin to live here on earth the blessed joy that we call "eternal life". One of the early fathers of the Church explained it this way: "Just as bread that comes from the earth, after God's blessing has been invoked upon it, is no longer ordinary bread, but Eucharist, formed of two things, the one earthly and the other Heavenly: so too our bodies, which partake of the Eucharist are no longer corruptible, but possess the hope of resurrection." And with each worthy reception of the sacrament, our imperfections are forgiven us and the hope of that resurrection increases until the wedding feast of Heaven is so close that we can almost taste it. Job, although he had only received God's grace in shadowy ways, had this desire: *from my flesh I shall see God; my inmost being is consumed with longing.*

Finally, we can add another perspective from which to draw consolation from the Eucharist. We are gathered here to offer the Holy Sacrifice of the Mass. How fortunate we are to have this last, enormous gift! Every celebration of the Mass, you must know, is the renewing of the sacrifice Christ made on the Cross on Calvary. He died for each and every human being who ever lived, lives or will live. And here today, on this altar, Jesus Christ will be offered especially for those who have died. There can be no more effective way of covering completely any shortcomings in their lives and ours. The blood of Christ has the power not only to cover our sins but to finish the transformation of life that was mortal into life that will never end. Christ has the power to conquer death, our last enemy. He is the reason why we need not fear death. *For I am certain that neither death nor life will be able to separate us from the love of God that comes to us in Christ Jesus, our Lord.*

Good and Faithful Servant

It is a commonly observed phenomenon that humans cry both when we are happy and when we are sad. Often we are both at once, which makes it a providential attribute, allowing us to express our mixed emotions with one sign, expressive of both, tears. We weep when we are sad especially when a life has ended under difficult circumstances or a beloved relative or a friend has been lost. But we weep, too, for joy. We are glad on account of the hope that is in us, a hope based on Jesus Christ. The death of a faithful Christian is the birth of a saint, for *precious in the sight of God is the death of his holy ones (Ps. 116. 15).*

To the eyes of faith, every new suffering is a challenge to rise above it to a new victory, and keeping the faith to the end, even through death, is final victory. Just when it seems death has won, we have won over it. Yet it is not altogether accurate to say that **we**'ve won, for it is impossible for us, mere mortals that we are, and fallen at that, to confront the mystery of suffering and death alone without being crushed. But in Christ we can be *afflicted in every way, but not crushed; perplexed, but not driven to despair; persecuted, but not forsaken; struck down, but not destroyed. (2 Cor 3. 8-9)* The Son of God who took flesh precisely to put death itself to death, dwells in us by grace. He is our strength, and the reason why we are able to draw victory out of apparent defeat. He makes us strong when we are weak; indeed, St. Paul rejoiced when was weak, because then the strength of Christ could shine in him.

Let us dwell for a moment on this mystery. Christ crucified is the ultimate reason why all the dark clouds of life are in fact lit up with a beautiful light behind. (It is as though sufferings are the rough wrapping paper of glorious gifts.) He is the ultimate mystery of our faith, and stumbling block to those who have no faith. Joy may seem like too much to ask for at a time of sorrow. Still, Christ's power gives more than the ability just to get through a situation. His grace enables us to rejoice in our sufferings: *Rejoice in the measure that you share Christ's sufferings,* said St. Peter.

So let us consider three reasons why tears shed should be mainly for gladness sake. First, we rejoice because we love Christ. We are able to share in His Cross, so that He did not have to bear the weight alone. We are able to say, "He has done so much for me, I will offer this for Him". Because *[Christ] died for all, .. those who live ... live no longer for themselves but for Him who for their sake died and was raised. (2 Cor 5.15).*

Second, we rejoice because suffering is a sort of fire that perfects us. It makes up for sins, increases virtue, and builds up merits. It is by sharing in Christ's sufferings that the saints in Heaven *washed their robes in the blood of the Lamb.* All we endure is not in vain, but of great value for redemption, ourselves and others. This Mass continues the process of applying Christ's saving sacrifice. It is the best way of uniting us to that perfect self-offering on Calvary so that we might be made ready to enter the wedding feast of Heaven. This Mass and our prayers make us like Christ's bride — without spot or wrinkle.

Finally, the third reason to rejoice is our hope of the reward that our illnesses and sufferings prepare us for. That reward is the fulfillment of our every desire, the attainment of the goal of our creation, the sight of God. Let our hope be fixed on this which we cannot see or experience yet, so that all that we can see and do experience does not overwhelm us.

Be Prepared

This very night your life will be required of you. I hope that when you hear of tragic deaths your first thought is: were they ready? Were they prepared for what the letter to the Hebrews tells us is a *terrifying thing, to fall into the hands of the living God?*

We all must do that one day. It is the only sure thing in life. The only criterion by which to determine if we have lived well or badly is whether or not we have prepared ourselves for that encounter. The rest of our existence — which lasts an eternity — depends entirely on that one moment when we are judged soon after death. Given these facts you would think that people would be a little more careful about the way they live. You would think they would have their eyes constantly fixed on eternity, determining their actions by this one criterion: is this action pleasing to the Almighty or not?

Most men live their lives as if they were going to live forever. As if there were no just judge, no Purgatory, and even no Hell. They live as if the only important thing were amassing wealth, or indulging appetites, or – and this is even more insidious – they live as if the only important thing were their hobby, or reading the newspaper, or working in the garden. They do many good or innocuous things, but if completely absorbed by them, without thought for the next life, these can be dangers. It's not rare in fact to find even quite religious people who do not think sufficiently of the great test that awaits them. St. Paul must have known some in Corinth to whom he said: *If for this life only we have hoped in Christ, we are of all men most to be pitied. (I Cor 15.19)*

It seems to me that perhaps the greatest error of our day – greatest both in breadth of acceptance and in the havoc it wreaks – is the error of presumption. Most people, including many religious people, think that going to Hell is hard and getting to Heaven is easy. This is for many even a corollary of *God is love*. Now it should give people who think this way pause to consider that Christ said the exact opposite: *Enter by the narrow gate; for the gate is wide and the way is easy that leads to destruction, and those who enter by it are many. For the gate is narrow and the way is hard, that leads to life, and those who find it are few. (Mt 7: 13-14)* Likewise, St. Peter quotes the book of Proverbs with approval: *If the righteous man is scarcely saved, what will become of the ungodly and the sinner? (I Ptr 4.18.)*

This doesn't mean that God is not a loving God. On the contrary, He has not only opened the way to salvation at the cost of the passion of his divine Son, but He has set up an institution that will communicate to us the power to become sons of God and will never falter in reminding us of all we must know and do to stay on the path of life. But as St. Augustine said: "God who created you without you, will not save you without you". Now, most people figure, I'll have time to put my house in order. True enough, I've heard of late-in-life and even death-bed conversions – they are beautiful things, but they are also rare. God allows Himself to be tempted but rarely. The ordinary course is that people drift away from the Church, the life of grace, and they just keep drifting. I never cease to be amazed – and horrified – that people in extremely precarious health can turn a deaf ear to a priest or to those who tell them to see one.

The priest's job is – stated crudely – to get people into Heaven. Like St. Paul, he strives to be *all things to all men to save at least some*. This may seem like a pessimistic remark; it is not. No one has ever had a firmer grasp on the universal and excessively indulgent plan of salvation wrought by God in Christ Jesus. But St. Paul also knows that it is a gratuitous plan; in other words, we are not born with a ticket to Heaven; we must be given one. It is first given, usually, into the tiny hand of a newly baptized infant. It is only lost by serious sin. Ordinarily, it can only be restored by confession to a priest. The sacraments are necessary for salvation because salvation is a gift; and that is how God ordinarily gives it.

Again, entrance to Heaven is not guaranteed by being a well-loved granny who volunteered at the hospital and won all the garden shows – these things one can do without grace. Heaven is merited only by receiving, appreciating, and preserving the gift of grace. The Second Vatican Council states for instance: "All children of the Church should nevertheless remember that their exalted condition results, not from their own merits, but from the grace of Christ. If they fail to respond in thought, word, and deed to that grace, not only shall they not be saved, but they shall be the more severely judged" What can we do, practically, to prepare ourselves for Judgment day? Are you always in a state of grace? Learn what Christ's Church expects of you, for you are responsible for it. Work on your virtues with more care than you work on your career. And should you ever fall, never delay confessing to the Lord who is ready to pardon. Receive all the sacraments frequently. Confessing is anticipation of judgment and also gives us help to live well.

Pray for a happy death. Ask St. Joseph and your Guardian angel to intercede for you. Offer your day to God with a morning offering and ask forgiveness every night.[Act of Contrition]. Pray the Rosary (be with us now and at the hour of our death), wear the scapular and gain indulgences for yourselves and the poor souls. To live as one prepared to meet God is not to live in fear. On the contrary, it enables us to live freed from the fear of death and judgment. Then, we will have true peace in this life and eternal peace in the next.

Vocation to Holiness

Of all the statements we can make about the human race, the least controversial may well be: "Nobody's perfect". We're so used to thinking that no one could ever be perfect that we think it would be foolish to set perfection as a goal. And yet, Perfect is the same thing really as holy. And we believe that many people have become holy – the saints, and the Blessed Virgin Mary. So maybe one can become perfect. Now we can say even more: it's not just that it is possible for some people to become perfect. We say that all people are called to be and should strive for it. Christ preaches it: *Be ye perfect*, said Christ, *as your Heavenly Father is perfect*. And St. Paul just addressed the believers in Corinth as *you who have been sanctified in Christ Jesus and called to be holy*. A vocation is a calling, and we have a calling to holiness. The Second Vatican Council emphasized this perennial teaching of the Church which has now been dubbed "the universal call to holiness".

This call to holiness is the call that is behind every other vocation. Consecrated life and Matrimony are the greatest and most common paths that one can walk in the vocation that we all have: to become saints. Now the sacraments of Holy Orders and marriage are also known as the sacraments of service. That is because a vocation is a form of life in which we commit ourselves to loving others in a more intense manner. It requires a certain irrevocable laying down of one's life for others: spouse, children, parishioners, etc. St. Therese of

Lisieux expressed most wonderfully how Love was behind every call to action issued by God: "If the Church was a body composed of different members, it couldn't lack the noblest of all; it must have a heart, and a heart burning with love. And I realized that this love alone was the true motive force which enabled the other members of the Church to act; if it ceased to function, the Apostles would forget to preach the gospel, the Martyrs would refuse to shed their blood. Love, in fact, is the vocation which includes all others…!"

Love is at the heart of every vocation because love is what makes us perfect. God first shares his holiness with us when He claims us as his own – at our baptism. At Baptism the baby becomes holy. However, the holy little baby must be taught as he or she grows up to treasure this gift. What a gift! "The gift in turn becomes task" in the words of John Paul II, as the child not only strives to preserve the gift intact but to increase it. The call to holiness never ceases in this life. On the contrary, as we take on specific vocations, our duty to become ever holier only increases. Feeble as her members are, the Church is always holy, and cannot lose it. The Church belongs to Christ irrevocably as his bride, and no matter how many of her members struggle or fall, she will remain the one, **Holy**, Catholic and apostolic church. Still, the sanctification of each member remains the main work of the Church.

Too often we think of holiness as an "extra", icing on the cake, as if God will be happy if we are good, decent people. But no – what Father would be satisfied if his children were somewhat happy, fairly safe, or just healthy enough? Our Heavenly Father wants us to be perfect like Himself! Indeed, our Lord warned us: *if your righteousness does not surpass that of the scribes and the Pharisees you will not enter the Kingdom of God.* Only the perfect can get into Heaven whether they are purified now or in Purgatory.

So let us all look at ourselves differently in the mirror. Even though we know our faults, miseries, and shameful pasts, we also know *that Christ Jesus came into the world to save sinners,* as St. Paul said, and though you might feel, like Paul, that *I am the foremost of sinners,* that must not dampen your confidence that He is able to make a saint out of you.

Blessed Even in This Life

Children and adults, people of every sort, all seek happiness. That is the goal of all human endeavor. This is also the point of religion, and here, at "the heart of Jesus' preaching" we are shown the way to happiness: how to be "blessed" in this life and the next. *These things I have spoken to you, that my joy may be in you, and that your joy may be full. (Jn.15.11)*

In order to understand the paradoxical nature of the Beatitudes, we must realize that there are two levels of happiness: natural and supernatural. Ever since the Fall, man has sought happiness in places where it is not to be found, which is sin. The wisest of men, the philosophers of old, made some progress, noting that happiness was never found where most people sought it, but in the virtuous life. We are well aware that we are made for something more, that our hearts are never satisfied, even by the love of other human beings. "Our hearts are restless until they rest in you" O God.(St. Aug.) God is happiness itself, blessed beyond all imagining. A*s it is written, "What no eye has seen, nor ear heard, nor the heart of man conceived, what God has prepared for those who love Him," (I Cor. 2.9)* "It comes from an entirely free gift of God: whence it is called supernatural, as is the grace that disposes man to enter into the divine joy" *(CCC 1722)*. Grace enables us to perform great works of virtue which produce fruits of peace and joy in us. But, so great is the beatitude to which we are called, that we are also given Gifts of the Holy Spirit, by which we are moved, if we cooperate generously, to even greater deeds. These acts are categorized in the Beatitudes of Christ. The seven gifts of the Holy Spirit, which we receive at Baptism, correspond to each of the seven Beatitudes, which are the heroic deeds Christians should perform through the action of the Spirit.

At this point, we can compare this supernatural happiness with the natural. Both are gained or lost by "decisive moral choices". Natural happiness is marked out by the commandments. They were given by Moses to the people of Israel as the condition for entering into the Promised Land, and enjoying its natural rewards. Our Lord, however, like a new Moses, lays down in His sermon on the Mount, the way for entering into the ultimate Promised Land of Heaven. These laws do not show one merely how to be just, but how to be a saint. For a good reason are saints also called "blessed". They are people who, by their lives of intense charity, begin to experience, on earth, the joy of the blessed in Heaven. Saints are notoriously happy, exuberant, although not by natural disposition; rather it comes from their exercising their share in God's nature which is to be perfectly Blessed. It would be a mistake, therefore, to understand the paradoxical message of the beatitudes as a call to forget about achieving happiness in this life and simply to hope for the happiness of Heaven. Sometimes Christianity is accused of doing that, of ignoring human misery saying that all will be compensated in the hereafter. But the joy of saints, who all suffer much more than most people, shows that this is not true.

In this life, we possess the joy to come by our sure and certain hope. Thus, Our Lord shows both the way to eternal happiness and to immense joy on earth. But it is not found where most people seek it, but in the Cross, for there we find love, and love is the key to happiness. "The greatest gift is bearing the cross with love" said St. Francis. The message of Our Lord is fully paradoxical: not only can we be happy despite the tribulations of this life, but we can be only be happy because of them. We must not fear any loss, any humiliation, any contradiction — all of them are so many opportunities to identify oneself with Jesus Christ. That is the essence of the Beatitudes: imitation of Christ. They are the secret to Christian perfection. because they are a portrait of Christ Himself. (cf. CCC 1717) He was poor — *Though He was rich He became poor for our sake (2. Cor. 8.9)*; He wept at the death of Lazarus, and more at the refusal of Jerusalem to convert; He told us to learn from Him for He was meek of heart; He excelled, of course, in purity, mercy, and *is Himself our peace (Eph. 2.14)*. To imitate Christ, and so share in His joy to the full, is only possible by His gift. So also we can achieve now a happiness beyond our dreams, only if we genuinely long for the happiness of the world to come.

Heaven on Earth

One of my grandmother's more characteristic adjectives was "Heavenly". She might describe a garden, a fragrance, a piece of music, or a person as "Heavenly". That really is the greatest adjective we can employ. We like to think that some things on earth give us an inkling of Heaven's delights, but St. Paul reminds us that *eye has not seen, nor ear heard, nor has it entered into the mind of man what God has prepared for those who love Him...* Why is it so hard to imagine what Heaven is like? Because, the main attraction in Heaven is nothing created or visible: it is God Himself.

Until then, can we experience anything that really is Heavenly? The answer is yes. We must be able to see something of God, here below, and become a little like Him, a little holy, for we know that is the condition for getting into Heaven. All the Saints in Heaven must have done a pretty good job of becoming saints on earth. How do we see God here below? Faith. It enables us to see truly, but hazily, what we will later see in the Beatific vision of Heaven. *Now we see in a glass darkly, then face to face.* Remember, that when we see Him, we shall

be like Him. Insofar as we see God now, by faith, we should be becoming like Him. Jesus even tells us in that same sermon: *Be perfect
as your Heavenly Father is perfect.* Now if we're going to follow in
the footsteps of Jesus and the Saints, along the way marked out by the
Beatitudes, we'll need more strength than we have on our own. This is
called: Grace. To all who gaze upon God in faith, He gives the ability
to act like Him, to share his nature, to really be "his son or daughter".
*My dear people, we are already the children of God, but what we are
to be in the future has not yet been revealed.*

Now we get an idea of where on earth we can find something really worthy of the adjective "Heavenly". It is a place where people are
getting a glimpse of the glory of God and are being transformed to
live like Him, lives of superhuman charity and virtue. That place is
the Church. The Church really is a bit of Heaven on earth, it is the
"seed and beginning of the Kingdom of God". Let us take this marvelous lesson to heart! Our citizenship is in Heaven, as St. Paul says.
We are simply sojourners here on earth, and we find a home in the
Catholic Church as in our heavenly homeland's embassy in hostile
territory. There we find Christ' vicar the Pope, but, again as St. Paul
said, we too are called to be *ambassadors of Christ.*

How terrible if we did not use our faith to seek for God, to see
Him better, to know Him more intimately! How terrible if bit by bit
we lost the ability to act like Him and his holy ones, like true children
of God. Let's not settle for a "false heaven on earth". Rather, let's love
the Church, our true Heaven on earth – the community of those who
see God in faith and strive to act like Him. If we do, our longing for
the true Heaven will grow, and it won't be long till we get there!

Sanctity

The liturgy presents us today with a message about holiness. A
message which contains both good news and bad news. The bad news
first, that very few people become saints, become holy. It's a universally accepted proposition that only a very few people actually reach
the potential of God's plan for them in this life. Only a very few become transformed in Christ, perfected in Charity, united to God here
below. And what a tragedy this is because life without holiness is
what Job described, 'drudgery, the life of a slave, just drags on, filled
with restlessness until the dawn, going by but without hope. *I shall
not see happiness again.*'

Why so few, we might ask, why so few become holy? The *Imitation of Christ*, a favorite book of many of the saints, explains why.

"This is the reason why there are found so few contemplative persons, because there are few who wholly wean themselves from transitory created things." So it is with both, those who miss Heaven altogether, and those that miss the Heaven on earth that sanctity is. They do so because they think it is too difficult to make all the changes needed, to leave hold of all the things that they are attached to. So that's the bad news.

Now the good news. The good news about sanctity is that it's not so difficult as it seems. There was a Polish tailor, earlier in this century, who heard this message preached one day at his church. The priest said it's not so difficult to become a saint. And he took it to heart, he believed it. He began to learn to pray. He bought a lot of books about the spiritual life, He denied himself many things, he even chose to remain single so as to devote himself to the Lord. But he worked as a tailor very hard, and he also worked in his spare time with youth groups, teaching them how to pray. He did this during the Nazi occupation of Poland during World War II and he risked his life to do so. He became a mystic and no doubt he became a saint and one of his young students became Pope John Paul II. He proved to this day that it's not so difficult to become a saint if you put your mind to it. That's the message of many who have ascended Mount Carmel, beckoning back for us to follow.

The suffering involved looks terrible from this side, but it's not really, for two reasons. The first is from St. Paul that the reward is so great. *So that to consider that the suffering of this present time is not worth comparing with the glory that is to be revealed in us.* But even in this life there are rewards that make these difficulties not so terribly daunting. Paul continues, *His glorious might strengthens us with all power for all endurance and patience and joy.* Both moral and physical suffering that is the price of holiness, is a small price, even in this life. So the Apostles were rejoicing that they were counted *worthy to suffer dishonor for the Name.* Nor is it very difficult to know how to approach God, how to find a way to union with Him. One of the greatest Mystics of the twentieth century, yet to be canonized, a Spanish Monk, wrote, "If we want to, we would become saints, it's much more difficult to become an engineer than a saint."

So here's a rough game plan for the would be saint. Two thousand years of Christian experience, during which time there have been many saints, show us there are three categories of the Christian in God's grace. The stage of the beginner is also called the purgative stage. That means that a great degree of effort is involved, eliminating deliberate venial sins, and the attachment to sin and the longing to go back to one's sins. And there's many who find this very, very difficult, as it is, very bitter. But there's a limit to how much purging we can do with our own willpower, mortifications, our pious practices, and so God must begin to purify our senses, our memory, our imaginations, and souls. And this intervention on God's part is known as the first night. After this begins the second stage of the proficient, also called the illuminative stage, here God begins to work more in the soul, teaching it, leading it to a darker but a very clear, certain understanding of the truths of the faith. Also to a more dreadful night of the soul which purifies the spirit, the intellect and the will. And after that second night if the soul hasn't turned back, as many do, we have to be very, very, generous, but if one doesn't, the third stage, the unitive stage is reached where the soul is united to God in a genuine prelude to Heaven with indescribable joys even in this life.

All this, brief and sketchy as it is, may sound a little bit fantastic, a little bit unrealistic for people who live in the world. Sounds indeed a little bit like a video game where you advance from mansion to mansion, St. Teresa of Avila calls these the seven mansions. Trying to avoid the pitfalls, fighting with the devil, following the guide of a spiritual director, this sounds a bit fantastic. But it is an itinerary by God which is intended for each and every one of us. Every single person, the Lord is calling to union with Him, even in this life. He wants each and every one of us united with Him and purged of all our imperfections even in this life, not in Purgatory, so we can step right into Heaven at the end of this life. That's God's plan. We're all called to be Mystics. And now you can't tell St. Peter if you meet him, that no one ever told you that.

You might be thinking, if it's so easy, why aren't you or some other people saints? The answer we could give is the one that Mother Teresa gave, when asked if she was a saint. She said, "I try to be, don't you. It's a simple duty for you and for me." We ought to at least be working on sanctity, working with all of our strength. God, we have to remember though, is totally sovereign and free in His gift of holiness to us, and normally He gives this gift only as a reward following a life of faithful, persevering cooperation with His grace. And what is this cooperation? The Lord Jesus, who didn't have to make any effort to be holy because He was the all holy one from the moment of His conception, nonetheless gives us the example of how to cooperate. We just heard it. Rising very early before dawn, He left and went off to a deserted place where He prayed. We too must seek out the face of God, which we see reflected in the face of Christ Jesus, who is still present on earth with us in this Holy Sacrament of the Eucharist. We can not see Him with our physical eyes, but with the eyes of faith, we must gaze upon Him, as often as we can, as long as we can. Asking Him to illumine our souls, and to bring us into this mystery which is union with His Father. It's morally necessary for salvation to make these efforts, absolutely indispensable, to grow in holiness. In prayer we seek out the One, union with whom, holiness is all about.

Christ provided us with all the means we need for growing in His grace. Prayer, as I mentioned, which is always in Him and through Him; the sacraments, especially the Holy Eucharist. "Receiving the Eucharist," St. Therese of Lisieux said, "is the quickest way to become holy," always into an ever more pure heart; and then right teaching, to study the doctrine of the Church, to know the mysteries that we may contemplate them more easily. Then we must strive to detach ourselves from all the obstacles, all that hinders us. At the end of the day those who are not saved, those who are not holy, there's only one reason, because they really didn't want to be. We have the example of a young Spanish saint who was beatified by Pius XII. She became a very holy Carmelite and died in 1950. when she was a young girl she went on a Confirmation retreat and they later found written in her notebook. "Today I have decided to become a Saint." If we make up our mind to do it, we can all be saints, just as that Polish tailor did.

Running the Way of Your Commands

Today's Gospel relates the encounter between Jesus and the rich young man. This is a meeting of extraordinary significance for understanding the Christian revolution in moral reasoning. Christian morality, of which the Catholic Church has always been the faithful proponent, can seem to many people excessively rigorous, uncompromising, even harsh. It seems it's made for perfect people, not for people like me. You may say, it's not fair, for "nobody's perfect". There is something in this: Christian morality is a roadmap to perfection. The Lord said: *if you would be perfect, go, sell what you have, and come, follow me.*

Do you want to be perfect? Don't we all? But we're afraid of saying so, because it sounds absurd, presumptuous and extremely difficult. Can't I just be a regular guy? How about above average? No, the Lord demands it of us: *"You, therefore, must be perfect, as your Heavenly Father is perfect" (Mt. 5.48)* And if we settle for anything less, like the young man, we must take leave of the Perfect Man and go away sad.

What will make us perfect? Love and love alone is the virtue that makes us perfect. Only Mark notes that *Jesus, looking at* [the young man], *loved Him*. Love is the context in which to think about morality, commandments and sin. The moral life is nothing but the loving response due to God for the many gratuitous initiatives made by Him out of love for us. (Veritatis Splendor) A good moral life is simply loving Him back. *This is the love of God,* says St. John, *that we keep his commandments* But we couldn't keep them unless God loved us first. Again John tells us: *We love, because He first loved us. (I Jn 4.19)*

The love of God is the source of our ability to fulfill the law, because the law is nothing but instructions on how to love. Christ details how we are to love God totally, especially in the Sermon of the Mount, He gives us the example by his own life, and, most importantly, He shares with us the power to do the same. Moses gave the commandments to mark out the minimum degree of love of God, of self-giving, to keep his listeners in communion with God. But, as we saw last week, He had to allow exceptions for "their hardness of heart". Only when Christ came to give us new hearts, when *the love of God has been poured into our hearts through the holy Spirit who has been given to us (Rom 5.5)*, only then did we become capable of keeping the commandments. What had been impossible to man before Christ, became no longer even "burdensome". Moreover, Christians began to "feel an interior urge *not* to stop at the minimum demands of the Law, but to live them in their 'fullness'" (VS 18). And so we return to our story, to the invitation: Do you want to be perfect?.

Christ makes clear that the commandments alone will not make us perfect, when He invites the young man to embrace voluntary poverty. Christ is announcing the "evangelical counsels" the vows taken by religious to live a life of poverty, chastity and obedience — to be "inseparable from the commandments" (2052). The commandments open the way to perfection and the counsels help us to advance on it. "Jesus shows that the commandments must not be understood as a minimum limit not to be gone beyond, but rather as a path involving a moral and spiritual journey towards perfection, at the heart of which is love" (VS 15) Peter and the other apostles had jumped at the invitation when they dropped their nets beside the sea of Galilee and left everything to follow Jesus. The vows of poverty, chastity, and obedience are helps to attaining perfect love of God more surely and quickly, but they are not necessary means. Still, whether we take formal vows or not, all Christians who want to be perfect must free themselves from the attachment to material possessions (poverty), from selfish gratification (chastity) and from their own will (obedience).

This certainly won't be easy. That's why the young man, amazingly, was able to resist even the loving glance of the Son of God. No, we mustn't be miserly with Christ who has given up everything for us. On the contrary, we must be generous, enthusiastic and cheerful — let us rush after Him, *Lord, widen my heart and I will run in the way of your commands.*

Work for the Greater Reward

This episode in the life of Jesus is related by all three of the evangelists. Obviously it struck them extremely strongly, as we see, they could only marvel, they were completely overwhelmed. This particular account by Mark stands out in its detail. It tells us, for instance, that the young man ran up, that he knelt before the Lord, that the Lord looked at him, that the Lord loved him. Mark tells us what Jesus told them when He addressed his disciples. He had a real message for them and they were completely overwhelmed. All these details come from Mark. Mark perhaps wasn't there but there's good reason to believe that Mark's account came from Peter. If you listen to that first letter of Peter it seems as if Peter is almost talking to that rich young man and all the rich young men in the world the way he's saying, look for the greater reward, look for the treasure that the Lord spoke of, *imperishable and incapable of fading or defilement,* which is kept in Heaven for you. Work for this and don't worry about any of the suffering. For a time you have to suffer the distress of many trials but this is just so your faith may be purified. Look for the great goal at the end. Remember it was Peter, also, who in another place in the gospel, says, *Lord, we have left everything for you.* And then our Lord promises, 'Yes, and you will have your reward in Heaven.'

Often we think of these passages only in connection with those who have a vocation to leave everything, to follow a path of obedience, and then don't follow it. But of course the Lord is speaking here to everybody who is not being generous with God, everybody who feels an indication from God to be generous and then turns away. Just as Jesus was sad and distressed, so also we must see it in that context, as a personal invitation from the Lord to be generous as He was generous with us, dying on the cross, and as a personal affront to Him whenever we, instead, are selfish. We have to remember that all of our Lord's invitations to be generous come from love. He doesn't love us, often, the way we love people. He doesn't try to do things that please them, no, the Lord when He loves someone, asks them to sacrifice. We have to look back at Him, with love, and say, yes Lord, following your example we will leave everything, trusting that You will reward us.

Becoming Saints

There are many, many potential saints in the world, but not so very many actual saints that we can meet. There's many potential saints in this room, a couple hundred perhaps. All of us have to make sure we don't stay potential saints, possible saints, but in fact, that we really and truly become saints. It seems that everybody goes through life waiting for something to happen to make them say, "Well now, I'll really begin to serve God." Everybody seems to be waiting for some sort of sign, waiting for a great prophet to come and shake us up, waiting perhaps for some other sign they are asking the Lord for. "Show us some great sign from Heaven then we'll reform our lives, then we'll do something great for God." Everybody seems to be waiting. We mustn't. We mustn't even wait if we're small to get older. We have saints in the Church canonized, such as St. Dominic Savio, only fourteen years old. The Holy Father canonized two of the children of Fatima who were even younger, I think nine and eleven. So you can't even wait to get older. You mustn't wait for anything.

The Lord Jesus, Himself, said there will be no other sign, there will be no other sign to get you going, except the sign of Jonah. What did He mean by that? He explains Himself more clearly in Matthew's gospel. He says, "Just as Jonah spent three days in the belly of the whale, so will the Son of Man spend three days in the earth." It's a bit of a prefiguration of the Lord spending three days in the earth after He was buried, after He died, then He rose on the third day. He's referring to His Resurrection. That is the sign, that no greater sign can be given, that it's time to change our lives, that God cares about us and He's going to give us His power to serve Him. No other sign will happen. That's why it was the greatest sign for the early Christians, that now, they had to live differently from all the Romans around them, now they had to live as Christians.

I want to read to you a few excerpts from some talks that were given in Rome by a Vietnamese Bishop. He spent thirteen years in prison, nine years in solitary confinement, for the faith. For weeks on end, he wouldn't see the sun, and sometimes for weeks on end he would be in total darkness all by himself. He was waiting there, almost going mad, thinking, 'Well this is useless, I can't do anything to help my people.' Then waiting, he said, "While in prison, everyone waits for freedom, every day, every minute. My mind was full of confused feelings, sadness, fear and tension. My heart felt lacerated by the remoteness of my people. But in the darkness of the night, in the midst of that ocean of anxiety, that nightmare, little by little I began to awaken. I must face reality. I am in prison, isn't this, perhaps, the best time to do something great. How many times in my life will I have such an opportunity again. The only sure thing in life is death. Therefore I must take advantage of the occasions that come by my way to seek to carry out ordinary actions in an extraordinary way. During the long nights of pressure I convinced myself that to live the present moment is the simplest and surest way to sanctity." In other words, not to wait for a better opportunity. He could do so much, even from sitting there in the dark out of love for God. "If I live each moment perfectly, my life will be saintly. The road of hope is paved with many small moments of hope."

Recognizing Sanctity in Others

It's an interesting rule of human nature that the Lord taught us today, that no prophet gains acceptance in his native place. And in other places in the gospel we see this, He was not accepted because they knew Him, "We know you, aren't you the carpenters son? We know your father and your sisters and brothers, you can't be who you claim to be." You see in the history of the Church, many saints, also, have gone unnoticed as saints by those around them, because they knew them well. This is true of Mother Teresa when she was just teaching geography in her former order, and other saints who were persecuted by their brothers and sisters in religion, St. John of the Cross, for instance. They didn't recognize them because they knew them so well.

We have to be careful of doing the same thing. There aren't perhaps many great saints among us that we don't realize, but there certainly are many potential saints that perhaps we don't realize. We don't think of them as what they are, truly potential saints in the making. Because we know each other so well, the faults and failings are all around us, we get used to each other, especially in families. One doesn't seem to think of these as truly, truly potential saints because we know their faults. But we have to remember that even sinners, of course, are potential saints. We have to remind them of this too, that God has created you to be holy. In a thousand different ways, especially the way we treat them, we have to make this known, that God expects each and every one of us to be truly, truly holy. It's a good thing to use our imagination for, to imagine those we come into contact with, transformed by the grace and power of God into genuine saints that one might read about in the history books.

We ourselves too mustn't fall into the same error, getting so used to ourselves and our failings and our habits, that we think that this is more or less about as good as I'll ever be. This would be false humility, we too are called to be saints. When we come into contact with people throughout our day, our only goal should be that, that contact, help them along this road towards sanctity. Because it's truly, truly possible. The Lord has picked a path for each and every one of us to become a great saint, and we can't ignore this potential just because we are so used to each other. We have to help each other, in particular, to suffer well, that's a way to holiness, and to pray well. In every way we can, let us help one another.

Hidden Sanctity

As great as St. Andrew is, Cardinal Newman in a little commentary here, points out that really his life is quite hidden. He says, "St. Andrew is little known in history, while the place of dignity and the name of highest renown have been allotted to his brother Simon, whom he, Andrew, was the means of bringing the knowledge of his Savior. Our lesson then is this, that those men are not necessarily the most useful men in their generation, nor the most favored by God, who make the most noise in the world and who seem to be principals in the great changes and events recorded in history. On the contrary, even when we are able to point to a certain number of men as the real instruments of any great blessings that shape mankind, our relative estimate of them, one with another, is very often erroneous."

A good lesson to draw from this feast is that, as Paul says, we are all called to be evangelists, even if we aren't all going to be those who make the great noise in salvation history. Think of any saint, or think for instant of John Paul II. Would we have a John Paul II if we didn't have his mother and his father, the tailor who taught Him to pray, all the friends he grew up with, even his Jewish friends, the seminarians he studied with, especially the one that was killed so young? We don't even know their names, the rector of the seminary, the cardinal who told him to be a diocesan priest, his professors, thousands and thousands of people, many of whom we don't know, many of whom he may not know were so influential in his life, are necessary to have a great saint. So this drama of salvation history has very few starring roles, most of them are in the background. This is especially true if you think of the way God works, mysterious ways of grace which are mainly moved by prayer. It's the nameless monks, the holy people, who really sustain the world and really move everything toward His consummation in the Kingdom of God .

So let us remember that if we feel insignificant and, for that reason, tend to despair of our role. Rather, if we can't preach or if we can't teach, or if we can't even go out of our house, we can always pray, we can always suffer, and we can always play a great role in eyes of the Lord.

Make Me a Saint

We can easily get blasé about the language of Scripture. We have to remind ourselves how tremendous it is. For instance, the Letter of John, *Who then is conqueror of the world?* Us. We who believe in the name of Jesus are conquerors of the world — to possess the Son of God within ourselves and to possess eternal life. All these marvelous promises in that one passage, which might remind us of what St. Peter, speaking in his second letter says, that *God has made to us, precious and very great promises.* Then he goes on to mention the greatest, which sums them all up, which is being partakers in the Divine Nature. Staggering statements which we have to always stop and appreciate!

It also gives us confidence. The kind of confidence that this leper had, that we can say, Lord if you will to do it , you can do anything for me. But we have to pray just as he did, that the Lord will cure us of our leprosy of sin, and then do many great things in addition. We have to be willing and confident enough to say, Lord, if you will to do so, you could make me holy. And hear the Lord say, I do will it. That's why I came. That's why I died.

This would be a beautiful prayer, Lord, if you will it, you could make me holy. You could make me like you, You could make me able to love the way You love. It's a prayer that He will surely answer. We don't pray for it explicitly, or often enough, anyway. "Lord, make me holy," Just for lack of trust, lack of hope. So, we mustn't be like that. Much better to be like the saints who startle us really, when they pray, 'Lord I want to be a great saint. I want to be a saint soon. Show me the way, Lord.' That's the way the Lord would like us to be, much more eager, much more trusting, much more ambitious in this way. So let us ask the Lord, "Lord, if you will it, You can make me a great saint." I'm sure the Lord does will it and He will help us.

Sola Caritas

Around the time of the Council of Trent, the beginning of the counter reformation, the Holy Spirit raised up a number of great saints in the Church. Saint Phillip Neri seems to have known them all, St. Ignatius of Loyola, St. Francis de Sales, St. Charles Borromeo. He knew also in his own life, what it takes to make a saint and that it was a simple matter. It's not a difficult matter to be a Christian, with many laws and requirements. It's a simple matter expressed in this Gospel, *to love one another as I have loved you.* The command that I give you is this, that you love one another. In fact, St. Phillip Neri took as his motto for his foundation, Sola Cartas, Love Alone.

He knew that the mark of a saint would be happiness. He said, "a servant of God ought always be happy." This was his characteristic, this is what attracted so many souls to him, his tremendous ability to be cheerful. The joy of cheerfulness. It can seem as if it is something that we can't on our own often produce, to be joyful. In fact, it is a gift of God, that's true. However, two things would help foster joy or cheerfulness in us, that St. Phillip Neri showed us. The first is that joy is a byproduct of other things. He endured many trials. For instance, his faculties for hearing confessions were taken away because of people calumniating him. That's what he loved most of all was hearing confessions, but he didn't allow that to take away his cheerfulness. So, enduring trials well, and also being detached from things. He once said, "If I had ten men who were totally detached from the things of this world, who wanted nothing but Christ, I would have the courage to convert the whole world with them." So, abnegation, detachment and humility. We only have some of his writings, just a few of his sayings, because apparently he burned them before he died and did other things so as not to attract the admiration of his fellow men. Through these various ways; humility, detachment, and mortification, joy turned up in St. Philip's heart as a by product.

Although one cannot perhaps produce joy in one's heart, one can act as if one were joyful and one can make oneself be cheerful. This, surely he did. He promoted song in his community to cheer up the pilgrims and made everybody sing. No doubt if he felt like singing or not, whether he was sick or not, I'm sure he sang and made himself act as if he were joyful. Then, joy follows. Joy comes later into his heart. So let us follow the great example of St. Phillip Neri and seek to be as happy as saints ought to be.

Christ the King

The Feast of Christ the King

Did you know that the Vatican has a radio station? Even if you did know that, you may not know that Vatican Radio has a theme song that they play between shows. *Christus vincit, Christus regnat, Christus imperat.* Christ conquers, Christ reigns, Christ commands. Before we start a new liturgical year, the Church leaves us with a final image: that of Christ reigning in glory. The image of Christ the King can be difficult for some, especially for natives of a democracy. It may seem to distance us from Him; or take away our dignity. Nonetheless, if properly understood, we can learn to love viewing Christ, as He truly is now, glorious in Heaven. To be reassured, we need only reflect on the fact that He is not like earthly kings. Rather, He came to serve and not be served. His weapons are truth and love. His throne was the cross and his crown made of thorns. In short, as He Himself said, *his kingdom is not of this world.* As evidence of this fact, Our Lord goes on to say that if his Kingdom were of this world, his subjects would fight for Him. This alerts us to the fact that if we wish to be his subjects we must fight for his kingdom. The Church on earth is known as the "Church militant" because, to us alone, falls the responsibility of struggling: the Church in Purgatory cannot help and the Church in Heaven has already triumphed. Therefore, we must know and defend the interests of Jesus Christ, *fighting the good fight* of faith. St. John identified three enemies that militate against the interests of Jesus and his followers: the flesh, the world and the devil. Let us see how we should fight each one of these enemies.

Firstly, we must wage war on the flesh. That is, we must fight the enemy within, which seeks to separate us from our Lord. Works of the flesh include not only *immorality, impurity, licentiousness*, according to St. Paul, but *idolatry, strife, jealousy, anger, selfishness, envy, and drunkenness (Gal. 5.19).* In short we must fight against all our appetites until they are brought into due order — not repressed, but made to follow the order set by our mind. Our mind must be in control of all we do, sovereign in fact. But we can only attain this natural nobility and integrity, if our minds are subject to Christ. Only then will His grace be at work in us, strengthening our minds' dominion over our appetites. St. Leo the Great explains this thus "all, regenerated in Christ, are made kings by the sign of the cross... for what is more king-like than to find yourself ruler over your body after having surrendered your soul to God?"

The second enemy of the Kingdom is the world. The "world" refers to that part of mankind which refuses to submit to the reign of Christ and fights tooth and nail against His followers. Many deny that the Lord is, by right, *the ruler of the kings of the earth (Rev 1:5)* We must fight unbelief with the same weapons that our Lord used on earth: goodness, kindness, humbleness of heart. That is the only way to win them over. But to win others over to the kingdom of Christ must be more than a hobby for us. This must be our very reason for being: *The reason I was born, the reason why I came into the world, is to testify to the truth.*

The third enemy we mentioned was the devil. Because Christ's kingdom is primarily not of this earth, its enemies also are not all of this earth. Insofar as we must fight spiritual powers, St. Paul recommends that we fight back with *the whole armor of God...the breastplate of righteousness, the shield of faith, the helmet of salvation, and the sword of the Spirit which is the word of God (Eph 6.13-16).* Even so, we seem often to be engaged in such an uphill battle. When one considers the Holocaust, or the progress of the culture of death through legal abortion and euthanasia, one wonders: is the devil winning out? How can Christ's Kingdom ever overcome? We must recall that it is not in keeping with God's plan to have the forces of goodness win out now, on earth. Christ's Kingdom only begins here on earth in the Church. It will not reach perfection until He comes in glory: *the Son of man coming on the clouds of Heaven.* For that day we must long with all our hearts, for then every tear will be wiped away. So let us pray the Our Father with sincerity, asking "Thy Kingdom Come!" There we will see Christ in splendor, as the hymn portrays Him: Christ conquering, Christ reigning, Christ commanding forever.

A Share in Christ's Authority

The people who observed Jesus were familiar with authority. Yet, they were amazed by Christ who *taught with authority* and who, obeyed even by the unclean spirits, commanded their obedience as well. We must have the same awestruck experience of contact with God's supreme authority, for it is only through recognition of it, and obedience to it, that we are saved. Authority in the church, like civil authority, comes from God, but directly. It is a share in Christ's own authority which He gave to his apostles. This is how the Second Vatican Council explains *(Lk.10.16):* "The bishops have by divine institution taken the place of the apostles as pastors of the Church, in such wise as whoever listens to them is listening to Christ and whoever despises them despises Christ and Him who sent Christ". What terrifying words when we think how often our Bishop and the Holy Father are criticized and their authority denied!!

While earthly authority is a service out of justice, the authority exercised by Christ and by Him, through his Church, is a service out of love and mercy. *I have come not to be served but to serve.* How beautiful it is to see that Christ, who by rights must have every power under his feet — even the powerful angels — does not force us into submission. Rather, He wields his authority so humbly, not imposing His truth or rule, but proposing it. Why? Because He wants to be obeyed only out of love, freely. The bad angels, having rejected a relationship of love, are nonetheless forced to obey against their will, but this is not God's original plan for them or us. The Pope is the servant of the servants of God, yet without losing his title to "supreme, full, immediate and universal power in the care of souls" (Christus Dom). In this the Pope is a wonderful reflection of Christ, all-powerful yet *meek and humble of heart*. He is "the sweet Christ on earth" (St. Catherine).

A second effect of the authority in the Church being from above, is that it is sacred. "No one can give himself the mandate and mission to proclaim the Gospel. The one sent by the Lord does not speak and act on his own authority, but by virtue of Christ's authority." *(CCC 875)* In honoring ecclesial authority, we honor Christ. In following the guidance of the Church we have the assurance of following the will of God. Coming from God directly, this sacred authority, makes sacred, sanctifies, those who allow themselves to be guided by it.

Today, then we have been invited to reflect upon the great gift that the authority of Christ, extended through time and space through the Church, is for us. We must ask ourselves if we are wholly responsive and obedient to this guide from Heaven. What can I do to fashion my life, more and more, upon the guidance of Christ? Or have I allowed a political understanding of power and authority to corrupt my faithful adherence to the Church? Do I view teachings and laws of the Church as made by men to be examined, skeptically, like the planks of a political party? Lord, we desperately need your guidance, your authority. Help us to submit freely and wholly to your ambassadors. In total obedience to You we find our freedom, for You are Truth and Goodness itself.

The Second Coming

The sun will be darkened, the moon will not shed its light, stars will fall out of the skies. Every year at this time, the Church reminds us of this reality; she wants us to consider the end of time at the end of the Church year. Just as we do at the end of a calendar year, or a fiscal year, so now we should make a reckoning of our lives. What have we made of our life this year? What did God want of me this year and every year? Have I fulfilled His expectations?

Examining one's life is something people hate to do. The main reason is that it is apt to lead you to do things you think you won't like. But, God's grace is always there. As St. Paul said, *I thank Him who has given me strength for this, Christ Jesus our Lord. (I Tim 1.12)* **Every** person is called to make a radical and conscious decision to serve the Lord with their whole life. Yes, the purpose of our life is to love, serve, and honor the one who made us, consciously and radically. You're probably thinking that many people, therefore, must be living lives that are futile and aimless. That is true. "The vast majority of men, it is said, lead lives of quiet desperation." Many Catholics included.

Why do so many people remain unmoved by such an awesome thought as the *Son of Man coming with power and glory, angels assembling the chosen, and sending* the rest *to everlasting horror and disgrace*? Well, we tend to think it unlikely that this will happen in our lifetimes for one thing. That was not the case for the first Christians. They thought that the first coming, the Incarnation of Our Lord, was a prelude to the second coming. There is an urgency which marked the early Church and which marks the Church today; it is not due so much to the possibility that world will end soon, but that the Kingdom is near. The true purpose of everything has been revealed and their orientation to the Creator restored; we rush to cooperate with the *subjecting of all things under his feet* regardless of whether the task is almost complete or not. *All things were created by Christ, in Christ and for Christ,* St. Paul declared. As believers we know this. We know the full truth about who we are and where we are going. If anyone asks us where we come from, the answer is: from Christ; where are we going? to Christ. How will you get there? Christ again. He is the mystery that envelops creation, the Alpha and the Omega. The Way, the Truth and the Life.

But still we hesitate, thinking there is time before the end comes. Jesus would not tell us when the end would be; He even speaks as if He did not know. He means that it is not important for us. One reason it is not important for us to know is that the end of **our** contact with the world is indeed imminent. Eternity is just a heart beat away. We will all experience judgment. We must live this life with that in view. What will it be like to meet the Judge? Well, that depends entirely on how we are living this life. St. Teresa of Lisieux longed to see the face of her Judge. All Christians are supposed to feel that way, which is why we pray "Thy Kingdom Come". And Paul looked forward to *the crown of righteousness , which the Lord, the righteous judge, will award to me on that Day, and not only to me but also to all who have* loved his appearing (*2 Tim 4.8*) But others will *cry out to the hills "fall on us" and to the mountains "cover us"* so great will be their dismay.

Let us judge ourselves before we are judged. Am I closer to the Lord Jesus than I was at this time last year? If not, I have wasted the year. Do I think I have maintained the same level of devotion, virtue, and faith? If so, I have actually slid backwards. Now is the time for developing a firm purpose of amendment. We must be honest and practical. Am I striving for union with Christ? What can I do to remove obstacles? What sin remains in my life? What virtue can I work on this year? Do I go to confession at least once a month?

Jesus wondered out loud during his life: when *the Son of Man comes will He find faith on earth?* Let us show Him that He would find faith. A strong, vibrant robust faith. A faith, in other words, that works through love, through deeds. We must be able to point to every choice in our life and say: "I do this out of my love for Jesus Christ. By it, I prepare myself and the world for his return. I long for that day. Come Lord Jesus! I am ready!" *May the God of peace make you perfect in holiness. May He preserve you whole and entire, spirit, soul, and body, irreproachable at the coming of our Lord Jesus Christ. (I Thss 5.23)*

The New Heavens and the New Earth

This last week of the year is a wonderful week. Christ the King, on Sunday and then a whole week to contemplate the last things, the glorious consummation of Christ's work, which for those of us who love the Lord Jesus — nothing but hopeful thoughts. Today we have thoughts of the New Heavens and the New Earth. It is a good idea to constantly stir up in our hearts this longing for Heaven. St. Bernard says today in the readings, in the Liturgy of the Hours, that God gives greater rewards to those who have greater desires. We must desire this gift of Heaven. Heaven as we know is often described as not being really a place but a state of communion, as the Catechism says, "communion of life and love with the Trinity, the Virgin Mary, the angels and the blessed." This is called Heaven. The scriptures today remind us that there is a mysterious aspect to Heaven which one has to use the language of place. This is this idea of the New Heavens and the New Earth.

Our Lord says that *the Heavens and the Earth will pass away.* Then, in the book of Revelations, *the former Heavens and the former Earth has passed away and the sea was no longer. I saw the New*

Heaven and a new Earth. Then comes the Holy City, the Church perfected down from Heaven. St. Peter, too, speaks of the New Heavens and the New Earth in which he says *righteousness dwells*. This image of a New Heavens and a New Earth is scripture's way of describing, in the words of the Catechism, "the mysterious renewal which will transform humanity and the world." It is described by some of the fathers as sort of a return to Paradise. Paradise is another word for Heaven for us, but it really means garden, as in Garden of Eden. So St. Ireneaus writes, "The world itself, restored to its original state, will be at the service of the just." So there is some sense in which the world will be restored to its original state, but much more, much more than the original creation. It would really be misleading to think that we would be back in Eden. Whatever we need to be happy, God will certainly give us.

The Second Vatican Council says, "At that time, the end of time, together with the human race, the universe itself, which is so closely related to man, in which it obtains its destiny through Him, will be perfectly reestablished in Christ." We can't image how this will be. This goes beyond what eye can see, or ear has heard or what enters into the mind of man. We can be sure that it will be perfect and we should long for it with all our hearts. Finally, St. Peter tells us to prepare for it thus, *Therefore, beloved, since you wait for these, the New Heavens and the New Earth, be zealous to be found by Him without spot or blemish and at peace .*

Evangelization

The Gift of Faith

Have you ever stopped to wonder why you believe and someone else might not? Consider, for instance, these two cases. I met a lector at St. Patrick's cathedral in New York who was a Jew. He grew up in a Jewish household in a Jewish neighborhood. But ever since he was a little boy he was attracted by the sight of the Catholic church he walked by. He loved to peer inside at the statues, and eventually he would sit inside secretly for long periods; later he attended Mass with a friend. He vowed that when he was older, when his parents had died, he would become a Christian. He did, and now he lectors at the Cathedral. Now compare that beautiful story with the case of a man I met recently who was born and raised Catholic, indeed he was an altar boy in this very Church for years. He received religious education and the sacrament of confirmation. Then as soon as he was out of high school, he stopped going to Church, never returning, not even to get married. For almost 20 years now he has not worshiped in church even for Christmas or Easter.

One man had hardly any chance or reason to be a Christian and he became a fervent one; the other had the faith served to him and turned away. What a curious thing is faith! It is a grace of God, yet, we have a role to play; like the residents of Antioch, we need to *be urged to remain faithful to the grace of God*. In other words, faith is a gift, unsought maybe even unwanted – yet it's a gift that can be rejected. God must give us the ability to believe – *no one can say Lord without the Holy Spirit* – and yet we retain the ability to say 'I will not believe'. *You reject [the word of God]* said Paul and Barnabus to the Jews of Antioch.

This freedom at the heart of faith follows from understanding the true nature of faith. It's not merely the assent to certain true propositions, contained in the Creed. Rather, the essence of faith is accepting not propositions, but the one who proposes them to us: namely, God. We assent to these truths because we believe Him who has revealed them. We don't decide if they are reasonable or demonstrable; rather, our acceptance of the whole faith – especially the parts we may not get — shows that we trust the one who reveals Himself. To believe then means that one has somehow encountered the one who reveals the full truth about God, namely, Jesus Christ. The believer encounters Him, even in a hidden way, and finds that He is trustworthy, He is somehow familiar to me. In the language Christ uses – faith is recognizing His voice. *My sheep hear my voice ... and they follow me.* Faith is following, entering freely and willingly into relationship with God, a relationship that is made possible by Jesus alone. Being divine and human, we can get to know Christ the Man, and at the same time get to know Him who dwells in light inaccessible. *Philip*, said Jesus, *he who has seen me has seen the Father... no one comes to the Father, but by me. (Jn. 14:9,6).*

What shall we think of the many thousands and millions of people who do not believe? First there are those who seem to have never had the chance to believe. We musn't forget that God *desires all men to be saved and come to the knowledge of the truth (I tim 2.4).* As a result every soul is invited by Christ to believe in Him; He finds a way to show Himself, whether by the words of an apostle, or by a hidden way, like to the young Jewish boy walking past the curious church. Sometimes it is only by means of what St. Justin called the "seeds of the word", truths which would one day lead the searcher to Christ, that He calls to a person, and, paraphrasing what St. Luke says about the Antiochians: *All who* are *destined for eternal life* come *to believe.* Now this doesn't mean that we will always be able to see an explicit act of faith on the part of all those who come to Christ: like the invitation, the acceptance, too, may occur in a hidden manner, known only to God. Still, this doesn't mean that we can sit back and let God do all the work! Paul feels the responsibility, like no man, to be *an instrument of salvation to the ends of the earth,* for *How,* he asks, *can they believe if they have not heard?* So Paul spent all his strength and used all his ingenuity insuring that as many people as possible heard the word preached with all possible force and persuasiveness, so that they might have every possible help in coming to believe. For, as we have seen, not all would accept the word, under the best conditions, so it must be harder still if no one has preached, and pleaded, given good example and loving support. Without going to the ends of the earth, we too must work to help people hear the voice of Christ.

What of those who, like the second man I mentioned, seem to reject the faith despite every effort? Very rare is the household that doesn't have a sheep or two who seems deaf to the voice of Christ, especially since Christ also said of his Church's leaders *He who hears you hears me.* We must, without ever giving up, try to show them something that they may never have seen before: that faith is a relationship with God. All of the rest of what we associate with our faith: the teaching of the church, especially on morality, the common prayer and the reception of the sacraments are means to help us maintain and intensify that relationship. But they are very necessary means, not optional as many of those who have drifted suppose.

Yet, let us learn from Paul and Barnabus again who – despite their rebuff were *filled with joy and the Holy Spirit.* They knew that although they were instruments of salvation, God is ultimately responsible for saving souls; He loves them all, more than we do, and nothing is impossible with God. Like all burdens, we must cast the burden of the unbelievers on the Lord, along with our prayers, so we can have joy. And, finally, we will console ourselves with the vision of St. John, the preview of who will be saved. Though we seem a little flock now, there we shall be *a great multitude, which no one could count, from every nation, race, people and tongue.*

Seeking Christ

We often forget that we are surrounded by people who really don't know who Jesus is. And yet, however indifferent or hostile we might imagine people are to the Message, they really aren't.

Zaccaheus endured the indignity of climbing that sycamore tree, because he *was seeking to see who Jesus was*. Yet he, the chief tax collector for an occupying army, and an extorter as well – was the last
person you might imagine wanting to know the Messiah. But Jesus
knew both, that Zaccaheus was the most unlikely disciple, and that he
desired to be one: that is why Jesus chose him: *Zaccaheus, come
down quickly for today I must stay at your house.* Zaccaheus perceived something of the goodness of Christ and was attracted by His
Person. He knew that amassing wealth had not made him happy, and
he kept searching for the fulfillment that only Jesus could provide.
This kind of person – one who is on the lookout for something of
value, something permanent, beautiful, true, solid, noble – and who
knows that they don't yet have it — this kind of person who is aware
of an emptiness inside that has yet to be filled – this is the kind of person that Christ spies from afar. He knows their name and He comes to
put an end to their meandering in an existential void: *The son of man
has come to seek and save what was lost.*

Sometimes we forget that Christ not only sought people out
where they lived and worked – in their boats, temples, streets, and
houses – but He told us to do likewise: Christ demands we also "Go
out to all nations and preach the good news, into the highways and by-
ways". How easily we forget that if Christians of days gone by had
been content to keep their faith to themselves, we would still be ven-
erating oak trees and scrutinizing crystals... and, by the way, such activities are getting popular again. Paganism is the fasted growing religion in many places, because we Christians have ceased to say:
"Friend, come quickly, I must have lunch with you today, and tell you,
show you, who this Jesus really is".

It's so easy to forget that the majority of people, even professed
Christians, really have no idea who Christ is — the vast majority. The
more one is involved in the Church – daily Mass, parish council – the
more one sees only committed Christians. One of the greatest dangers
– and sources of strife in the Church – is this inward gazing, this
forgetfulnes of that great majority of men, still leading lives of quiet
desperation, and of our duty to unite in finding ways to reach them.
That is our mission: that is the reason for the existence of the Church:
to be the universal sacrament of salvation, the means by which all
men learn who Jesus is and so come to believe in Him. You will find
that no more rewarding occupation can be found than searching for
lost souls, winning their friendship, introducing them to Christ, and
hearing the echo in your heart of His words to Zaccaheus: *Today salvation has come to this house.*

Spiritual Fruitfulness

Moses was reminded that to come into the presence of God is not something to be presumed or taken for granted. St. Paul asks in the second reading whether we are worthy to stand before God. What is it that we can present to Him that will, as James says "cover a multitude of sins"? God definitely doesn't want us to appear empty handed when we come to Heaven and Jesus describes this expectation as "bearing fruit" in this life, or "making interest" on the gifts we've been given.

But what is the fruit we are to bear? What is spiritual fruitfulness? To be fruitful, fertile is to reproduce: "be fruitful and multiply". In the natural realm, to generate an image of ourselves. Spiritual life is no less fruitful, only the life that is to be passed on here is not **our** life, but the life of grace which we received from God. The image to be reproduced in others is not **our** own, but the image of Jesus Christ. If we are spiritually fruitful we are communicating to others the beauty of knowing, loving and *imitating* Jesus Christ, and they begin to do the same. In Paul's words, who was "father" to so many, *be imitators of me as I am of Christ.*

The Catholic Church is a body, the body of Christ, and it is alive, vivified by the Spirit of God. It has been growing, since it was but a dozen fisherman, until it is a billion worldwide. It cannot stop growing, it is fertile by nature. Yet, individual Christians can remain sterile. If no one upon seeing his life is attracted, fascinated, challenged, and moved to do likewise, then that Christian is sterile and the genuine Christian spirit is not in him. This is an infallible measure of the Christian life. Do people merely stare at us and say "That's fine for you" or do they desire to follow the Way? Do they ask us "what is the reason for the hope that is in you? And "Brothers, what must we do?

Is this standard difficult? Yes it is. Christ shows this by coming so soon to look for fruit, and in the other case, out of season. It is a terrible challenge: to inspire others to live the Christian life. But we cannot avoid it, and we can do it with grace. A major cause of the vocations crisis is right here: those who are living in religious orders and priesthood are not living it radically, generously enough, or many young people would be attracted. Shall we blame the culture? Our spirit is precisely to overcome the culture, not be overcome by it! Of course, parents must examine themselves: am I passing on the life of grace to my children? Saint John Vianney was very strict with parents reminding them that God would demand an account of them for this fruit of their lives most of all. We must add, however, that children are

free, and parents can only do so much. Moreover, there is no use lamenting one's mistakes, but keep fighting: the best spiritual parenting
is done late in life and even after death.

What is the secret to this supernatural fecundity? God is always at
work. He is attracting souls to Himself. He has spread the Church all
over the world. On our own we cannot convert one single soul, we
cannot persuade anyone of any bit of the truth of the Gospel. We must
trust totally in the power of God, **His** love, to work with us and in us.
The Holy Spirit is represented by Fire and we can see this same ardent
love that spreads all over the world in the Fire that burned the bush
without consuming it. This is not a destructive fire but one that is in
fact fruitful. This is why the burning bush has been seen also as a
symbol of the holy purity of the Virgin Mary whose womb by the
power of the Holy Spirit brought Christ to the world without losing its
virginal state. It is this same Spirit and only this Spirit that can make
us also instruments of engendering Christ in the world around us.

Zeal for Christ

We must consider this phenomenon of zeal today because Elijah
exemplified it, John and James distorted it, and every good disciple
should be characterized by it. Our Lord is clearly showing us that his
disciples must not be half-hearted, hesitant, or mercenary – they must
be zealots, in a good sense of the word. Zeal is a "necessary effect of
loving something" it is "the vehement movement of a lover towards
the thing loved". It accompanies "ardent" (burning) love. Like fire, it
consumes: *zeal for thy house will consume me.* Now from this very
concept we can begin to see that zeal is a good thing on one hand – we
can't claim to love something if we aren't 'fired up' about it – and yet
it can get out of control very easily.

Now, when we love something for our own sake, our zeal, though
originally legitimate, can very easily become distorted and selfish. In
English, the word for this has evolved into a new word: jealous. This
originally good movement of the soul easily becomes a disordered desire. It has been said that "Jealousy is more self-love than love"
(Rochefoucauld). When the object of our love is not our own personal
good, but the good of another, one might suppose that zeal is always
laudable. Not so. The first danger is that the good we love with a zealous love can turn out to be a false good. Thus, St. Paul was moved by
zeal to persecute the early Church because He thought this to be good.
We must always examine whatever "cause" we might be interested in
– is it worth being zealous about? When we have only one life to live,

which is unanimously agreed to be short, and very often shorter than we ever imagined – do we really want to spend our energies and stir up our passions over trivial or vain matters? Should we not concern ourselves only with what will promote the Kingdom of Christ – that is, with what will sanctify souls and make God better known and loved? What marvelous results St. Paul obtained when he turned his burning heart away from the Old Law and towards the Crucified and His concerns alone – namely the spreading of the Gospel to every creature. Then, as he would explain, *the love of Christ urged* him on to become all things to all people so as to save at least some.

There is a second way one can err, however, even when one is zealous for the good of others, and even when the good is genuine and important, our zeal can be immoderate. This was the problem of James and John. They were genuinely concerned about the honor due to their Lord, but they did not know **how** to be zealous for God. How will the glory of God, the object of their love, best be promoted? Not by destroying their enemies, but by winning them over with love and patience. This was the way of Christ. We have a wonderful example of zeal in the person of the Holy Father. Speaking to all Christians, especially the lay faithful, he wrote: "To all people of today I once again repeat the impassioned cry with which I began my pastoral ministry: "Do not be afraid! Open, indeed, open wide the doors to Christ!" Thus it's clear that missionary zeal is proper to every disciple. Thus Figuratively, while you remain in your families and community, you must experience what it means to have no place to lay one's head, no time to bury one's father, etc. In other words, it is not enough to be a strong member of a church community, but the laity must be ready to part with the familiar, the comfortable, the easy, for the good of souls and the glory of God.

Very often we Catholics act like mice because we are afraid of being perceived as zealots. We don't speak up when we see that others are in error or choosing the wrong path. Sometimes an exaggerated respect for other's independence or feelings makes us conclude that it's none of our business. Like Cain we say *"Am I my brother's keeper?"* But the fact is, if we loved God and loved our brother, we would burn with that vehement movement called zeal that would make it so hard to stand by while either God is offended or our neighbor drifts in sin. But our zeal will not generally be unwelcome, if it is born of true love for our neighbor and desire for his ultimate good.

We do not call down fire from Heaven to destroy, but to renew. We call down the Holy Spirit to renew the face of the earth. To convert hearts. We must dispose our neighbor with whatever words will help. This is the sort of zeal that will please God. This was Christ's objective: *I have come to cast fire on the earth and how I wish that it were burning already.* Our zeal for souls and for God's glory will be the measure of how much this Holy Spirit has been poured into our hearts.

Proclaiming the Name of Jesus

"Mission must therefore be the passion of every Christian; a passion for the salvation of the world and ardent commitment to work for the coming of the Father's kingdom." That is the message of the Holy Father for every Christian on this World Mission Day. Is it your passion, your single consuming passion which in some way directs all that you do, to make Christ known? If mission were not the passion of the early Christian church, we would not be Christian ourselves. Listen to Paul speaking to the Thessalonians, the oldest part of the New Testament: the word has *sounded forth.... your faith in God has gone forth everywhere... with the goal that all men might serve the true God* and await the coming of his Son with confidence.

Much has changed in the last two thousand years, but not the mission of Christ's disciples. Pope John Paul II, speaks the same language: "As the Father sent the Son, so the Son sent the Church to the ends of the earth. She has one mission, one message of salvation, which comes from God and is destined for all of mankind, so that, redeemed from sin, everyone might become a son of God." The measure that you seek to make Christ known is the measure of your love for Him. Yes, the connection between love of God and love of neighbor is so apparent. If you love God, you will think of Him and speak of Him, like a young person in love, you will want to tell others about Jesus. You will want to give Him the one thing He so desires, a sinner come back. *There will be more joy in Heaven...* You cannot claim to have love of God without love of neighbor. What greater love can we show than giving our greatest gift. If you are a Christian, this is your greatest asset — you would sacrifice anything for it, even life. How can you *love your neighbor as yourself* if you would not work to communicate that gift to them?

We know that example is necessary to back up our words if we are to proclaim the gospel. Still, it is a trap to think that one can fulfill one's duty by a good example alone. When the Pope came to Denver for the World Youth Day, he made this point very clear. We are all responsible. Remember, there are twenty-four people out there for each one of you. God depends upon your cooperation. "World Mission Day invites all believers to be missionaries in their own lives." There are two common myths about Evangelization. The first is that it is the job of the priests and the second is that coming into the Church is not necessary for salvation. When you see a grocer, your doctor, your mailman, do you wonder... does this person know Christ? Why do I deserve to have an intimate relationship with Christ and he doesn't? Why do I deserve certain hope and him fear and question mark? The Church is not asking you to be imprudent, offensive, rash, but if we have genuine love for our neighbor, we will be able to see the moments and areas in which the person is open to the message. We will seek to bring them one step further, one step at a time, with great respect for their conscience and presumption of good will.

Moreover, we must be efficient. It does no good to flail at random, to stand up and begin to preach. The Church has always organized into ranks with strategies, like "an army in battle array" (cf. Song of songs) Today especially she is regrouping in what is called the New Evangelization, which means "new ardor, new expression, new methods". More is required than last week's donation. God demands your whole heart and soul and mind and strength to be put into the practical love of God which is apostolic action. We all have time to be a Christian. One must begin by making the mission the guiding force of all we do. That is why we wear the clothes we do, say what we say. That is why, ultimately, we eat and breath — to live for Christ, for his service, for the spread of his Kingdom. Then, we will also see that our priorities have been uneven. We will see that we have time to devote to specifically apostolic works. Yet, it will always cost. There is no mission without the Cross. It is what we proclaim and the means by which we proclaim it.

Preaching the Gospel

In this gospel Our Lord Jesus gives very specific instructions to evangelists, to those who would preach the gospel. This is what the Church has been doing for these two thousand years. The evangelist, whatever his role, whether it be literally walking from nation to nation as a missionary like Paul or whether it be a missionary at one's place of work or in his community, has this characteristic which our Lord makes very clear, that they must be detached from this world. They must not carry unnecessary belongings, they must not have a traveling bag, they must not delay themselves along the way. They have a task and they must be divested of everything that might stand in the way. Also we see that the world has this ability to attach itself to us and us to attach ourselves to it, to become an obstacle. So he mentions this, *Enamored with the world, you have left the preaching task and gone off to Thessalonica.* It's love of the world that gets in the way of preaching the gospel.

St. Ignatius of Antioch has a startling statement for all those who would wish to be evangelists. He says, "Do not speak about Jesus Christ as long as you love this world." Do not even say the name of Jesus Christ, we're not worthy of it, if we love this world, so opposed are they. So opposed in what sense? Obviously not everybody in the world is supposed to leave their houses and bank accounts and so forth to preach the gospel. So in what sense is it opposed? In what sense do we have to leave it? I would suggest three ways, maybe they also go in order.

First, we must leave the need, the desire, to be accepted and respected by the world. If it admires us, fine, but if it thinks we're crazy, so much the better. The next thing one has to be willing to give up is comfort, the world offers comfort, and an unwillingness to sacrifice, and that makes it very impossible to preach the gospel. So giving up acceptability, comfort and then even security, even being willing to put that on the block in some way or another. We always try to cover every possibility and not trust in God's providence, but the Lord, here, says you'll be given what you need to eat and drink, whatever you need will be given to you.

So how do we apply this in individual cases? We just have to look around to see wonderful examples. One, very obvious one, those who try to have, if they are able, large families. I think of my parents who had eight children, but none of their friends had, I think, over five children. They thought it was crazy, obviously, so there goes respectability, and on top of that having many children can even cut into your comfort and even into one's security. One has to really trust providence to have such a family. That's just one little way that you see how everybody can detach themselves from this world and in some way preach the gospel. But there's many other beautiful examples. All of us can find a way to preach the gospel if we don't get caught by the world.

Apostolic Spirit

Christianity has been given a bad image. It is for women, for wimps, for pacifists. We tend to preach only *Let the children come to me*, and not *I have come to cast fire on the earth.* Anyone who thinks that religion is boring or Jesus is for the weak should meditate on this.

I have come to cast fire on the earth, and how I wish that it were burning already. That is the voice of an apostle, of *the* Apostle, the one who was sent from the Father to the world with a mission to accomplish. From Him, all apostles take their name and lead. Our Lord knew that His mission required paying the ultimate price, laying down His life. This was the *baptism* that He looked forward to, that He was *in distress*, not out of fear so much as out of yearning that His Father's will be accomplished. The word that Our Lord uses is the same used to describe being pressed by a crowd or a high fever. It expresses His inability to sit still, to be comfortable, while there was work to be done. It is the same feeling that all apostles must have. St. Paul was likewise *constrained* by the Word entrusted to him *(Acts. 18.5)* so that he told the Corinthians: *the Love of Christ constrains me, because we are convinced that one has died for all.*

In our day we have a great need of apostles. There is a need for the light of the Gospel in a world that is cold and dark. *I have come to cast fire on the earth.* "How I wish it were already kindled, fanned into flame by the Holy Spirit, and leaping forth in good works" (St. Denis the Carthusian). The Holy Spirit is the one who is responsible for making apostolic hearts. He is the one who transformed the Twelve from cowards locked in a rented room into apostles willing to defy any authority out of obedience to the will of God. The Holy Spirit came upon them as tongues of fire. *Our God is a consuming fire. (Heb. 12.29) The Love of God poured into our hearts by the Holy Spirit* is the fire that makes the heart of an apostle. Like fire, this love first of all purifies. If we love God we will be truly sorry for having offended Him. We will never be content with a certain level of virtue but continually strive to be better, to be holy. When we put God's will first, as did Jesus Christ, we can see everything in a new light. When we are consumed by love for Him, we are not blinded to other goods, but we see them in proper perspective. The fire that the Holy Spirit enkindles in our hearts makes us restless to make Christ known. That is the measure of your love of Christ: do you desire to make Him known? When you are speaking with someone, are you anxious to find out if they know Christ or are estranged from Him or His Church? Do you take real, bold steps to bring them around? Christ need not be the one thing we talk about, but He must be in everything we say. He must be the motivation, the background, the purpose of all we do.

Our love for Jesus Christ, if we let it show, will catch on to those around us. Why are we so timid? [Why are you becoming a priest? Because I love Jesus Christ] Why do you go to Church? Because I love Jesus Christ. This is the key element of the heart of an apostle: love, personal and passionate, for Jesus Christ. Do you love Jesus Christ? Is He the center of your life, the ultimate motivation for all you do? If so, you will not be able to contain yourselves. *We cannot but speak of what we have seen and heard. (Acts. 4.20) With so many witnesses in a great cloud on every side of us,* should we not *throw off what hinders us*? How can we fail to catch the fever, to be pressed by the desire to preach that the Christ is Jesus, that He has died for us, that if people repent and believe they can be saved? It is almost surreal to be bored with religion, to find it unchallenging. If you find the Catholic religion boring, it is not the Catholic religion but a false substitute for it, a combination of routine and dull religious practice. The true faith is a challenge, a mission, an all-encompassing and totally engrossing phenomenon that makes one's life so different and exciting that those who don't believe seem to be walking dead, zombies, people who have missed the boat of life and are simply wasting their time on earth. Being an apostle is a full time job. Because we have been baptized, we all are called to evangelize.

Soul of the World

The Christian is a helper to the doctor of souls; cured at Baptism of the mortal illness of sin, we must strive to avoid relapses. We must live in the world, without becoming part of the world. Our job is to diffuse His life-giving Spirit among the world, without being overpowered by the spirit that holds the world captive and moribund.

How shall we avoid becoming contaminated ourselves while in the world? We who have been called out of darkness into the light of Christ and his holiness, must refuse with all steadfastness to return to the ways of the world. An early Christian explained that *[Christians] dwell on earth but are citizens of Heaven...the immortal soul dwells in a mortal tabernacle. So Christians sojourn among perishable things, but their souls are set on immortality in Heaven.* We must test every opinion, every entertainment, every fashion, every pleasure that the world affords, holding it up to the light of Christ. Strong in faith, like Abraham, we must keep our eyes set on God's eternal promises.

Disciples of Christ must imitate Him in his "prophetic office"; like Him we will be met with misunderstanding, ridicule, and opposition. "Let [lay persons] not hide this their hope then, in the depths of their hearts, but rather express it through the structure of their secular lives in continual conversion and in wrestling *against the world rulers of this darkness, against the spiritual forces of iniquity (Eph. 6.12)."*

"...[T]he laity become powerful heralds of the faith in things to be hoped for if they join unhesitating profession of faith to the life of faith." "[Married Christians] by example and by their testimony, convict the world of sin and give light to those who seek the truth." *(LG 35).*

"Do you know what the Devil's first temptation is to the person who wants to serve God with dedication? It is human respect." (Cure d'ars) It can be a subtle temptation since it can appear that we are being charitable, building unity, tolerating the weaker in faith... but all these can easily be masks for our own cowardice. *Whoever denies me before men, I also will deny before my father who is in Heaven.* We think of Peter, who for fear of consequences, did not take sides with Jesus. Let us not think of the repercussions; often this moment of vacillation, of giving into an all too human prudence allows the moment to go by. Even humanly speaking, it is impossible to please all people all the time. There is only one person we need care if we are pleasing and fear displeasing: Jesus Christ.

To the Nations

Today is World Mission Sunday. Today we celebrate the efforts and achievements of missionaries, who preach the Gospel in so many ways. Mission has been an essential part of the nature of the Church ever since Christ ascended into Heaven saying: *Go therefore and make disciples of all nations.* Today we think particularly of the classic sort of mission, traditionally called *ad gentes*, to the nations, ever since St. Paul set as his goal to preach to nations who had never heard of Christ, leaving St. Peter to his mission among the Jews. There were those who thought that the Second Vatican Council's generous affirmation of all that is true and good in world religions would lessen the need for missionaries. The opposite is the case: the religious instinct that thrives in so many forms is seen as a preparation, an invitation, a call for the full truth of Christ to be explicitly preached and embraced.

To some this sounds patronizing; perhaps even like a renewal of cultural imperialism. No indeed, quite the opposite: we come as the Lord did: a servant to all. Just as Christ came *not to be served but to serve*, so also the genuine apostle, beginning with St. Paul, is a servant. *For what we preach is not ourselves, but Jesus Christ as Lord, with ourselves as your servants for Jesus' sake. (2 Cor 4.5)* And again: *For though I am free from all men, I have made myself a slave to all, that I might win the more.(I cor 9.19)* The missionary is a servant in three senses. First of all, Christians have known from the beginning that our Gospel is most often preached effectively without words, but by service. While service must not substitute for boldly articulating the *kerygma*, even in difficult situations, nonetheless, silent love can open doors and minds as nothing else. Think of the Missionaries of Charity, Mother Teresa's order, who have taught about Christ in virtually every nation on earth by their loving, whole-hearted service to the poorest of the poor. A missionary is a servant also in a second sense. We come offering help to a humanity in need; we have what all men are seeking — a relationship with the Father in Heaven through his Son, Jesus Christ. This great gift which we certainly don't claim to have merited or discovered by our own powers, we propose to and never impose on the rest of the world, respecting the particular genius of each people's culture and the sanctuary of each person's conscience.

Even though we are engaging in humble service we must take great care that those we help do not feel patronized. This is always a danger. As St. Vincent de Paul said of material service: "It is for your love alone that the poor will forgive you the bread that you give them". Likewise, and more so, when we offer another person the truth about God and Man revealed in Jesus Christ, we had better do so with love. The mission is urgent then in two senses: firstly due to the needs of the people, because their longing for truth is so great and they are desperate to have the peace and joy of knowing Christ. But the missionary endeavor is also urgent because love must be its driving force: *The love of Christ urges us*, says Paul again, drives us out to discover more and better ways to bring Christ's message of healing love to a broken world.

Finally, missionaries are servants in a third sense, in the sense that Christ uses the term in reference to the First Reading from Isaiah: suffering servants. To be a real missionary one must put oneself out for others, be willing to die for them. Just as Christ was not received, so also the service that his apostles offer to a sinful world is often rebuffed in the harshest manner. We must not forget that we are living in a century of martyrs and many of them have been missionaries. In God's mysterious providence, it is the great sacrifices, including the ultimate sacrifice of laying down their lives, which builds up the Church. The Cross attracts. "The blood of martyrs is the seed of Christians".

Now what can each of us do to help the mission ad gentes? Certainly, give money. But also pray and sacrifice: St. Therese became the patroness of the missions without leaving her convent!! Also we have in this parish dozens of potential evangelists, young boys and girls whom God is calling to leave everything and go make disciples of the nations. They will never do it, if they do not hear stories, true stories of heroism, such as that of Isaac Jogues and Jean de Brebeuf. If children grow up not knowing who these North American martyrs were, we have failed them and the mission. They must know them so that grace can work in their souls, too, so that their hearts, too, will yearn with St. Jean, "My God, it grieves me greatly that you are not known, that in this savage wilderness all have not been converted to you, that sin has not been driven from it. My God, even if all the brutal tortures which prisoners in this region must endure should fall upon me, I offer myself most willingly to them and I alone shall suffer them all". Thank God that he did or we might not be Christians ourselves!

Fortitude in the Service of God

Barnabus must have been a man of exceptional courage. He accompanied Paul and the evangelist Mark on the first missionary journey ever. Now it is no small thing to give your goods to the Church and become a missionary, in any age. To be the first man, along with Paul, to ever preach to Gentiles, makes us stop in admiration. What enables a man to do this? The answer is given by the Holy Spirit: *Set apart Barnabas and Saul for me for the work that I have called them to*. The Holy Spirit enabled them to carry out the amazing things they did. When the Holy Spirit directs a person's actions enabling them to do more than virtue is capable of, even virtue elevated by grace, we are in the realm of Gifts of the Holy Spirit. We know that there are seven, and one is Fortitude. Barnabas must have had it in abundance. It would have given him the courage to overcome fear and hardship not only because faith told him God would help, but because God supplied him with unshakable confidence and unconquerable assurance.

The gift of fortitude is not only available to us all, but we all need it if we are to carry out the Christian life. The Holy Spirit has a job for each of us, too. We all know people who either have never heard the Gospel or live as though they never had. We cannot admire the likes of Barnabus without hearing him say what He said to the people of Lystra who thought he was Zeus: *What are you doing? I am of mortal nature like yourselves*.

There is no reason that we cannot do great things, like Barnabus, if we also appeal to the Spirit to give us His gift of fortitude. We must not think that we are exempt from this responsibility if we have already lived most of our life or chosen a career other than being a missionary. There is always someone you can convince of the truth of the

Gospel and you will need fortitude to do it. Fortitude enables us to exercise an unflagging energy in the practice of virtue and in the service of God, be brave before all manner of danger or difficulty, suffer the greatest sorrows with joy, live the "heroism of the little", dying as martyrs drop by drop.

Serving God with Dedication

"In Christ we have already reached the heights of Heaven" says Leo. In this sense then the Kingdom exists even now. But the fulfillment of the Kingdom remains a transcendent event. It cannot occur in the scope of human history but must end time as we know it, bringing *a new heavens and a new earth (Rev. 21.1)*

There is a great desire in the hardened heart of fallen man to see his ambitions fulfilled in this life, not in some life to come. So much of the time, money, and effort, spent in this world is marred by the fact that it is directed, not towards the building up of the Kingdom of God, but the pursuit of an illusory goal, a perfect society of peace, health, and harmony, without Christ. Steering clear of this error one can also fall into another. If we cannot build a perfect world here below, why not simply wait, doing nothing until the Lord returns. The thought of the second coming should leave us with an increased desire to labor to prepare the world for it. The fact that it can come at any time, the fact that it is already growing among us, means that *time is short (I Cor. 7.29)* in every age. This is why, when the apostles stood gazing Heavenward at Jesus' ascending form, the two angels rebuked them: *Men of Galilee, why do you stand looking into Heaven?* What are you doing? Get to work.

Time is precious since it's a finite commodity, not only for the world, in general, but for us. *For what is your life?* asks St. James. *It is a vapor which appears for a little while. (Jas. 4.14)* Every moment is an opportunity to grow into a better image of God, to prepare ourselves to meet Christ. Only in time can we build up merit for a greater reward in Heaven. We cannot be sure that we will have more than today or even the rest of today. So...*While we have time, let us work good*, as the Apostle Paul said to the Galatians. Apostles do not say "Time is money" but "Time is souls that can be won over to Christ". To willfully waste time is a sin. St. Bonaventure: "No loss is of greater moment than the loss of time". We cannot give Christ our spare time, after we are done doing everything else we feel like.

Consider, first, the time Christians waste watching television. If you come anywhere near that national average, consider that it might well be a sin, even if you only watch the Discover channel. Besides, *idleness teaches much evil (Sir. 33.27)*, and gazing at too much television, when one's soul is made for the vision of God, is opening the door to the degradations that are sinful.

Consider time wasted talking. Christians should have much to do, but little to say. We can talk so much about God and so rarely **to** God. We can go about in circles talking of apostolic plans and get very little done. And again, immoderate chatter leads so quickly to sins: dissipation of spirit, criticism, vainglory, and so on. Even without alluding to evil talk, Our Lord warned that for every useless word we must render an account on Judgment day. *(Mt.12.36)*

A third area in which we could gain so much time: avoiding useless activity. Everyone in the world is short of time, so busy, but busy at what? We always have time to do His will. Are we working for food that will not satisfy? Think for example of a man who uses up the precious few hours he could spend with his family working overtime so as to buy a new car when the old one would do. Think of the mother who goes back to work, juggling young kids, when no one would starve if she stayed at home. Think of the millions of hours of activity expended without the agent ever stopping to ask: Does God care if I do this or not? Does He want it? Will it contribute to His great plan or not? Are my priorities, His? If you are rushed, stressed, or anxious — and we all are at times — it is a sure sign that your desires are not in line with His, and among other things, you are wasting your time.

I say "your" time, but it is His time. We are his servants, his useless servants and may God forbid that He come back and find us getting drunk and beating the housemaids as in the parable. *Abide in Him*, says St. John, *so that when He appears we may have confidence and not shrink from Him in shame at his coming*. On that day we will never regret any effort we made for Him, as we see the degree of love shown by our use of time fixed for all eternity. Like runners who give their all for two minutes to have a place in record books forever, let us give our all and *finish the race*.

Mary Mother of the Church

Evangelization Retreat

We just had the feast of Our Lady of Guadalupe. I don't know how familiar everybody is with the origin of this miraculous image. In the Liturgy of the hours, there is an account written in the sixteenth century by an Indian who lived contemporaneous with Juan Diego, the Indian who saw the Blessed Virgin. The most interesting part, perhaps, of the Miraculous events in Tepeyac in Mexico is that it had only been less than forty years after the Spanish arrived, and up to then the Franciscans had been trying without success to make converts of a very difficult lot of people. The Aztec were in full swing with human sacrifice, only five years before over twenty thousand young people had been sacrificed in four days in an Aztec festival. They were hard to convert for that reason and also because of the language barrier, because of the distance barriers, and because the rest of the Spanish were terrible witnesses to the faith. They were enslaving the Indians, and even imprisoning and scourging the priests who tried to protect them. It was hopeless, with very few converts. But within nine years of this miracle, this miraculous image, nine million Indians were baptized. They were real Christians, they passed on the faith and they became missionaries themselves to the rest of South America.

As the Holy Father put it in the document that closed the Synod of the Americas recently. "It was no question that the Blessed Virgin Mary played a decisive role in the Evangelization of America." And still she does, so she was awarded, not only the title the Mother of Evangelization, but of the New Evangelization which the Holy Father is encouraging us to undertake. "Today more than ever, dear brothers and sisters, your apostolate is indispensable in order for the Gospel to be the light, salt and yeast of a new humanity. Because of this, today more than ever, it is necessary for Christians, illuminated and guided by faith, to know the Church for what she is, in all her beauty and sanctity, to love her as their own Mother."

That little phrase there is one of the themes that I wanted to communicate tonight. The Church as our Mother, the Blessed Virgin as our Mother. The two are intertwined. The Blessed Virgin Mary is the type, the exemplar, the height of the Church. Very many things that we say of the Blessed Virgin Mary, we say also of the Church. The Blessed Virgin Mary's one concern is with bringing others to Christ and this is the mission likewise of the Church. There's a beautiful passage in the second Vatican Council comparing Mary to the Church. Both Virgins, both Mothers, both temples of the Holy Spirit, and so forth. Listen to this phrase of Paul VI here, talking to the people of Mexico about Our Lady of Guadalupe, "Mary remains hidden. Mary exhorts us to make Christ the center and summit of the whole Christian life. She remains hidden in supreme humility so that the image of her Son might appear to humanity with all its incomparable brightness. For this reason, true Marian devotion reaches its fullness and its most rightful expression when it is a path to the Lord and directs all its love toward Him, just as Mary knew how to do."

So that's the key phrase. "True Marian devotion is a path to the Lord." The more we come close to Mary, the closer we'll be brought to Christ. It's as if her whole reason for being is to be an evangelist, though she never really preached. What evangelization means, is bringing people to Christ. We can see her doing that in various ways in her life. As soon as she heard that Christ Jesus was within her, 'she made haste,' says the Gospel, down to her cousin Elizabeth to bring the Lord to her, and more specifically to John the Baptist. As soon as she came into his presence the grace of Christ touched the baby, John the Baptist, in the womb and he leapt for joy. He was sanctified in the womb of his mother. So there we see Mary bringing Christ right away to others. While she was waiting for Christ to be born, the Advent time, she immediately went out, doing what she could to help Christ arrive in people's hearts. So likewise as we're waiting for Christ to come again, the second time, it can't be just a passive waiting, just sitting back and waiting for Christ to come. We have to use that waiting time to make haste to everyone we can and somehow bring Christ to them.

That would be to imitate Mary, that would be real Marian devotion. Real Marian devotion according to the second Vatican Council is "imitation of her virtues." She kept on showing Christ to the world, to Joseph, to the shepherds, to Simeon, and at Cana, she is the one who initiates Christ's mission, bringing Christ to the world there too. In a beautiful phrase at the beginning of the Holy Year, the Holy Father says, ... "and the Blessed Virgin Mary continues to lay the Christ Child in the cradle of the Church through every generation." What Mary did, showing Christ to the Shepherds, she continues to do through the Church, in every generation, showing Christ to the world.

I'll just say a word about her virtues, the three big ones, Faith, Hope and Charity. Of course Mother Mary is known for her Faith, a woman of Faith. That's the key virtue for uniting us to God. St. John of the Cross said, "The greater one's faith, the closer one's union to God." Mary had to walk by faith. We mean for her, everything was not clear about the future, about what the angel's greeting meant. She was troubled, and it says several times, she pondered these things in her heart. Faith doesn't mean that everything is clear, but that everything is certain. So she was certain about the things that God said, even if she couldn't see how this was going to be. For that reason she was in so close union to God. This is from the Holy Father, "In the faith which Mary professed at the Annunciation as the Handmaid of the Lord, and in which she constantly precedes the pilgrim people of God, the Church strives energetically and constantly to bring all humanity back to Christ, its Head, in the unity of His Spirit." This is another expression of both Mary's desire to bring humanity to Christ, and the Church having the very same reason for being. But it's in Faith that that's done. Faith is very attractive. People are attracted by it.

If you want to know how to be truly devoted to the Blessed Virgin Mary, you have to read the book *True Devotion to Mary* by St. Louis de Monfort. The Holy Father said that this book changed his life. So that's a pretty good recommendation. This little paragraph here says, "Lastly, you never think of Mary without Mary thinking of God for you. You never praise or honor Mary without Mary joining you in praising and honoring God. Mary is entirely relative to God. Indeed I would say that she was relative only to God, because she exists uniquely in reference to Him. She is an echo of God, speaking and repeating only God. If you say Mary, she says God. When St. Elizabeth praised Mary, calling her blessed because she had believed, Mary, a faithful echo of God, responded with the canticle, my soul magnifies the Lord." So the idea there is, if one has enough faith in God, to be so closely united to God, one is like an echo of God and the goodness of God will attract people through you. Another way of saying that, is that holiness is attractive, so holiness and mission are linked.

In the phrase of the Holy Father, "The universal call to holiness (we're all called to be saints) is closely linked to the universal call to mission. Every member of the faithful is called to holiness and to mission." And it's saints, He says, who will spread the Gospel. So we must work on our faith, with Mary's help. Mary's great faith was strong enough to support ours, just as we must use the faith we have, a gift from God, to support those who are weaker in the faith. We can't wait until we feel that we have this tremendous faith so that we want to go out and preach on the street corners before we actually go out and do anything. That will never happen. So before anything is very clear and we have no questions, which was even the case for Mary, we have to take the faith we have and realize that's strong enough to help somebody else.

The next virtue is hope. Mother Mary is a great example of hope. Just think of what St. Elizabeth said about her. Blessed is she who believed that the promises of the Lord would be fulfilled. And then as she goes into her Magnificat she lists a whole number of promises, that the hungry would be filled with good things and so on. So she trusts in God's mercy. This is why, because of her tremendous hope, she is attributed as intercessor. Of course we believe, that she was so closely united to God, that whatever she asks will be given to her. We could say she is almost all powerful, because anything she asks, God will give her. The power of the intercession of Mary! Now this some-times could be imagined as her rescuing people from God's wrath. That would be an absurd way of thinking of her intercession, that she's standing between us and God to protect us from God, or even that God put her into the economy of salvation so that she would save people that He wasn't concerned about. That notion of intercession would be completely wrong. Rather, what intercession is, is that someone has such faith in God as Merciful Father and knows that God has a universal call to good will, and they cooperate with that. So when we say that Mary's interceding for us, it's not like in a caricature of a family where the mother goes between so that the father won't get angry with the child, nothing like that. Rather God wants to save ev-erybody and has planned to do that most effectively through using the cooperation of others, and first among them is the Blessed Virgin Mary. So He has willed to give His gifts of grace to the world through her requesting them, just as He's willed to give certain gifts to the world through our requesting them, through our prayers. This gives us merit when we cooperate and is helpful to us to be able to call on those who are closer to us than the ungraspable, mysterious God.

It's because of this great hope in God's mercy and love, that Mary's intercession is so valuable and ours will be all the more effec-tive the more we believe, the more we hope in God. The Church today really is afflicted by a lack of hope, and that's why there is so little evangelization going on. The Holy Father keeps saying that there is a Springtime ahead of us, if people will just believe it. We imagine it's so hard to bring someone to the Lord, but why do we think that? If you think back to the early days, back to 1531, they were coming in droves. It's so possible for people to be attracted by the beauty of the faith, if we really have that hope, that expectation, that what we have is so good, that God's promises are so wonderful, that holiness is so attractive, that the Church is so beautiful. As soon as they hear about it, then they'll want it. It's true, people really are starving for that. Just as Mary is that universal intercessor, all graces come to us through her, likewise, the Church is the universal Sacrament of Salvation. All people will come to Christ through it. There's that connection always between Mary and the Church.

The last virtue is love. Usually when we think of love in relation-ship to God we think of it in terms of spousal imagery which is the way the Holy Scripture presents it to us and Mystics and so forth. But in this connection of evangelization, the sort of love we must think of is maternal, maternal love. Listen for instance to this quote from the Second Vatican Council, "The Virgin Mary in her own life, lived the example of that Maternal Love by which all people should be fittingly animated to cooperate in the apostolic mission of the Church, on behalf of the rebirth of men." Remember our goal, that we all get reborn by grace, born again by grace. So the love that wants to have people be reborn is a maternal love. You could say a jealous love. You see everybody in the world like a child that you want to help. Jealous and zealous comes from the same word. So we say missionary zeal, we have this jealous love for this person that we are responsible for, that has been entrusted to us and we want good things for that person, just as a mother would for her child.

St. Augustine goes so far as to say that the predestined of this world, the elect, the just, are enclosed in Mary's womb and that they come to life only when their good mother brings them forth into eternal life. The expression for giving birth is the gift of life in a lot of languages. So when we reach the light of Heaven, it's as if being born from the womb of the Church, the womb of the Blessed Virgin. Another sense in which we speak about maternal love, is that Christ will be born in people. The Church in her apostolic work, also rightly looks to her who brought forth Christ, so that through the Church, Christ may be born and increased in the hearts of the faithful also. So just as Mary gave birth to Christ, so also the Church gives birth to Christ in people's hearts. And the two things really fit together, us being reborn and Christ being born in us. They fit together in a beautiful phrase of St. Paul's, which he said to his new converts. "I am in labor with you, until Christ is born in you."

Just a footnote about love, it always costs. Mary was given to us as Mother at the foot of the Cross, "Behold your Mother." And being a mother in this sense requires sacrifice. "I am in labor with you…" Labor means sacrifice. In fact that's always going to be the case. Remember the blood of Martyrs is the seed of Christians, from the persecution of the Church, from the sorrow of Mary, from the Passion of Christ, comes to the world all the fruits of redemption. So as we want to imitate the Blessed Virgin Mary's love, we have to ask the Lord for hearts big enough to desire to sacrifice for our brothers that Christ may be born in them.

Sanctity of Life

Children

There is something fascinating about the face of a child, especially a baby. Christ especially loved children, as He loved the poor, because they were particularly vivid images of love, which is to say, of God. We must look at children who are still young enough to have never actually sinned. They are images of God; as Mother Teresa says: "There we see the face of God". As a result, when we help little children we must do so with genuine charity; that is to say, we must love God, by loving them. We must honor and praise Him, who is made, in some way, visible and tangible in little children. If we appreciate the beauty of innocent children, we will, as Christ did, also develop a greater abhorrence for all the attacks upon them. Christ speaks of scandal, the deformation of their souls. This is a common tragedy; indeed it is the rule. This is why the twenty-year-old who has the same attractive innocence of a five-year-old is a rare exception. Yet it is possible: the man who heard St. Thomas Aquinas' last confession could not but exclaim: "He has the soul of a five-year-old".

There are other attacks upon children in our day. Not only their souls but their lives are in danger. All attacks upon them are attacks upon God. Given what we said about the patent value and God-like beauty of children, those who seek to destroy them must be considered evil in the fullest sense of the word. Just as the good angels protect the children interceding before the Father, the evil ones, the devils, and their allies on earth, seek to kill children through abortion, pornography, and many other evils. We must view all this with eyes of faith: the evil forces which seek to destroy the Church, strike at the cell of that society, the family, and they seek to ruin the family by attacking its most vulnerable element: the child.

Let us pray to Christ, who was Himself a little child. He remained always child-like in pure innocence and did not use his omnipotence to keep Himself from suffering the attacks upon Him. Let us pray to Him to help us see attacks on children as attacks upon Him, allowed for the same purpose, the redemption of the world. But we pray also that as many of these pristine images of God as possible be kept free from harm.

Fatherhood

This Mass was offered in honor of St. Joseph because we need his protection, of course, as head of families, but also his example of fatherhood . The crisis of fatherhood, as we know, is really at the heart, or a major part of the culture of death. This is becoming more and more recognized, of course, and more and more written about. If we only stop to think about what a different picture it would be if fathers really were fathers. How few women would really choose abortion if the boyfriend, if that's the case, was a true father and said, "I will take responsibility," even after making a terrible blunder — or if her own father said, "I will be a real father to you." As we all know, you know better than I, most women who get abortions, it's because of a lack of support from the men in their lives, or even pressure from the men in their lives.

So, we pray to St. Joseph, that fathers everywhere will learn to develop his great virtues. Obviously he is known first and foremost for his chastity. Speaking of Bishops and priests, St. Paul says, "How could someone take care of the household of the Church, if he can't yet manage his own household?" Likewise we could say, "How could someone manage his own household, be a good father, if he can't manage himself, if he can't control himself and his passions." So chastity is essential to be a good father. We pray that St. Joseph will increase this virtue and intercede for fathers everywhere, that they might develop it and of course the other virtues that he had — self discipline, prudence, courage, patience, generosity, wisdom, all of these things — that fathers may all develop St. Joseph's virtues.

The crisis of fatherhood, we must also admit, is largely caused by women, insofar as the feminist movement is a major antagonist in this problem of developing genuine fathers. What many people in this movement are after, is not equality but power. It's an attack on the role of the father or let's say authority in general. This became clear to Cardinal Ratzinger within the context of the all male priesthood. We also, in the priesthood feel the crisis of fatherhood. It is normally assumed that the call for female priests is a call for equality but maybe this isn't really so. This became clear to Cardinal Ratzinger when one of the leading proponents, a feminist theologian in Germany, began to study more about the priesthood and saw that priests are themselves servants of the Church — that they are called to be obedient servants, and as she pondered this she realized that women didn't really want to do that, in her view. She said, "We don't want to be priests, women priests. Rather what we need to do is abolish the priesthood all together." So then Cardinal Ratzinger observed that, maybe the problem there is not so much wanting to be equal, but rather wanting to do away with authority, and that might be at the heart of the matter.

The crisis of fatherhood, their failure to play the role of head of the household is because the whole concept of the head of the household has largely disappeared. This is no doubt, in part, because of authority being confused with power, which it mustn't be. There's many confusions here. One is confusing authority with power, another with freedom as license, another is order meaning superiority and inferiority. None of this need be the case. We need only to look at **The Father**, the Heavenly Father, who in the Blessed Trinity is first, is source, origin of all the Persons, yet is in no way superior to the other Persons. So, in God's plan, all things are possible. It is possible, if we model our family on the Blessed Trinity and live with grace, which transcends nature, it is indeed possible to have an order without any hint of superiority or lording it over other people.

So we should see the family and the role of father in this light, a mystery to plumb, a beautiful thing, and not something to resist. Chesterton points out the famous statement which is quoted by Pius VI , "The husband is the head of the house, while the woman is the heart of the house." In other words if we truly understand the family in God's plan and not according to our understanding of power struggles, we would see that the family transcends all that. If we get right to the heart of the matter, the crisis in fatherhood is really a crisis in belief of God. A book has just come out to that effect which looks at the great atheists of our day and sees that all of them had terrible relationships with their father. If people really understood, if people really lived and experienced the love of a father and all of these virtues of self control, discipline, mercy, strength, prudence and so on, they would be led, helped anyway, to accept that there really is such a Father in Heaven. The contrary is the case, if they don't experience that, they tend to have difficulty in thinking that a Heavenly Father does exist. As we know, the culture of death, is really an atheism, a refusal to believe that God exists and that we must order our lives and our world according to His Fatherly plan. Also, we have to remember that it was Jesus Himself, who taught us that God truly is a Father. It was His Holy Spirit that enabled us to really, as St. Paul says, cry out "Abba — Father " and have these familial relations with the almighty God who otherwise may have seemed so distant.

So let us bring all of these concerns for our families, for our culture, for our world before Jesus who taught us so much about family, and about the true nature of God. Let us ask Him to have this true view of things, and the virtues that St. Joseph showed us, flourish in our society again.

Christian Motherhood

When we think of the ideal of motherhood, we must recognize that we are holding up something that is truly from above. It is something which has natural foundations but which, like all things, has been made new by Christ. Doubtless it is true that there are many worthy mothers who never got the opportunity to know Christ explicitly, but only His Spirit, at work in hidden ways, could make them love in a way that fully merits the title of mother.

We must remember, that all things human, including motherhood, needed to be made new by Christ. If we're not careful, the maternal virtue of being welcoming and open to life can turn into a selfish claim to a child at all costs, legitimate prudence can become fearful distrust of Divine Providence. Or the characteristic of being nurturing and gentle can get distorted into doting, spoiling the child. The necessary detachment which allows children to live their own lives can become an excuse for giving up the effort to help them grow as persons and Christians. Surely, all mothers experience their need for God's help when they find themselves unable to love, even their own children, with the intensity and constancy that they wish they could; frequent confession is a great help to them in a task which really does take supernatural grace to be accomplished well!

In our day and our culture, more than in any other time or place, authentic motherhood is under assault. Motherhood, that is, understood as a unique, irreplaceable, absolutely vital mission in the church and society, to which women are called by God. If mothers are seen as the heart of families, which are the cells that make up the Church and civilization, it becomes clear that they need thorough preparation, unflagging support and lots of grace. But as the values that mothers are primarily charged with transmitting – such as love of God, generosity, self-sacrifice, purity of heart, love of beauty, even life itself – as these goods are devalued, the role of mother gets reduced to giving birth only. This is the direction we are heading: a culture of death is a culture where motherhood has been degraded into virtual oblivion. It's also a culture where the new commandment of love is losing its greatest witness.

Fortunately, as long as there is a Church – and there always will be – there will be true Christian mothers. One of the happy parts of being a priest is working with so many sterling examples of this noble breed, and helping them in various ways to live up to the exceptional demands of their calling. This is one of the Church's primary tasks, and the Church is equipped for it – she's referred to as "holy Mother church" for a reason. Through the Church, children of God are generated, nourished, instructed, consoled, healed and so on. The Church's defining characteristic is that love – that God-given, self-sacrificing, other-directed love – which makes mothers great: *they will know you are Christians by your love*, and they will know that you are mothers by this same love.

The Church has been a sign of contradiction and a beacon of hope to the world for these past twenty centuries. In, with and through this Mother, individual mothers can also stand up to the culture and take issue with it. They can resist being deformed by the culture and instead take the initiative in re-forming it. Mothers are the first agents in forming our culture, for they can make the deepest impact upon the way of thinking and acting of the next generation. They must guard their children like the lioness, but with fortitude that comes from the Holy Spirit!

Fortunately, also, there is someone who can give direction, protection, help and good example to Christian mothers. There is, we could say, a mother of Christian mothers, who is always near at hand: that is the Blessed Virgin Mary. She is the first woman to be made new by Christ. She was prepared and sanctified so that none of Eve's guilt touched her. While the Church will only be beautifully adorned, *without spot or wrinkle*, at the end of time, Holy Mary already is and always has been perfect, totally beautiful, the image of what the whole Church shall be. How eagerly Christian women, young and old, should study the person of Mary. How did she think, and speak and pray? How did she spend her time? How did she do chores? Did she complain on the way to Egypt? Surely not! Was she not – in receiving the wise men — the model of humility for those mothers whose children excel? And was she not also the model of strength at Calvary for those whose children are handicapped or insulted or already taken back to God? Mother Mary, show us all, mothers and those who learn from them, how to love, how to live this new commandment. Help us to receive communion, the Sacrament of Love, as you received it, with perfect devotion, every day of your life after your Son ascended into Heaven. Finally, continue to renew this world of ours in the way that God has planned: through our Holy Mother the Church, through the families that make it up, and through those families' mothers .

The Elderly

If we consider, what is aging? What is it but the corruption of what we love so greatly, our flesh, our bodies. Like all suffering and death it is an effect of original sin. We have to remember all the wrinkles and crows knees that people hate to get, one of the main reasons is that they are reminders of the fact that we will have to die. Reminders that we will have to carry with us at all times. We, who fear the end of life, have often tried to find a fountain of youth. In our own day we find that, more and more, in the cosmetic industry and the great interest in health products. All this can be seen as part of our fear of getting old, because we fear death itself. So many vain attempts have been made to stop time, rather than to profit from the time we have.

There is a way to grow younger every day, even as our body grows older. This way is the spiritual life, just as our Lord Jesus said, "Unless you become as little children, you will not enter the Kingdom of God." Little children, as we know, are pure of heart, outgoing, trusting, dependent, genuine, unselfconscious, humble, always living in the present, always full of trust and full of love. We must become like them. When we do, we will become younger, more and more youthful in a very real and meaningful way. Becoming like little children, in the sense the Lord means, is the work of grace. As Paul describes it, "So we do not lose heart, though our outer nature is wasting away, our inner nature is being renewed every day," being renewed by grace, the true fountain of youth which flows from the heart of Christ. When He came back from the dead He said, "Behold I make all things new," or all things young again.

Christ speaks for us in the Gospel passage we just heard on many different levels. So when He says, "Some of you here have come a long distance," we can think of Him referring to the journey of life. Those who have traveled furthest on life's journey are the elderly. Christ is referring perhaps, in this prophetic action of His, to the journey of life because He is foretelling this provision of food for that journey. Lest we faint on the way, lest we collapse on the way to Heaven, He has given us food which is the Holy Eucharist. That's the food that renews us, that's how we're kept young, through that bread of Angels. St. Ireneaus, one of the earliest fathers of the Church, went so far as to call the Holy Eucharist the antidote to death and the medicine of immortality. In fact, that most incurable disease, which is aging itself, the Lord has cured by giving us the Bread of Life.

Let us renew then our efforts to appreciate the Lord's plan to make us children of God, to renew us in mind and body through His gift of grace. We may have indeed wasted many opportunities to grow in God's grace, but if youth is a characteristic time for hoping, and old age for regretting, in the Lord's economy all that can be changed. In Christ, all of our regrets, time wasted, time not profited from, can be swallowed up in His mercy. He is God, for whom a thousand years is like a single day, a watch in the night. He can make up for all of our failings and in the order of grace, we will have nothing to regret but only eternal life of Heaven to look forward to.

God's Gift of Life

Leprosy, untreated as it had to be in Biblical times, was a terminal illness. These ten men, like Naaman the Syrian, were dying. I'm sure that when they were cured they were all beside themselves with joy. They all appreciated the value of having life restored to them – a healthy and possibly lengthy life back in their families. It's only natural to respect life, an obviously good thing, especially when it's endangered. However, the Samaritan stands out, because he was not only happy to receive his new lease on life, but *he was grateful*. He knew that it was a gift from God.

It is Respect Life week in the Catholic Church in the United States. But if we simply celebrate life as a very good thing, a beautiful, valuable phenomenon — we fall short. Life is *a gift of God*. If our respect for life does not lead us to fall down in adoration, praise and thanksgiving of the Creator, it is lacking. What's more, if we do not give God his due in this way, we will soon find ourselves lacking respect for the lives He has made.

The Second Vatican Council includes this sage statement: "The creature without the Creator vanishes … through the forgetting of God, the creature itself is lost sight of." Where are man's rights to life and liberty more trounced than is atheistic systems which pay lip service to the greatness of man, while squashing the lives of each man in particular? Indeed, we could go so far as to say that an infallible index of the genuine religiosity of a person, society or civilization is its treatment of innocent life.

If the image of God which is the human person is not jealously guarded, no matter how small or weak, how old, or how deformed, then God is not loved, adored, respected, or thanked for his gift of life. Every attack on an innocent human being is an attack on God. We must draw close to the one who called Himself Life itself: I am the Resurrection and the Life. For this gift of life, eternal life, we must never stop thanking God and praising Him in a loud voice.

The Gospel of Life

There was a landowner who planted a vineyard. Jesus explains his image in terms of the Kingdom: *Therefore, I say to you, the kingdom of God will be taken away from you and given to a people that will produce its fruit.* This Sunday, we are to reflect upon a particular aspect of the Gospel, namely, the Gospel concerning Life, to see if we are producing the fruit that the landowner expects. Are we gradually turning our society into a civilization of love, where life is an ever more sacred, treasured, value? This is our mission, and yet it seems that Christian countries, the developed West, is leading the world in attacks upon life! It is from the West that landmines and weapons are sent to the developing world, along with methods of population control that seek to eliminate poverty by eliminating the poor. It is in the Christian West, where medical ethics began, that doctors now are avidly pursuing reproductive technologies, embryo experimentation, and cloning without any regard for the human dignity of the tiny persons at their mercy. It is in the Christian West, finally, that death is sought as a solution to serious crime problems and to the great expense of caring for the terminally ill. Countries that consider yourselves civilized, that have been sown with the seeds of the Gospel, *Why,* [the Lord is asking] *why when I looked for the crop of grapes, did it bring forth wild grapes?* The Lord *looked for judgment, but see, bloodshed! for justice, but hark, the outcry!*

It would not be right to simply catalogue the increasing attacks upon life. We could allow ourselves too easily to point the finger at those who commit these crimes, failing to examine ourselves. The Holy Father insists, on the contrary, that we need to renew "a culture of life within Christian communities themselves. Too often it happens that believers, even those who take an active part in the life of the Church, end up by separating their Christian faith from its ethical requirements concerning life…With great openness and courage, we need to question how widespread is the culture of life today among individual Christians, families, groups and communities in our dioceses" (*Evangelium Vitae*) How widespread is the culture of life in my heart? in my family? in my parish?

By now we are familiar with the term which so aptly describes the breadth and depth of the anti-life animus: "the culture of death". Acknowledging that hostility to life has become a part of Western culture, provides us Christians with two reasons to make this humble self-examination, proposed by the Pope. First, anti-life values could not have replaced Gospel of life values without the cooperation of many who call themselves Christian. If we were actively infusing our culture with Gospel values, the forces of evil would not be able to triumph. Imagine the impact on our culture if the tens of millions of Catholics who live in the United States were advanced in the virtues of chastity and humility, of charity, patience, and self-denial.

The second reason for us to examine ourselves on the subject of the culture of death, is that a people are not only the creators of their culture but the products of it. We can hardly live in a society that is busy enshrining the most barbaric acts as rights, without being affected ourselves. From all sides we are being encouraged to adopt the philosophy of the wicked tenants in the Lord's parable. They respected no moral norms, objective truths about good and evil, but followed only their own self-interest. Short term benefits, instant gratification, and the exaltation of their own will, blinded these tenants to what they knew in their hearts to be right. Having committed certain injustices, denying the landowner his due and maltreating his emissaries, they were emboldened to pursue greater gains and commit greater crimes. They set their hearts on the whole inheritance, saying to themselves, *Come, let us kill him.* They rejected the stone, the foundation stone of a just society, who is Christ and his Gospel, which affirms that there are some acts which must never be committed or condoned. Finally, they incurred, as our society has also, the curse of Isaiah: *Woe to those who call evil good and good evil, who put darkness for light and light for darkness... woe to those who are wise in their own eyes, and shrewd in their own sight... who acquit the guilty for a bribe and deprive the innocent of his right!* (Is. 5.20-23)

We know from the parable that the Lord is all powerful and will win out in the end. Yet, He delays his return in the hope that some of these tenants will repent. There is time, and the time is now, to transform this culture of death into a culture of life and a civilization of love. "At the heart of every culture lies the attitude man takes to the greatest mystery: the mystery of God" (*Centesimus Annuis*) The culture of death will be converted by the return of belief in God — not lip-service, but a real, practical belief in God the Father, the Creator of each and every man, woman and child no matter how small or weak, in his own image. This belief in God, our Father, who so loved the world that He sent us his only Son, would turn our nation around.

How can we contribute to this enormous task? Most importantly, we must be responsible tenants of the vineyard of our own souls and our families. We must see to it that we are completely and totally converted to belief in God the Father and his Son Jesus Christ. This is eternal life! How, for instance, can we claim to see the image of God in our neighbor and still watch movies that glorify violence and immorality? *Whatever is true, whatever is honorable, whatever is just, whatever is pure, ... if there is anything worthy of praise, think about these things.* Yes, let the kingdom of God be extended within us, and it will spread also to our neighbors.

Signs of Contradiction

That Christian dogma which has been called the most obvious is also the one that is most often overlooked. We don't notice it, although we are looking right at it. It is the background of our lives; original sin. The effects of original sin are so powerful that even the Jews, blessed with the law, could not help but tend to evil. And we too are affected: despite the benefit of two thousand years of Judeo-Christian tradition, we live in a country that can call evil good and good evil with the greatest of ease. We seem even worse off than the pagans: idolizing ourselves, our freedom, and making war on our children.

The antidote to original sin and its effects — a darkened intellect and a weak will — is grace. When people are moved by grace they tend to God, and so they come into conflict with a fallen world that tends to evil. They become a "sign of contradiction", like Our Lord, and like Him, they are hated by the world. Thus St. Vincent of Saragossa suffered the most barbarous treatment from enemies of goodness rather than hand over his copy of the Gospels to be desecrated. Why, we must ask ourselves, do so many Christians do a much greater disservice to the Gospel by condoning abortion, even though they are not even under threat of death? Why do we fear the label of "extremist" or "fanatic" more than St. Vincent feared the rack?

Undaunted, signs of contradiction we must be. In the pro-life fight which is far from over we must hear Christ's words: *is it lawful to save life or to kill it?* And we must not be mute so that *He look around angrily* at us *grieved at our hardness of heart*. Only grace will overcome hard hearts, enlighten darkened intellects. Let us pray for it and for the grace that will give our weak wills the courage to be signs of contradiction to a fallen world.

Martyrdom

Most Catholics only see red vestments on Pentecost, but in fact they are most usually worn as a reminder of blood, the blood of martyrs. Since we don't celebrate these feasts and memorials when they fall on Sundays, those who cannot make it to daily Mass may not recognize the Church's great emphasis on the value of martyrdom.

Why the emphasis? Because martyrs are witnesses – this is the translation of the Greek word – and they are witnesses of the most eloquent kind to that dogma which is at the heart of our faith: namely, the resurrection. If it's true that Christ is risen, and that you too will live forever with Him, body and soul, then you won't mind dying to keep his law. Willingness to die for the faith and morals is the greatest proof that we will live forever by that same faith. Today's world needs witnesses to the resurrection as never before. Firstly, this means that we need to hold up martyrs, not less today, but more. The Holy Father has done just this. Throughout his pontificate he has returned again and again to the theme of martyrdom, but never so earnestly as during the Great Jubilee, when he wrote: "...the Church in every corner of the earth must remain anchored in the testimony of the martyrs and jealously guard their memory." The truth about the resurrection is the key to hope in an age of despair.

No clearer sign of this despair is needed than the increasing acceptance of euthanasia in the once Christian west. Shocking and incredible though it is, until this week, doctors in Oregon had legally given lethal doses of drugs to patients who wanted to die. God's law, his sovereignty over life and death, duty to family and community meant nothing to these people when confronted with a painful disease. How different from the noble youths of Judah who willingly suffered much more terrible pains rather than breach God's dietary statutes! These had fortitude because they knew their bodies would rise again; the people in Oregon who killed themselves had no such faith, no hope, and no fortitude. Have we become a people which does not even have the natural nobility of ancient Rome expressed by one of their poets thus: "Count it the greatest sin to prefer life to honor, and for the sake of living, to lose what makes life worth living." (Juvenal)

However, just when we might have given up hope, we have heroes again. We hear stories of real people willing to endure suffering and risk death to preserve and defend the law of God, to promote justice, and to demonstrate love. But whether we are called to martyrdom of blood or not, we are all called to be witnesses to the Resurrection. We must *walk in newness of life*. We must live detached from the world even, as St Paul dramatically puts it, letting *those who have wives live as though they had none*, (*1 Cor 7:28*) that is with eyes fixed on Heaven, not clinging to earthly realities. Our tendency must be to pray, *our conversation in the Heavens*, our tongue free of evil. We must honor God's law in the least matter, especially in regard to purity: *every other sin which a man commits is outside the body, but the immoral man sins against his own body*, which is meant to be a temple of the Spirit, now and in the world to come. Those who see us will think that we are already living *like the angels in Heaven*. And, finally, we must be willing to sacrifice, to make efforts, to do good to all, without counting the cost, motivated by the same yearning for everlasting life that motivates martyrs. For as St. Cyril says: "The root of every good work is the hope of the resurrection".

The Splendor of Truth

What must we do to have eternal life? It is the great question of the Gospels which the rich young man asked Jesus. It is the question that the first converts asked the apostles on Pentecost: *Brothers, what must we do?* It is the question that split the Protestants from the Catholic Church: are good works required or is faith alone sufficient? It is a question of enormous import.

There is a temptation to emphasize deeds to a fault. This was the temptation of the Jewish converts to Christianity. They underestimated the power of the Cross which has so sanctified those who are reborn in baptism that they have no need of the myriad prescriptions of the law which sought to make the chosen people worthy of their God. All these were but preparations for the great transformation of God's people into the Church of Christ. Henceforth, they needed no temple, but they were to *be God's temple (I Cor. 3.16)*. What in the future was to set them apart? How would God's chosen people be discerned?

Christ gave the answer of course: *they will know you are my disciples by your love*. Christ, then, and the apostles with Him have put emphasis upon the heart not external observances. At this point, however, we encounter the opposite temptation to the legalism of the early Jewish converts. If they erred by saying that morality is entirely exterior, others err by saying it is entirely a private matter. If Christ is calling us to a new commandment of love, who is to judge if we transgress it? Some go so far as to say that people who commit abortion — knowingly and willingly — may be making a loving choice. Enemies of Christ have come among his present day disciples disturbing them and unsettling their minds, but with this new error, the removal of all objective standards.

As in the days of old, when the apostles, the foundation stones of the Church, wrote that first encyclical letter, so in our day, their successors, led by John Paul II, have come to the rescue with a letter, called *Veritatis Splendor*. This is a profound affirmation of what is apparent from the Gospels: Jesus Christ did not abolish the Law but He fulfilled it. Thus He responded to the rich young man: *If you wish to enter into life keep the commandments*. These are a summary of the deeds that represent the bare minimum we must do if we are to achieve happiness through loving and being loved. In other words it is impossible to love God or our neighbor when we knowingly and freely violate the commandments. Those who live together before marriage cannot have true love because their actions, which speak louder than words, tell a different story of selfishness and disregard for God. For Christ says: *If any one loves me he will keep my word... Those who do not love me do not keep my words. He who says 'I know Him' but disobeys his commandments is a liar, and the truth is not in him; but whoever keeps his word, in him truly love for God is perfected.*

The key is that some acts are of themselves incapable of leading to the happiness that God had called us to, regardless of our intention. It is impossible to love God as the goal of our life and choose — knowingly and freely — something that cannot lead us towards Him. If we take Jesus at his word we will have to admit that there is much work to be done. It is no secret that many people are not living by the commandments that lead to life. Whether or not they come back depends upon us: the radical witness of our lives, evident holiness, standing out from the crowd. We must also speak the truth in a timely and charitable manner, but without fear or human respect. We must heed the Pope's call to: "show the inviting splendor of that truth which is Jesus Christ Himself. ... Only the Cross and the glory of the risen Christ can grant peace to [man's] conscience and salvation to his life."

Living the Truth

The Church is a mother to her children, and she will not give them evil gifts. When the People of God cry out: "Show us Jesus Christ! Preach the Gospel to us! Tell us how to attain eternal life," the Church responds, bolstered by her charism of infallibility, with the authentic Gospel entrusted to her by Christ Himself. Her goal, like any mother's, is only that her children be happy. Our Lord said: *Ask and you will receive that your joy may be full. (Jn. 16.24)* He sought to impose no useless burdens on his disciples, but only a light burden and a sweet yoke. Holy Mother Church does not wish to bind up unnecessary burdens either, as the Pharisees did, but she will preach the whole truth, *in season and out of season.*

We only fully discover who we are and what we must do to be happy through the revelation of Jesus Christ, the perfect man. Nonetheless, a great number of truths of our nature, written deep upon our hearts by the hand of God, are being ignored or denied, especially in the area of family life. The document, known as *Humanae Vitae*, af-

Making God the Joy of Our Soul

firmed that God, in his wisdom, arranged that man and woman should cooperate through an act of love with the creation of each new human being. If spouses, consciously and freely, do anything to frustrate the life-giving potential of their married love (that is, by contraception or sterilization), they sin gravely. We must celebrate the courage of Paul VI in reminding the world of this truth, and thank God for enlightening the Church on this matter. We also pray for the many Catholics who have failed to understand or accept this essential element of the Church's moral doctrine. Many have suspected their mother of giving them a snake when they ask for a fish. Let us pray for these wayward children that the Father give them the Holy Spirit as He has generously promised to do for all who ask!

It is not possible to try to explain now the many theological, psychological, social and medical reasons which combine in a sort of symphony to show that Paul VI was indeed speaking on behalf of the Creator and Redeemer of Life when he reaffirmed the unlawfulness of contraception. Rather than present arguments, let us consider the fruit that has come from the general acceptance of contraception, for from its fruits we can know the tree. The first bad fruit that Paul VI predicted in his letter was promiscuity. Certainly, the last thirty years have seen a dramatic increase in that. A related bad fruit is divorce. As soon as the Anglicans allowed contraception in 1930, the divorce rate among Protestants began to rise. A few decades later, when Catholics began to use contraception in significant numbers, the divorce rate among us began to rise, too. Why? The couple cuts themselves off from God, the source of love. The man begins to objectify his wife. Her dignity as a woman, the giver of life, is devalued. She feels unloved, and distance between them grows. Mother Teresa mentions the third bad fruit of contraception. "Once that loving is destroyed by contraception, abortion follows very easily." Our present Pope affirms "[T]he popularization of artificial contraception leads to abortion, for both lie — though at different levels — on the same line of fear of the child, rejection of life, lack of respect for the act or the fruit of the union, such as it is established between man and woman by the creator of nature." Technology has now blurred the distinction further so that, tragically, many Catholics have become active cooperators in the culture of death.

Yet there is hope. As the Lord surveys the Sodom of our time, He may be able to find "ten just men" amongst it. There are brave and generous Christians who will always be "the soul of the world", a witness of authentic love in a culture of hedonism and death. We must convince the world that God has not given his children a scorpion when they asked for an egg. He knows what is good for us; He made us. The Church's stand on contraception is not a cold, useless, man-made rule. Rather, *Humanae Vitae* is part of the Gospel law of liberty; it liberates couples for authentic Christian love. As John Paul II encouraged some Indonesian bishops: "Let us never fear that the challenge is too great for our people. They were redeemed by the precious blood of Christ. They are his people... It is He, Jesus Christ, who will continue to give the grace to his people to meet the requirements of his word... what is impossible with man is possible with God."

What remains for us is to be what we are: a new creation, a people set apart: *Be not conformed to this world, but be transformed by the renewal of your mind*, said St. Paul. If you cannot see the beauty of Humanae Vitae, *Seek and you shall find*. If you cannot imagine ever being able to live it: *Ask and you shall receive*. Never think you have no alternative to sin, but *knock and the door will be opened to you*.

Shepherds and Wolves

Providentially the readings today fit perfectly with the life and significance of St. Ireneaus and also compliments what was in the liturgy on Monday where the Lord warned us so sternly not to judge anyone. But remember how nuanced that commandment was because today He gives us criteria for judging. Not judging the interior state of their soul so as to make an unnecessary condemnation, which is indeed beyond even the scope of our right and duty, but to be able to judge the actions of others, especially teachers or prophets, so as to discern whether they are true or false prophets.

The criteria the Lord gives us is by the fruit that they bear. In particular the fruits of the Holy Spirit. Do we discern those? Especially in light of St.Ireneaus, the fruit of peace. From the time of Israel there have always been false prophets. This of course is part of the history of our Church. The book for which St. Ireneaus is best known is called, *Against Heresy*. Indeed he spent his life defending the true faith as the opening prayer indicated and trying to build up peace in the Church. The great fruit that one should see from a true prophet, a true teacher, is peace and harmony with the Church Universal and especially its Universal Pastor.

In our own day, we have to say it with sadness, we have a new and particularly grave problem with false prophets in that, in a way, it's become institutionalized. It's always been the case that a priest here or there has broken faith. All the great heresies began with priests, be it Arias, Phelagius, Luther, Calvin, and so forth even to our own day.

For many, the idea of dissent from the received teaching, the universal teaching, has become, you could say fashionable and widespread, beginning in 1968 with Humanae Vitae. Notice that word dissent is linked to dissention, lack of peace. So you see right there the bad fruits. Unfortunately it has become so widespread in seminaries and universities that, you could say, almost that the majority of the theologians teaching there are not entirely in union with the Church Universal. Along with this has come an abdication of the role of Shepherds. The Bishops, of course, are asked to watch over the flock and protect them from the wolves on the prowl but many Bishops have just taken a passive role letting the theologians fight it out among themselves.

The tide is turning though, we can be pleased that the Holy See has intervened in many ways, for instance, drawing attention to this explicitly and publicly in the encyclical *Veritatis Splendor* especially in the moral sphere, as well as issuing an instruction on the proper role of theologians. Now it is trying to strengthen the Bishops by appointing many new and strong ones as well as approving norms for theologians teaching in Catholic Universities. So there's hope for the future, but in the meantime, of course, we all must be aware that this is the historical moment the Church is moving through. We must be on our guard against the wolves and look for those fruits, the fruit of obedience, humility, and above all union and peace with the Universal Church.

The Little Ones

In the Gospel today, Christ speaks with passion about the need to defend the *little ones*. He wants to see them flourish in health of body and soul so as to take their place in his Father's Kingdom which *belongs to such as these*. How could He defend these little ones without remembering how little children, the Holy Innocents, were slaughtered upon his coming into the world? How could He speak of them without thinking ahead also to how, two millennia down the road, millions of innocents would be slaughtered every year by abortion? What would his disciples be doing about it? God forbid they should be found idly standing by or worse contributing to the culture of death — *it would be better for them to have a millstone tied around their necks...*

Today is Respect Life Sunday. Respect Life Sunday in an election year, when abortion is one of the major issues on the table. This is cause for serious reflection. Let it also be an opportunity to reaffirm the Church's position that no one — absolutely no one — is beyond the reach of the mercy of God and the power of his grace. Women who are frequently victims of abortion and the misguided doctors and politicians who perpetrate it can be brought back to Christ, and for this we must hope and pray and work.

The Second Vatican Council reaffirmed the legitimate autonomy of the political world, practical questions of how best to build prosperity and achieve security are not for the Church to answer. But what happens when politicians stray from the arena in which they enjoy a legitimate autonomy? What happens when those charged with ordering society to promote the good of man deny what is essential for his good? When those whose job it is to devise laws of man presume to rewrite the laws of God? In such cases, which are none too rare, the Church intervenes. Loud and clear, and often all alone, she has condemned the platform of the communist party which sought to destroy the individual, of the Nazi party which sought to destroy the Jews, and of the fascist parties and dictators which sought to destroy the Church and overrun human rights. Surely no one would say that she did wrong in these situations.

Why then is it any wonder that the church will object when a political party condones and promotes the death of innocent children? Just as Pius IX forbade Catholics from voting for fascists, so should Catholics consider themselves forbidden to vote for pro-choicers. This is not about telling you for whom to vote, but for whom you may not vote; there is a difference. No candidate will be perfect. The day is far in the future when earthly politics will produce a platform fully imbued with the Gospel. When weighing the pro's and con's of the various candidates this election year, however, we must be sure to remember that all issues are not of equal importance. Cardinal Bernadin is remembered for promoting the whole range of life issues with the image of Christ's "seamless garment," lest, while we fight for an end to abortion and euthanasia, humane ways of dealing with violent criminals, and providing health care and housing be forgotten. Nonetheless, he reminded Catholics that "a consistent ethic of life does not equate the problem of taking life with the problem of promoting human dignity". Rather, as the Bishops as a whole have pointed out, abortion and euthanasia are "preeminent threats" because "they directly attack life itself, the most fundamental good and the condition for all others" (*Faithful Citizenship*).

Is it consistent with faithful citizenship to be a single-issue voter? Does our faith require it in the present circumstances? The reason this question causes so much difficulty is that the term "single-issue voter" is ambiguous. If we mean "is it reasonable to vote for a candidate who is right on one very important issue, regardless of whatever else he might say?" The answer would be "certainly not". There are a number of issues important to our country and to our faith upon which a candidate should be evaluated. However, if we mean "is it reasonable to consider a candidate *disqualified* because of his stand on a single issue?" The answer is "Absolutely!". Even if a candidate combined all the best qualities of the four presidents on Mount Rushmore, it would be absolutely wrong to vote for him if he also called for something terrible, like a return to slavery, or the expulsion of Jews from the country. In other words, the right position on one issue should not be sufficient to win a Catholic's vote, but a wrong position on one issue should be sufficient to lose it.

Moreover, terrifying as it is to unmask the depths of the incoherence of the human heart, almost half of the "active Catholics" — defined as attending Mass every Sunday, probably subscribing to religious publications and belonging to a Church organization — almost half of these voted to re-elect our current president. (Clinton) What blindness and deafness! What pitifully unformed consciences. Many there are who, with eyes only for the state of the economy, do what St. James accused his contemporaries of: *fattening your hearts in a day of slaughter.*

In conclusion then, no one can be both a coherent Catholic and a supporter, neither an enthusiastic nor a reluctant supporter, of a pro-choice politician. We are Christians, when we are in church, when we are in the privacy of our homes, when we are inside the voting booth. We are always Christians. And if the quarter of our country that is Catholic acted in a manner coherent with their Christian faith, the *little ones* we remember today would be alive for tomorrow.

The Mystery of Evil

The Gospel tells us that the Lord was unable to work any miracles in his own land. Unable! The Almighty, the Omnipotent God was unable to do something! How can that be? We know this only makes sense to talk this way when what is predicated of God is something contrary to his perfect nature. So we can say that God is unable to lie. God is unable make a stone so heavy that He cannot move it and so forth. So it also must be contrary to God's nature, to his wisdom and his goodness to work a miracle for unbelievers. So we can say, He not only will not, but can not, answer prayers unless they are uttered with faith. Perhaps this thought sheds some light upon the mystery of why God who is capable of miracles of grace, and why He who is able to convert any heart, no matter how hardened, and who wills that all men be saved and come to the knowledge of the truth, apparently stands by impotently while souls reject it. We need his grace to approach and He offers sufficient grace to all, yet we can withdraw by our own power. We can resist the pull of the Almighty One, and this is a mystery to ponder. People are allowed to take offense at Him, and that word really is to be scandalized by Him.

This doctrine, that we can resist grace, is something that the Protestants couldn't accept, so they fell into a heresy, saying that God must not be offering his grace to the hardened sinner, which is false. *My grace is sufficient for you*, the Lord said to St. Paul. He could have added, but you can resist it. So we see Jesus preformed all the signs that were foretold of the Messiah. *Go and tell John what you have seen and heard, the blind receive their sight, the lame walk, the lepers are cleansed, the deaf hear and the dead are raised up. The poor have the good news preached to them and blessed is he who takes no offense at me,* the Lord said. Yet, miserably, there were many who could see Him perform all of those signs and still be scandalized, offended by what they did not want to see, namely, a humble Messiah, from their own surroundings who would have to carry a cross and would ask us to carry one too. So they managed to close their eyes to the obvious fact of God with us. Their obstinacy was such that it amazed Jesus, He was amazed at their lack of faith. And isn't it amazing that anyone would persist in unbelief when the truth is so apparent, that anyone would choose evil and sin when goodness and virtue are so beautiful, when a Gospel life is clearly to one's own best interest. This is the mystery of evil.

What happens when not just one or several people, but a whole nation stubbornly refuses God's invitation to communion in truth and love. Then it becomes like the Israelite people that Ezechial was describing, *a nation of rebels, who rebelled against Me, a people hard of face and obstinate of heart who heed and resist, for they are a rebellious house.* If we are faced with such a nation, we too must be amazed that it should happen that a whole people is led to deny the obvious and shun what is in it's own best interest, rejecting, not only what is needed for the pursuit of happiness, but even for the very survival of civilization. This unfortunate state of affairs is ours.

Who among us could celebrate July fourth this year, claiming to be both a proud Christian and a proud American? It's impossible, when just days earlier the highest court in the land affirmed as a right, a God-given right, they said, enshrined in our nation's founding documents, something so dreadful that we can't even describe it. They refused to describe it in their documents and I certainly won't describe it here. Is this the freedom we cherish and celebrated as we tried vainly to have a happy fourth? Must we not be like Jesus, amazed at the hypocrisy of man?

I know of many women who have had abortions, usually under great stress or great duress, who have great, good hearts and are renewing their relationships with the Lord Jesus. But the lawmakers and the judges and the medical professionals, who can calmly and dispassionately decree death, have cold — blooded hearts. Those five justices did not err out of stupidity. The problem is not their IQ's, but their corrupt wills and their faithless hearts. This leads to a darkening of the intellect and even to the extinction of basic human emotion. They can see a diagram of the procedure such as was printed in the Catholic Review this week, and keep right on their deadly course. If the young women were told half of what is happening, most of them would refuse to abort. Many of our nation's leaders are, on the contrary, spiritually living dead, moral zombies, hell-bent like on their macabre mission of defending and extending the culture of death.

If it's faith in Christ Jesus, who is the Truth and the Life, that would have purified and elevated our culture and kept it from sliding into barbarism, we must ask, if we seek to lay the blame somewhere, we must ask, who is primarily responsible for maintaining and extending that salutary faith in these United States? The answer is you and me. Christians, and especially Catholics, since we have the fullness of the saving truth and the means for acquiring grace left by Christ to His Church. This is what makes our current crisis all the more painful, all the more galling. Because the Church under Clinton cannot say what the Church under Nero said, "You are the problem, we are the solution." No, we have to admit that Catholics as a whole are part of the problem. Thanks be to God that the one glimmer of hope in that disastrous decision was that three of the four dissenters were the three Catholics on the court. Thanks be to God for that.

Still as the Holy Father reminds us in *Evangelium Vitae,* "We need to begin the renewal of a culture of life within Christian communities themselves. Too often it happens that believers, even those that take an active part in the life of the Church, end up by separating their Christian faith from its ethical requirements concerning life." Among the certain objectionable ways of acting, must certainly be included, voting for pro-choice politicians. With sixty-two million Catholics in a country only four times that size, we should be able to lead the nation back to sanity. Your single vote is not much perhaps, but it had better not go to support a man or woman who intends, like Herod, to

destroy the innocent. That Catholics vote in equal or greater propor-
tions for such people, is a great scandal! And that not a few of these
politicians, call themselves Catholics and are allowed to do so, is even
more scandalous. Such scandals will only cause the next generation to
take even more offense at the message of Christ Jesus.

So in conclusion, we have to listen again with new ears to the
Carpenter, the Son of Mary. We must not say that He is a mere man
with a culturally restricted and historically conditioned message. We
must hear His voice speaking to us, His demanding, revolutionary,
life-changing, history-making message. We must not resist, we must
not be afraid to be transformed or we will never transform our land.
Let Him perform a miracle of grace on you, in your heart, in your
family, in this parish, then in this state and country.

How long, for instance, must we worship in the shadow of a killing machine? How long before we hear those words, "Does not that
banner still wave over the land of the free and the home of the brave?"
In answer, No, it does not! Anyone who is free to kill their child is a
slave, of passion and ideology. "And prison," says Henry David
Thoreau , "is the only house in a slave state in which a free man can
abide with honor." So when we Catholics are willing, en masse, in a
group, to be jailed for the truth, then we will be able to say that once
again our nation's flag flies over a brave people. And may God bring
that day to pass, very soon.

Sons of Light

Until God is the object of genuine worship, people will not see
clearly right from wrong. The exaltation of abortion as a right, as
something to be defended and even celebrated as progress, recalls
Our Lord's next words addressed to the Pharisees who scoffed at his
teaching: *You are those who justify yourselves before men, but God
knows your hearts; for what is exalted among men is an abomination
in the sight of God.* "Abomination" is a reference to pagan sacrifice.
This abomination is the destruction of the image of God, which is the
child.

In the Gospel, Our Lord reminds us over and over again that there
are two kinds of people in the world. Sons of light and sons of darkness, the wheat and the tares, citizens of the city of God or of the
world (Augustine), those on the narrow road and those on the wide
and easy path to destruction. Is everything that black and white? Indeed, on judgment day there are only two possibilities. But it remains
true, of course, that conversion is always possible in this life both

from good to bad, or from bad to good. One can convert from bad to good, for this reason we must pray for them. But, just as there is potential for good in the sons of darkness, there is potential for evil in our ranks. "The only thing necessary for the triumph of evil is for good men to do nothing." (Burke) We must examine ourselves. Why is it that we are in such a spiritual stupor, that we need to be woken up to such an outrage? Isn't it because many Catholics have begun to think like the sons of darkness? Do you not realize that it is Catholics, called to be sons of light, that are responsible for the evils we have? The Catholic vote put in a pro-abortion president and governor. We must teach Catholics now more than ever so that the culture of death does not swallow them up.

We are enlightened at baptism, but how quickly that light gets extinguished if we are not taught, if we are not helped to become convinced that we are created by God to love and serve, that we were redeemed by his Son, that we must preserve his Spirit in the temple of our souls and respect it in others. Making a sacrifice of our wills and lives in service to Him is authentic worship in spirit and truth. This is also what will win for us this battle against the sons of this world. We are sons of light, because we are sons of God who is Light and followers of his son who is the Light of the world. We must see things as they truly are. We must expel from our hearts the influence of our pagan culture which allows us to live in peace, to pass by an abortion clinic without revulsion, without pangs of conscience. Then we can pray and work to expel that evil from our midst, and hopefully to win over some of the sons of darkness. May the Lord help us to do all of this and soon.

Demonic Influences

We tend to think of demonic possession as extreme cases where the devil has power over the movement of a person's limbs or over their tongues, where a person speaks strange languages, always against their will. Indeed the devil never, ever has power to move our will. But we could also speak of possession when the devil simply exercises his power to move, not our exterior limbs, but our interior faculties, our imaginations, our memories, passions, etc. Again, it can be against our will, that's why we call these temptations.

What if a person then gives his assent to those movements? The devil can lead them very far indeed. This is a sort of possession. The scripture uses this language, for instance, in the case of Mary Magdalen. Tradition doesn't imagine that she was anything but very immoral, but scripture tells us that Jesus cast seven devils out of her. More famously, Judas, himself at the last supper, we're told the devil entered into him. He then went out to commit a great crime. Likewise we just heard James saying that the wisdom of this world is earth-bound, kind of animal, brutish, even devilish. There's no other way to explain the great evils that we've seen. You think of the most terrible atrocities of the Nazi's for instance, it's demonic influence, there's no other explanation.

We have to have this very real understanding, the understanding of the Church, when we try to confront evil in our world. Just as we believe, for instance, that here in this Church, there are angels gathered around the tabernacle, always adoring the Lord night and day. We have to have the same understanding that in an abortion clinic, where those terrible evils take place, there are devils gathered there exercising their influence on those who work there. Gathered, perhaps we can imagine, like vultures sitting up there on top. This is how Christian art has depicted the influence of the devils upon our society. Another example of the Church's real understanding is the first prayer that the priest says, putting on his vestments, "Lord place upon me a helmet of salvation to overcome the assaults of the devil."

Regarding the case of abortion, where we see more clearly than anywhere else, that demonic influence, the Holy Father made reference to this very Gospel passage because the last line in many older manuscripts is 'this kind you can drive out only by prayer and fasting.' All of you who are daily communicants, have to remember, that gift of God comes with a great responsibility, namely, it's a spiritual battle against evil. Building up the Kingdom of God is a spiritual battle. St. Paul says, "We do not fight against powers of this earth, but against Principalities and Dominions, against these angels, these devils. So you're in the front lines of that. Every day you have to ask the Lord, *'increase my faith, increase my faith.'* You have to every day make advances in prayer and in austere living so that you can be better soldiers in this fight. Then surely we will overcome.

Holy Hour for Life

We need to lay down our life as witnesses to the Lord. *You also are witnesses because you have been with me from the beginning.* We must be witnesses to the world that doesn't want to see that witness or hear that witness. *I chose you out of the world; therefore the world hates you.* All this is very familiar to those who are in the pro-life battle. It's a funny battle in that it's not really two people — one wants to win and the other to lose, but rather one side, namely us, wants the other side to win too. It's the same fight that our Lord Jesus came to fight. We want them to be winners. We want them to be happy. We know what will make them happy. That's what we're trying to convince them of. It's the same dreadful battle that Our Lord was engaged in, trying to give us what will make us happy, and many of us not wanting to receive Him.

We see also in this passage that the world does not accept us because it does not know God. This is identified by the Holy Father as the heart of the problem of the culture of death — that they don't know God. We must be witnesses to God and to Christ and also to the love that Christ came to teach us, which makes us more human, which makes us seek this self sacrificing love. For that reason we lay down our lives.

So now is the time to take refuge in the Lord , to come back into the shelter of his house and to draw strength from Him, Him truly here present. Especially because on all of our minds is, "How long , Lord, must this battle go on? God doesn't give signs as to how long we have to be fighting. His work is furthered by keeping us in the dark, often, because then the virtue of hope gets purified and strengthened. We aren't basing our hope upon encouraging signs we may find, but soley upon His word. He said that if we are faithful, He will win the victory for us. He said, *Fear not Little Flock, for I have overcome the world. Ask and you shall receive.* His word has to be enough for us. We do not need encouraging little signs. On the contrary, we know that the successes, as we look at history, always comes as a surprise. What greater example than the fall of Communism, expected by no one. All of these great evils have fallen all of a sudden because evil is really a sort of straw man. It seems absolutely impregnable but, in fact, it is very weak. It has no foundation. So the Lord would have it fall very quickly. The devil himself puts on such a great show, that he could scare anybody, but in fact he is afraid of even a little child in the state of grace.

We never know the day or the hour of when the Lord will come to our rescue. The second coming, we don't know when it will come. It will come as a surprise. Our own death will come as a thief in the night. Those are good things and we have to look forward to them with hope. Likewise, this victory, when it will come, will be a surprise. So, we have to keep our hope always strong because it will come. We must hope, and hope very big. We have to ask God during this Holy Hour to glorify Himself, glorify Himself in this manner and to give us an occasion to praise His mighty works. Let the whole world see how powerful He is.

So, it's a time to stir up our hope. It's also a time to remember that all of the sacrifices that are required during the rest of this fight and all of the sacrifices that we've made, every single prayer, every single endurance of an annoyance, or a discomfort, whether seen or unseen, is not ever wasted but saved up jealously by our God, who loves every tear that is shed out of love for Him. He is saving it all up and it's growing on one side of a balance. At a certain moment one side of the scales will tip and we will be surprised by the joy of the Lord coming to our rescue. So let us continue to pray with such sentiments of hope and gratitude in the Lord who loves us so much.

Respect Life Retreat

Knowing Ourselves

The goal of the first talk is to know ourselves somewhat better. This is not an easy thing, there is a psalm which said, *The interior of man and his heart is an abyss.* St. Augustine wrote, "Now I am to myself a great question." To know who we are, is certainly the foundation on which we need to construct the Christian, which is a human, become perfect. So let us ask the Lord in this meditation, for great humility. Why don't people look at themselves more often in the mirror of prayer, quiet, alone in their room? Because to know ourselves is very difficult, to look at ourselves. So let's ask the Lord for courage.

Why don't we take St. Peter as our model. Peter, who thought he knew himself well. Remember the first time the Lord came to him, coming off his fishing boat there on the Sea of Galilee and he fell down before the Lord and said, *Depart from me for I am a sinful man.* He thought he knew himself. But Peter was not yet purified, was not yet humble. He was given great graces, he was called to such a high vocation, such a great role in the Church, perhaps he trusted too much in himself, perhaps he didn't know himself so much, know how weak he was so he said, *I Lord, would never betray you.* But of course he did. He only began to really know himself after having denied the Lord three times. Remember the Lord came out and looked at him. We have to ask the Lord to turn His gaze upon us especially when we're in front of Him in the Blessed Sacrament. Ask the Lord, 'Look at me the way You did Peter.' And after that Peter really began to know himself. And of course he went outside and wept bitterly for his sins.

The first thing to know about ourselves is that we're creatures. Being creatures means we're contingent beings, we didn't have to be, we've been called out of nothing. It's important to remember that, that on our own we are nothing. The Holy Scripture attests to that in *Isaiah 40:15. Behold the nations are like a drop from a bucket, and they are counted as the dust on the scales...All the nations are as nothing before Him...* And so that should include each and every one of us. This of course could lead to despair if one focused only on one's nothingness. And it did lead the preacher in Ecclesiasticus in that direction. *I said in my heart, with regard to the sons of men, that God is testing them to show them that they are but beasts, that the fate of the sons of men and the fate of the beasts is the same, as one dies so dies the other. All is vanity, all go to one place all are from the dust and turn to dust again. Who knows if the spirit of man goes upward and the spirit of the beast goes down to the earth.* He at least knew himself which was something, but that's all he focused on, that's all he knew, his littleness, his nothingness, that he was vanity. We mustn't stop there.

To know ourselves, we must not only realize that we're a creature, but we must think, 'God created me for a purpose, what is that purpose?' If we are to know ourselves we must know why we exist. Even the pagans knew that. Plato said, "The unexamined life is not worth living." In our times people have lost the inclination to ask those questions, that there be a purpose in anything. They've tended to deny that they've been created for a reason, but of course Christians mustn't think that way. We have to realize that God has made us for a purpose and that our entire value consists in that. That He has a role for us, and so fidelity, absolute fidelity to whatever His will is — our worth depends upon it.

Another consideration. Of all the creatures that God has made, that He's called into being out of nothing for some reason, the human being is unique in one thing, that we're the only one that can fail to achieve the purpose for which we've been created. No dog can be uncanine, but a human being can be inhuman. We're the only ones that can fail. Not only can we fail, but we all do. Except for the Blessed Virgin Mary, every human being called into creation from Adam to us, have failed in some degree to achieve the purpose for which we were created. We were created to serve God, and yet we're unable to do so. Even the Lord said that we have to confess that we are useless servants. Although we are such useless servants, nonetheless, we tend not to be sufficiently grateful, we never thank the Lord for having called us into being and we tend to ignore Him, even after showing us such great love. So all of these things made Pascal, who was a very holy man, besides being a great mathematician, exclaim, "What sort of freak then is man, how novel, how monstrous, how chaotic, how paradoxical, how prodigious! Judge of all things, feeble earthworm, repository of truth, sink of doubt and error, glory and refuse of the universe!" We're everything all together. Because, looking at what we have in common with creatures and how we can actually fall below them by not achieving our purpose, we're also vastly high above them with our soul. Our soul is outside of time. It's called by the second Vatican Council "a seed of eternity". St. Thomas Aquinas calls it in a certain sense infinite, because it can contain all things, it can know all things. It can even, not comprehend, but come into contact with the Infinite, Himself, God.

So we have this greatness in us also. Which is why we say then that we are made in the image of God. The eighth psalm is a beautiful thing to meditate upon. *When I look at Thy Heavens, the work of Thy fingers, the moon and the stars which Thou has established, what is man that Thou art mindful of him and the son of man that Thou dost care for him? Yet Thou hast made him little less than a god and dost crown him with glory and honor, Thou has given him dominion over the works of Thy hands, Thou hast put all things under his feet, all sheep and oxen and also the beasts of the field, the birds of the air and the fish of the sea, whatever passes along the paths of the sea. O Lord, our Lord, how majestic is Thy name in all the earth!*

That's the secret to our glory, and also our true and ultimate purpose, because we have a soul, which can even attain the knowledge of God, we can give God glory. We're the only creatures that can directly praise and glorify God, and that is our highest calling. St. Ireneaus went so far as to say, "the glory of God is man fully alive." So we have this paradox, glory and refuse of the universe all at once. And what makes the difference? It's our free will, it's the one thing that separates us from the beasts. Free will is not only the reason for our glory, but why Pascal called us wretched and below all the animals, feeble earthworm. It's our ability to make choices. We never ponder enough what a difference our every choice can make.

Consider some of the choices that have been made. The choice made by a young girl on which the salvation of the world depended. When Mary said 'be it done unto me according to thy word, compared to the choice made by the crowd that cried out, 'we would choose that you release Barabas, not Christ. The choice of Pilate, when he said, 'I did not want to condemn this righteous man,' yet he chose that it was better than possibly angering Caesar. We too make many choices which have a great difference in their effects. A doctor gives the example of a twenty-year-old woman who had an ultrasound and found out that her baby had Edward's Syndrome. It is characterized by se-

vere mental retardation, congenital heart disease, cerebral malforma-
tions, eye defects, cleft lips and a skin problem, ridges, all over the
skin. A priest was there for the delivery and to everyone's surprise, the
baby lived because the mother had chosen to give her that opportunity. She lived and thrived and brought joy to this couple for over a
year. They loved this baby as much as any couple could love a child.
They chose life and became heroes, much more holy. This other
woman, the thirty-three-year old mother of two girls, insisted on having an amniocentesis which had a chance of hurting the baby. Despite
the risk and against the doctor's advice, she insisted upon knowing.
Over the doctors better wishes the amniocentesis was performed, sub-
sequently he learned that the reason the woman wanted it was to find
out the baby's sex. When she discovered it was another girl, she
aborted the baby. What power of choices the Lord gives us! We can
choose to be saints or we can choose to be sinners.

C. S. Lewis makes this point in an essay entitled the *Weight of
Glory*; "All day long we are in some degree helping eachother to one
or the other of these destinations, to Heaven or to Hell. It is in light of
those overwhelming possibilities, it with the awe and circumspection
proper to them, we should conduct all our dealings with one another,
all friendships, all loves, all play, all politics. There are no ordinary
people, we have never talked to a mere mortal. Nations, cultures, art,
civilizations, these are mortal and their life to ours is as the life of a
gnat, but it is immortals with whom we joke, work, marry, snub and
exploit, immortal horrors or everlasting splendors. By our choices we
decide which we will be."

That's the paradox. We have the potential in us to be both. And
what makes the difference? What makes us either an immortal horror
or an everlasting splendor? Our choices. St. Thomas Aquinas said, "to
be human is to be more than human." We don't really have the choice
to be ordinary people, certainly not ordinary Christians. We either
choose to be united to Christ, transformed into a Saint, or the only
other option, the terrible one, which puts us below the beasts. There is
a famous old statement, 'the corruption of what is best is the worst',
so we end up worse than we naturally would have been. But to be an
ordinary human being is not an option. My mother always quotes my
brother when he was little. She was somehow explaining this to him
before bed, and he said, "You mean I can't just be a regular guy?" She
said, "No, that's not an option for us to be a regular guy, we're either
saints or sinners." You're either with Me or against Me, said the Lord
Jesus. Bad choices, which we call sins, actually return us to nothingness. Remember we came forth from nothingness and sins lead us

back in that direction. Good choices unite us with He who Is and give us a greater share in reality. That's also why sinners are so similar, they become bland, every sinner is boring, one like another. But saints are all different, they become more and true to what they are, more of an image showing a particular facet of the Lord Jesus.

The other element to know ourselves, which we've already touched upon here, is the fact that the superiority of our soul over matter, doesn't exhaust our greatness. Rather, our greatness lies in the fact that we are offered this grace, which is supernatural, above our nature. But part of our nature is to have a potential to be transformed by grace. In other words, we're naturally called to communion with God, we naturally look for that, we naturally long for that. Quoting John: *That which was from the beginning, which we have heard, which we have seen with our eyes, which we have looked upon and touched with our hands, concerning the word of life, the Life was made manifest and we saw it and we testify to it and proclaim to you the Eternal Life which was with the Father and was made manifest to us. That which we have seen and heard, we proclaim also to you,* and why? So that you may have fellowship with us, to have communion with us. And our fellowship is with the Father and His Son, our Lord, Jesus Christ.

Christians, even in this life, have that communion with the Holy Trinity, the whole Trinity, dwelling in our hearts, in our souls, and us in God. That's to know what we're really made for, this is to know ourselves. At our Baptism we're given all that. It's a whole new life, a whole new divine life, it's called the supernatural organism. On top of our nature, our body and soul we're given this other life with all of its own properties, able to attain our supernatural end and three of the virtues, Faith, Hope and Charity. They unite us to God. This tremendous gift, we have to be sure to meditate upon. Remember how our Lord Jesus, in John, chapt. 4, was talking to the woman at the well. *If you knew the gift of God,* if you stopped to know yourself, to know not only how miserable you are but to know what God has made you for, to know what He's given you, to not take it for granted, to know that while on our own, truly we can do nothing, in Him we can do all things. We cannot lay claim to any of the good we do, all that is His power of grace at work in us. We can only claim the sins that we do. This is important, to know ourselves, to progress in this self-knowledge.

The Lord actually protects us perhaps, from seeing the half of our miserableness. Only when saints really grow in holiness do they really grow also in this humility, this ability to see how really wretched we are. This sounds, when we read it, as if they're really exaggerating, ridiculous, sort of false humility. They see themselves as so wretched, the most wretched of all. Not really, it's not exaggerated, they're seeing themselves more truly. We're protected from seeing it because we'd despair at once if we saw ourselves as we really are. Yet it's a grace we should ask for, because it's truth and so it does also produce joy. St. Claude de Colombiere writes, "I know of no greater joy than to discover some weakness in myself I did not realize before. I often taste this joy and shall always have it, when God gives me His light when I am examining my conscience. I firmly believe, and in this I find joy, that God guides those who give themselves up to His leadings and He takes care of the least things that concern them."

So we should examine our conscience and ask the Lord to look at us and help us like Peter, to know our real miserableness. Remember how Our Lord took Peter aside and said, *Peter, do you love me?* and Peter said, *Yes, Lord, I love You.* And the Lord said again, *Do you love me?* and Peter said, *Yes, Lord, You know that I love You. You know that I love You. (Jn. 21)* And yet he must have wondered deep down, Why is the Lord asking me three times? Maybe he realizes that, I say that I love Jesus, I think that I love Jesus. And so do we. But do I really love Jesus? We have to not answer so quickly. Peter himself, tradition says, almost didn't have the love to be a martyr. There's that church in Rome on the road, under the Appia, where allegedly he had a vision to strengthen him, the Church of Quo Vadis.

So let us ask the Lord for that grace, the many, many graces He has for us this short weekend. He can do things very quickly, like the Christmas Carol, all in one night. That we might really, really know ourselves. That we might not stop at the superficial, but try to find the vices deep down that cause me to do the things that I do. Those vices, those seven capital sins are never dead, not in any saint. They keep growling and working, underneath the surface, tempting us to fall. So we really have to put our finger on what causes us the most trouble, where should we put our vigilance this year, where should we put all our efforts in transforming ourselves, cooperating with His grace.

The Interior Life

This talk is on the interior life. It's not so much a meditation as an instruction. So what is the interior life or as St. Francis de Sales calls it, the devout life? It's important to know because in the Church of our day we often hear people say, "Where are we going to find volunteers for this or workers for that?" As if what the Church lacks is hands to do things. That's a big mistake. They should be saying where are we going to find a few saints. If we just had a few holy people, people with a real interior life... unfortunately among Christians it can be a rare thing, yet so few of them can do so much. The devil apparently said to the Cure d' Ars, "If there were three more priests like you I'd be finished." The idea being, that with just a very few holy people, the Lord can do tremendous work through them. This interior life, this life of holiness, we might ask ourselves, who's called to it? I think by now we know that everybody's called to it. The second Vatican Council reemphasized this, that every single Christian is called to perfection. Holiness then, is not an option, but if we're called to it, it is for us a duty. When someone asked Mother Teresa if she was a saint, she said, "I try to be, don't you. Holiness is a simple duty for me and for you."

One of the recent Popes said, "Ideals, if authentic, are not dreams but duties." So much the more, the interior life, which is nothing but union with God. If this is what we were created for, our reason for being, then it's a duty. Why do we think we should only be united to God in Heaven? We should be united to God from the beginning, in this life. "Therefore," the second Vatican Council continues, "all the faithful are invited and obliged to holiness, let all of them see that they direct their affections rightly, lest they be hindered in their pursuit of perfect love by the use of worldly things, let those who use this world not fix their abodes in it, for the form of this world is passing away." And Christ, of course, called all to holiness when He said *'Be ye perfect as your Heavenly Father is perfect.'*

St. Thomas explains that this means to be perfect in Charity, this is the essence of holiness. That's why the earlier quote said, "The fullness of Christian life, the perfection of love." An anonymous author wrote, "Do not be surprised that man should be an imitator of God. If God wills it, if God gives us the ability, than we can be imitators of God, we can be perfect." The word life has come up quite a bit, the interior life, the devout life, the fullness of Christian life. What kind of life is it? It's a new life and it's the divine life. The Interior Life is the life of God, that He shares with us. We have it very small, in seed form, at Baptism, and we develop in the interior life and it grows until it blossoms and that's what Heaven is. The Liturgy of the Hours has a prayer around Epiphany time: 'Without surrendering Your Divinity, You wondrously took our humanity, Grant that our lives may press to a fuller participation in Your Divinity.' That's what the interior life is, a participation in the divinity, in God. St. Thomas Aquinas says about Christmas, "He assumed our nature so that He might make men gods." This is what St. Augustine calls the great exchange. God takes from us our human nature and gives to us His divine nature. Obviously only Christ Jesus had two natures, one human one divine. But we come as close as one can without having two natures because we share in the divine one. We have the human one, we share in the divine one. St. Peter says in his letter to those newly baptized, *you've become partakers in the nature of God, the Divine nature.* That's what grace is, you've become a new creation in Christ with this new life, it has its own laws, its own goals, its own characteristics.

So now let's examine the essence of this interior life. There are two aspects to look at, the more contemplative and the more active. St. Elizabeth Ann Seton gives an indication of the essence of it, "I will tell you what is my own great help, I once read or heard that the interior life is but the continuation of our Savior's life in us. That the great object of all His mysteries is to merit for us the grace of His interior life and communicate it to us. It being the end of His mission to lead us to the sweet land of promise, a life of constant union with Himself." It means to share His life, to have Him living in us — this is the interior life. This is a great mystery, that's why it is to be contemplated. This is why the Church is holy. The Church is indefectibly holy, because the Church is made up of persons whose holiness is a participation in Christ's own, truly members of His body. It's the holiness of Christ that makes the Church holy. Thus we can say the Church continues permanently the Incarnation of the Word in history until the end of time.

These truths obviously need to sink in, that's why meditation, mental prayer is so key. This one important aid to developing an interior life that I'll mention is from a book *The Soul of the Apostolate.* The point of the whole book is that the apostolate, the active life is utterly worthless and in vain without a serious interior life. He says here, "Since we are convinced that no active worker, priest or layman, will have truly profited from the reading of what has been said so far unless he is fully determined to set aside a certain time every morning for mental prayer. Fidelity to mental prayer will guarantee this life of Christ, without mental prayer it is morally impossible. Base your interior life on its absolutely necessary element, morning mental prayer." St. Teresa of Avila said, "the person who is fully determined to make a half an hours mental prayer every morning, cost what it may, has already traveled half his journey." Without mental prayer the day will almost unavoidably be a tepid one. Those are strong words, but it stands to reason. If we don't really strive with all of our wills to unite ourselves to the Lord Jesus, (and the emphasis on morning because then one would derive an indication of what to do the rest of the day, how to follow His will), how can we expect to have union with the Lord?

This mental prayer should be elaborated on, and there are some beautiful descriptions in the document of the Congregation for the Doctrine of the Faith on what Christian meditation really is. They were concerned with the influx of Eastern non-Christian forms of meditation. "The meditation of the Christian in prayer seeks to grasp the depth of the Divine in the salvific works of God in Christ, the Incarnate Word, and in the gift of His Spirit, these divine depths are always revealed to him through the human earthly dimension." Remember what St. Elizabeth said, that the great object of all His mysteries is to merit for us the grace of His interior life and to communicate it to us, all of His mysteries, His baptism, His instituting the Holy Eucharist, His passion, anything that the Lord Jesus, come in the flesh, did, is one of His mysteries, and it's through that earthly human dimension that we reach the Divine. No one comes to the Father except through Me, said Christ Jesus. Any other methods err. St. Teresa of Avila also emphasized this. If your meditations aren't on the humanity of Christ or something like the Sacraments or the Church, something that He instituted, in time, to unite us to God, they aren't going to lead you to God. Prayer is, most importantly a dialog between two persons, the soul and God. Between our freedom and His freedom, and therefore at the heart of it is love. The goal of mental prayer says St. Teresa of Avila, "is not to think much but to love much." Not to just empty oneself but to let God fill one.

Speaking of that, they mentioned the centrality of the Eucharist for the interior life as the Source and the Summit of the life of the Church, the very Word Incarnate present invisibly in the Eucharist as the beating heart of the Church. Her very life, nourishing her holiness constantly with His own. This shows us how it is that the Church can claim to be the Incarnation of Christ through time, she has the very Word Incarnate at her heart. In receiving the Eucharist, it's the only food which doesn't turn into our substance but rather we turn into it. We become what it is we partake of, namely we are turned into Christ, and the members of His Body. Not only can we not become holy without the Holy Eucharist but we can not even avoid sin. It's impossible to lead a Christian life even on a mediocre level without receiving the Holy Eucharist. Again the Second Vatican Council, "In order to reach perfection, the faithful should use the strength brought out to them by Christ's gift [the Holy Eucharist] so that following in His footsteps and conformed to His image, doing the will of God in everything, they may wholeheartedly devote themselves to the glory of God and the service of their neighbor.

So that brings us to the more active part of the interior life. Prayer is essential to having a fruitful life of activity, of virtue. On the other hand, without that striving all day long for virtue, one is not going to progress in prayer, union with Christ, at all. So these two elements go hand in hand. Union with God is above all love, and love means doing the will of the Beloved. Prayer is seeking, "What is Your will, O Lord, what is Your will for my life?" And then, "Give me the strength to do it." Enlighten my mind to know what you want and inflame my heart to do it. Again Elizabeth Ann Seton, "And what was the first work of Our Dear Savior's life? You know it was to do the Father's will. Well then the first end of our work is to do the will of God. Secondly to do it in the manner He wills, thirdly to do it because it is His will."

So the interior life and the life of holiness is synonymous with doing the will of God. This also has sort of an active and passive part because a good part of doing the will of God is seeing absolutely everything that happens to us as the will of God. Seeing everything that we didn't choose as sent to us by the Lord Jesus, as something that not only are we to accept but embrace as sent by Him. And this book is a classic book, *Abandonment to Divine Providence*. I'm going to read a big chunk of this so you get the idea of how important it is to embrace everything that happens as the will of God. He says the fact that a leaf falls from a tree cannot happen without the will of God. The Lord Jesus, Himself, says, not a sparrow falls from the sky without My Heavenly Father willing it. He never wills a sin, but He does will that we suffer from the sin. It's wrong to say that God willed that Pilate turn Jesus over to be crucified, but it's true to say that He willed His Son to be crucified in that manner. Everything that comes into our life is, only because God allows it for our good, for the good of those who love God. "Once we can grasp that each moment contains some sign of the will of God, we shall find in it all we can possibly desire so there is nothing more reasonable, more excellent, more holy than His will. Can any variation of time, place or circumstance add anything to its infinite value? If you are taught the secret of finding its presence in every moment of your lives, then you possess all that is precious and extremely worthwhile, what is it that you want, those of you seeking perfection? Give your desires free reign setting absolutely no limits, no boundaries to them. Listen to me, let your hearts desire the infinite, for I can tell you how you can fill them. There is never one moment that I can not show you how to find whatever you desire, the present moment is always overflowing with immeasurable riches, far more than you are able to hold. Your faith will measure it out to you, as you believe, so will you receive. Love too is also a measure, the more you love the more you will want and the more you will get. Every moment the will of God is stretched out before us like a vast ocean which the desires of our heart can never empty, but more and more of it will be ours as our souls grow in faith and trust and in love."

That's the interior life growing in Faith, Hope and Love. What he's saying is that if you want to be united to God at any given moment, there's only one way and it's to be doing His will. So at any moment of your life one can be perfectly united to God and filled with his riches if one's totally doing His will. The other aspect of embracing His will is not only accepting the things we have no choice in, but rather the more difficult, the things we have to decide to do. Knowing what is the will of God, what about that? That, of course, which is a perennial problem, becomes clearer the more that we advance in other virtues such as recollection, life of silence, simplicity, detachment from all inordinate desires and through mortification, austerity. All of those and many other virtues, as they grow, will clear the way and make it easier to see, what is the will of God. There won't be as many competing demands on us.

One of the problems people in the world have is that it always seems they have too much to do. That they're frantic doing things. Remember that peace also comes from doing the will of God, because God would never will that you have twenty-five hours of work in a twenty-four hour day. God is not unreasonable like that. It's obviously our will, we make a list of things that we think should be done, or we think God wants done, that's too much for us. God is only going to will that you do what you can do, He's never going to will that you do more than you can do. So if you feel that you have more to do than you can do, think, what is God's will? The rest I'm not going to do.

Obviously our conscience is the thing that God gives us to know His will, that's why it's called the voice of God resounding in our hearts. And so the more delicate our conscience is, the more precise it is in judging what's right and what's wrong, what is God's will in each and every circumstance of the day, the more we're going to know what God's will is. And so to make it more delicate of course, examination of conscience and frequent confession are essential. Another thing to help us know what the will of God is, is something called co-naturality. As we grow in grace, as we grow in virtue, it becomes much simpler to know the will of God, even without a whole lot of reflection or analysis, it becomes almost second nature. The virtues, especially the infused virtues, the ones that come with grace, become second nature, it becomes natural to do the will of God, to do the good. Less thought is required.

And finally one other help in finding the will of God, and remember if it were impossible to know the will of God, God wouldn't expect us to do it. So obviously it is possible to know the will of God. That's what the gifts of the Holy Spirit are there for — that's another thing that we received at Baptism. The gift of counsel, of wisdom, etc.. these gifts are there to help us know the will of God, especially in extremely difficult situations or where there's no time for reflection. That's where the Holy Spirit can guide us, but of course one has to be a little way along in the Spiritual life to have those gifts really functioning. That's the definition of the Mystical life, to have the gifts of the Holy Spirit really active.

Here's three laws of the Interior Life. First of all the law of growth. Remember, it's a life, living things grow, all living things. And the life of grace is not less so, it's more so. If it's not growing, its dead. That's why spiritual progress and constant striving for holiness is so essential. It's like an airplane, if it's not going forward, its headed for a crash. We should remember always, that our place in Heaven is determined by the love we have arrived at, at the moment we die. So run the race without stopping. We're not like angels who at one instant arrive at a certain level of holiness, no, the Lord, for us, makes it a process. This is incidentally one of the tragedies of abortion, that these children aren't given the opportunity to grow in holiness to the fullness that they might have achieved. Certainly we believe that they're living in the Lord, as the Holy Father says in *Evangelium Vitae*, but are they living the highest level of union with the Lord that they would have, if they'd had the opportunity to develop their spiritual life?

St. Elizabeth Ann Seton again, "Perseverance is a great grace, to go on gaining and advancing every day, we must be resolute and bear and suffer as our blessed forerunners did. Which one of them gained Heaven without a struggle?" This is the law of struggle. Life, the interior life is always going to be a fight. Remember, we're fighting against a fallen nature, and other enemies also, the world and the devil, that's why the Church on earth is called the Church Militant. We need to have that spirit. The Interior life is always a soldier type spirituality. It'll always be the way of the cross. Again Elizabeth Ann Seton, "What are our real trials, by what name shall we call them. One cuts out for herself a cross of pride, another one a causeless discontent, another one a restless impatience or a peevish fret-fullness." It's important to see that our big crosses come from our very own natures, our very own vices, our very own passions, interestingly. Our sufferings are caused by our disordered passions. You have to accept them humbly, that this is one of those things that gives us a trial in this life, that makes life a struggle. Remember always St. Paul who was having some struggle he was going through in the interior life (we're not sure what it was). He called it the angel of Satan to beat me. And He asked the Lord three times to take it away, and what did Our Lord say? *My grace is enough for you.* So also when we keep fighting against something that we keep confessing, that's okay, it's a cross that the Lord is giving us, that the fight against it perfects us.

The third law, the law of Increase. Remember since this is a Divine gift, a Divine power it must be given us. There's three ways that we receive an increase in this gift, prayer, sacraments, and meritorious good works. So prayer, we must ask for an increase in grace, an increase of Faith, Hope and Charity. We already saw that the Apostles said, *Increase our Faith.* St. Paul calls for an increase of Hope, *May the God of Hope fill you with all joy and peace in believing, so that by the power of the Holy Spirit, you may abound in Hope.* And then he also prays for an increase in love, *And it is my prayer that your love may abound more and more with knowledge and all discernment.* So we have to pray for it, ask for it. Then the second way the interior life increases, is through all the sacraments, the ordinary channels of God's grace. It is the ordinary manner of contact with the humanity of Christ, the sacraments. The Catechism, if you have the version with pictures, has a picture of the woman with a hemorrhage touching the hem of Christ's garment. Why? Because through the sacraments we actually touch, have contact with the Body of Christ, and that's what heals us. The third way is meritorious good works. Whatever we do, no matter how small, is not small if it's done with grace, if God asked us and if it's done with grace. Mother Teresa says, "Do small things with big love." The most menial tasks of our day can make up for whatever's lacking in the sufferings of Christ. If it's done with grace, if it's His love working in us. Every single act. The interior life is simple, it's not easy, it's simple. It's loving God. It means the one you love, you do what pleases Him. It's centered on Christ. If Christ is not at the center of the interior live it's empty. It's easier to be a saint than to be an engineer. It's not hard, we make it hard. It's taking away anything that hinders us and leaving only Christ at the center of our lives.

It's occurred to me that everyone focuses so much on the interior life, on spiritual progress, you can begin to think, well, isn't this a little bit egotistic? But remember, first of all becoming holy is a good act of love for God. That's what it is, being holy, it's loving God. So it's certainly not going to be egotistical, and also your progress in holiness is the only way to help any person in the world that you may love. We'll only be useful to others in bringing them to happiness in this life and the next, as we are holy ourselves. It'd be a big mistake to think of the interior life, as one would say, exercise, "I really should do it for myself." It's completely for others, also it's obviously the best thing you can do for yourself. All of those goods fit together but it's improper to think of it as self absorbed or egotistical in any way.

Faith

This meditation is on faith. Members of the Church must live the same faith, hope and charity. These virtues make up the Christian life and so it's critical if we're going to renew the Christian life, to stir them up. For this meditation let our petition be, in the words of one of the prayers that we pray during the Epiphany season, "Father, You revealed Your Son to the nations by the guidance of a star, lead us to Your glory in Heaven by the light of faith." That star is the image or a symbol of our faith, that leads us to Christ, and just as it led those three kings to salvation, so also our faith will lead us.

We might consider in our meditation *Mark 9:14-29*, Jesus, immediately after the Transfiguration. What does He encounter? A boy possessed by a mute spirit. ...*What an unbelieving lot you are, how long must I remain with you, how long must I endure you....* The father of the boy says, *if, out of the kindness of your heart you can do anything to help us, please do.* And Jesus says, *If you can? Everything is possible to the one who trusts.* The father immediately responded, *I do believe. help my unbelief.* We see one example how the Lord was surprised and astonished by people's lack of faith, that someone would say to Him, the Son of God, 'If you can do any thing, please help?' He's astonished at their lack of faith. Jesus not only marvels at the people's lack of faith, calling the disciples often, *Oh men of little faith*, but also He marvels at peoples' great faith at other times, such as the Centurion's, *'Not even in Israel have I found such faith'(Mt.8:10)*

The lack of faith is spoken about, amazingly enough, almost as disarming the Lord's omnipotence. He did not do many works there because of their unbelief. *(Mt. 13)* One of the other Gospels said, ...He could not work any miracles there, because of their unbelief. Just as the lack of faith seems to almost obstruct the omnipotence of God, on the other hand, faith, seems to confer upon those who have it, a sort of omnipotence. *(Mt.21)* Jesus answered them, *Truly I say to you, if you have faith and never doubt, you will not only do what has been done to the fig tree, but even if you say to this mountain, 'Be taken up and cast into the sea,' It will be done, if you have faith.* Then again the Lord said, *Even if you had faith the size of a mustard seed, even the tiniest bit of faith, you could say to this sycamore tree, Be rooted up and planted in the sea and it would obey you.* This is what we need, because we're trying to move mountains, the mountains of evil that have built up so quickly in our society and which no natural power can move but faith could move them, even just a little faith could move these mountains of evil that are in our society.

So what is this faith more precisely, this faith that we tend to take for granted? It was something we received at Baptism and something that was fostered by our parents in childhood usually. We tend to take it for granted as if it's just part of us. We have to remember there are a lot of people who don't have faith, and people who don't have faith and wish they did. So we have to thank God that we have this gift of Faith. *We always thank God, the Father of our Lord, Jesus Christ when we pray for you,* says Paul, *because we have heard of your faith in Christ Jesus and of the love which you had for all the saints, because of the hope laid out for you in Heaven.* There we see all three of these virtues all together, because of your faith, of the Love you have and because of the hope laid out for you in Heaven. These three virtues are not arbitrarily chosen by St. Paul as a creation of the Church, and they're not just names given to certain pious sentiments, they are real powers given to the soul by God.

Faith is the first and most fundamental which unites us to God. That's why they are called theological virtues, because they have God as their object and they unite us to God. Faith is the first which unites us to God, unites our intellect to God but not without our will, remember the intellect and our will are parts of our soul. It's defined as the submission of our mind and will to God who reveals Himself. Hope and love more completely unite us to God. The former by the desire for the reward that the Lord will give us, and the second, love or charity, the most perfect, out of a desire to be united to God for the good that He is in Himself. Charity is the only one of those three that will remain forever, the other two are just for our journey.

Faith is a real light, it's called the light of faith and it's a real reflection of that light of glory that we call the Beatific Vision. Because it's the true light of God, that light by which we can glimpse God. As St. Paul said, *through a glass darkly.* It's necessary for salvation because it unites us to God. The Council of Trent wrote: "Hence in the very act of justification, together with the remission of sins, one receives through Jesus Christ, in whom one is inserted, the gifts of Faith, Hope and Charity. It adds, faith without hope and charity neither unites a person perfectly to Christ, nor makes him a living member of His Body. Therefore, it is rightly said that faith, by itself, if it has no works is dead, quoting the letter of James.

Of all the choices we make in life, choices which are so decisive, the choice to believe is the most fundamental, the most dreadful. The choice of whether to believe in the Son of God, is a choice that every human being that reaches the age of reason, must make. When we possess faith, it's not something we can take for granted. I remember in the seminary, a Sri Lankan Bishop came and told what happened to him that day. He had gone for a walk in Rome and ran into one of his classmates from when he was studying in the seminary in Rome. His classmate was a German who had gone on to become a theologian. But there on the street he said to his Sri Lankan friend, whom he hadn't seen all those years, "You know I write books about God, but I myself do not believe." He had lost the faith and it had become just an intellectual exercise. He was now so full of anguish. The Sri Lankan Bishop said to him, good advice, "Go back to Germany, go see your mother and tell her what you have told me. She's the one who first taught you the faith, and she's the one who can rekindle it, if anyone on this earth can." So it's nothing to take for granted, no matter where we are in the spiritual life, we can lose our faith, can let it bit by bit grow cold.

We have to remember that it's not a feeling, it's something we choose, it's always a choice. And it's a choice we have to make every single day especially when the feeling is not helping, but just the opposite. If you go to church and feel nothing, even feel like a pagan and even, as some saints have felt, as though they're not going to be saved. All those are just trials to make it more meritorious for you to make that act of faith and say, "No matter how I feel, Lord, I believe, I want to believe more and more. Because this is what unites me to God first and fundamentally, and we have to ask every day. The apostles, themselves, asked the Lord, *Lord, increase my faith.* So we must make the same request.

The spiritual director of St. Margaret Mary, St. Claude de Colombiere, wrote, "It is an error to think that faith, is so entirely a gift of God, that it is not within our power to increase and strengthen it." Our faith is full of paradoxes. Here's one. Faith is entirely a gift of God yet it is within our power to increase and strengthen it. Saint Claude again, "Some admit that they have very little faith and excuse themselves on this account for their bad lives. Therefore when they are reproached for their lack of faith, it makes no more impression upon them, than if you had told them that they did not have the gift of miracles." It's a gift, but it's an ordinary gift that the Lord offers to everyone, anyone who seeks it. So if we don't have the gift, or the gift grows cold, it's for lack of seeking. He who seeks God, always finds God. If this weren't the case, the Lord wouldn't have reproved everybody who had little faith. Always we have to remember that faith is a gift which we have to desire with all our hearts. *My soul thirsts for thee, my flesh faints for thee as in a dry and weary land where no water is. So I have looked upon thee in the sanctuary, beholding thy power and glory, because thy steadfast love is better than life. My lips will praise thee, I will bless thee as long as I live. I will lift up my hand and call on thy name. My soul has feasted...and my mouth praises thee with joyful lips when I think of thee on my bed and meditate upon thee in the watches of the night. For thou hast been my help and in the shadow of thy wings I shout for joy.*

Faith should have that effect of filling our lives with joy. Remember always, it's the seed of glory, it's the very life we'll be living in Heaven, of the Beatific Vision and that's why if faith grows, grows strong, this life begins to be a heaven on earth, a true communion of the angels and saints, a true presence of the Lord which the soul begins to feel could never ever be broken. Also for our consideration, finally, since we cannot take the Lord Jesus as our model for faith, since He saw the Heavenly Father directly, beheld His face, had the Beatific Vision here on earth, the person we can really look toward as a model for our faith is the Blessed Virgin Mary, Virgin most faithful. If St. Paul praises Abraham, our father in faith, so highly, so also Mary, and much more, would be the one who conquered and earned all the things she did through faith alone. Elizabeth was the first to praise her for that, *Blessed are you who has believed in the promises of the Lord.*

St. Louis de Monfort who is the great apostle of Mary, says, "Mary will share her faith with you. Her faith on earth was stronger than all the patriarchs, prophets, apostles, and saints. Now that she is reigning in Heaven, she no longer has this faith, since she sees everything in God by the light of glory, however, with the consent of Almighty God, she did not lose it when entering Heaven, she has preserved it for her faithful servants in the Church militant. Therefore the more you gain the friendship of this noble queen and virgin, the more you'll be inspired by faith in your daily life. It will cause you to depend less upon sensible and extraordinary feelings. It is a lively faith motivated by charity, enabling you to do everything from no other motive than that of pure love. It is a firm faith, unshakeable as a rock, prompting you to remain firm and steadfast in the midst of storm and tempest, it is an active and probing faith, which like some mysterious pass key admits you into the mysteries of Jesus Christ and of man's final destiny and into the heart of God, Himself. It is a courageous faith, which inspires you to undertake, without hesitation, great deeds for God and the salvation of souls. Lastly this faith will be your flaming torch, your very life with God, your secret fund of Divine Wisdom, your all powerful weapon to enlighten those who sit in darkness and the shadow of death. It inflames those who are lukewarm and leads to the goal of fervent love, it restores life to those who are dead through sin, it moves and transforms hearts of marble and cedars of Lebanon, by gentle and convincing argument, finally this faith will strengthen you to resist the devil and other enemies of salvation." So let us not omit to ask the Blessed Virgin to also increase our faith in us.

Hope

Every single minute is a grace for the Lord, you never know when He might give you an insight, and it's so easy to drown out His voice and so let's be very generous. One of the characteristics of the faith is that it has that unified, ever-new quality to it as long as it's held by someone with real faith, no matter if they're very learned or not... This makes me think of the Catechism of the Catholic Church which had been written by lots of different people but it fit together so that it made one integrated whole. One of the bishops who was given it to review said, "Yes, this is the faith. This is the faith of my mother, the faith my mother taught me." Even though she probably didn't know half of the things that are in there, it's still the same faith integrally whether it be held by a charcoal burner, or Cardinal Ratzinger... any way that was the last talk.

Now we speak about hope. Faith gives rise to hope. In the first letter of *Peter (3:15)*, he says, *Be ready to give reasons for the hope that is within you.* It's not a baseless hope, it's based on our faith. It's a crisis of truth in our culture that we've seen a loss of purpose, consequently a loss of hope. There has been a rise of interest in eastern mysticism and the new age movement which really say that there is no truth, there's no law, you can do whatever you want. At the heart of them is great pessimism. It's the greatest problem of our day, lack of hope and despair. We see an exaggeration of what Pascal mentioned in his day, man hurts himself in hedonism, workaholism, drugs, suicide, existentialism. It's certainly the characteristic of our day, hopelessness. As a result it's not a coincidence that the Holy Father's book is called *Crossing the Threshold of Hope*. It's at the heart of the abortion question. I heard on the feast of the Holy Innocents, Fr. Benedict Groeschel preaching in the cathedral in New York on this topic and he said, out of the nine million people in New York there's probably not nine that believe that it's a good thing to kill a baby. There's so many abortions in New York, he says, because people are afraid to think. He used the analogy of those soldiers in Bethlehem who killed the babies for Herod. They really didn't want to do that. They just didn't want to think about it. They were afraid to think of resisting the order. And this fear is a lack of hope.

Why are you cast down, O my Soul. Why are you disquieted within me. Hope in God for I shall again praise Him, my help and my God. (Ps. 33) God is the source of our hope, the object of our hope. Remember, all these theological virtues have God as their object. Hope unites us to God as the source of every good thing that we could want for ourselves. Hope of eternal happiness, of union with Him, brings us joy in this life. Hope is always for something that's not yet obtained, yet it gives us a certain possession of those things even in this life. That's why we have the Beatitudes. *Blessed are those who are sorrowful, Blessed are those who are poor*. How's that? Because those people possess in Hope the rewards promised them, even though they are sorrowful in this life, they have some sort of joy because they possess the reward in some way.

We can hope for things in time. Other things can be the object of our hope in so far as they are ordered for our salvation. We can hope for anything in so far as it helps us toward that goal. As a text to look at we could focus on St. Paul who has many wonderful things to say about Hope. Consider for instance, *Romans 8:18* to through the rest of the chapter.

I consider that the sufferings of this present time are not worth comparing with the glory to be revealed in us. For creation waits with eager longing for the revealing of the sons of God. All creation is sharing in our hope, he says. *"We know that the whole creation has been groaning in travail, together until now, waiting for the redemption of our bodies. For in this hope we are saved. Now hope that is seen is not hope. For, who hopes for what he sees? But if we hope for what we do not see, we wait for it with patience. The Spirit is within us, we know that in everything God works for the good of those who love Him and are called according to His purpose.* Then he closes with the great hymn of triumph, *If God is for us, who can be against us. He who did not spare His only Son, but gave Him up for us, will He not give us all things with Him?... Nothing will separate us from* the love of Christ, the love of God through our Lord, Jesus. St Paul is the one who said, *I know the one in whom I have trusted*, and *Hope against hope*. He is the apostle of hope we could say.

In *2 Cor. 1:8*, He says: *For as we share abundantly in Christ's sufferings so through Christ we share abundantly in comfort too. If we are afflicted it is for our comfort and salvation. If we are comforted it is for your comfort that you experience when you patiently endure the same suffering that we suffer. Our hope for you is unshaken for we know as you share in suffering so you share in our comforts... On Him we have set our hope that He will deliver us again.* To fail in hope, is a very dangerous thing. St. Thomas says it's not the worst sin, but it's the most dangerous. If one falls into despair what will get one out? One has no hope to pull oneself out. Despair is described as the sin against the Holy Spirit. Not that God couldn't forgive any sin but he who falls into despair is giving up on being forgiven and that's why Christ says he can't be forgiven. So we constantly have to renew our hope. We have to make sure we aren't trusting in and basing all our happiness in things that are passing away. *Woe to those who go down to Egypt for help and rely on horses, who trust in chariots because they are many and horsemen because they are very strong but do not look to the Holy One of Israel or consult in the Lord.(Is.31)*

Make sure that the Lord is the basis of our hope. Prayer is an expression of hope as we heard St. Paul mentioning. The condition for fruitful prayer is that we pray with hope, with confidence that our prayers are going to be heard. St. Therese of Lisieux says, "You get what you hope for and we just don't hope big enough." We have to remember when we pray we are not trying to change God's will, that's impossible. We pray for what will happen in accord with the will of God. But our prayer is part of God's providence. It has a real effect on and hastens what will happen. When we pray the Our Father, we say Thy kingdom come. Obviously His kingdom is going to come. He's going to triumph whether we pray or not, but He gives us the great dignity that by saying that prayer we are actually contributing to the hastening of the coming of the kingdom of God. All the things we pray for – if we pray for an end to abortion, abortion will end. When we pray, it will end sooner. This is why hope does not disappoint (another quote of St. Paul). Because what God wills, God gets. As we mentioned before, He doesn't will evil, but He may will that we suffer from evil caused by other people. So we have to be ready when we pray to realize that God may bring some good out of the prolongation of an evil. We must not get discouraged because the ultimate triumph is delayed.

God does will the passion of His Son, He wills suffering for us,

He wills that we should suffer and that we should have this battle with evil. God could stop abortion all at once. It's part of His Divine Providence to have us tested in the fire. Why get discouraged if evil is not conquered in a day. He brings good out of evil, greater good. And so we need that great faith in Him that He is all powerful and know that He does bring good out of evil so that we don't lose hope. We have to remember that Hope, in all it's gloriousness, when things are really difficult, when we are very low. His power always shines forth in weakness. This is the good He brings out of evil. He let's these unbelievably terrible things happen...just think of Auschwitz. Have you ever seen the picture of the Holy Father entering in the cell where Maximillian Kolbe died? That's a beautiful thing that could not have happened if God had not allowed Auschwitz. The Vicar of Christ standing in that same place where Nazi murderers were killing holy people. We see that the Nazis are gone, but the Vicar of Christ is there. Another place we see that is in the Coliseum in Rome. In the Coliseum there is a big cross set up in the stadium. Think of how the world powers were feeding Christians to the lions here, and now there is a big cross right about where the emperor used to sit. So there is great glory for God represented in these images. The triumph of good over evil. For goodness to triumph, evil has to be given a bit of a reign.

We needn't get discouraged. Hope is the power to know that no matter how terrible something is, He allows it to be so terrible so that He can show His great power. I heard recently of a priest who came to give witness on the 50th anniversary of the Holy Father's ordination. He'd had a very strange life as a priest, almost entirely in a communist prison camp, in Albania or somewhere. Almost as soon as he was ordained he was captured by the communists and put into a sort of prison where he was very cruelly treated. One of the cruel things they did to him was that they waited until Christmas Eve, his first Christmas Eve as a priest, I think, and then they came and put him in a very cold bathroom upstairs and they stripped him and beat him. They left him unconscious and when he finally came to he realized that it was Christmas Eve and he was lying frozen on this floor, aching all over. But he said that in his heart was great, great joy. There's no natural explanation for that, except that the Lord shows His power in our weakness. He allows the devil to do his worst so that we come out unscathed. He allowed Job to have all those trials so that Job could say, *I will trust in Him. Even if He should kill me, I will trust in Him.*

So we have to increase our hope in this pro-life battle that can seem so miserable. We have to especially, constantly ask the Lord to increase our hope and also affirm with Acts of Hope such as we said this morning. Look how full of hope the Holy Father is. He says in *Evangelium Vitae*, "In this great endeavor to create a new culture of life we are inspired and sustained by a confidence that comes from knowing that the Gospel of Life itself is growing and producing abundant fruit."

Even if things seem to be getting worse, he says things are getting better in the eyes of faith. The Church is that way, he says, like the kingdom of God itself, so the Church, like the people of Israel, they seem to be constantly being overcome by their enemies. Yet this little group of faithful, called the Anawim, somehow survived and somehow just kept growing. The kingdom of Israel kept growing and could not be crushed. It's the same with the Church, what Jesus called his little flock. It's always a little flock that the world always seems to be crushing, almost in danger of extinction. But it just keeps growing, keeps getting stronger – it's a mysterious way of growing. It's the same in this battle for the salvation of the world, no matter how miserable it seems at every moment, though it seems we're slipping back, we're actually making progress.

The Lord lets the odds get very much against us, again to show His power. We should remember the story of Gideon *(Judges 7:2-8)*. The lord said to Gideon, *The people with you are too many for me to give the Mideonites into their hands lest the people flaunt themselves against Me saying my own hand has delivered me...*

That's the way the Lord works! He'll say in our case, "Got rid of that abortion clinic with a handful of people." The fewer the better to show the Lord's power. We have to imagine the best possible thing happening there. We have to hope big, something instead to honor the Lord, for instance a chapel – a place to make reparation for what went on there. Such as places where terrible things occurred that have been turned into chapels in other places. So imagine something like that, imagine the best thing that you can. Imagine the conversion of the doctor involved, imagine anything you want, and know that God's plan is even better than anything you can imagine. You can't hope big enough. We should expect miracles of grace, not only in others, but in ourselves. What holds us back is that terrible temptation to say, "I can't really be a saint, I'll just be the ordinary Christian. We must remember *Isaiah (52:10)*. *The Lord is there and what is He not powerful enough to do?* And you'd better not say He's not powerful enough to transform my heart. That would be a false humility.

We can't say Christ is our model of hope so we take Our Lady of Hope. Remember Our Mother Mary stood by the side of the cross. She was not despairing at all. She was standing there knowing that the

Lord had a plan, knowing that, as the Holy Father says in *Evangelium Vitae*, "It is precisely this blood, the blood coming from the cross, that is the most powerful source of hope. Indeed it is the foundation of the absolute certitude that in God's plan He will be victorious." *Death is caught up in victory. O death, where is your victory? O death, where is your sting?* For that reason, sad though she was, Mother Mary is not at all despairing beside the cross.

Charity

Our faith that conquers the world is a living faith, a faith that works through charity. Charity is then the force that conquers the world, the evilness in the world, all that is opposed to Jesus and His Reign. The weapon is Charity. When we speak of love and charity, there's a great danger of being trite. Why? Because love is universally appreciated. We hear it on radio songs, we see it on postage stamps. Everyone seems to think it is something good, that we should strive for. That's not what the Lord, Jesus is talking about, that kind of love that we naturally have, that everyone strives for. No, He lifts it to a New Commandment. *Love one another as I have loved you.* This love of which we speak, so far from being something trite, is completely revolutionary with the coming of the Lord Jesus. It's what distinguishes the Christian like a brand upon our foreheads. Everything that we do is distinguished by this. *By this all men will know you are my disciple, by the love you bear one another.* Every activity of the apostolate should find in Charity its origin and driving force and should be distinguished from every kind of social work. That's why Mother Teresa always said, "We are not social workers!"

It's Charity, it's different from philanthropy, from anything on a human level. Why? Because Charity is again a theological virtue, the greatest of the theological virtues. A gift from God which we receive at Baptism and we lose by mortal sin. Someone who has committed a mortal sin cannot perform acts of charity, properly speaking. This love is not a feeling or a passion. There is a love that is a passion, Christians have this too. Love those brownies, whatever, that's natural, that's part of God's plan. But Charity, this virtue of love, is a decision of the will, a decision to move toward what the mind knows as good. Precisely to move toward the greatest good, God Himself. The object of Charity is God, Himself. We love all other things for God's sake. So God is the only object of our Charity and we love everything else for His sake.

It's impossible to choose what's good consistently since we're fallen and especially at the cost of self renunciation. The greatest act of love, *greater love than this no man has than to lay down one's life for another.* This is impossible to human beings without God's help. To fulfill the commandment He gave us, to love one another as I have loved you, is impossible except by wills transformed by grace. God doesn't destroy the nature but transfigures it by grace. Grace alone allows us to opt for the God we cannot see no matter the pull of nature, even the pull of self preservation. With Charity we can choose to die for the Lord. What the Holy Father says about martyrdom is very true. It's pretty clear now that it's the major theme in all the Holy Father's teachings in the third part of *Veritatis Splendor.* "You can keep the moral law if you're willing to die." He's been holding up the examples of the martyrs. He's going to canonize 120 martyrs of the Spanish Civil War this year. On and on, in all different places, it's a major theme. And He's not afraid to say that Christians should be willing to be martyrs.

So we can compare this Divine love – of Charity — with human love. Human love, on a human level, even the most sublime married love, is very different. First comes attraction, passions and sentiments, then for that to become real love the two individuals have to make a decision. "I'm going to love this person no matter what, even should the sentiments disappear." On a human level too, love, properly speaking, is a decision, but it usually comes later. It's the opposite with Divine Love. At the beginning God hides and even presents us with the Cross. 'Follow Me on the way of the Cross', and there is nothing attractive about the Man of Sorrows. There is no comeliness in Him. So we're called to make the decision first and to follow Him without any consolations. Then, mysteriously, later on when one has chosen the cross, then comes the joy, then the passions and the whole being can cooperate in the love of God.

In this case of Charity, unlike Faith and Hope, we can take Christ Jesus as our model. This is what makes us perfect, charity. Be ye perfect as the Heavenly Father is perfect, as Christ is. In one sense it is impossible for us to be as perfect as God, in the second sense of perfection, we'll only be perfect in Heaven. 'Only in Heaven will I be fully a man,' (*St. Ignatius of Antioch*). In a sense, we can in this life reach the height of the Christian perfection of charity. To be perfect in charity is to be perfect. Then you can say someone is simply perfect. In some other virtue, such as justice, you say he is a perfectly just man. Someone who is perfected in courage, you could say is a perfect soldier. But if you say someone is a perfect man, he is perfected in charity. In this we can use the Lord Jesus as our model.

The Incarnation – that He would give up the joys of Heaven, even if He was never going to suffer, but just lead a quiet life here with Mother Mary. What a terrible sacrifice, to take on the limits of human nature — the humiliation of God to dwell in the flesh. And then of course one can meditate on the charity, which goes beyond comprehension, dying such a painful, lonely death for sinners. These two aspects in today's Liturgy of the Hours, leaving Heaven for earth was like the bridegroom giving a pledge and dying for us was the dowry. Those two great acts of love on Christ's part, were two parts of wedding human nature. The first was the engagement, the second was the dowry. That's a beautiful way of seeing the Lord's love. He's the bridegroom. This love that He has for us, this love we imitate, is a very personal love, the love of the beloved who wants to wed each one of our souls, take them to Him. This distilled revelation boils down to three words: *God is Love*. This is the revelation that corresponds to the revelation in the Old Testament to Moses in the burning bush, *I Am*. So God revealed then that He is existence, the only necessary being, the source of all truth, and in the New Testament that that Necessary Being is a person who is consumed with love for us.

Christ is not only our model. We don't just try to love Him as He loves us. But if we have charity, we actually have Him within us, working in us, so that the love we have is not so much our wretched attempt to imitate Him, as it is our participation in His own love, in His Charity. And that's why we can merit salvation. That's why Fr. Hardon says always, always, always any act done, any act, no matter what, done in a state of grace, done with Divine Charity in us merits salvation for us or for someone else. And that's a beautiful doctrine for those of us who aren't called to be martyrs, to shed our blood necessarily, because we can do great things even without shedding our blood. Here in a different book, St. Francis de Sales writes; "It may very well be that a small act of virtue executed by a soul in which reigns burning charity, has more value than martyrdom itself sustained by another person who has a somewhat languid, tepid or weak divine love." Some little act of charity can be worth more, like the widow's mite, exactly like that, because of the love she had in giving that tiny bit of money. It had more value than the great thing done by someone with little love.

A case of that is here in this book written by a great Cistercian mystic who lived during the time of the Spanish Civil War. He was living a hidden life and was sent to peel turnips. He says little devils are following him, giving him battle. His brother was off at the front, doing great things, he probably wanted to be a great saint himself and here he was sent off to peel turnips. He says, "Why did I leave my house to come here, in this cold, to peel these ugly vegetables?" He's even tempted against his superiors. He says, "I forget about all that and take refuge in silence and turn to the Blessed Virgin. 'Why am I doing this?'" Then he gets the answer. Peeling turnips for love of Jesus Christ. He says, "It could be that the very least actions of life done in the name of Jesus Christ such as opening or closing one's eyes could win for us Heaven. To peel turnips with real love of God can give Him more glory and give to us more merit than the conquest of the Indies." He finishes his morning work with total joy just peeling turnips and rejoicing in his heart. He had such love in his heart, he describes it as a volcano of love. It doesn't matter to God that it was just spent peeling turnips. Now that I think about it maybe housewives peel a lot of turnips – do it with great love!

There are three results of living a life of love. The first is joy. Anyone who is holy should be joyous! The virtue of charity needs to be regulated by the gift of the Holy Spirit, and that's wisdom. In the original translation its related to the word savor. The fruit of the gift of Wisdom is that we relish, delight in Divine things, we should find sweetness in it. As the psalm says, *Taste and see how good the Lord is!* That goes along with charity, that gift of wisdom and it turns the most bitter things into pleasant things. The same saint talks about savoring the cross, it becomes for him the greatest delight when he has sufferings. Which is obviously impossible, it's the opposite of the natural way. On a supernatural level, when charity is developed, the greatest suffering, because it is an opportunity to love more, is all the more pleasing to us. This is the wisdom of the cross that St. Paul talks of. This is the power of the cross. *For Christ did not send me to baptize but to preach the gospels but not with eloquent wisdom lest the cross of Christ be emptied of its power.* This wisdom is craziness to the world and the wisdom of the world is folly with God. So the result is joy, no matter what, it's impossible to take joy away from the Saints!

Freedom is essential to the whole concept of love because it is making a response to that call. The founder of the Legionaries of Christ, Father Maciel writes, "My vocation is, to my mind, a creation by God in every instance of my life, my freedom, subjected out love, is always on the watch so that nothing will tarnish the fidelity and totality of my dedication to the Beloved at every instant of this new creation, each instant is a new call." Remember that God has a will for us in every single moment and when we choose to do His will it's responding to that call of love that He makes to us at every single moment. It's the way to be united to our Beloved in every single moment, this produces great freedom in the soul. That's why this new law is called the law of liberty. What's called the law of liberty constrains us. Paul says that the love of Christ forces us to pick up our cross. Yet we call this freedom. It's a paradox. "Freedom," the Holy Father said, when he came to the states, was, "the ability to do what we ought, not the ability to do what we want." Later on when our flesh gets subjected, when all of those passions have been formed through virtues so that they more correspond to what's truly right, then also we want with our lower levels what we want with our will. But at first it will always be a cross.

Finally a third effect of charity is zeal. Fr. Maciel continues, "This word love, encompasses all the daily varieties of our being, our desire and our doing, a continuous self-giving and a devouring fire to bring as many people as possible to share the knowledge of God's kingdom. Love becomes the decisive motive of my interest in others and their happiness." Remember this love is the love of God, it is the decisive motive of my interest in others. That means everybody. I can only really love people, even my family, if I'm loving them for Christ's sake. A lot of people are lovable in their own right. We tend to love them naturally. But we can't love them, as Jesus wants, to the degree that God wants, unless we're loving them for sake of Jesus. Like Mother Teresa who loves those beggars with that great love, because she loves them for Jesus' sake, she sees them as actual or potential other Christs, members of His body. Then you can really love Jesus, then you can love your neighbor with a boundless love, because it's real charity which is always ultimately directed toward the Lord.

So if the world is dry like kindling it can be conquered by the love of God, by the consuming fire, but it's only going to get to the world through us. That's the Lord working. We have to be little sparks, little sparks of God's love, we have to ask Him to transform our very useless human love into a little participation in that consuming fire that is the love of God. It's not something that we can do on our own, so we have to pray for it. We have to pray that the Lord will enable us to love, and this is the difference in this love we have for God. We should pray all the time, I want to love you, Lord. I want to love you more. How much I want to love You! Admitting, I don't love You the way I want. If you said this to a person, I don't love you but I wish I did, they'd be offended. But God would not. God loves it when you say to Him, I don't love you as much as I should, but I want to love You more. In the words of the psalm, *Widen my heart that I may run after you in the way of your commands.* So let's ask the Lord, going before Him to give us that love.

References

CCC — Catechism of the Catholic Church

NMI — Novo Millennio Ineunte – Pope John Paul II

LG — Lumen gentium, Vatican II (Dogmatic Constitution of the Church)

GS — Gaudium et spes, Vatican II (Pastoral Constitution of the Church)

Dominus Iesus — Congregation for the Doctrine of the Faith

Dom. Viv. — Dominum Et Vivificantem, Pope John Paul II

Centesimus Annus — on Rerum Novarum, Pope John Paul II

Faithful Citizenship — U.S. Conference of Catholic Bishops

RP — Reconciliatio et paenitentia, Pope John Paul II

DM — Dives in Misericordia, Pope John Paul II

FC — Familiaris Consortio, Pope John Paul II

AMCII — Ascent to Mount Carmel, book II, St. John of the Cross

DS — Denzinger Sconmetzer

Red. Mater — Redemptoris Mater, Pope John Paul II

ST — Summa Theologicae, St. Thomas Aquinas

Mun. Deus. — Munificentissimus Deus, Pope Pius XII

Mys. Fid. — Mysterium Fidei, Pope Paul VI

Imitation of Christ — Thomas a Kempis

Triumph Through the Cross — St. Louis de Monfort

The Soul of the Apostolate — Dom Jean-Baptiste Chautard, O.C.S.O.

Abandonment to Divine Providence — Father J.P. Caussade, S.J.

Letter to the Knights of
Columbus, Feb. 2002

Dear Brother Knights,

Be not afraid! That happy command issued frequently from the lips of Our Savior, before and after His resurrection, for He knew his disciples needed encouragement to face the great challenges and trials ahead. The road to Heaven is a narrow and steep one, and the dangers along it are many. Our beloved Holy Father made those words his own on the night of his elevation to the chair of Peter, telling the whole world the same thing: *Non abbiate paura!*

As many of you will have already heard, I am leaving Baltimore for some time. As you read this, I should be in St. Petersburg, beginning to help build up the Catholic Church in Russia. Those words of Christ, echoed by Pope John Paul II, are a great consolation to me. How could we undertake any mission or any apostolic work unless we had been promised victory? Fear is unnecessary – not to mention, unbecoming — when success is assured. If we work for Christ we will succeed, although the success we achieve may not be of a tangible or qualitative sort. Christ won His victory on the Cross, a fact we cannot forget. And we seek no other glory here below.

We all have a mission. Each one of us has a path marked out, not by fate, but by a loving Father, an omnipotent and omniscient God who knew us from the foundation of the world (Eph. 1.4) and who guides all things to their end. If we knew what He expected of us, we would faint with fear. So He reveals his will bit by bit to those who pray and who trust that He will help us through it all. Never lose your ambition to do great things for God! Never think that any one of us was created to be an average Christian. Why not have a world filled with great saints? Why not be one more of them? Christ will be with you every step of the way, reminding you that fear is useless. Have great peace and joy in your heart and in your council. And please pray for me upon occasion.

With Gratitude in Christ,
Fr. Cummings

Easter Sunday II — 02

Peace and Grace to you all from Our Risen Lord,

When I saw this article in the Osservatore Romano, I was of course reminded of many happy memories and dear friends because they are "fellow workers,"as St. Paul said, in God's Kingdom. High on the list of blessings that came to me at St. John's was learning first hand how true it is that the family must be "the way of the Church." Primarily through it, do the laity exercise their baptismal share in Christ's priesthood (teaching, praying, governing) and only through it will a civilization of love come about. The first thing the communists did – as if by some perverse instinct — besides closing churches, was to separate families, make all women work, take over the education of youth and encourage the practice of abortion. It will be big work to set society back up — it's foundation of faith and family.

How much the world needs the Church ("the soul of the world"), and how much the Church needs holy families! I do encourage you all to persevere every day, dispite all the difficulties, making your homes peaceful sanctuaries where the precious souls entrusted to you by the Creator can grow up into the wonderful saints God intends them to be. Persevere also in your extra apostolates, helping other families in various ways, as well as with your example and prayer.

I will keep praying for you all. I know how difficult family life can be. Receive all those crosses as means to grow holy; they come from Our Father in Heaven, even as He laid the cross on His own Son. And may the Spirit who raised Him from the dead, who united the early Church in thought and action, who is within you, bind your families together and lead your apostolates forward with assurance.

Yours in Christ,
Father McLean

Fr. McLean Cummings is a priest from the Archdiocese of Baltimore who is now serving the Church in St. Petersburg, Russia. The youngest of eight, he was ordained June 6, 1998 and spent his first years as a priest at St. John the Evangelist Church, in Severna Park, Md. He graduated from Harvard University with a philosophy degree, received a Bachelor's in Theology from the Pontifical Athenaeum Regina Apostolorum, and a license in philosophy from the Pontifical Gregorian University. He received his Master's in Moral Theology from Mount Saint Mary's Seminary in Emmitsburg, Md. Before entering the Seminary, he tutored immigrants and inmates, helped in soup kitchens, and worked on the editorial staff of the Catholic Youth Magazine, "You!" (formally called Veritas). While at St. John's, Father Cummings became involved in, and helped to direct, many ministries including visitation of hospitalized, homebound and nursing home patients, the Respect Life Committee and Evangelization Team. His dedication encouraged many to pray several times a week in front of the abortion clinic and to participate in door to door evangelizing throughout the community. It's likely that Father Cummings is missed most of all as a confessor and spiritual director, leading many to a deeper, more faithful life of prayer and inspiring them to strive for holiness in their particular state in life.

We ask your prayers for the spread of the faith in Russia, for an increase in vocations, and, in particular, for the priests who are now working there. There is such a great need to evangelize since the fall of Communism, especially in light of Our Lady's promise at Fatima, that peace would come to the world through the conversion of Russia. After nearly a century of suffering and persecution, surely the Church will soon be blessed by the fruit of the sacrifices of so many of the faithful. Don't forget that your prayers and sacrifices can do so much also! If you wish to support the Church in Russia or just learn more about the current situation there, please contact: **Aid to the Church in Russia, P.O. Box 1077, Great Falls, Va. 22066-1077. Email: info@aidrussia.org.**

All donations for this book are greatly appreciated (no matter how small). What is not used for printing and shipping costs will be given to assist in this great work of restoring the faith in Russia. To make a contribution or to obtain additional copies of this book to share with family and friends, write to: **John or Miriam Lademan, 1677 Pleasant Plains Rd. Annapolis, Md. 21401, or call (410) 757-5682.**